AAUSC 2012 Volume – Issues in Language Program Direction

Hybrid Language Teaching and Learning: Exploring Theoretical, Pedagogical and Curricular Issues

Fernando Rubio (Editor)

Joshua J. Thoms (Editor)

Stacey Katz Bourns (Series Editor)

D1317924

HEINLE
CENGAGE Learning·

Australia • Brazil • Japan • Korea • Mexico • Singapore • Spain • United Kingdom • United States

HEINLE
CENGAGE Learning·

AAUSC 2012 Volume – Issues in Language Program Direction: Hybrid Language Teaching and Learning: Exploring Theoretical, Pedagogical and Curricular Issues
Fernando Rubio,
Joshua J. Thoms and
Stacey Katz Bourns

Editorial Director: P. J. Boardman

Publisher: Beth Kramer

Editorial Assistant:
Gregory Madan

Managing Media Editor:
Morgen Gallo

Executive Brand Manager:
Ben Rivera

Market Development Manager:
Courtney Wolstoncroft

Executive Marketing
Communications Manager:
Jason LaChapelle

Rights Acquisitions Specialist:
Jessica Elias

Manufacturing Planner:
Betsy Donaghey

Art and Design Direction,
Production Management, and
Composition: PreMediaGlobal

For product information and
technology assistance, contact us at **Cengage Learning
Customer & Sales Support, 1-800-354-9706**

For permission to use material from this text or product,
submit all requests online at **cengage.com/permissions**
Further permissions questions can be emailed to
permissionrequest@cengage.com

Library of Congress Control Number: 2012950573

ISBN-13: 978-1-285-17467-9

ISBN-10: 1-285-17467-4

Heinle
20 Channel Center Street
Boston, MA 02210
USA

Cengage Learning is a leading provider of customized learning solutions with office locations around the globe, including Singapore, the United Kingdom, Australia, Mexico, Brazil and Japan. Locate your local office at: **international.cengage.com/region**

Cengage Learning products are represented in Canada by Nelson Education, Ltd.

For your course and learning solutions, visit
www.cengage.com.

Purchase any of our products at your local college store or at our preferred online store **www.cengagebrain.com.**

:engage.com and log in to access

Printed in the United States of America
1 2 3 4 5   16 15 14 13 12

Contents

Introduction

Theoretical Views

Pedagogical and Curricular Concerns

Acknowledgments

Just like it takes a village to raise a child, it takes a large team of dedicated people to produce a volume like this. We are greatly indebted to Stacey Katz Bourns, our series editor, for her patient guidance through the process, from the call for papers to the final editorial touches. Her incredible attention to detail, elegant sense of style, and organizational skills helped us stay on task and translated into a much better final product than we would have been able to produce by ourselves.

Our heartfelt thanks goes to the AAUSC editorial board for helping us narrow down and shape the scope of this volume, for suggesting names of potential contributors, and for volunteering to review manuscripts. In particular, we want to express our gratitude to all those board members who served as reviewers for our volume: Heather Willis Allen, Catherine Barrette, Carl Blyth, Heidi Byrnes, Robert Davis, Charles J. James, Carol Klee, Cheryl Krueger, Glenn Levine, Judy Liskin-Gasparro, Hiram Maxim, Kate Paesani, H. Jay Siskin, Johanna Watzinger-Tharp, and Mary Wildner-Bassett. We are also grateful to a number of other scholars, including Luis Cerezo, Lisa Dewaard, Nancy Guilloteau, Angelika Kraemer, Nicole Mills, Eduardo Negueruela, Mary O'Donnell, Ana Oskoz, Sue Otto, and Amy Rossomondo, who agreed to review manuscripts and provided invaluable suggestions to us and to the authors.

Of course, the volume would not have been possible without the authors' contributions. The quality of their work, their flexibility, and their patience with us while working through numerous drafts made our job rewarding and enjoyable.

Finally, we want to express our gratitude to Heinle Cengage Learning for their continued support of the AAUSC Issues in Language Program Direction series and, in particular, to Beth Kramer, our publisher, who provided guidance throughout the entire process.

Fernando Rubio and Joshua J. Thoms
Editors

AAUSC Editorial Board 2012

Annual Volumes of *Issues in Language Program Direction*

1998 *Research Issues and Language Program Direction*
Editor: L. Kathy Heilenman

1997 *New Ways of Learning and Teaching: Focus on Technology and Foreign Language Education*
Editor: Judith A. Muyskens

1996 *Patterns and Policies: The Changing Demographics of Foreign Language Instruction*
Editor: Judith E. Liskin-Gasparro

1995 *Redefining the Boundaries of Language Study*
Editor: Claire Kramsch

1994 *Faces in a Crowd: The Individual Learner in Multisection Courses*
Editor: Carol A. Klee

1993 *The Dynamics of Language Program Direction*
Editor: David P. Benseler

1992 *Development and Supervision of Teaching Assistants in Foreign Languages*
Editor: Joel C. Walz

1991 *Assessing Foreign Language Proficiency of Undergraduates*
Editor: Richard V. Teschner

1990 *Challenges in the 1990s for College Foreign Language Programs*
Editor: Sally Sieloff Magnan

Abstracts

ROBERT BLAKE

Best Practices in Online Learning: Is It for Everyone?
In this chapter, I advocate for the need to use technology in the foreign language (FL) curriculum and describe different conditions under which technology fits into the curriculum, including the implementation of online courses. This implies, of course, that not all online courses are the same by any stretch of the imagination, just as not all in-class, face-to-face (F2F) classes produce the same learning experience. Many in the language teaching profession seek to compare directly online learning with an imagined *gold standard* represented by F2F classroom learning. I examine the difficulties in doing this type of comparative research, which is fraught with numerous uncontrolled individual variables that make asking the question, "Which is better?" unproductive for the field. I try to explain why some quarters of the FL field persist in refusing to accept online courses into the FL curriculum for normal course credit despite the growing use of online courses in higher education. Finally, I consider the questions of whether or not the online learning environment constitutes a good fit for everyone. I present evidence that online language learning presents a difficult avenue of study for certain students, but it also promises to be a most excellent alternative for others. Suggestions are made for what could be a more fruitful research agenda concerning online language learning and the computer-assisted language learning field.

CARL S. BLYTH

Opening Up Foreign Language Education with Open Educational Resources: The Case of *Français interactif*
The general goal of this chapter is to examine the open education movement in order to understand its impact on foreign language education. More specifically, this chapter explores the intersection of blended foreign language learning and open educational resources (OERs). The affordances and challenges of OERs are summarized and discussed. A case study of *Français interactif*, an OER developed at the University of Texas at Austin, illustrates openness in many of its unique features, including an open development process based on feedback from a community of users, a modular design, and an open license. Suggestions are given to language program directors about how to join the open education community of practice.

LUIS CEREZO

Beyond Hybrid Learning: A Synthesis of Research on E-tutors Under the Lens of Second Language Acquisition Theory
A growing number of studies in second language acquisition have investigated the pedagogical effectiveness of hybrid learning curricula, where traditional face-to-face instruction is supplemented by technology-mediated learning. Less attention,

however, has been devoted to fully online curricula, where learners work independently with interactive technology such as e-tutors. Increasingly, though, academic institutions are including online learning as a critical component of their strategic plans. Many provosts and deans are already asking language program directors to make complex and unprecedented logistical decisions to implement online curricula, and to the extent possible, these decisions should be informed by the results of empirical research. This chapter provides a synthesis of existing research on online second language learning with e-tutors, with a focus on grammar. This synthesis is geared around three central questions. The *whether* question addresses whether e-tutors can facilitate second language grammar development per se and compared with other instructional technologies; the *why* question addresses why e-tutors can be pedagogically effective on the basis of second language acquisition theories; and the *which* question addresses which specific e-tutor features promote the highest grammar learning outcomes, thus contributing a more precise picture of what an ideal e-tutor should look like. The chapter closes with a set of recommendations for further research.

LARA DUCATE, LARA LOMICKA, AND GILLIAN LORD

Hybrid Learning Spaces: Re-envisioning Language Learning
As institutions of higher education are encouraged to do more with fewer resources, educators and administrators are increasingly contemplating "hybrid" or "blended" learning. Various studies have asserted that enhancing course content through technology can support in-depth delivery and analysis of knowledge and increase student satisfaction. The chapter addresses some of the primary theoretical issues at stake in the implementation of hybrid courses into second language learning while also providing case study examples of ways in which Web 2.0 technologies can be used to make the most of our new educational landscape. Second language acquisition theories are also discussed with respect to their implementation in hybrid learning before taking a critical look at tools that have been used in face-to-face contexts and adapted in blended or hybrid courses at undergraduate as well as graduate levels. These examples are provided to showcase the ways in which technological tools can enable the enrichment and extension of the classroom setting in both traditional and alternative settings.

SENTA GOERTLER

Theoretical and Empirical Foundations for Blended Language Learning
Fully and partially online courses are on the rise in colleges across the country. Although administrative and logistical reasons often dominate the discussion and the planning of partially or fully online courses, as language educators, we must also consider the potential benefits for language learning. This chapter first presents a quick summary of research on blended learning (BL). The main portion of the chapter focuses on a discussion of the relationship between second language acquisition theories and different computer-assisted language learning formats as they relate

to hybrid and online learning. The next section presents arguments in favor of BL based on confirmed second language acquisition processes. The chapter concludes with recommendations for curricular design of BL and online learning.

AMY E. ROSSOMONDO

Integrating Foundational Language and Content Study Through New Approaches to Hybrid Learning and Teaching

The focus of this chapter is foundational foreign language teaching and learning that integrates content and language study in a hybrid environment. It offers a detailed description of how the open-access, web-based *Acceso* project implements an approach to intermediate-level Spanish study, consonant with recent discussions of integrated language and content instruction at all levels of instruction by means of a broad range of computer-assisted language learning applications. The chapter also argues for a characterization of *Acceso*'s content as "hybrid" with respect both to its collaborative development and maintenance and to how student engagement of this content is facilitated inside and outside of the classroom. Finally, the chapter discusses the benefits and challenges of developing and implementing such a project from a language program director's perspective, as well as directions for its future.

SUSANNE ROTT

Complementary Functions of Face-to-Face and Online Oral Achievement Tests in a Hybrid Learning Program

Recent research has attended to various aspects of oral tasks. Yet there has been very little analysis of how different test tasks and formats are complementary in terms of the skills they elicit. Moreover, the feasibility of conducting oral tests online has not yet been well examined. The current exploratory investigation compared students' linguistic and interactional competencies in three commonly used oral exam tasks: teacher–student interview, role-play, and monologue. The interview and the role-play were conducted face to face (F2F), and the monologue was conducted in an online format. The data collection was based on third-semester German learners' three- to five-minute responses to a speaking prompt and analyzed for aspects of communication, interactional, discourse, lexical, and grammatical competence. Results showed that in the online monologue and the F2F interview, students demonstrated similar language abilities that complemented language abilities demonstrated in the role-play.

FERNANDO RUBIO

The Effects of Blended Learning on Second Language Fluency and Proficiency

In an effort to address the needs of a new digital generation of students and remain fiscally efficient in times of budget strains, many departments have decided to move some components of their language programs to the online format and design courses that combine traditional face-to-face (F2F) instruction supplemented with online components. A number of studies have compared the effects of these blended courses with traditional courses, but the findings have either been inconclusive or have proved no significant differences. This chapter presents the results of a study comparing the proficiency and fluency gains of two groups of first-year students of Spanish at the university level. One of the groups completed two consecutive semesters of F2F classroom instruction in a traditional format, meeting four days a week. The second group enrolled in two semesters of beginning Spanish in a blended format that combines two F2F sessions per week with two "virtual days." In addition to measuring speaking and writing proficiency levels according to the American Council on the Teaching of Foreign Languages scale, the study provides a more fine-grained, quantitative analysis of a number of features typically associated with fluency. Results show that even though differences are not noticeable when comparing overall proficiency levels, a quantitative analysis of fluency features reveals some interesting differences between the two groups.

FERNANDO RUBIO AND JOSHUA J. THOMS

Hybrid Language Teaching and Learning: Looking Forward
The introductory chapter discusses the current state of affairs in hybrid or blended second language teaching and emphasizes the main issues that need to be taken into account when starting or maintaining a hybrid FL course. After providing a summary of the content of the different sections of this volume, the chapter closes with our view of how blended language teaching and learning will continue to evolve and contribute to the ever-changing landscape of FL education.

JOSHUA J. THOMS

Analyzing Linguistic Outcomes of Second Language Learners: Hybrid Versus Traditional Course Contexts
This chapter reports on a small-scale empirical study that analyzes the speaking and writing gains of students enrolled in an introductory Spanish language course taught in a traditional, face-to-face context and a second, introductory Spanish language course that was delivered via a hybrid course format. Both were college-level courses taught by the same instructor. The overarching research question investigated in this project is the following: what are the differences in speaking and writing gains of students enrolled in each of the two types of courses over the course of an academic semester? Results indicate that there were no statistically significant differences between students in the traditional and hybrid courses with respect to speaking gains. However, there were statistically significant differences regarding writing ability because students in the hybrid course improved more versus students in the traditional course. Reasons for these differences are delineated and future areas of research are offered.

DOLLY JESUSITA YOUNG AND JASON PETTIGREW

Blended Learning in Large Multisection Foreign Language Programs: An Opportunity for Reflecting on Course Content, Pedagogy, Learning Outcomes, and Assessment Issues

From the new millennium to the present, colleges and universities have experienced increased pressure by government-funded agencies, academic administrators, and the technology industry to integrate technology into higher education for the purpose of reducing instructional costs. On the surface, the concept of blended learning (BL) may appear apparent, but actual application is complex, particularly for large multiple section foreign language (FL) elementary and intermediate university-level programs. Few published accounts exist that examine issues of curriculum and pedagogy as these play out in BL instruction in this context. This chapter documents the evolution of BL up to the present time, surveys past and present BL programs across the nation, considers the discourse present in disseminating information about them, and gleans characteristics of the programs based on the available public and published documents. In an effort to move beyond the current discourse used to describe BL instruction in this context and as a way to reflect on curricular and pedagogical issues, we examine the variables, processes, and considerations that go into redesigning a large multisection Spanish course at this level. Our purpose is not to provide a model for curricular and pedagogical decision making in BL instruction for elementary or intermediate FL programs but to reflect on the unique contexts in which curricular and pedagogical issues are considered. Without curricular planning and careful consideration of pedagogies, we cannot adjudicate whether and how BL instruction should or can be judged positively. Without reflection on the various contexts and pedagogies, programs will be reacting to outer circumstances rather than reflecting deeply on issues pertaining to adult instructed language learning.

Chapter 1

Hybrid Language Teaching and Learning: Looking Forward

Fernando Rubio and Joshua J. Thoms

The topic of this 23rd volume in the AAUSC Issues in Language Program Direction series is relevant to our readership and timely for our profession. Hybrid language teaching and learning, also referred to as "blended learning" (BL), has become an increasingly popular model for the delivery of foreign language (FL) courses at the college level in the United States. Several factors have contributed to the proliferation of hybrid models of instruction in various institutions. Some include a more thorough understanding of how computer-assisted language learning (CALL), when informed by second language acquisition (SLA) theories, can facilitate learners' abilities to access input and produce output more effectively in the second language (L2), notice and correct linguistic errors more efficiently, and interact more easily with native speakers of the L2 to understand facets of the L2 culture better, among other benefits. In addition, many FL textbooks now incorporate interactive online components that allow an instructor or a language program director (LPD) to be more creative and flexible when planning a course and determining what can be taught in and outside of the classroom. Yet another factor that plays a role in the growing number of hybrid course offerings is the economy. Given the economic downturn in recent years, many institutions' budgets have been cut, which has directly affected how FL programs—both large and small—deliver their courses. In some instances, administrators in universities have suggested that FL programs adopt a hybrid learning or BL model to use resources more efficiently versus severely reducing the number of sections of FL courses offered or eliminating FL programs altogether.

Regardless of the reason for the increase in the number of hybrid courses being offered throughout the United States, it is clear that blended teaching and learning is quickly becoming an essential alternative in many FL programs. Specifically, in addition to the option to enroll in a traditional face-to-face FL course, several FL programs now offer students the possibility to take the same course in a hybrid, blended, or fully online format. Therefore, we believe that it is important for our profession to understand the power of different technologies to provide a solid foundation for the design of BL contexts and the theoretical underpinnings that may justify their integration. Although this volume does not claim to have all the answers to the many questions that the recent explosion of BL has raised, we believe that it will guide our readers into aspects of blended teaching and learning that can be of specific interest to them.

In a 2006 review of hybrid learning, Buzzetto-More and Sweat-Guy predicted that hybrid learning was "poised to cause a paradigm shift in higher education" (p. 153). However, unlike other disciplines, particularly mathematics, FL is a latecomer to the blended world. In fact, no research was available on blended FL courses until Adair-Hauck, Willingham-McLain, and Youngs (2000) evaluated Carnegie Mellon University's program. Since then, CALL researchers have investigated a variety of issues related to FL hybrid courses and have provided insight into the effects of hybrid FL courses on L2 learning and teaching. This volume contributes to that ongoing research effort and provides readers with some useful and practical information that university administrators, LPDs, instructors, and students should consider when experimenting with FL hybrid courses. Although several chapters in this volume offer insights into the various issues that need to be taken into consideration when starting or maintaining a hybrid FL course, we would like to briefly underscore some of those issues here.

Hybrid Foreign Language Courses: Issues to Consider

Before highlighting some of the essential aspects of FL hybrid courses that LPDs and administrators need to consider when creating or implementing these kinds of courses in their FL programs, it is first necessary to define what is meant by hybrid or blended teaching and learning. The definition of *blended teaching and learning* can take a broad approach in which technology is seen as a supplement to a traditional course without substantially altering its approach (for more definitions, see Graham, 2005; Heinze & Proctor, 2004; Nicolson, Murphy, & Southgate, 2011). On the other hand, a more narrow definition, such as the following one adopted by Laster, Otte, Picciano, and Sorg (2005), can also apply: "Courses that integrate online with traditional face-to-face class activities in a planned, pedagogically valuable manner; and where a portion (institutionally defined) of face-to-face time is replaced by online activity." When using the term *hybrid or blended FL course*, we are referring to the aforementioned definition by Laster et al. (2005)—using technology and online projects to replace some portion of face-to-face class time with the aim of reducing in-class contact time without sacrificing the quality of instruction, the learning experience of students, or the learning outcomes of the course.

We now turn to some of the main issues that are important to consider for any LPD who is given the task of creating or maintaining a hybrid FL course. These insights come from our experiences as LPDs who have been in charge of one or more hybrid courses in large FL programs.

Time and Resources

Although hybrid models can afford students and teachers a number of benefits related to L2 learning and teaching, it is worth mentioning early on that implementing and maintaining an effective FL hybrid program can be challenging if LPDs are not allowed the necessary time and resources for this endeavor. Specifically, LPDs need to consider a variety of issues when creating an FL hybrid course or when adapting a traditional course to be taught in a hybrid format. Much of the initial learning phase requires time for LPDs and the instructors who may be asked to help design and implement an FL hybrid course.

It is therefore imperative that anyone considering implementation of an FL hybrid course (e.g., deans, department chairs, or LPDs) realize that those involved with the implementation of the hybrid course need to be provided the essential resources upfront. That might mean that an LPD or instructor be given a course release to spend time (a) researching the various formats hybrid or blended courses can take, (b) experimenting with or understanding the various technologies to be incorporated in the course, (c) working with the publisher of the textbook to see if additional online content can be made accessible to students in the future hybrid course, and (d) familiarizing potential instructors with what a hybrid or blended teaching approach entails, among other tasks. To reiterate, this initial investment in time and resources helps to ensure that all aspects of the FL hybrid course be fully addressed and developed.

Course Redesign and Training for Instructors

In her discussion on the relationship between SLA theory and CALL, Chapelle (2009) reminds us that "based on their work with technology in other domains, most people would probably readily agree that technology alone is not the answer, but that a real solution will draw on technology in a manner that is informed by professional and scientific knowledge about SLA" (p. 750). As the methodology and SLA experts in their programs, the LPDs have the responsibility to pay attention to what we know from SLA theory and consider what aspects of the acquisition process lend themselves best to technology integration and why so they can create the optimal blend of face-to-face and online experiences that will result in improved learning.

Foreign language programs differ in their situational factors and intended goals and outcomes, but a well-designed blended course always starts by establishing the desired results, determining what constitutes appropriate assessment evidence, and then building a learning plan that takes maximal advantage of the face-to-face time with students and of the avenues opened up by interaction with or through a computer. Input, output, feedback, and interaction are aspects of the language acquisition process that are considered crucial by most SLA theories. Therefore, LPDs who are considering embarking on the design of a blended course should take into account and take advantage of the ways that technology changes how we access and interact with input, produce output, and provide and react to feedback. Additionally, a variety of collaborative tools and social networking sites can promote learner autonomy, collaboration outside the classroom, and access to authentic materials and native speakers. Several chapters in this volume provide excellent reviews of technology tools—many of them not necessarily designed for teaching purposes—that provide favorable conditions for language acquisition.

The integration of all or some of these options and the resulting augmented role that technology assumes in a blended course should also translate into pedagogical changes in the classroom. Unfortunately, this is not always the case. More than 20 years ago, Garrett (1991) warned that "technology that can be taken for granted is already light years ahead of the profession's ability to integrate a principled use of it into the classroom and the curriculum" (p. 74). Again, the role of the LPD must be to start with a 3,000-foot view of his or her language program, determine what technology is practical and advisable to use based on sound theoretical principles, and then make ground-level decisions regarding what elements of a course can benefit from moving to the online environment and how this move should alter the pedagogy of the face-to-face components. One of the safest approaches is to make sure that there is a seamless connection between what students do online and what happens in the classroom so that even though the medium may change, the overall objectives remain the same.

It is also worth noting here that the instructors asked to teach a hybrid course need to receive adequate training about what hybrid courses are and how the various technologies incorporated in a particular blended course can be used in a pedagogically sound manner. Given that many of the lower-level courses, particularly in large FL programs, are staffed by graduate student teaching assistants (TAs) in many universities in the United States (Maxim, 2009; MLA Ad Hoc Committee on Foreign Languages, 2007), it is likely that TAs will be given the task of teaching a hybrid course in any given FL program. Although many TAs make use of a variety of technologies on a daily basis outside of their academic lives, few receive training in their FL programs regarding how technology can be integrated in their teaching (Thoms, 2011). As a result, LPDs considering the implementation of hybrid courses in their FL program need to provide extensive, ongoing training to TAs regarding how various technological applications work and how they can be used in their assigned hybrid FL course. LPDs should also consider involving TAs early on in the process of creating hybrid courses because some graduate students will be able to contribute their extensive knowledge about how specific technologies (e.g., Twitter, wikis, and social networking sites such as Facebook and Ning) can be integrated into the hybrid FL course syllabus.

The Cost Versus Quality Debate

The experience of a significant number of institutions across the country has demonstrated that redesigning courses to the blended model can result in important savings. The National Center for Academic Transformation (n.d.) provides a full report on the degree of success, financial and otherwise, of more than 100 programs in a variety of disciplines. After the field has established that blended contexts do not have any negative effects on acquisition and that they are a legitimate alternative to other curricular options, we have to move past the need to justify their existence based solely on the financial benefits that an institution can accrue from implementing blended courses. Perhaps the financial focus should turn from institutions to students and the discussion should revolve around how BL may lower the cost of education as we discuss below when we mention the marriage of blended teaching and open educational resources.

In any case, quality should remain the central consideration when deciding on a course design or redesign. Interestingly, of the many submissions that we initially received for this volume, none addressed the practical advantages of BL as an answer to budgetary or space concerns or enrollment pressures. On the contrary, as the different sections of the volume clearly indicate, our profession understands that the decision to "go blended" should be considered as an opportunity to facilitate the integration of content and language from the introductory levels of instruction, address the needs and draw on the strengths of a variety of learners, foster the formation of communities of learners, improve linguistic outcomes, and adopt pedagogies that are well grounded in SLA theories.

Assessing the Effectiveness of Hybrid Course(s)

Language program directors need to focus their energy on designing courses that are pedagogically sound and based on what we know from current theories of language acquisition about the benefits of integrating technology. As blended models continue to evolve, assessment will have to adapt as well. But rather than using the traditional face-to-face course as the benchmark against which blended (and online) courses need to be measured (see Blake, Chapter 2), assessment needs to address how new modes of delivery meet the needs of a changing student population, in terms of both facilitating their linguistic gains and addressing their social and cognitive needs.

Our profession understood years ago that teaching with technology meant a lot more than simply making materials available to students online. Likewise, an assessment plan for a blended course cannot be an online replica of how students are assessed in a traditional class. If we test not only *what* we teach but also *how* we teach, assessment in the blended course needs to be significantly redesigned to reflect how students learn when technology is an integral component of the learning process. Although linguistic indicators are a good starting point, assessment should not stop there. A successful program also needs to look at other aspects of the learning process and gauge the impact that technology integration may have on issues such as student satisfaction and retention, ability to adapt to different learning styles, or ability to facilitate learner autonomy, among others. Of course, only if the results of the assessment are then used to revise and refine the course redesign will we be able to effectively close the assessment loop. Because the ultimate goal of any redesign should always be enhancing program effectiveness and raising program standards, all constituents (other faculty, graduate student TAs, undergraduate students, administrators), not just the LPD, need to be involved in the assessment process.

What This Volume Offers

The remaining 10 chapters in this volume, organized in five sections, offer readers insights, reflections, analysis, and guidance related to creating, maintaining, and assessing the effectiveness of a hybrid FL course. Although some of the chapters report on empirical research related to the benefits of hybrid courses for L2 learning and teaching, all of them offer valuable information to LPDs who are in charge of creating or sustaining a hybrid FL course.

This chapter, coupled with the second chapter, introduces some of the fundamental issues related to offering hybrid FL courses. LPDs are offered some practical advice from Robert Blake, who, in his chapter "Best Practices in Online Learning: Is It for Everyone?" presents readers with a number of concerns that LPDs should consider when implementing hybrid and fully online FL courses in their programs. In addition to exploring reasons why some still question whether or not a hybrid or fully online FL course should be afforded equal credit as a traditional FL course, Blake goes on to explain that hybrid courses are good alternatives for certain kinds of students but may not be suitable contexts of learning for all students. Specifically, he reports on research indicating that conscientiousness is an important personality trait that can determine a student's success in an FL hybrid course. That is, students who are diligent and dedicated to their academic work in general are those who will perform well in the FL hybrid course environment.

The second theme of the volume explores a number of theoretical issues about principles of SLA that need to be considered when designing a hybrid FL course. In Chapter 3, "Theoretical and Empirical Foundations for Blended Language Learning," Senta Goertler discusses the connection between CALL and SLA theory and the ways in which theory should both inform the design of blended courses and drive the research conducted in them. Her chapter presents seven different formats of CALL: CALL tutorials, intelligent CALL (iCALL), computer-mediated communication (CMC) with peers, CMC across cultures, online communities, games, and simulations. Goertler discusses how each tool can be beneficial from one or more theoretical perspectives. The chapter concludes with a review of how BL can respond to some of the common understandings of the SLA process and provides a list of practical recommendations for anyone interested in designing a blended course.

Chapter 4, "Beyond Hybrid Learning: A Synthesis of Research on E-tutors Under the Lens of Second Language Acquisition Theory," written by Luis Cerezo, offers a review of research conducted to date on the effectiveness of e-tutors, which constitute an essential component of a number of blended FL courses. Cerezo focuses on the success of e-tutors as opposed to other pedagogical approaches to promote grammatical competence. Following SLA theory, the author argues why e-tutors are effective and discusses which e-tutors have the potential to be most effective. The chapter serves as an excellent basis upon which LPDs can make decisions regarding how to deal with grammar pedagogy in a blended environment.

The third theme of the volume addresses several curricular and pedagogical concerns. In Chapter 5, "Hybrid Learning Spaces: Re-envisioning Language Learning," Lara Ducate, Lara Lomicka, and Gillian Lord offer a perspective on the changes that the profession is undergoing as a result of the inclusion of Web 2.0 technologies in the pedagogical tapestry of L2 teaching and their potential to promote collaborative learning. Their chapter reviews the theoretical underpinnings of the justification for the implementation of hybrid courses, particularly for the crucial role that some Web 2.0 tools can play in them. The last section of the chapter reviews a number of case studies of the successful use of blogs, wikis, Facebook, and Twitter in language courses. It provides examples for LPDs and instructors of how to use these tools effectively.

Chapter 6, "Introducing Blended Learning in Large Multi-Section Foreign Language Programs: An Opportunity for Reflecting on Course Content, Pedagogy, Learning Outcomes, and Assessment Issues," by Dolly Young and Jason Pettigrew provides an overview of the implementation and maintenance of hybrid courses in a large, multi-section, Spanish language program at the University of Tennessee. Their chapter provides an overview of BL programs implemented across the country over the past decade. They emphasize the fact that in most cases, the motivations behind the implementation of blended courses and the way the redesign is reported revolves around issues of cost savings, course delivery, and instructional components rather than pedagogical or curricular issues. In an effort to move beyond the way that BL courses are normally described and to provide LPDs with some useful guidance, they offer a detailed account of how curricular and pedagogical issues were considered from the development stages to the implementation of the beginning Spanish BL course at the University of Tennessee.

Learning outcomes is the fourth theme of the volume and consists of three chapters. In Chapter 7, "The Effects of Blended Learning on Second Language Fluency and Proficiency," Fernando Rubio reports on a study comparing linguistic gains of students enrolled in beginning-level face-to-face and blended Spanish courses. The results show no significant difference in the proficiency gains made by the two groups. However, when looking at a number of quantifiable measures of writing and speaking fluency, the data point to a small advantage for students who enrolled in the blended courses. The results suggest that a fine-grained analysis of fluency may be a better way to measure differences in linguistic gains after short treatments that are typically not enough to elicit measurable gains in proficiency.

In Chapter 8, "Complementary Functions of Face-to-Face and Online Oral Achievement Tests in a Hybrid Learning Program," Susanne Rott discusses the advantages of combining in-class oral activities with online asynchronous tasks and the benefits for language development of this blended approach. She reports on a study comparing the type of language produced by students in three oral exam tasks: a teacher–student interview and role-play, both done face to face, and a monologue recorded online. The students in the monologue condition showed the highest level of linguistic complexity but, interestingly, they did not think that the medium allowed them to demonstrate their real abilities in the language. The results of the study should give instructors pause when deciding what tasks to assign to the online as opposed to the face-to-face component of a blended course.

In Chapter 9, "Analyzing Linguistic Outcomes of Second Language Learners: Hybrid Versus Traditional Course Contexts," Joshua Thoms reports on an empirical study that compares gains made in speaking and writing by two groups of students enrolled in a hybrid and a face-to-face version of an elementary Spanish course. Although the results of the speaking assessment confirm what previous studies found, namely that there is no significant difference in speaking skills between the two groups, his data indicate a significant advantage in writing gains for students enrolled in the hybrid version of the course. Thoms speculates that the advantage may be attributable to increased writing practice built into the design of the hybrid version.

The volume ends with a final theme that explores a topic that is relevant to hybrid or online FL courses: open access concerns. In Chapter 10, "Opening Up Foreign Language Education: The Case of *Français Interactif*," Carl Blyth gives an overview of the open education movement and its overall impact on higher education. He discusses how the adoption of open educational resources (OERs) in FL courses may facilitate and improve blended teaching and learning. The chapter includes a case study of the French OER *Français Interactif* and shows how a diverse community of users finds ways to adapt the program to their particular needs. The chapter ends with suggestions for language professionals about how to take advantage of the open education movement.

The final chapter of the volume, Chapter 11, "Integrating Foundational Language and Content Study Through New Approaches to Hybrid Learning and Teaching" by Amy Rossomondo, presents the open-access Spanish program *Acceso* as an example of hybrid design and hybrid implementation. The chapter describes how the collaborative process that resulted in the development and maintenance of *Acceso* (more than 70 faculty, instructors, and graduate TAs and several different units on campus) benefits all stakeholders. It closes with a reflection on how open-access hybrid courses with a literacy-based approach can help address the challenges of integrating language and content in introductory-level FL courses while facilitating the development of digital literacies.

Looking Forward

Every year since 2005, The New Media Consortium has published the annual Horizon Report, which identifies key trends and challenges in the integration of technology in higher education. The 2011 report (Johnson, Smith, Willis, Levine, & Haywood, 2011) identifies two key trends that are crucial for understanding some of the justifications for the growth in popularity of blended teaching and learning. One has to do with the flexibility that we have come to expect in an increasingly mobile world in which students move across time and space and in and out of interaction with technology: "People expect to be able to work, learn, and study whenever and wherever they want" (p. 3). The other key trend emphasizes the changing nature of working and learning, no longer an individual endeavor: "The world of work is increasingly collaborative, giving rise to reflection about the way student projects are structured" (p. 3).

These two tendencies have crucial pedagogical consequences that our profession will need to be prepared to address, and we believe that BL can move us in the right direction. Our profession needs to come up with teaching and learning materials and practices that reflect the ways students learn outside the classroom and the ways we interact in the workplace. Because this initiative is unlikely to happen at a large scale within the traditional publishing venues, particularly in languages that are less financially attractive for publishers, we as a profession need to take advantage of the possibilities opened up by the surge in open-access and open-source educational resources. In *The Power of Open*, Casserly and Ito, respectively CEO and chair of Creative Commons, remind us that "the field of openness is approaching a critical mass of adoption that could result in sharing becoming a default standard for the many works that were previously made available only under the all-rights-reserved framework" (2011, p. 5). As Blyth (see Chapter 10) and Rossomondo (see Chapter 11) very convincingly argue in their chapters, a combination of open and closed materials as well as online and printed ones is already used successfully at some institutions and may become "the new blended," a new way of organizing formal learning that resembles the way people learn and interact with information today. As teachers and students continue to demand and expect more and better technology integrated into L2 courses, the cost of producing these teaching materials through the traditional channels will continue to spiral up with the corresponding increase in cost to students. Again, the open movement may provide a way to facilitate technological advances in L2 teaching without increasing the already high cost of higher education. In any case, we look forward to the various ways in which blended language teaching and learning will continue to evolve and contribute to the ever-changing landscape of FL education.

References

Adair-Hauck, B., Willingham-McLain, L., & Youngs, B. E. (2000). Evaluating the integration of technology and second language learning. *CALICO Journal, 17* (2), 269–306.

Buzzetto-More, N., & Sweat-Guy, R. (2006). Hybrid learning defined. *Journal of Information Technology Education, 5,* 153–156.

Chapelle, C. (2009). The relationship between second language acquisition theory and computer-assisted language learning. *The Modern Language Journal, 93,* 741–753.

Garrett, N. (1991). Technology in the service of language learning: Trends and issues. *Modern Language Journal, 75,* 74–101.

Graham, C. (2005). Blended learning systems: Definition, current trends, and future directions. In C. J. Bonk & C. R. Graham (Eds.), *Handbook of blended learning: Global perspectives, local designs* (pp. 3–21). San Francisco, CA: Pfeiffer.

Heinze, A., & Procter, C. (2004). Reflections on the use of blended learning. *Education in a Changing Environment.* Salford, United Kingdom: University of Salford, Education Development Unit. Retrieved May 31, 2012, from http://www.ece.salford.ac.uk/proceedings/papers/ah_04.rtf.

Johnson, L., Smith, R., Willis, H., Levine, A., & Haywood, K. (2011). *The 2011 Horizon Report.* Austin, TX: The New Media Consortium. Retrieved May 27, 2012, from http://net.educause.edu/ir/library/pdf/HR2011.pdf.

Laster, S., Otte, G., Picciano, A.G., & Sorg, S. (2005, April). Redefining blended learning. Paper presented at the Sloan-C Workshop on Blended Learning. Chicago, IL.

Maxim, H. (2009). An essay on the role of language in collegiate foreign language programmatic reform. *Die Unterrichtspraxis, 42,* 123–129.

MLA Ad Hoc Committee on Foreign Languages. (2007). Foreign languages and higher education: New structures for a changed world. *Profession, 12,* 234–245.

Nicolson, M., Murphy, L., & Southgate, M. (Eds.). (2011). *Language teaching in blended contexts.* Edinburgh: DunedIn Academic Press.

The National Center for Academic Transformation (n.d.). *Project descriptions sorted by degree of success.* Retrieved May 28, 2012, from http://www.thencat.org/PCR/Proj_Success_all.html.

The Power of Open. Creative Commons. Retrieved May 28, 2012, from http://thepowerofopen.org/.

Thoms, J. (2011). Investigating foreign language graduate student instructors' perceptions and use of technology in the classroom. In H. Maxim & H. W. Allen (Eds.), *Educating the future foreign language professoriate for the 21st century* (pp. 192–211). Boston: Heinle Cengage.

Chapter 2

Best Practices in Online Learning:
Is It for Everyone?

Robert Blake

The foreign language (FL) coordinator or department contemplating integrating technology into the curriculum should reflect on a number of topics before, during, and after implementation, namely,

- the rationale that motivates the use of technology in the FL curriculum in the first place;
- the different conditions under which technology might be used (which implies, of course, that not all online courses are the same by any stretch of the imagination);
- the reasons why some FL professionals refuse to accept online courses for university credit or as a way to satisfy the language requirement;
- the fallacies underlying the profession's assumption that all face-to-face (F2F) classes are better than online options;
- the factors that potentially doom a comparative line of research that poses the simplistic question: "Which is better—F2F or online?"
- the affordances and limitations of the online learning environment that may not present a good fit for some students while promising a most excellent alternative for others.

In addition to making reference to other researchers' work in presenting this overview of online language learning, I will be drawing on my own experience as a teacher of a hybrid first-year course in Spanish at UC Davis for the past six years, the creator of a fully virtual Spanish course with materials from *Tesoros* (a first-year program that has evolved from the CD format to DVD and later to *Moodle* and now is being readapted to a *SoftChalk* and SAKAI platform). As director of the UC Language Consortium (http://uccllt.ucdavis.edu), I have acquired other insights into online learning by serving as a producer for an online first-year Arabic course, *Arabic Without Walls* (http://arabicwithoutwalls.ucdavis.edu/aww/) that has been taught in a virtual format to University of California students, first from UC Berkeley and later from UC Irvine. Currently, I am helping to produce *Arabic Encounters* for the advance-level and Flagship programs. Finally, I helped finance the last stages of development for the online Quechua Language materials, *Ucuchi*, developed by the late Roger Andersen at UCLA with input from UC Davis (http://quechua.ucla.edu/), a unique labor of love for this extraordinary applied linguist.

The Need for Technology in the Foreign Language Curriculum

If any graduate candidate goes to an MLA interview and is asked, "Do you use technology in your teaching?" no one would be so outdated as to reply with a flat, "No." Technological competence is now an addendum to almost every job posting in our field. Accordingly, no one would deny the importance of using technology in support of learning, least of all with respect to learning foreign languages, but the reasons underlying why it should be integrated into the curriculum are not immediately obvious. The idea that technology is important for FL teaching and learning even made its way into the 2007 Modern Language Association (MLA) report on foreign languages and higher education with a brief recommendation about reforming the teaching of language and culture by having the language departments train their graduate students to use technology in language instruction and learning (MLA, 2007). But even this enlightened report seems to view technology merely as a set of tools rather than part of a larger fundamental cultural change in the way we teach languages or, more accurately, in the way that students themselves *learn* language—or learn anything for that matter.

The wild success of social computing and gaming—*Facebook* has started to sell market shares, and *Halo 2* grossed more than $125 million on the first day of its release in 2004—should be enough to alert us to the fact that the rules of engagement are changing. Our students love to *do* things using the desktop or laptop computer, the iPad, or the iPhone. Not only do students enjoy using technology to accomplish mostly any task, but they are also willing to spend significant amounts of their time outside of class working on language homework if technology is added into the mix. This accounts for the recent interest in harnessing video games for the purposes of language learning (Gee, 2007; Peterson, 2010; Thorne, 2008; Thorne, Black, & Sykes, 2009), because students intrinsically appear to enjoy learning via a game format. They love to play—well, we all love to play—as I have talked about in other presentations about the power of *homo ludens*, the human being who plays (Blake, 2011b). To the frustration of many of us classroom teachers, our students want to *play* on these devices practically all the time even in class when we don't want them to. Quite frankly, as I struggle to learn first-year Arabic, I find that I am using the *Google* translation app on my iPhone to support learning this difficult noncognate language.

From a broad cognitive point of view, learning a second language (L2) requires an enormous amount of time on task. This should not surprise us because, as children, we spent an enormous amount of concentrated time learning our first language. For L2 development, whether judging by the Interagency Language Roundtable scale, the American Council on the Teaching of Foreign Languages (ACTFL) guidelines, or the European Framework benchmarks, it takes about 600 hours to reach what we can loosely call *functional proficiency* in a Romance language, which is a category I language. For a category IV language, such as Arabic or Chinese, the time greatly increases, to around 2,200 hours (http://www.dliflc.edu/archive/documents/DLPT_Credit_by_Exam_Policy.pdf).

With respect to learning in general, Malcolm Gladwell (2008) suggests that 10,000 hours are needed to become an expert in some area. He cites the example of Bill Gates to prove his point. Mr. Gates was a student at the University of Washington when time sharing became available, making working on the computer mainframe relatively inexpensive, which allowed Gates hours and hours of practice to perfect his skills and ideas. In my own case, I have calculated that I reached 10,000 hours of Spanish language study sometime around the end of my PhD studies—a rather neat fit into Gladwell's metaphoric calculation.

In the case of our students, then, time on task is crucial to success in L2 development. If students enjoy using technology to learn, if they leverage more of their out-of-class time this way so as to continue their contact with the target language, then it is a positive extension of the time spent in the classroom. Our job in academia is to help structure that extra time in the most advantageous fashion possible, which does not mean any random application of available technology but a well-articulated coordination of the tools and best practices that exist.

The last argument that can be marshaled in favor of incorporating new technologies into the heart of the FL curriculum deals with the issue of access to instruction for less commonly taught languages. Even if all universities wanted to teach all the world's languages, the supply of language instructors is severely limited in many of the most crucial languages. People's time and collocation to educational institutions are also limited. Online instruction may be one way to provide access to students on any given campus—or more simply, anywhere—to courses at another university to obtain the necessary beginning levels of language study that will eventually feed into programs offered abroad or at other institutions. Likewise, online language maintenance courses at the intermediate high and advanced levels have their place, too, an application of technology that has not escaped notice at the U.S. Departments of State and Defense.

This vision, of course, presupposes that the United States will minimally continue to value speaking world languages even while Harvard's former president Larry Summers (2012) predicts that the emergence of English as the global language, along with better machine translation programs in the face of the world's vexing language fragmentation, will all become serious disincentives to investing further in language study in higher education. Needless to say, some of our campus administrators might echo these thoughts and comfort us by saying that higher education is already producing the next generation of Middle Eastern professionals with uniquely *English-only* expertise—but few in that region of the world would share this egocentric view. Or perhaps their reasons are much more venial—short-term money savings in response to difficult financial times without forethought to any future consequences beyond the next few fiscal years. In any event, technology can help in this arena, as my previous experience with online Arabic, Quechua, and Punjabi has shown me, if implemented in an intelligent manner with the support of the language faculty.

Online Learning: Types and Tools

The different curricular roles for technology can be broadly described as *blended* (using technology as a supplement to classroom instruction), *hybrid* (providing instruction both in class and online), and completely *online* language learning (Blake, 2011a). These delivery formats, along with the mix of the technological tools used therein, overlap in many cases with the differences in nomenclature having more to do with the percentage of content that is delivered online (for a detailed classification, see Kraemer, 2008). Allen and Seaman (2010) have characterized the hybrid learning format as representing the best of both worlds in the sense that it provides learners with all the conveniences of online learning while still maintaining the traditional F2F link found in the classroom experience. According to their recent Sloan report concerning online learning in general, a 25 percent increase in online enrollment occurred in 2008, the last year of their study (Table 2-1). This means that 30 percent of all college students now take at least one course online, including language courses. In terms of content alone, 30 to 79 percent of the course materials for higher education are delivered online in a blended or hybrid format. Allen and Seaman define *hybrid learning* as a course in which a "substantial proportion of the content is delivered online, typically uses online discussions, and typically has a reduced number of face-to-face meetings" (p. 4). What remains to be discussed is whether the learning styles of all students allow them to thrive in these technologically supported learning environments, a topic we shall enjoin shortly below.

Within these three main delivery formats, substantial portions of a course can involve computer-mediated communication (CMC) of either an asynchronous

Table 2-1. Postsecondary Total and Online Enrollments for Fall 2002 Through Fall 2008

Fall Term	Total Enrollment	Annual Growth Rate Total Enrollment (%)	Students Taking at Least One Online Course	Annual Growth Rate Online Enrollment (%)	Online Enrollment as a Percentage of Total Enrollment
2002	16,611,710	NA	1,602,970	NA	9.6
2003	16,911,481	1.8	1,971,3976	23.0	11.7
2004	17,272,043	2.1	2,329,783	18.2	13.5
2005	17,487,481	1.2	3,180,050	36.5	18.2
2006	17,758,872	1.6	3,488,381	9.7	19.6
2007	17,975,830	1.2	3,938,111	12.0	21.9
2008	18,199,920	1.2	4,606,353	16.9	25.3

NA, not available.
Adapted from Allen & Seaman, 2010.

(deferred-time communication such as instant messaging) or a synchronous na-ture (i.e., real-time communication). The CMC tools themselves vary from offer-ing students the ability to exchange just text; text and audio; text and video; or text, video, and whiteboards (see Lafford & Lafford, 2005; and any of Robert Godwin-Jones's columns on *Emerging Technologies* published in *Language, Learning & Technology*). Understandably, applied linguists have devoted much attention to examining how CMC exchanges take place from an interactionist, social-cultural, or discourse perspective. Some researchers have endeavored to determine whether CMC is at least as effective as classroom F2F exchanges in promoting oral proficiency development (Blake, 2011a).

Simplifying a great deal of previous research in this area, CMC exchanges all seem to provide additional language practice, whether or not they can be clas-sified as exactly equivalent experiences to F2F interactions. In Gladwell's (2008) context of a prerequisite 10,000 hours, then, it is irrelevant to ask whether CMC can replace F2F exchanges: More is always better, and students need more and more in order to reach just functional proficiency (600+ hours), as well as a more advanced state of bilingualism. But chat sessions undoubtedly add greatly to lan-guage development, as can be seen from the following student comments col-lected two years after having enrolled in an entirely virtual first-year Arabic course (S'hiri & Blake, forthcoming). In this course, students were asked to chat both with classmates and instructors using *Wimba Voiceboards* that provided text and audio exchanges.

> I enjoyed the chat sessions and I feel I learned a lot from them. They were probably the more intensive part of the class and they helped me keep the rhythm throughout the semester.

> One key to a successful class, and indeed a successful education is the student-to-student interaction that takes place [in the chat sessions]. For that, I'd like to say a special thanks to those of you who took time to correspond with me, even a little.

> I loved the fact that part of our grade was to constantly commu-nicate with the professor, TA, and classmates (though late at night when I still had a ton of homework to do, I didn't feel the same way!!):-> I am thankful for it and for the struggle.

> Student X and I met, on average, four times a week [online via *Wimba*] and went through the assignments together. I found this very helpful, because not only did it force me to put aside a few hours each day to study Arabic, it also gave me the opportunity to practice speaking Arabic with a peer (those online chats can be terrifying), work through questions we had, and have the real-life interaction of the standard real-life class.

The value of CMC exchanges like the ones reported above can be confirmed by the explosive popularity of social computing (i.e., *Facebook, LiveMoca, Twitter*, and *texting* in general), which offers the profession another avenue to engage lan-guage students outside the classroom, especially with respect to tandem learning (i.e., pairs of students learning each other's native language) with the goal of also developing intercultural competence. While tandem learning has enjoyed much success (Schwienhorst, 2008), these online collaborations have sometimes led to some unpleasant breakdowns in communication, as has been reported in the literature (Belz, 2002; Ware, 2005; Ware & Kramsch, 2005) and should not be undertaken without considering the obstacles to intercultural understanding, especially when the dialogue is mediated through technology. As with almost every activity carried out inside or outside of the classroom, careful selection and planning of the task itself help to guarantee a felicitous exchange and mitigate the possibilities of the type of breakdowns chronicled in the literature.

In addition to CMC tools described here, a plethora of other Internet 2.0 tools afford helpful ways of delivering engaging language materials and activities, including interactive web pages, blogs, wikis, clouds, apps, bots, and tutorial computer-assisted language learning (CALL) databases that can respond to frequent errors with finely tweaked feedback messages (Heift, 2010a). How instructors mix and match these components is entirely up to their own discretion and creativity. This helps explain why comparing one hybrid course to another is such a difficult research proposition—in other words, comparing technologically supported courses is as hard as comparing one F2F teacher with another. Methods, tasks, personalities, and individual student factors vary wildly. Before moving on to tackle the acceptance of online learning by our profession and the pros and cons of doing comparative studies, let me illustrate what a single Internet tool can accomplish for our L2 students.

The Case of *LangBot*: A Student Vocabulary Instant Messaging Buddy

As researchers in vocabulary development have clearly shown (Cobb, 2007; Nation, 2001; Nation & Waring, 1997), L2 reading is next to impossible without a critical mass of vocabulary items. Fully independent reading requires knowledge of close to 3,000 of the target language's most frequent words and the ability to guess words in context demands that the student knows approximately 95 to 98 percent of the words contained in a particular text (Nation, 2001). Most first-year courses optimistically expect students to learn approximately 1,000 of the most frequent words, although when dealing with category III (e.g., Russian, Filipino) and IV languages (e.g., Chinese, Arabic), that figure might be unrealistically high. Subsequently, the jump to second-year language courses saddles students with drastically increased vocabulary demands in order to ramp up to the increased load of L2 reading and listening skills.

LangBot, developed by Scott Payne at Amherst College (https://www.amherst.edu/aboutamherst/news/faculty/node/144997), is an *app* intended to help students increase their vocabulary both in breadth (i.e., more words) and in depth (i.e., a better semantic network with more connotations) by providing a vocabulary *buddy* via their iPhones, iPads, or computers. As shown in Figure 2-1, *LangBot* can be accessed through any instant messaging (IM) program (e.g., Instant Messenger, iChat) and then questioned for word translations in Spanish, Chinese, or German. The Spanish version of *LangBot* returns a translation for each query and then prompts the user to see the word in context as provided by a selection

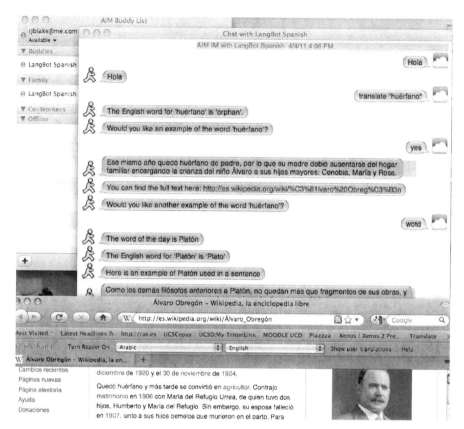

Figure 2-1. Instant messaging Interface for *LangBot*.

from *Wikipedia*. Students can also ask to see the word of the day selected from a list of the most frequent 3,000 words in Spanish (following guidelines given by Davies, 2006), adjusting for the learner's specific linguistic level. *LangBot* keeps a record of each student's requests that is also available for the instructor to see. Whenever the student asks for a pop quiz on vocabulary, *LangBot* retrieves the student's search history and customizes the exam to that student's particular needs.

Kelly Bilinski Arispe, a PhD candidate at Davis, decided to test out whether or not three groups of L2 Spanish learners—novice high, intermediate low, and intermediate high—who used LangBot for only one quarter would experience more vocabulary growth than those who had no access to this vocabulary *app*. She tested the groups before and after with an instrument that probed vocabulary breadth and depth via the phone following protocols adapted from Meara's approach to vocabulary acquisition (Read & Nation, 2009). The results are quite surprising and can be found in Tables 2-2, 2-3, and 2-4, with the asterisks indicating significance at the $p < .05$ level. Table 2-2 shows that all three groups using *LangBot* added significantly more words to their vocabulary (i.e., breadth) compared with those who did not use this *app*. Similarly, the correlation found in Table 2-3 confirms that among the *LangBot* users themselves, the more students used *LangBot* by sending messages and queries, the more progress they made in their vocabulary breadth, an observation

Table 2-2. Analysis of Variance for Access to *LangBot* Across Levels According to Vocabulary Breadth

	Treatment		
Vocabulary Breadth	**Access (μ ± SE)**	**No Access (μ ± SE)**	**df**
Beginner	1.36 ± .74* (n = 25)	0.23 ± 0.49 (n = 32)	1
Intermediate low	3.40 ± .44* (n = 20)	2.27 ± 0.57 (n = 22)	1
Intermediate high	2.48 ± 0.39* (n = 25)	0.29 ± 0.49 (n = 18)	1

*$p < .05$ within rows.

Table 2-3. Pearson Correlations for *LangBot* Messages and Breadth and Depth Scores

	Messages
Breadth	.245*
Depth	−.003

*$p < .05$

Table 2-4. Analysis of Variance for Access to *LangBot* Across Intermediate Levels According to Vocabulary Depth

	Treatment		
Vocabulary Depth	**Access (μ ± SE)**	**No Access (μ ± SE)**	**df**
Intermediate low	2.45 ± 1 (n = 20)	4.3 ± 1 (n = 22)	1
Intermediate high	4.62 ± 0.92* (n = 25)	1.47 ± 0.79 (n = 18)	1

*$p < .05$ within rows.

that again speaks to the importance of time on task with respect to L2 development. But with respect to vocabulary depth, as shown in Table 2-4, only the intermediate high students were able to restructure their semantic nets in more meaningful ways as a result of the extra practice afforded by *LangBot*.

The Acceptance of Online Courses by the Foreign Language Profession

I am always astonished, if not taken aback, when I meet with university committees on courses to find that many faculty members assume that all F2F classes are inherently better than any online classes without any regard to size, lecture versus discussion format, or the instructor's classroom talents (or lack thereof). It is simply not the case that a poor instructor lecturing 300 students necessarily creates a superior learning experience to other formats, including online options. Obviously, one smells fear stemming from a belief that technology will replace instructors and the established way of doing things, thereby robbing students of the magical presence of the instructor, along with any justification for charging steep tuition fees for an elite undergraduate experience. We all know that good teachers are wonderful and bad teachers may do damage to students' progress, but good teaching depends on a host of individual factors. Bad teachers using technology still most probably add up to a discouraging educational experience. Likewise, merely being physically present in the same classroom should not constitute the gold standard of teaching or learning from the student perspective—it works both ways. Achieving a sound curricular design should always be the responsibility of the faculty and the overriding concern, whether or not the delivery method involves technology partially, as in the instance of a hybrid course, or completely, as in the case of an online class. Nevertheless, many language professionals persist in fearing technology despite the fact that language instructors must clearly be involved at all stages of design and implementation of an online curriculum.

Many instructors fear that these new technologies will be used by cash-conscious administrators to reduce the faculty and make class delivery less expensive by increasing class size. First of all, the few cost/benefit analyses that have addressed this question have shown that using technology only marginally saves money without necessarily improving student performance in any significant way (Maher, Sommer, Acredolo, & Matthews, 2005; but also see Herman & Banister, 2007, for a rosier estimation of savings for online delivery). Second, only asynchronous formats have any chance of implementing drastic increases in the number of enrolled students, but online language courses should ideally involve a synchronous CMC component to stimulate oral proficiency, making them as time intensive as, if not more so, than F2F classes. Third, choosing not to include CMC opportunities turns the online class into little more than an electronic workbook, which is not what our profession should have in mind when contemplating online education.

Again, the proper use of technology can increase student access through anytime anywhere learning and the sharing of faculty among different institutions, which is something that the FL profession is just beginning to explore. For students, some prefer to work in a hybrid manner because it fits their preferred learning styles, others enjoy the flexibility offered by working online, and still others do not thrive very well in these new digital learning environments—a topic I will return to below.

With respect to granting college credit for online language courses, many faculty members demand to see the research on the teaching effectiveness for online courses as a prerequisite for taking any action to legitimize this format. When language instructors contemplate approving credit for distance learning language courses, the phrase *equivalent educational experience* seems to dominate the discussion, a slippery notion based on the premise, again, that all courses delivered in the classroom already share equivalent experiences. The truth is that language courses, whether delivered *in situ* or online, enjoy certain affordances while suffering from other specific limitations. To a great degree, the differences among same-level language courses owe more to the individual talents and limitations of each instructor and the quality of the learning materials they use rather than the format itself. This is not to imply that the course format will not also shape the nature of the learning environment in significant ways (Thorne, 2003). Although the exercise of equating courses delivered by different instructors via different formats remains an elusive goal, making sure that students can move seamlessly back and forth between in-class and online learning experiences should be possible and, moreover, constitutes an absolute faculty responsibility for a well-articulated language curriculum with online options. Because L2 development is a slow process, as previously discussed, each learning experience along the way should be, above all else, stimulating, motivating, and well articulated. Clearly, there exists more than one pathway to reach the goal of becoming bilingual—no matter how much some in our profession value the in-class format over any other avenues of language study, such as independent study, hybrid classes, online courses, or study abroad.

Returning to the issue of comparative studies, the present-day language assessment tools are often inadequate to tease out significant differences in linguistic proficiency, especially among the first-year student population (see discussion in Blake, 2009; Blake, Wilson, Cetto, & Pardo-Ballester, 2008, pp. 123–124). This is hardly surprising when one considers the limited vocabulary (<1,000 words) and limited time on task entailed in the first-year curriculum: minimally, only about 150 hours. This is just the nature of the possible gains that can be achieved during the first year of L2 language study, not a criticism of any student, teacher, or curriculum; the brain is still overwhelmed with processing issues that mitigate against the short-term memory holding items long enough to be converted into permanent memory (i.e., the implicit knowledge system). A new plateau seems to be achieved around the 200-hour mark, which is intuitively captured by the ACTFL rubrics of *Novice Low, Novice Mid,* or *Novice High*—which is a more diplomatic way of describing the situation in contrast to the brutally frank nomenclature used by the Interagency Linguistic Roundtable scale of *0* or *0+.* In other words, students need about 200 hours of instruction or contact with the L2 in order to bump up from the first-year plateau to the next level of *intermediate.* Accordingly, measuring progress during those first 200± hours remains a difficult task fraught with problems, at least with the present assessment tools, which clouds our ability to track student progress in the first year.

This is exactly what we found at UC Davis comparing the placement results for in-class, hybrid, and completely online Spanish learners (Blake et al., 2008)—no clear separation among student scores from course 1 to 3 no matter what format of instruction was used. We used *Versant for Spanish* (Pearson), an assessment instrument designed to determine oral proficiency automatically as graded by the aid of voice recognition software and a parsing algorithm, which gives a score from 20 to 80 points. *Versant* depends heavily on a well-known psycholinguistic technique of sentence repetition: students cannot repeat what does not reside in their long-term memories or what has been called their interlanguage grammar.

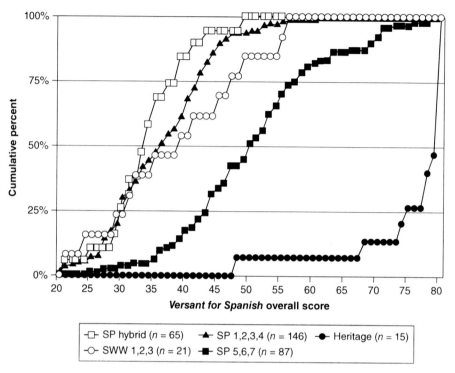

Figure 2-2. Comparison of *Versant* scores among in-class, hybrid, and online students.

For the 258 in-class students, the *Versant* scores separated the students into three statistically observable groups: beginners consisting of students from quarters 1 to 4 (the first 200 hours of instruction), intermediates from quarters 5 to 7, and heritage speakers. In other words, the *Versant* test recognized two separate plateaus for the non-heritage students in the lower-division curriculum, as shown in Figure 2-2. The scores for the in-class students from quarters 1 to 4 were then bundled together and compared with the placement scores for the hybrid and online students at the end of their respective series. Among all of these first-year students—in-class, hybrid, or completely online—there were no significant differences in the placement scores notwithstanding the different delivery formats.

Although small-scale studies comparing discrete CMC or vocabulary treatments abound in the literature, very few comparisons of full-scale mainstream online course delivery are available (White, 2006, p. 259). Some notable exceptions for foreign languages are the following: Adair-Hauck, 2000; Blake & DelForge, 2007; Cahill & Catanzaro, 1997; Chenoweth & Murday, 2003; Chenoweth, Ushida, & Murday, 2006; Cziko & Park, 2003; Green & Earnest-Youngs, 2001; Grgurovic, 2007; Hampel, 2003; Hampel & Hauck, 2004; Lamy, 2004; Scida & Saury, 2006; Soo & Ngeow, 1998.

No significant difference between the in-class students and the online students was the most frequent finding from these comparative studies for first-year language study. Occasionally, the online students performed slightly better but never worse. Obviously, the number of uncontrolled and uncontrollable variables—namely, the talents of different instructors, different types of students, different technological tools, different tasks, different delivery modes, different time frames—abound and will continue to confound this comparative line of research. But because we are all in L2 education for the long haul (10,000 hours or bust!), I suggest that our profession should concentrate more on making the curricular design the very best it can be with or without technology and providing students with well-articulated options to different learning formats whenever possible.

Is Online Learning for Everyone?

The previous presentation of online learning is not meant to give the impression that just because online learning appears to provide a legitimate education option in pursuit of L2 development (like many other activities, too), everyone should therefore be required to learn languages this way or all F2F classes should be abandoned. A sound language curriculum provides options for its students; one size should not have to fit all. Accordingly, I want to end this panoramic review of online language learning by briefly considering the question: Is online learning for everyone?

At the UC Davis campus, we recently finished a study that examined certain personality and cognitive factors that might align with successful hybrid language experiences (Blake & Bilinski Arispe, forthcoming). All 64 informants studied introductory Spanish with multimedia materials supported by synchronous chat sessions (video, voice, text). Personality and cognitive traits were probed using the Big Five Inventory scale (BFI) and the Shipley Institute of Living Scale (SILS), respectively. The BFI (John, Naumann, & Soto, 2008) measures personality traits according to extraversion, agreeableness, conscientiousness, openness, and neuroticism; the SILS (Senior, 2001; Zachary, 1991) measures verbal and abstract intelligence. Both are reliable measures heavily used in psychological studies. The results were correlated with final grades, not an ideal measure of a felicitous online learning experience, but then again, most students who get As or Bs tend to take more language classes, and most students who get Cs, Ds, or Fs tend to slough off or drop out. In that sense, grades are not a bad measure of a positive learning experience. Linguistic proficiency of the Oral Proficiency Interview (OPI) ilk was not of interest for this particular study. Course satisfaction and proficiency are not unrelated, however: if a student drops out, the chances that further L2 development will occur are most probably minimal.

The quantitative data revealed two trends. First, the BFI trait of **conscientiousness** had a highly significant, positive correlation with final grades for these online students, as can be seen in Table 2-5—it was the only factor that even came close to statistical significance. Second, with respect to learners' preferences shown in Table 2-6, low-verbal learners (per SILS) highly favored working with online materials, as opposed to learning in class or chatting online; this was shown by the negative but significant correlation in the first row of Table 2-6.

Table 2-5. Pearson Correlations for Social Factors and Learner Preferences According to Final Grade

Social factors and Learning Preferences	Final Grade	
	Correlation	Significance
Extraversion	.183	$p = .149$
Agreeableness	.055	$p = .668$
Conscientiousness	.381	$p = .002^\dagger$
Neuroticism	−.022	$p = .862$
Openness	−.137	$p = .280$

$p < .05.$
$^\dagger p < .01.$

Table 2-6. Pearson Correlations for Cognitive Factors According to Learner Preferences

	Tesoros Online Materials		Synchronous CMC Sessions		Class Meetings	
Verbal intelligence	−.316	$p = .012^*$	.014	$p = .916$	−.002	$p = .987$
Abstract intelligence	−.222	$p = .080$	.028	$p = .829$	.055	$p = .666$
Shipley score	−.321	$p = .010^\dagger$	.036	$p = .777$	.044	$p = .734$

$^*p < .05.$
$^\dagger p < .01.$
CMC, computer-mediated communication.

On the one hand, the results suggest that students who take control of their own learning experience will perform well within the hybrid learning environment; on the other, low-verbal learners benefit in particular from the ability to work online at their own pace.

There is little doubt that students will increasingly be directed to enroll in hybrid courses as the popularity of this format continues to grow in higher education among administrators and teachers alike. In this study, we examined the question of whether or not all language students are equally ready to take advantage of this new online learning environment. To make informed curricular plans, language departments need to have a clear understanding of which types of students are likely to have a positive online language learning experience. Students, for their part, need to know what will be expected of them in these new learning environments. Although measuring language proficiency gains in hybrid learning formats also constitutes a legitimate area of research, more attention needs to be directed to what social and cognitive factors might condition a successful online L2 learning experience.

These very preliminary results point to the BFI personality trait of conscientiousness as an important element for success in the hybrid environment. Conscientious learners make goals and have a clear plan for their learning process. In a word, they are self-motivated and less subject to or dependent on the type of constant teacher reinforcement that is uniquely available in a supportive, F2F classroom, but not all classrooms are equally supportive, of course. This is *not* to say that successful in-class learners are *not* conscientious but rather that conscientiousness stands out prominently as the principal BFI indicator of success in this hybrid environment. In L2 acquisition and CALL circles, the construct of learner autonomy seems to echo the similar concept, as Sinclair's (1999, p. 310) comments illustrate:

> The establishment of self-access and learner resources centers, the increase in distance learning programs, and a greater involvement of IT in language tracking all demonstrate this professional concern with empowering learners to be more effective and more independent in their language learning.

In practical terms, students should receive explicit advice before enrolling in hybrid and online formats that a high degree of conscientiousness will be required in order to do well. An intriguing research question would be whether or not a personality trait like conscientiousness can be primed with explicit training. Researchers also need to explore whether or not certain online interface features might stimulate conscientiousness for online language learners in more efficient ways.

The second finding of this study suggests that low-verbal learners enrolled in a hybrid language class are greatly assisted by the existence of online materials that permit large amounts of self-study and language practice, such as was possible with a program like *Tesoros* for Spanish (Blake & Delforge, 2008) or *e-Tutor* for German (Heift, 2010a). Accordingly, low-verbal learners might better benefit from a hybrid course or even a blended course that incorporates some type of online component that provides a space for self-paced learning (also see Heift, 2010b)—this finding brings us back to the importance of tutorial CALL, which has been ignored somewhat of late in the excitement over social computing and CMC studies.

One speculation might suggest that these preferences expressed by low-verbal learners might have something to do with the rapid pace and verbal delivery common to F2F interactions and the modern communicative classroom. Low-verbal learners during the first year of L2 language study might simply be overwhelmed by fast-talking native or near-native instructors who are trying to model real-life speech as demanded by the communicative classroom, our own gold standard. These low-verbal students appear to require more time for individual language study and practice during which they can fully control the pace of their own learning. Again, I am returning here to Gladwell's (2008) metaphor of the 10,000 time-on-task hours needed to reach proficiency.

Finally, although strong preferences for synchronous chatting did not emerge in the quantitative data of this study, our students expressed in the exit interviews a pronounced enjoyment for chatting in synchronous computer-mediated communication (SCMC) in Spanish without the pressures normally encountered in F2F contexts (i.e., "the freedom to make mistakes" and "do relaxed talking"). But running small-group synchronous CMC sessions is time consuming and human resource intensive—not exactly music to the administrator's ears. But I would argue that CMC sessions should be *de rigueur* for all online courses.

Conclusions

Overall, the CALL research supports the idea that hybrid and online language courses constitute a responsible option for the FL curriculum, especially for students who are strongly self-motivated or conscientious. Hybrid courses with an online self-study component empower individual language study and provide the needed practice that gives a needed advantage to the low-verbal learners in particular. By the same token, a synchronous chat component will help maintain course quality and oral proficiency, although mitigating the ability to scale up the class size in the online format.

Whether or not hybrid courses represent *the best of both worlds,* as Allen and Seaman (2010) have suggested, is not really a necessary claim. Hybrid language courses are a good fit for conscientious, high-verbal, and even low-verbal learners—and that covers a significant proportion of our student population. Now the language profession must endeavor to create and implement online materials that adequately provide a curriculum that includes pedagogically sound chatting tasks as well as tutorial CALL and, along the way, train a new generation of graduate students how to teach in this environment even when most of the permanent faculty has never done so.

On a more cautionary note, I have said little about what contribution online language learning can make toward the attainment of advanced proficiency, a level where subtle but crucial pragmatic and cultural knowledge comes into play. What affordances, if any, can online courses offer in lieu of having access to the benefits offered by study abroad (Davidson, 2007)? That question would be very pertinent for the *Arabic Encounters* materials being prepared now for advanced Arabic students at UC Davis—but that is another story for another time.

The processes involved in learning online are just beginning to be examined with a focus other than the proverbial comparative question, "Which is better?" Many interesting challenges await us in the CALL field as practitioners carefully integrate technology into the FL curriculum.

References

Adair-Hauck, B., Willingham-McLain, L., & Earnest-Youngs, B. (1999). Evaluating the integration of technology and second language learning. *CALICO Journal, 17*(2), 269–306.

Allen, I. E., & Seaman, J. (2010). Learning on demand: Online education in the United States, 2009. Babson Survey Research Group. Retrieved August 5, 2010, at http://www.sloanc.org/publications/survey/index.

Belz, J. A. (2002). Social dimensions of telecollaborative foreign language study. *Language Learning & Technology, 6*(1), 60–81. Retrieved December 10, 2006, at http://llt.msu.edu/vol6num1/belz/.

Blake, R. (2009). The use of technology for second language distance learning. *The Modern Language Journal, 93,* 822–835.

Blake, R. (2011a). Current trends in online language learning. *Annual Review in Applied Linguistics, 31,* 19–35.

Blake, R. (2011b). *Homo ludens,* los videojuegos y las TICs y el aprendiz de ELE. *FIAPE IV,* Congreso internacional, April 23–26, 2011. Retrieved February 3, 2012, at http://www.anpenorge.no/fiape/IVcongreso/actas.html.

Blake, R. & Shiri, S. (2012). Online Arabic Language Learning: What Happens After? L2 Journal, 4, 230–246. http://escholarship.org/uc/item/0bf3r8g1.

Blake, R., & Bilinski Arispe, K. (forthcoming). Individual factors and successful learning in a hybrid course. System.

Blake, R., Wilson, N. L., Cetto, M., & Pardo-Ballester, C. (2008). Measuring oral proficiency in distance, face-to-face, and blended classrooms. Language Learning & Technology, 12(3), 114–127.

Blake, R. J., & Delforge, A. (2007). Online language learning: The case of Spanish without walls. In B. Lafford & R. Salaberry (Eds.), The art of teaching Spanish: Second language acquisition from research to praxis (pp. 127–147). Washington, DC: Georgetown University Press.

Cahill, D., & Catanzaro, D. (1997). Teaching first-year Spanish on-line. CALICO Journal, 14(2), 97–114.

Chenoweth, N. A., & Murday, K. (2003). Measuring student learning in an online French course. CALICO Journal, 20(2), 284–314.

Chenoweth, N. A., Ushida, E., & Murday, K. (2006). Student learning in hybrid French and Spanish courses: an overview of language online. CALICO Journal, 24(1), 115–145.

Cobb, T. (2007). Computing the vocabulary demands of L2 reading. Language Learning & Technology, 11, 38–63.

Cziko, G. A., & Park, S. (2003). Internet audio communications for second language learning: A comparative view of six programs. Language Learning & Technology, 7(1), 15–27.

Davies, M. (2006). A frequency dictionary of Spanish: Core vocabulary for learners. New York: Routledge.

Davidson, D. (2007). Study abroad and outcomes measurements: The case of Russian. Modern Language Journal, 91(2), 276–280.

Gee, J. (2007). What video games have to teach us about learning and literacy. New York: Palgrave.

Gladwell, M. (2008). Outliers: The story of success. Boston: Little Brown and Company.

Green, A., & Earnest-Youngs, B. (2001). Using the web in elementary French and German courses: Quantitative and qualitative study results. CALICO Journal, 19(1), 89–123.

Grgurovic, M. (2007). Research synthesis: CALL comparison studies by language skills/knowledge. Retrieved on February 7, 2012, at http://tesl.engl.iastate.edu:591/comparison/synthesis.htm.

Hampel, R. (2003). Theoretical perspectives and new practices in audio-graphic conferencing for language learning. ReCALL, 15(1), 21–36.

Hampel, R., & Hauck, M. (2004). Towards an effective use of audio conferencing in distance language courses. Language Learning & Technology, 88(1), 166–182.

Heift, T. (2010a). Developing an intelligent language tutor. CALICO Journal, 27(3), 443–459.

Heift, T. (2010b). Prompting in CALL: A longitudinal study of learner uptake. Modern Language Journal, 94, 198–216.

Herman, T. & Banister, S. (2007). Face-to-face versus online coursework: A comparison of costs and learning outcomes. Contemporary Issues in Technology and Teacher Education, 7(4), 318–326.

John, O. P., Naumann, L. P., & Soto, C. J. (2008). Paradigm shift to the integrative Big-Five Trait taxonomy: History, measurement, and conceptual issues. In O. P. John, R. W. Robins, & L. A. Pervin (Eds.), Handbook of personality: Theory and research (pp. 114–158). New York: Guilford Press.

Kraemer, A. (2008). Formats of distance learning. In S. Goertler & P. Winke (Eds.), Opening doors through distance language education: Principles, perspectives, and practices (pp. 11–42). CALICO Monograph Series (Vol. 7). San Marcos, TX: CALICO.

Lafford, P., & Lafford, B. (2005). CMC technologies for teaching foreign languages: What's on the horizon? *CALICO Journal, 22,* 679–710.

Lamy, M. N. (2004). Oral conversations online: Redefining oral competence in synchronous environments *ReCALL, 16*(2), 520–538.

Maher M. W., Sommer, B., Acredolo, C., & Matthews, H. R. (2005). What are the relevant costs of online education? In J. E. Groccia & J. E. Miller (Eds.), *On becoming a productive university: Strategies for reducing costs and increasing quality in higher education.* Bolton: Anker Publishing Company.

Modern Language Association. (2007). Foreign languages and higher education: New structures for a changed world. Retrieved February 23, 2012, at http://www.mla.org/flreport.

Nation, P. (2001). *Learning vocabulary in another language.* Cambridge, UK: Cambridge University Press.

Nation, P., & Waring, R. (1997). Vocabulary size, text coverage and word lists. In N. Schmitt & M. McCarthy (Eds.), *Vocabulary: Description, acquisition, and pedagogy* (pp. 6–19). Cambridge, UK: Cambridge University Press.

Peterson, M. (2010). Computerized games and simulations in computer-assisted language learning: A meta-analysis of research. *Simulation & Gaming, 41*(1), 72–93.

Read, J., & Nation, P. (2006). Meara's contribution to research in lexical processing. In T. Fitzpatrick & A. Barfield (Eds.), *Lexical processing in second language learners.* Clevedon, UK: Multilingual Matters.

Schwienhorst, K. (2008). Learner autonomy and CALL environments. New York: Routledge.

Scida, E. E., & Saury, R. E. (2006). Hybrid courses and their impact on student and classroom performance: A case study at the University of Virginia. *CALICO Journal, 23,* 3, 517–531.

Senior, G., (2001). Shipley Institute of Living Scale. Retrieved on February 20, 2009, at http://www.usq.edu.au/users/senior/69301/Shipley.htm.

Sinclair, B. (1999). More than an act of faith? Evaluating learner autonomy. In C. Kennedy (Ed.), *Innovation and best practice in British ELT.* London: Longman (in association with the British Council).

Soo, K., & Ngeow, Y. (1998). Effective English as a second language (ESL) instruction with interactive multimedia: The MCALL project. *Journal of Educational Multimedia and Hypermedia, 7*(1), 71–89.

Summers, L. (2012, January 20). What you (really) need to know. *The New York Times.* Retrieved February 23, 2012, at http://www.nytimes.com/2012/01/22/education/edlife/the-21st-centuryeducation.html?_r=1&emc=eta1.

Thorne, S. L. (2003). Artifacts and cultures-of-use in intercultural communication. *Language Learning & Technology, 7,* 38–67.

Thorne, S. L. (2008). Transcultural communication in open internet environments and massively multiplayer online games. In S. Magnan (Ed.), *Mediating discourse online.* Amsterdam: Benjamins.

Thorne, S. L., Black, R., & Sykes, J. (2009). Second language use, socialization, and learning in Internet interest communities and online gaming. *Modern Language Journal, 93,* 802–821.

Ware, P. (2005). Missed communication in online communication: Tensions in a German-American telecollaboration. *Language Learning & Technology, 9,* 64–89.

Ware, P., & Kramsch, C. (2005). Toward an intercultural stance: Teaching German and English through telecollaboration. *Modern Language Journal, 89,* 90–105.

White, C. (2006). Distance learning of foreign languages. *Language Teaching, 39,* 247–264.

Zachary, R. A., & Western Psychological Services (Firm), (1991). *Shipley Institute of Living Scale.* Los Angeles: Western Psychological Services.

Chapter 3
Theoretical and Empirical Foundations for Blended Language Learning

Senta Goertler

Blended and online learning are clearly on the rise (cf. Allen & Seaman, 2010) in general and appear to be on the rise in foreign language learning contexts as well. Blake (2011) pointed out that online course enrollment increased more than 10 times the increase in overall enrollment, thereby confirming an exploding trend in favor of online learning. Although the trend and the logistical benefits of blended and online learning due to the temporal and geographical flexibility are well known (cf. Blake, 2011; Goertler, 2011a; Kraemer, 2008a), less is known about blended and online learning and its foundation within second language acquisition (SLA) research and theory. This chapter argues that blended and online foreign language (FL) learning is not just a trend but that it also supports and reflects SLA theory and research.

This chapter focuses on the connection between SLA and blended learning. First, I will briefly review comparative research investigating the outcomes of face-to-face (F2F), blended, and online courses. The main part of the chapter focuses on the foundation of various computer-assisted language learning (CALL) formats within different SLA theoretical approaches. This section is introduced by a short review of commonly described SLA theories followed by a description of relevant CALL formats and concludes with a section outlining the connection between SLA theory and the CALL formats and their role in a blended language course. After discussing a theoretical basis for blended learning, I will quickly review what we know about SLA from research and describe its role in blended language classes. Finally, the chapter will conclude with recommendations for curricular design in a blended course.

What We Know So Far

As already mentioned, so far we know that blended and online learning is steadily increasing. Statistics, however, do not give any indication of how blended courses are designed and implemented. A blended or online course can take many different CALL formats and can be based on different teaching approaches or founded in different theoretical perspectives. Means, Toyama, Murphy, Bakia, and Jones (2009) define the following curriculum-related moderator variables as part of their presentation of research on blended and online learning: (1) pedagogy or learning experience (instructor-delivered expository or independent, active, or collaborative interactive), (2) computer-mediated communication (CMC) with the instructor (asynchronous only or asynchronous and synchronous), (3) CMC with peers (asynchronous only or asynchronous and synchronous), (4) media features (text-based only or text and other media), (5) time on task (more online than F2F or more F2F than online), (6) one-way video or audio, (7) computer-based instruction elements, (8) opportunity for F2F time with the instructor (during instruction, before or after class, or not at all), (9) opportunity for F2F time with peers (during instruction, before or after class, or not at all), and (10) opportunity for practice and feedback provided (p. 29). These different materials and implementations necessarily influence how effective a course is and how effective the delivery format is (see also Blake, 2011). The choices made in response to these 10 variables also imply different theoretical stances and different assumptions about language learning. This chapter argues that a blended course can make sense from an SLA perspective if SLA theory and research is taken into consideration in response to these 10 variables and if SLA is integral to course design and implementation.

Research results on blended learning, regardless of implementation variables, have been positive. The U.S. Department of Education commissioned a meta-analysis of blended and online learning, which found that blended learning was the best learning environment followed by online learning (Means et al., 2009). This meta-analysis of 176 studies showed the same trend across fields and learner types. Grgurovic (2007) collected comparative studies on CALL in a database. She summarized the results related to specific skills (learned or taught) and the level of integration of the online materials. In a follow-up meta-analysis of 25 studies included in the database, Grgurovic, Chapelle, and Shelley (2007; as cited in Chapelle, 2010) concluded that blended and online learning yielded better results. Because meta-analyses came up with favorable results for blended and online learning, it is only logical to conclude that individual comparative studies show similar results for blended, online, and F2F language classes (Chenoweth, Ushida, & Murday, 2006; Goertler, 2011b; Sanders, 2006). It follows that studies focused on self-reported or measured improvement across one semester without a control group also discovered language development (Banados, 2006; Goertler, 2011b; Kraemer, 2008b; Madyarov, 2009; Strambi & Bouvet, 2003). Naturally, the success of the course depends on the design of the course as was mentioned earlier. Additionally, the kind of success that can be measured depends on the research design. Moreover, the instruments and the data analysis procedures also influence the results. Contradicting results as have been found when looking at specific skills (see summary in Goertler & Winke, 2008) can be explained by variability in course design, as mentioned earlier (Blake, 2011).

Another reason for variability in course effectiveness of blended and online FL learning is that online learning may involve different processes of learning and different outcomes compared with traditional F2F learning (Blake, 2009). Furthermore, as Garrett (1991) has implied and Sykes (2012) has argued, it may be time to let go of a comparative research methodology for understanding the learning process and outcomes in blended learning, at least from the perspective of SLA research and theory. Comparative studies may provide interesting information for administrators but are not actively contributing to SLA research, which is much more interested in how people learn in different contexts (see also Chapelle, 2010). Therefore, SLA theory and research needs to inform both the design of blended courses as well as the research methods and research questions investigated in these learning contexts. To set the stage for such investigations, this chapter will now discuss the connection between SLA theory and research as it relates to the online components within a blended course.

Second Language Acquisition Theoretical Foundation for Various Computer-Assisted Language Learning Formats in Blended Courses

Computer-assisted language learning practitioners (cf. Chapelle, 1997) and researchers (cf. Blake, 2007; Chapelle, 2009) have long called for CALL research and material design to be theoretically grounded in SLA. Although not all theoretical assumptions and empirical results are applicable to a technology-enhanced language learning environment, CALL must turn to SLA theory and research to understand language learning processes and to apply that knowledge in materials and course design. Because of the differences between the F2F and CALL learning environments, White (2006) has argued for the development of a distinct theoretical framework specifically for online learning. Although I will return to such a proposal at the end of this chapter, the focus here is on what we already know from SLA theory and research and how it is relevant for blended courses.

In a blended language class, F2F learning activities may enhance and reinforce online learning activities and vice versa. It is crucially important that these two environments and the learning opportunities within them complement each other by being based on either the same SLA theoretical perspective or complementary SLA perspectives. Because most SLA textbooks provide insights into how to apply those theories to the F2F portions of the course, this chapter particularly focuses on the SLA theoretical foundation for the online components of a blended course.

Chapelle (2009) has argued that computer-mediated language instruction makes sense from any SLA theoretical perspective. Yet naturally, different kinds of computer-mediated language instruction implementations are better supported by some SLA theories than others. Since the birth of SLA theory, the field has expanded dramatically, and it is beyond the scope of this chapter to focus on all SLA theories. Instead, I will focus here on theories typically highlighted in review books and articles of SLA theory (see, for example, Gass & Selinker, 2008; and VanPatten & Williams, 2007a; for a discussion specific to CALL, see Chapelle, 2004, 2007, and 2009; Thorne & Smith, 2011; and Youngs, Ducate, & Arnold, 2011), including universal grammar, processability theory, interactionist perspectives, sociocultural theory, and language socialization (Table 3-1). Then I will describe different formats of CALL (Appendix 3-1) and provide information about which theoretical perspective is best suited for the format, keeping in mind that any blended or online course may use a variety of these formats (see also Blake, 2011; Kraemer, 2008a).

The formats of CALL discussed in this chapter are an expansion of Blakes's (2011) model, which separated CALL into tutorial CALL (traditional and

Table 3-1. Second Language Acquisition Theoretical Perspectives

Universal Grammar (White, 2003, 2007)	**Type of Approach: Linguistic**

Universal grammar assumes that everyone has the innate ability to learn languages. Universal grammar is the representation of all grammars of all languages. All languages are guided by the same principles but are differentiated based on the parameters of a language. When a child first hears a language, no parameters are set; upon processing the input, parameters will be set, and the language is learned. Perspectives differ as to the availability of UG during second language learning (see Gass & Selinker, 2008, for further discussion). A new process of learning might be necessary, parameters may need to be reset to account for the second language, or one may access the initial stage of the universal grammar to set a separate set of parameters for the second language.

Processability (Pienemann, 1998, 2007)	**Type of Approach: Psycholinguistic**

The basic assumption of procesability theory is that language learning as a consequence of language comprehension and as evidenced in language production only occurs when the language processor is ready. This in turn means that there is an order in which aspects of the language can be processed. The theories assumes a processability hierarchy that dictates what can be processed when (i.e., what can be learned when).

Interactionist Perspectives (Gass, 1997; Gass & Mackey, 2007)	**Type of Approach: Psycholinguistic**

This second language acquisition perspective is based on the assumption that interaction is key to learning. During interaction, input has to be processed to be comprehended input, which then may allow for noticing differences between the target language and the interlanguage rules. During output within interactions, learners can test the hypotheses they have formed about the second language. Whereas comprehended output can serve as positive feedback on the hypotheses, the negative feedback received during negotiation of meaning of incomprehensible output can lead to noticing of differences and subsequent adjustment to the interlanguage (i.e., learning).

Sociocultural Theory (Lantolf, 2000; Lantolf & Thorne, 2007)	**Type of Approach: Social**

Sociocultural theory assumes that learning is collaborative, mediated, and situated. Language is one form of mediation between the human and the environment. The process of learning (including language learning) follows the pattern of being regulated by objects, regulated by others (typically more experienced), and eventually being self-regulated. At the point of self-regulation, something is learned or internalized; however, this is not a constant stage, and something internalized at some point in time may no longer be internalized later. Analyzing expert language and imitating it is a step in language learning. Another key concept in learning under sociocultural theory is the zone of proximal development, which is the distance between what a novice can do without assistance or scaffolding and what he or she can do with assistance. This is also the window in which language learning occurs.

Language Socialization (Duff, 2007; Ochs, 2002)	**Type of Approach: Social**

For a novice to become a legitimate, accepted member of a community, the novice is socialized through language and at the same time socialized in how to use language. Socialization is further complicated in second language learning because of the already existing membership to one or several first language communities and the correlating first language identity.

intelligent CALL [iCALL]), social computing (CMC), and games. For this chapter, a more fine-graded categorization was selected to highlight differences from SLA theoretical perspectives and in response to the 10 variables presented earlier. The categories are (a) CALL tutorials, (b) iCALL, (c) CMC with peers, (d) CMC across cultures, (e) online communities, (f) games, and (g) simulations. Yet this list of tools is not exhaustive, and more online tools could be used in a language class. Considering the space limitations of this chapter, other features such as using online content for authentic input, corpora, concordancers, online dictionaries, and other tools for analyzing language and trouble-shooting linguistic problems will not be discussed here (for a review on those topics, see Lafford, Lafford, & Sykes, 2007).

Introduction to Second Language Acquisition Theory

Before discussing how CALL elements of a hybrid course are supported by SLA theoretical perspectives, I will first summarize the main theories (see Table 3-1 for an overview). The theories can be divided into their approaches, which are typically related to the field of origin as well as how they define and account for where and how learning occurs. The theories were divided into the following categories: (a) linguistic (universal grammar), (b) cognitive and psycholinguistic (processability theory, interactionist perspective), or (c) social (sociocultural theory, language socialization) theories. The main difference between these approaches is whether they assume that language learning is an innate ability (e.g., universal grammar), part of general cognitive processing and psycholinguistic learning, or deeply embedded in social interactions. Table 3-1 indicates the type of approach for each perspective and summarizes its most salient features.

Formats of Computer-Assisted Language Learning

The CALL formats were divided into those that include a human-to-human interaction via the computer versus those that are an individual human-to-computer interaction. Naturally, simulations and games can span over both of these categories and are therefore included in their own category. The human-to-computer category was further divided based on the quality of feedback and strategies for material organization (i.e., tutorial CALL versus iCALL). The social technologies were grouped into three categories: CMC with peers, CMC across cultures, and online communities. The factors that differentiate social technologies are (a) the purpose of the communication and (b) the typical interlocutors. CMC with peers and CMC across cultures account for classroom activities only. During CMC with peers, students communicate with people at their language level, thereby limiting the opportunities to benefit from expert–novice interactions. In CMC across cultures, students communicate with people who are experts in the language and typically also from another culture, thereby making expert–novice interactions possible but adding cultural differences as an added difficulty in the communication. Although these communications with peers and members of the target culture are also part of building online communities, the online communities in focus in the separate online communities category are focused on online communities that already exist outside of the class and that are organized around a theme or a task. The focus of communication in such online communities is on the content or tasks that these communities engage with rather than on a specific cultural or linguistic mission. Furthermore, members of these communities are typically from a variety of countries and cultures choosing one or multiple languages as their medium of communication. This different purpose, as well as the types of interlocutors, changes the integrateability of different theoretical perspectives.

Games and simulations share some commonalities with CALL tutorials and iCALL as well as with social media. Games and simulations as part of a blended language course are even more complicated to categorize and therefore were included in their own categories. A game or simulation may be focused on language learning or simply include speakers of another language; they may include only learners, members of the target community, or other multilingual participants or players. Simulations necessarily and games potentially include nonplayer characters or prerecorded interlocutors. These features make them a mixed category and heterogeneous in nature. The difference between the two is that simulations simply simulate a task or an interaction without an engagement with the actual task or real interlocutors.

In Appendix 3-1, I provide a definition of each CALL format, summarize the features of the format, list examples, and point out the best matching SLA theoretical perspective from the ones described above. However, in the following sections, I will explain how these formats are supported by SLA theory and what role they might play in a blended language learning environment. Chapelle (2009) also provides an informative overview of the connection between CALL and several of the theories mentioned here. Although there is some overlap between Chapelle's (2009) discussion and the discussion here, the former is limited to CALL in general and does not address blended learning specifically.

Computer-Assisted Language Learning Tutorials

Computer-assisted language learning practitioner tutorials are computer–human interaction based, are typically skill based, and provide feedback based on a limited answer key. As indicated earlier, this CALL format is most supported by universal grammar. A CALL tutorial provides learners with input, which can trigger parameter settings. Additionally, a CALL tutorial may highlight first language (L1) and second language (L2) contrasts to provide more practice on features that differ between the two languages to allow for adjustments to parameter settings in contrast to the L1. CALL tutorials are also considered effective from a behaviorist perspective because they provide instant feedback and by cognitive theories that support a development from declarative or explicit knowledge to procedural or implicit knowledge, suggesting that through repeated practice, paths are strengthened or processes become automatized (see Gass & Selinker, 2008, for a more detailed discussion). Because no interaction with a human is part of these CALL formats, this is not considered helpful from those theoretical perspectives that assume the locus of learning in or through interactions such as the interactionist perspectives, sociocultural theory, and language socialization. For it to be beneficial from those perspectives, transfer from practice in controlled settings to natural conversations has to be possible. Considering these limitations from a social perspective on language learning, there are also implications for the role of CALL tutorials in a blended course. CALL tutorials would likely be part of homework or online class time as individual work reinforcing a concept learned in class. Given the technical limitations, such tools should primarily be used for controlled exercises with limited student production so that the program can provide accurate feedback. The teacher could facilitate the learning with these tools and maximize their benefits by assigning exercises that target a learner's weakness. A typical assignment would consist of completing a specific set of exercises, which some learners may complete quickly and for which others may need more time. The teacher can use the program internal reports to make decisions on what to review in class based on learners' successful completion of the exercises.

Intelligent Computer-Assisted Language Learning

Computer-assisted language learning practitioner tutorials and iCALL overlap, but iCALL has more capabilities. Because of the intelligent feedback and the computer-adaptive progression of materials, other theoretical frameworks in addition to the universal grammar apply as well. From a processability theory perspective, iCALL carries the advantage of being able to control the sequencing of materials. The learner, the teacher, and the program can select materials based on a learner's current capabilities and can thereby dynamically react to a learner's performance with new materials. As is the case with CALL tutorials, the lack of interaction causes problems from a social perspective on learning, although the availability of intelligent feedback allows for computer-aided scaffolding. Parser-based iCALL programs allow the software to score and provide feedback on even longer productions (Fryer & Carpenter, 2006). When such a program's feedback is based on previously (or concurrently) collected and coded learner corpora (see discussions in Blake, 2007; Pendar & Chapelle, 2008), the program can provide more accurate feedback. Presumably, the learners who produced the language in the learner corpus are at a similar developmental stage and would have similar problems as the learners engaging with the program, which should allow the current learners to receive scaffolding on the structures currently being processed. If the developer or designer also keeps in mind the processability hierarchy in his or her choice of amount and type of scaffolding depending on the error source, these programs can be even more effective. The application of these programs in a blended course is similar to CALL tutorials, but because of the more sophisticated nature of these programs, less teacher feedback and guidance are required during the implementation phase. A typical assignment in this type of program might be similar to CALL tutorials or require a set amount of time or is dependent on when the student reaches a certain level. The advantage of the time limit is that each student must spend the same amount of time with the program. However, because of individual differences, such as language aptitude, students' results may differ radically. Program reports can be used by the teacher to develop individual learning paths and programs rather than following a one-size-fits-all approach.

Computer-Mediated Communication With Peers

Computer-mediated communication with peers indicates activities and tasks that require learner–learner interactions via computer technologies. CMC tools vary in the nature of the interactions. For example, a blog may be less conducive to a discussion than a discussion forum. However, the blog may be better suited for reflections than the discussion forum or a synchronous chat. CMC has typically been implemented and studied from an interactionist perspective. CMC, similar to other forms of interaction, allows for noticing, feedback, and negotiation of meaning and thereby enhances language learning (for discussions, see Blake, 2009; Kern, 2006; Sauro, 2009). Often, the medium slows down interactions among students compared with synchronous F2F discussion, which has been confirmed to result in more salience and thereby increasing opportunities for noticing and subsequent learning (see Ortega, 1997, for a summary). Additionally, as the work by Smith (Smith, 2003, 2008; Smith, Alvarez, Torres, & Zhao, 2008; Smith & Gorsuch, 2004) has shown, learners receive feedback not just from the interlocutor but also through scrolling and rereading portions of their own and the interlocutor's language production as well as through the consultation of other resources (e.g., online dictionaries, textbooks). The synchronicity of the medium influences the nature of the interactions, the type of feedback one receives, and students' ability to process the input. Some argue that interactions in CMC may take a different pattern from F2F interactions (see Fernandez-Garcia & Martinez-Arbelaiz, 2002; Smith et al., 2003).

Because of its social nature, peer interactions can also be seen as beneficial from a sociocultural theory and a language socialization perspective. Sociocultural theory, however, puts more of an emphasis on expert–novice interactions. From a language socialization standpoint, CMC with peers can be helpful but only in socializing learners to be part of a community of learners of the language. One may also argue that because learners are communicating with each other, their native-like input is limited and their primary input may be nontarget like, which may negatively impact their language learning. Because this form of CMC is limited to course members, it can be used during F2F or online time. It can therefore serve as a connection between the F2F and the online components of a course. The main purpose of CMC activities is to practice communication in a slowed-down format or when F2F is not an option. Payne and Whitney (2002) have argued that such interactions even when completed in text-based programs can improve communicative ability and oral proficiency. The teacher's role is to carefully design tasks that require and inspire communication and collaboration. The teacher can also provide feedback after reviewing the records of the interactions or an end product to be created during the CMC activity.

Computer-Mediated Communication Across Cultures

Naturally, this CALL format shares a lot of similarities with the previous format. The key difference is that these interactions occur between novices and experts. Because during CMC across cultures, the learners interact with an expert, these interactions are seen beneficial from the perspective of any theory that sees native-speaker input as an important trigger (e.g., universal grammar) or mechanism for learning. Similar to the above, CMC across cultures allows for input, pushed output, the negotiation of meaning, feedback, and noticing. It is thereby supported by interactionist perspectives on SLA. Most significantly, this form is supported by sociocultural theory because the learners are communicating with a native speaker (expert–novice interactions), and assuming the tasks are meaningful, scaffolding can occur and learners can move from being regulated by others (the native speaker) to self-regulation. From a language socialization standpoint, CMC across cultures also offers students the opportunity to be socialized into a cross-cultural community (for more, see the discussion on online communities and the work by Hanna & de Nooy, 2003). Because of the nature of the conversation with native speakers, there may also be limits to the effectiveness of these interactions. For instance, native speakers may not be able to adjust to the language learner, which means that the input is not comprehended by the learner. This, according to the interactionist perspective, as an example, can then undermine student learning. Arguing from a processability standpoint, the native speaker input may not be processed because of the learner's developmental stage and may therefore not result in learning. Furthermore, the challenge of navigating both a higher language proficiency as well as cultural differences may lead to an overloading of the working memory, and this may hinder the learning process. Additionally, from a practical standpoint, organizing such exchanges can be cumbersome and a logistical nightmare (see, for example, Belz, 2003). Typically, these interactions occur on students' own time in coordination with their partner(s). The teacher will organize the logistics and set up the exchange. The exchange may include other components as part of the class (e.g., reflective blogs, collaborative wikis). Some of these components may be part of the F2F time or additional online components. Previous research has made it clear that these communications are effective if learners are left alone but that they may lead to miscommunications, which need to be debriefed during F2F class time (see Belz, 2003). These debriefing sessions would best be done during class time in the privacy of the classroom and with instructor guidance.

Online Communities

Online communities heavily use CMC. Online communities relevant for blended courses are (a) the course itself, (b) already existing target-language communities, and (c) multilingual, transnational communities. Here the focus is on online communities consisting of members from around the world with a shared interest. Many of the advantages and cautions are mirrored in what was discussed under the previous two CALL formats. The interesting aspect about online communities, from a sociocultural theory perspective, is that the expert–novice role can be two-fold in an online community. For example, a German tree worker may be an expert on safety standards in the tree industry in Germany but not an expert in English. While exchanging ideas with an American tree worker, the German tree worker is an expert on the topic but is a novice for the language. Thus, the two interlocutors can scaffold each other in different ways. Online communities are especially supported by and interesting from a language socialization perspective on language learning. Because online communities based on shared interests are mostly not defined by national borders, the status of one's L1 does not limit access in transnational communities (see Friedman, 2010). Online communities are communities of practice and learners can be socialized into these communities (see also discussion by Thorne, Black, & Sykes, 2009). Online communities may also serve as a transitional place for more traditionally defined target communities (see, for example, Lam, 2004). From a blended course perspective, three types of online communities are relevant: (a) the class itself, (b) a transnational or cross-cultural online community, and (c) target-language or target-community online communities. It is important in online and blended classes that a sense of community is established within the course using the F2F time as well as online platforms. Connecting learners with online communities that include language users of the language being studied can enhance the possibility of lifelong learning and lifelong use of the language. The teacher's role is to set up community platforms for the course, introduce existing online communities, be an active member in the class community, and strategize and debrief with students on how to become a legitimate member of online communities. When using already existing communities, the teacher can guide learners through analyses of interactions to help them become more accepted members of those communities and thereby have more opportunities for language learning.

Online Gaming

Because online gaming can include so many different formats, its theoretical foundation varies according to the game type. The place-based mobile game *Mentira* (Sykes, 2010), for example, includes peer-to-peer interactions as students work together to clear their name and understand the game, interactions with the game itself in an attempt to receive good clues, and interactions with members of the community in the neighborhood in which the murder mystery takes place. In all three interaction realms, learners receive feedback and input and have to produce output. Other games may be less interactive but still include feedback.

The big advantages from the SLA perspective for gaming in general are the individualized feedback and individualized paths (as discussed under iCALL); the opportunity for real, simulated, or rehearsed interactions (see discussion on CMC); and the incidental focus on language learning. A counter-argument can also be made from a cognitive perspective that the game playing itself demands so much cognitive processing that none is left for language learning. Overall, however, games show great potential for language learning, especially in online and blended environments, yet the astronomical development costs make them almost impossible to implement at this time (Blake, 2011). Designing effective games requires skills that language teachers do not have (e.g., programming, graphic design, game theory), and additionally, this process requires financial resources that are typically not available to language programs. Hence, although games offer great benefits to language learning and are a wonderful addition to a blended language learning class, they are unrealistic in almost all contexts at this point. If commercially available, a game could form a connection between the classroom and online activities by creating a transition between the two.

Simulations

Simulations are somewhat problematic in their relation to SLA theory because they are often simulations of interactions without being real interactions. Furthermore, these simulations do not always include feedback. For simulations to be beneficial, transfer has to be possible from the practiced simulated interactions to real-life interactions (see Sydorenko, 2011, for further discussion). Yet in a blended classroom, simulations play an important role because the decrease in F2F class time means students have less time to interact with other students. Hence, simulations are an effective way to allow for practice of responding to different prompts as preparation for actual conversations during class time and beyond.

Blended Courses and Second Language Acquisition Theory

To summarize, a comprehensive online course that uses a variety of CALL features has the potential of being based on and supported by a variety of SLA theories. What may be seen effective from one SLA perspective may not be seen as effective from a different theoretical perspective. For example, although participating in iCALL tutorials may be seen as beneficial from a processing theory perspective, these activities are not seen as beneficial from an interactionist perspective because they do not involve human-to-human interaction even though the programs do offer immediate and intelligent feedback. Moreover, an online component not only has to be supported by SLA theory and best pedagogical practices (including articulation with the F2F components), but also has to be logistically feasible. Although iCALL tutorials that provide intelligent parser-based feedback created from a coded learner language production corpus are preferred over scoring based on a simple limited answer key, it does not mean that they are readily available for every program and every language. High costs are involved in developing such systems, and likely only commonly taught languages will have access to such tools. Likewise, engaging games with three-dimensional graphics and a plethora of tasks, feedback, and opportunities for failure are extremely expensive to create and are at this point outside of the budgetary possibilities of language programs (see also Blake, 2011). These words of caution should not stop blended learning teachers and course developers from attempting to approximate these most ideal tools.

Observations from Second Language Acquisition Research and Their Implication for Blended Courses

After reviewing SLA theories, CALL formats, and the SLA theoretical foundation for different CALL types in blended language classes, I now turn to confirmed observations about SLA and how they can be addressed in blended language classes.

The focus in this section is on the 10 observations—things we know about SLA—identified by VanPatten and Williams (2007a, 2007b).

VanPatten and Williams (2007b) outlined 10 observations from SLA that any SLA theory needs to be able to explain (for a discussion on how the theories mentioned above address these observations, see Ortega, 2007; VanPatten & Williams, 2007a):

> (1) Exposure to input is necessary for SLA. (2) A good deal of SLA happens incidentally. (3) Learners come to know more than what they have been exposed to in the input. (4) Learner's output (speech) often follows predictable paths with predictable stages in the acquisition of a given structure. (5) Second language learning is variable in outcome. (6). Second language learning is variable across linguistics subsystems. (7) There are limits on the effects of frequency on SLA. (8) There are limits on the effect of a learner's first language on SLA. (9) There are limits on the effects of instruction on SLA. (10) There are limits on the effects of output (learner production) on language acquisition" (pp. 9–12).

Observation 1

Online and blended learning increase the opportunity for and the variety of input (observation 1), which is necessary for language learning. Additionally, digital tools make it possible to enhance and modify the input either before exposure (by developers or teachers) or during exposure (by the learner). At the same time, F2F oral input is more limited, and learners have the opportunity to ignore vast portions of the input from the online resources (for a summary of studies on learner online behavior, see Fischer, 2007). In a blended learning environment, input can include enhanced and digitally annotated input and slowed-down input in CMC during the online portion as well as the oral modified input from an expert speaker enhanced by gestures and facial expressions with room for negotiation of meaning in the F2F portion of the class.

Observation 2

Because language learning can occur incidentally (observation 2), making available a varied source of language input and language learning opportunities increases the chances of such incidental SLA. A blended course can simply make more resources available than a course that does not include online portions or does not include F2F components. Yet it all depends on what the learners do with the input and how they are encouraged to interact with the materials.

Observation 3

As pointed out earlier, learners learn more than what they are exposed to in their input (observation 3). In online portions of language courses, patterns can be highlighted and students can be led to self-discover structures and lexical items through the use of language corpora and analytical work with language corpora and concordancers to experiment with language and analyze the input they receive.

Observations 4 to 6

VanPatten and Williams's fourth point is that learners move through the acquisition process in a somewhat predictable order. This can, as pointed out in early sections and in Chapelle's (2009) discussion of the relationship between CALL and SLA, form the basis of sequencing and feedback in blended and online courses, and because of the asynchronous nature of the courses, students can be guided to navigate through these sequences at varying speeds (see also the earlier discussion on iCALL). This flexibility in practice and presentation of materials also supports the next two points: the variable outcome (observation 5) and the variability across linguistic subsets (observation 6). In the online portion of blended courses, students can be encouraged to move through the materials in an individualized fashion that addresses their particular aptitude for language learning and their strengths and weaknesses in the linguistic subsets of their current language proficiency. Then class time can be used for a more systematic presentation of content and for practice of language structures and skills.

Observations 7 to 10

VanPatten and Williams's last four points put into perspective the previous points by pointing out the limited effects of frequency (observation 7), L1 (observation 8), instruction (observation 9), and output (observation 10). These points, on the one hand, mean that no matter how great the course design and the course delivery, learners may still not succeed. On the other hand, it also implies that frequency and instruction can have a positive effect. The repetition that the online medium offers can play an important role but is not a guarantee. Instructional and practice materials can be replayed as many times as a learner would like in a blended course. This is a crucial advantage of online versus F2F presentation of materials. Because the effect of instruction is limited (observation 9), more time can be spent on practice modules with extensive feedback, which of course seems more natural to an independent course delivery such as an online course than an F2F course. In online components of a course, the speed of communication can also be slowed down, thereby making the processes involved in interaction and output more salient, which may increase the positive effects of output, as has been suggested by CMC research (see previous discussion on CMC).

In conclusion, blended learning may have some inherent advantages that can facilitate student learning. Blended learning courses may especially help motivate students, and students can gain greater language proficiency through a well-designed blended course compared with a well-designed F2F course or a well-designed online course. As pointed out at the beginning of the chapter, this has been confirmed by research.

Recommendations for Curricular Design and Research Methodology

To reiterate, from the discussion of SLA theory and SLA observation and their relation to blended language learning, a combination of CALL formats is beneficial. Different CALL formats work better depending on the SLA theory. Similarly, different CALL formats can address different necessary components of successful language learning. Of particular interest is a combination of iCALL tools and CMC that includes online communities and gaming (see also Blake, 2011). Well-designed iCALL tools and games make it possible for a learner to go through the material at his or her own pace and following his or her own path while receiving valuable, detailed, individualized, and targeted feedback. The online communities and other CMC environments would allow for input, output, negotiation of meaning, and identity formation in an FL, a crucial part for any social perspective on language learning. Therefore, a well-designed online and blended course should include a variety of these tools (see also Kern, 2006, for a discussion of different roles tools play). Goertler (2011a) provides more information about general curricular recommendations for online and blended learning. General principles of curricular design and innovation apply here as well such as the needs and goals of the stakeholders, available resources, articulation within the course and beyond, assessment of learning outcomes and curricular innovation, and the willingness to engage in a long-term iterative process (see also suggestions by Barrette, 2008; Means et al., 2009; Pelz, 2004; White, 2006).

Following are some concrete recommendations for blended instruction derived from SLA theory and based on current knowledge of SLA processes:

- Conduct a needs analysis to determine language level, developmental stage, and computer literacy skills;
- Design materials and tasks for both online and F2F environment that address realistic learning goals and are based on SLA theory;
- Build into the course data collection and data analysis procedures, so that you can continuously conduct formal and informal evaluations of the course using both qualitative and quantitative data and research methods;
- Prepare yourself for an iterative curricular design process because technological advancements and the information from the research on previous iterations will influence subsequent iterations of a course;
- Use the increased input and especially enhanced input options;
- Provide opportunities for various interaction opportunities, including (a) audio, video, text based, and F2F; (b) asynchronous and synchronous; (c) simulated or real; (d) with a variety of interlocutors such as peers, teacher, and other language speakers from a variety of communities;
- Whenever possible, use individualized programs that are adaptive to learners' performance;
- Whenever possible, use reports and analysis tools to improve teaching materials and learning tasks and to adjust to learners' developmental stages;
- Offer a range of practice opportunities, both skill and structure-based as well as communicative tasks in both online as well as F2F environments;
- Teach and provide assistance with technology tools to avoid cognitive overloading caused by technological difficulties;

- Include a variety of media to address multiple learning styles;
- Facilitate learning by teaching learners effective strategies to navigate both F2F and online class tasks;
- Whenever possible, provide immediate feedback through interlocutors or the computer or the materials;
- Make sure that the teacher and learner roles are consistent in both the online and the F2F component of the class.

Conclusions

In conclusion, blended and online learning offers potential benefits for language learning and has been found beneficial for language learning. Unfortunately, hybridization of the curriculum is often driven by logistical concerns rather than by a focus on improving the language learning process. In this chapter, I have argued that blended learning can be and should be based on SLA theory and research.

Yet curriculum development does not happen in an institutional vacuum and is constrained by logistical and monetary concerns. As has been alluded to before, unfortunately, the best tools are the most cumbersome and expensive to develop and may never make it into mainstream language instruction, especially in smaller languages. Moreover, the logistical considerations may override some of the pedagogical motivations. For example, although it is considered beneficial from an interactionist perspective on SLA to include interactions in the online as well as the F2F portion of the course, the design variables given by an administrator might not allow for such interaction. The course may have only one assigned instructor for multiple sections with the support of graders as a cost-saving mechanism. Given those circumstances, it would be unrealistic to have communicative tasks during F2F class time. Likewise, if the majority of the students do not have access to high-speed Internet, many of the CMC tools will not work sufficiently fast to be effective for language learning and practice. Hence, one must find a balance between following best practices derived from SLA research and SLA theory while also working within the institutional constraints.

One also has to keep in mind and continuously inform all stakeholders that a blended or online course cannot be the same as a traditional course and therefore cannot have the same results. This is not a judgment of better or worse results, but simply going through the language learning process a different way and engaging in different language use will result in different language abilities. This, of course, poses a problem in places where a course is offered in online, blended, and F2F delivery formats.

I will close this chapter by pondering on SLA in the 21st century. As social media and massively multiplayer games steadily increase in popularity, the likelihood that students will engage in language practice through these media may be much greater than the likelihood that they will use an FL on a daily basis in any other format. If that is the case, then do we, as language educators, need to adjust our curricular goals for the students? Moreover, as technology-enhanced, blended, and online learning courses increase and more learners have participated in them, will that change the learning culture and even the learning processes? How will those changes impact language learning processes? I close this chapter with the argument that SLA researchers need to learn more about language use, practice, and learning in online communities inside and outside the classroom in order to broaden SLA theories to account for a variety of language learning and language use settings.

References

Allen, I. E., & Seaman, J. (2010). *Learning on demand: Online education in the United States, 2009.* Retrieved July 30, 2010, from http://www.sloanconsortium. org/publications/survey/pdf/learningondemand.pdf.

Banados, E. (2006). A blended-learning pedagogical model for teaching and learning EFL successfully through an online interactive multimedia environment. *CALICO Journal, 23*(3), 533–550.

Barrette, C. M. (2008). Program administration issues in distance learning. In S. Goertler & P. Winke (Eds.), *Opening doors through distance language education: Principles, perspectives, and practices* (pp. 129–152). San Marcos, TX: CALICO.

Belz, J. (2003). Linguistic perspectives on the development of intercultural competence in telecollaboration. *Language Learning & Technology, 7*(2), 68–117. Retrieved July 30, 2010, from http://llt.msu.edu/vol7num2/belz/default.html.

Belz, J., & Thorne, S. (2006, Eds). *Internet-mediated intercultural foreign language education.* Boston: Heinle & Heinle.

Blake, R. (2007). New trends in using technology in the language curriculum. *Annual Review of Applied Linguistics, 27,* 76–97.

Blake, R. (2009). The use of technology for second language distance learning. *Modern Language Journal, 93*(Focus Issue), 822–835.

Blake, R. (2011). Current trends in online language learning. *Annual Review of Applied Linguistics, 31,* 19–35.

Chapelle, C. (1997). CALL in the year 2000: Still in search of research paradigms? *Language Learning & Technology, 1*(1), 19–43. Retrieved July 30, 2010, from http://llt.msu.edu/vol1num1/chapelle/default.html.

Chapelle, C. (2004). Technology and second language learning: Expanding methods and agendas. *System, 32,* 593–601.

Chapelle, C. (2007). Technology and second language acquisition. *Annual Review of Applied Linguistics, 27,* 98–114.

Chapelle, C. (2009). The relationship between second language acquisition theory and computer-assisted language learning. *Modern Language Journal, 93*(Focus Issue), 741–753.

Chapelle, C. (2010). The spread of computer-assisted language learning. *Language Teaching, 43*(1), 66–74.

Chenoweth, N. A., Ushida, E., & Murday, K. (2006). Student learning in hybrid French and Spanish courses: An overview of Language Online. *CALICO Journal, 24*(1), 115–145.

Duff, P. (2007). Second language socialization as sociocultural theory: Insights and issues. *Language Teaching, 40*(4), 309–319.

Fernandez-Garcia, M., & Martinez-Arbelaiz, A. (2002). Negotiation of meaning in nonnative speaker-native speaker synchronous discussions. *CALICO Journal, 19*(2), 279–294.

Fischer, R. (2007). How do we know what students are actually doing? Monitoring students' behavior in CALL. *Computer Assisted Language Learning, 20*(5), 409–442.

Friedman, D. (2010). Becoming national: Classroom language socialization and political identities in the age of globalization. *Annual Review of Applied Linguistics, 30,* 193–210.

Fryer, L. & Carpenter, R. (2006). Emerging technologies: Bots as language learning tools. *Language Learning & Technology, 10*(3), 8–14.

Furstenberg, G., Levet, S., English, K., & Maillet, K. (2001). Giving a virtual voice to the silent language of culture: The CULTURA project. *Language Learning & Technology, 5*(1), 55–102.

Garrett, N. (1991). Technology in the service of language learning: Trends and issues. *Modern Language Journal, 75*, 74–101.

Gass, S. (1997). *Input, interaction, and the second language learner.* Mahwah, NJ: Lawrence Erlbaum.

Gass, S., & Mackey, A. (2007). Input, interaction, and output in second language acquisition. In B. VanPatten & J. Williams (Eds.), *Theories in second language acquisition* (pp. 175–200). Mahwah, NJ: Lawrence Erlbaum.

Gass, S., & Selinker, L. (2008). *Second language acquisition: An introductory course.* New York: Routledge.

Goertler, S. (2011a). Blended and open/online learning: Adopting to a changing world of language teaching. In N. Arnold & L. Ducate (Eds.), *Present and future promises of CALL: From theory and research to new directions in language teaching* (pp. 471–502). San Marcos, TX: CALICO.

Goertler, S. (2011b). For a smoother blend: Lessons learned from blended instruction. In S. Huffman & V. Hegelheimer (Eds.), *The role of CALL in hybrid and online language courses. Selected papers from the eighth annual conference on technology for second language learning.* Retrieved September 25, 2011, from http://apling.public.iastate.edu/TSLL/2010/pdfs/goertler_2011.pdf.

Goertler, S., & Winke, P. (2008). The effectiveness of technology-enhanced foreign language teaching. In S. Goertler & P. Winke (Eds.), *Opening doors through distance language education: Principles, perspectives, and practices* (pp. 233–260). San Marcos, TX: CALICO.

Grgurovic, M. (2007). *Research synthesis: CALL comparison studies by language skills/knowledge.* Retrieved November 1, 2007, from http://tesl.engl.iastate.edu:591/comparison/synthesis.htm.

Hanna, B., & de Nooy, J. (2003). A funny thing happened on the way to the forum: Electronic discussion and foreign language learning. *Language Learning and Technology, 7*(1), 71–85. Retrieved February 24, 2012, from http://llt.msu.edu/vol7num1/hanna/default.html.

Heift, T. (2002). Learner control and error correction in ICALL: Browsers, peekers, and adamants. *CALICO Journal, 19*(3), 295–313.

Heift, T. (2005). Inspectable learner reports for web-based language learning. *ReCALL, 17*(1), 32–46.

Heift, T. (2010). Prompting in CALL: A longitudinal study of learner uptake. *Modern Language Journal, 94*(2), 198–216.

Kern, R. (2006). Perspectives on technology in learning and teaching languages. *TESOL Quarterly, 40*(1), 183–210.

Kraemer, A. (2008a). Formats of distance learning. In S. Goertler & P. Winke (Eds.), *Opening doors through distance language education: Principles, perspectives, and practices* (pp. 11–42). San Marcos, TX: CALICO.

Kraemer, A. (2008b). Happily ever after: Integrating language and literature through technology. *Die Unterrichtspraxis, 41*(1), 61–71.

Lafford, B., Lafford, P., & Sykes, J. (2007). Entre dicho y hecho . . .: An assessment of the application of research from second language acquisition and related fields to the creation of Spanish CALL materials for lexical acquisition. *CALICO Journal, 24*(3), 497–529.

Lam, W. (2004). Second language socialization in a bilingual chat room: Global and local considerations. *Language Learning and Technology, 8*(3), 44–56. Retrieved September 25, 2011, from http://llt.msu.edu/vol8num3/lam/default.html.

Lantolf, J. (2000, Ed.). *Sociocultural theory and second language learning*. Oxford: Oxford University Press.

Lantolf, J., & Thorne, S. (2007). Sociocultural theory and second language learning. In B. VanPatten & J. Williams (Eds.), *Theories in second language acquisition* (pp. 201–224). Mahwah, NJ: Lawrence Erlbaum.

Madyarov, I. (2009). Designing a workable framework for evaluating distance language instruction. *CALICO Journal, 26*(2), 290–308.

Means, B., Toyama, Y., Murphy, R., Bakia, M., & Jones, K. (2009). *Evaluation of evidence-based practices in online learning: A meta-analysis and review of online learning studies*. U.S Department of Education, Office of Planning, Evaluation, and Policy Development, Policy and Program Studies Service. Retrieved July 30, 2010, from http://www2.ed.gov/rschstat/eval/tech/evidence-based-practices/finalreport.pdf.

Nagata, N. (2002). BANZAI: An application of natural language processing to Web-based language learning. *CALICO Journal, 19*, 583–599.

Ochs, E. (2002). Becoming a speaker of culture. In C. Kramsch (Ed.), *Language socialization and language acquisition: Ecological perspectives* (pp. 99–120). New York: Continuum Press.

Ortega, L. (1997). Processes and outcomes in networked classroom interaction: Defining the research agenda for L2 computer-assisted classroom discussion. *Language Learning & Technology, 1*(1), 82–93. Retrieved July 30, 2010, from http://llt.msu.edu/vol1num1/ortega/default.html.

Ortega, L. (2007). Second language learning explained? SLA across nine contemporary theories. In B. VanPatten & J. Williams (Eds.), *Theories in second language acquisition* (pp. 225–250). Mahwah, NJ: Lawrence Erlbaum.

Payne, J. S., & Whitney, P. J. (2002). Developing L2 oral proficiency through synchronous CMC: Output, working memory, and interlanguage development. *CALICO Journal, 20*(1), 7–32.

Pelz, B. (2004). (My) three principles of effective online pedagogy. *Journal of Asynchronous Learning Networks, 14*(1), 103–116. Retrieved July 30, 2010, from http://www.ccri.edu/distancefaculty/Online%20Pedagogy%20-%20Pelz.pdf.

Pendar, N., & Chapelle, C. A. (2008). Investigating the promise of learner corpora: Methodological issues. *CALICO Journal, 25*(2), 189–206.

Pienemann, M. (1998). *Language processing and second language development: Processability theory*. New York: Benjamins.

Pienemann, M. (2007). Processability theory. In B. VanPatten & J. Williams (Eds.), *Theories in second language acquisition* (pp. 137–154). Mahwah, NJ: Lawrence Erlbaum.

Sanders, R. (2006). A comparison of chat room productivity: In-class versus out-of-class. *CALICO Journal, 24*(1), 59–76.

Sauro, S. (2009). Computer-mediated corrective feedback and the development of L2 grammar. *Language Learning and Technology, 13*(1), 96–120. Retrieved on September 25, 2011, from http://llt.msu.edu/vol13num1/sauro.pdf.

Smith, B. (2003). Computer-mediated negotiated interaction: An expanded model. *The Modern Language Journal, 87*(1), 38–57.

Smith, B. (2008). Methodological hurdles in capturing CMC data: The case of the missing self-repair. *Language Learning & Technology, 12*(1), 85–103. Retrieved July 30, 2010, from http://llt.msu.edu/vol12num1/smith/default.html.

Smith, B., Alvarez-Torres, M. J., & Zhao, Y. (2003). Features of CMC technologies and their impact on language learners' online interaction. *Computers in Human Behavior, 19*(6), 703–729.

Smith, B., & Gorsuch, G. J. (2004). Synchronous computer mediated communication captured by usability lab technologies: New interpretations. *System, 32*(4), 553–575.

Strambi, A., & Bouvet, E. (2003). Flexibility and interaction at a distance: A mixed-mode environment for language learning. *Language Learning & Technology, 7*(3), 81–102. Retrieved July 30, 2010, from http://llt.msu.edu/vol7num3/strambi/default.html.

Sydorenko, T. (2011). *Exploring the potential of rehearsal via automatized structured tasks versus face-to-face pair work to facilitate pragmatic and oral development.* Unpublished doctoral dissertation, Michigan State University, East Lansing, MI.

Sykes, J. (2010, June). *Design and implementation: Mobile, place-based games and language learning.* Paper presented at the annual meeting of the Computer Assisted Language Instruction Consortium (CALICO), Amherst, MA.

Sykes, J. (2012, February). *Digital game-mediated language learning: From ideas to implementation.* Keynote presented at the Second Language Studies Symposium, East Lansing, MI.

Sykes, J. M., Oskoz, A., & Thorne, S. (2008). Web 2.0, synthetic immersive environments, and mobile resources for language education. *CALICO Journal, 25*(3), 528–546.

Sykes, J., & Reinhardt, J. (forthcoming, 2012). *Language at play: How digital games can inform, enhance, and transform L2 pedagogy. Theory and practice in second language classroom instruction.* J. Liskin-Gasparro & M. Lacorte (Series Eds.). Upper Saddle River, NJ: Pearson-Prentice Hall.

Thorne, S. (2003). Artifacts and cultures-of-use in intercultural communication. *Language Learning & Technology, 7*(2), 38–67. Retrieved July 30, 2010, from http://llt.msu.edu/vol7num2/thorne/default.html.

Thorne, S., Black, R., & Sykes, J. (2009). Second language use, socialization, and learning in internet interest communities and online gaming. *Modern Language Journal, 93*(Focus Issue), 802–821.

Thorne, S., & Smith, B. (2011). Second language development theory and technology-mediated language learning. *CALICO Journal, 28*(2), 268–277.

VanPatten, B., & William, J. (2007a, Eds.) *Theories in second language acquisition* (pp. 97–114). Mahwah, NJ: Lawrence Erlbaum.

VanPatten, B. & William, J. (2007b). Introduction: The nature of theories. B. VanPatten & J. Williams (Eds.), *Theories in second language acquisition* (pp. 1–16). Mahwah, NJ: Lawrence Erlbaum.

White, C. (2006). Distance learning of foreign languages. *Language Teaching, 39,* 247–364.

White, L. (2003). *Second language acquisition and Universal Grammar.* Cambridge: Cambridge University Press.

White, L. (2007). Linguistic theory, Universal Grammar, and second language acquisition. In B. VanPatten & J. Williams (Eds.), *Theories in second language acquisition* (pp. 37–56). Mahwah, NJ: Lawrence Erlbaum.

Youngs, B., Ducate, L., & Arnold, N. (2011). Linking second language acquisition, CALL, and language pedagogy. In N. Arnold & L. Ducate (Eds.), *Present and future promises of CALL: From theory and research to new directions in language teaching* (pp. 23–60). San Marcos, TX: CALICO.

Appendix 3-1. Computer-Assisted Language Learning Formats

Name	Definition	Features	Example	SLA Theory
Tutorial CALL (see also Blake, 2011)	A computer program with skill-based exercises that provides immediate feedback based on a preprogrammed answer key	• Individual interaction with the computer; no human-to-human interaction • Typically a focus on grammar or vocabulary (i.e., skill-based exercises) • Typically exercises with limited answer options • Typically self-grading and providing immediate feedback • Sometimes with explanations of errors or correct answers or indication of location of errors • Sometimes includes access to glosses and grammar explanations • Typically produces records for the teacher (correct and incorrect answers; number of attempts; whole class overall performance)	*Quia* workbooks	Universal grammar
iCALL (see work by Heift, 2010, and Nagata, 2002)	A computer program with skill-based exercises that provides immediate intelligent feedback. Feedback is based on previously coded errors often based on a learner corpus; the feedback is parser based and can therefore provide feedback even on longer productions	• All features mentioned above • Feedback can be based on previously coded learner corpus and be parser based • Feedback could be enhanced by speech recognition software • Students may be guided through the program based on an initial placement test and performance on subsequent lessons • May include more nuanced feedback • May include different scaffolding elements to assist learners in developing a more native-like response • Typically provides more detailed records to the teacher (correct and incorrect answers; time in the program; number of attempts needed; scores on tests; progression through the program)	*E-tutor* (see Heift, 2002, 2005, 2010) *Tell Me More* (see Blake, 2011)	Processability theory

Name	Definition	Features	Example	SLA Theory
CMC with peers (for overview, see Kern, 2006)	A computer medium that allows for synchronous or asynchronous communication via text, audio, or video with other learners	• Communication among peers using computer technologies (which can include mobile devices) • Learners can engage in different kinds of tasks depending on the tool (e.g., reflecting via a blog, completing jigsaws or a role-play via a chat, discussing topics in a chat or discussion forum) • Learners can be engaged in asynchronous CMC (e.g., discussion forum, blog, email) or synchronous CMC (e.g., Skype, chat) • Some tools keep a record of the communication others do not • Collaborative tasks can also be integrated by using additional tools such as wikis • Students can also be asked to share their work and provide each other with feedback via CMC tools	Tools such as discussion forums, chat, email, *Skype*, and *Facetime* used for learning in peer–peer interactions	Interactionist perspectives
CMC across cultures (Belz, 2003; Belz & Thorne, 2006; Thorne, 2003)	A computer medium that allows for synchronous or asynchronous communication via text, audio, or video with native speakers	• Same as above with the important difference that interactions are with a native speaker from a target language community • Typically, these communications are organized by the teacher and involve L1 class–L2 class or student—native speaker partnerships • Sometimes the partners have to work together for common goals or discuss specific topics; other times the partnership is more loosely defined • Typically, these exchanges are integrated into the class and reflected upon during class	Tools such as above used for cross-cultural exchanges; see, for example, *Cultura* (Furstenberg, Levet, English, & Maillet, 2001) project	Sociocultural theory

(continued)

Name	Definition	Features	Example	SLA Theory
Online Communities (see also Thorne, Black, & Sykes, 2009; and work by Hanna & de Nooy, 2003)	A group of people who share a common interest and typically are remote from each other who use CMC technology to form an online community on an online platform or in a virtual world	• A community of people using an online platform to communicate, share, and update each other; this could be limited to the class, include the class, or be independent of the class • Some of these platforms may include elements of CMC mentioned above or gaming as mentioned below	For learners: *English, baby!* Online groups by interest: http://www.treebuzz.com/ Virtual worlds: *Second life* Social media: *Facebook, Google+*	Language Socialization
Gaming (Sykes & Reinhardt, forthcoming)	A digital game that is task based and designed for semistructured play involving problem-solving, negotiation, feedback, and the freedom to fail	• Games can be mechanical or interactive • Games engage learners in tasks for the purpose of completing short- and long-term goals within the games; every player move receives feedback by either advancing or not in the game; failed attempts can result in learning • Games can be played individually, against other players, or collaboratively against other teams • In the language classroom, two categories of games are relevant: games designed with a language-learning focus such as Julie Sykes' *Mentira* (Sykes, 2010) and games that are played globally in multiple languages with transnational and translingual interactions such as *World of Warcraft* • Games may be played stationary (e.g., *Wii*) or mobile (e.g., *Mentira*) • Games may use real identities, avatars, or pseudonyms	*World of Warcraft* *Words with Friends* *Mentira*	Mixed

Name	Definition	Features	Example	SLA Theory
Simulation	An online platform that simulates real interactions with the language or culture being studied	• These environments could be simple as the *Conversations* program developed by the *Center for Language Education and Research*, in which one can create simulated conversations by recording multiple connected prompts for a learner to respond to • More complex environments allow learners to navigate a three-dimensional environment in which they have to complete tasks with NPCs; they may have several answers available to select from, and the response from the NPC will depend on the selected response	*Conversations* *Croquelandia*	Mixed

CALL, computer-assisted language learning; CMC, computer-mediated communication; L1, first language; L2, second language; NPC, nonplayer character; SLA, second language acquisition.

Chapter 4

Beyond Hybrid Learning: A Synthesis of Research on E-tutors Under the Lens of Second Language Acquisition Theory

Luis Cerezo

For several reasons—logistical, theoretical, pedagogical, and evidence based (Goertler, 2011)—higher education institutions are increasingly advocating for technology-enhanced curricula for second language acquisition (SLA). Research in this field of inquiry has grown exponentially, and recent literature reviews concluded that technology can be effectively used to develop different areas of a second language (L2) (Abraham, 2008; Egbert, Huff, McNeil, Preuss, & Sellen, 2009; Felix, 2005a; Hubbard, 2005; Peterson, 2010; Stockwell, 2007). Even more interestingly, recent meta-analyses of developmental studies found greater effect sizes for conditions using technology than conditions based on other forms of instruction, including face-to-face (F2F) instruction (Grgurovic, Chapelle, & Shelley, in preparation, as cited in Chapelle, 2010; Zhao, 2003) and individual study with printed texts (Taylor, 2009). These results presage a bright future for technology-enhanced language learning (TELL), although several limitations should be considered. For example, more replications and longitudinal studies are needed; also, studies must exert tighter control over external and internal factors (e.g., time on task, type of pedagogical practice, amount of exposure to input, and learners' individual differences); and existing meta-analyses are based on a small pool of studies, so their results must be interpreted with caution (see also Felix, 2005b; and Norris & Ortega, 2010, for a discussion of issues in meta-analytic literature).

From a different perspective, it is important to avoid overgeneralizations when making claims about technology because TELL can take many forms, and each of them may yield very different learning outcomes. For example, whereas in *hybrid or blended* curricula, 30 to 80 percent of F2F meetings are replaced by online discussions, in *online or open* curricula, this percentage is surpassed (Allen & Seaman, 2011). Additionally, curricula can incorporate *technology-mediated* or *technology-based* components, depending on whether learners respectively use technology to interact with other humans or to work independently. Overall, much ink has been spilled to discuss different types of TELL environments in descriptive studies, action research studies, and position papers. However, among the studies that used pretest–posttest designs to measure L2 development, the majority have focused on hybrid and technology-mediated learning (e.g., Tang, Yin, & Lou, 2009). The field has caught full speed and new studies in computer-mediated communication (CMC) appear in journals issue after issue. In contrast, relatively few developmental studies have investigated online learning, in which F2F instruction is dramatically reduced or eliminated, and even fewer studies

have investigated technology-based learning, in which learners work independently with technology without interacting with a teacher or a peer (Blake, 2009;
Cerezo, 2010; Hulstijn, 2000). In this latter scenario, so-called *e-tutors* occupy a
central role. An e-tutor is software that, in addition to displaying language input,
has the capability of engaging learners in some sort of pedagogical practice and
evaluating their responses, parsing them as correct or incorrect, and reacting accordingly by, for example, providing modified input or corrective feedback (see,
e.g., Levy, 1997; Taylor, 1980). There are different types of e-tutors, depending on
how they process learners' responses (with or without natural language processing tools) and how they react to them (with or without using learning modeling
techniques) (see Heift & Schulze, 2007; Schulze, 2008, for a review).

By nature, the development of an e-tutor involves expertise in two different
areas, linguistics and computer science. For this reason, scholarly research on
e-tutors is spread out over a wide range of journals—of applied linguistics, computer science, computational linguistics, and educational technology—and is not
easily accessible. As a result, TELL researchers often have the perception that the
literature on e-tutors is very limited (Schulze, 2008). Although this is not the case,
research on e-tutors is largely descriptive, and only a fraction of studies have investigated whether and how e-tutors may facilitate L2 development by using pretest–posttest designs, especially in the realm of grammar (e.g., AbuSeileek, 2009;
Cerezo, 2010; Nutta, 1998). This relative lack of developmental studies is particularly striking in light of the growing presence and potential of e-tutors inside and
outside academia. Outside academia, the sales of commercial e-tutors (e.g.,
Rosetta Stone, Tell Me More, or *Rocket Languages*) are booming; inside academia,
more and more university administrators are pushing for the adoption of online
learning curricula—65 percent of 2,500 surveyed institutions in the United States
reported that online learning is a critical component of their long-term strategic
plans (Allen & Seaman, 2011). Several factors may have caused this imbalance of
research. For example, product developers may be reluctant to finance investigations on e-tutors because they do not see an immediate return on the investment,
and research-granting agencies may deride the "applied" nature of these investigations (Hulstijn, 2000). Also, from a pedagogical perspective, some researchers
are more interested in using technology as a medium rather than a tutor because
it best befits their perception of language learning as socially constructed knowledge. Or, from a motivational perspective, some teachers and scholars may perceive e-tutors as a potential threat to their jobs, so they choose to ignore them
(see, e.g., Blake, 2001, 2007, for a review of teachers' negative attitudes toward
technology).

Additionally, e-tutors are not only underresearched but also underreported in
research syntheses and meta-analyses. Although e-tutors have been discussed at
different lengths in specialized publications on TELL (e.g., Blake, 2009; Heift &
Schulze, 2007; Schulze, 2008), they remain largely ignored by wider scope publications on SLA. For example, none of the four major meta-analyses of empirical
literature on corrective feedback (Li, 2010; Lyster & Saito, 2010; Mackey & Goo,
2007; Russell & Spada, 2006) included an e-tutor study. One wonders why this is
so. Some may argue that studies on computerized feedback are not informative

to oral interaction literature because the sources of feedback are fundamentally different. However, computerized feedback is ultimately a human product, and e-tutors are likely to provide more consistent feedback in terms of type and frequency, which ultimately results in more tightly controlled studies (see, e.g., Hulstijn, 2000; Sanz, 2000; Tsutsui, 2004). From a different perspective, others may argue that modality should not be overlooked and that oral and written feedback should be analyzed separately. However, on the one hand, some meta-analyses did include studies of written feedback in CMC (Li, 2010; Mackey & Goo, 2007), and on the other, computerized feedback does not necessarily have to be written, as illustrated by recent research with prerecorded oral feedback (Cerezo, 2010).

Addressing these gaps, the present chapter provides a synthesis of empirical research on e-tutors for L2 grammar development, revolving around three central questions. First, the *whether* question addresses whether e-tutors can effectively promote L2 grammar development per se and compared with other types of instructional technologies based on workbooks, videos, and F2F. Second, the *why* question addresses why e-tutors can promote L2 development in light of three psycholinguistic or psychocognitive theoretical approaches: the theories of dual coding and multimedia learning, the noticing hypothesis, and the interaction framework. And third, the *which* question addresses which e-tutor features promote the highest L2 grammar development outcomes, focusing on the type of computerized practice and the type of computerized feedback. The chapter closes with a summary of findings and a set of recommendations for further research on e-tutors.

Literature Search and Selection Criteria

The following sections provide a thematically organized synthesis of published and unpublished primary sources on the use of e-tutors for L2 development with a focus on grammar. To qualify for this synthesis, a study had to meet all of the following four criteria: (a) The study involved the use of an e-tutor, understood as software that has the capability of parsing learners' responses as correct or incorrect, responding accordingly; thus, if the study involved the use of software to merely display L2 input, it was excluded (e.g., Doughty, 1991; Robinson, 1996). (b) The e-tutor was the only source of instruction; studies in which e-tutors were used as a supplement to other type of instruction, such as F2F, were excluded (e.g., Sagarra & Zapata, 2008). (c) The study measured L2 grammar development in the form of learning outcomes (e.g., accuracy, latency or fluency, complexity). (d) The study involved a pretest–posttest design; if assumptions were made based only on posttreatment measures, the study was excluded (e.g., Chen, 2006).

To identify primary sources, four techniques were used. First, the reference lists of published literature reviews and meta-analyses were consulted. Second, two electronic databases were searched, Linguistics and Language Behavior Abstracts (LLBA) and ProQuest Dissertations & Theses (PQDT). Search queries were based on combinations of the query phrase *second/foreign language* with the following terms: *computer-based instruction, computerized instruction,* computerized tutors, e-tutors, electronic tutors, distance learning, online learning, open learning, CALI, CALL, CASLA, iCALL, MALL, TELL, and WELL. No time bracket was selected—retrieved sources included years up to 2011. Third, the reference lists of recent doctoral dissertations were consulted. And fourth, feedback from both colleagues and anonymous reviewers was incorporated.

Retrieved sources were classified in three sections, depending on whether they were informative to the *whether, why,* or *which* questions discussed below. This synthesis is by no means exhaustive; rather, its purpose is to provide tentative answers to important questions about e-tutors under the lens of SLA theory.

The "Whether" Question: Whether E-tutors Can Promote Second Language Grammar Development

Since Nagata's (1993) seminal publication, at least 20 empirical studies have used pretest–posttest designs to investigate whether e-tutors can successfully facilitate L2 grammar development. Interestingly, all of the retrieved studies answered this question affirmatively, showing that independent work with e-tutors can be pedagogically effective for specific L2 grammatical structures, learners, and contexts (AbuSeileek, 2009; AbuSeileek & Rababah, 2007; Bowles, 2008; Camblor, 2006; Cerezo, 2010; Hsieh, 2007; Lado, 2008; Lin, 2009; Medina, 2008; Moreno, 2007; Morgan-Short & Wood Bowden, 2006; Nagata, 1998a, 1998b; Nutta, 1998; Petersen, 2010; Rosa & Leow, 2004; Sachs, 2011; Sanz & Morgan-Short, 2004; Torlaković & Deugo, 2004; Watts, 1989). Additionally, a fraction of these studies compared the effectiveness of e-tutors against other instructional technologies. In Watts's (1989) study, e-tutors were compared with non-interactive videos; in Nagata's (1996) study, they were compared with instruction based on workbooks; and in Nutta (1998), Torlaković and Deugo (2004), AbuSeileek and Rababah (2007), Abuseileek (2009), and Petersen (2010), the comparison group was F2F instruction.

In Watts's (1989) study, 30 adult English students of beginning French interacted with two different versions of the *Dès le Debut* video series for four hours total. One group watched a traditional video and completed exercises in paper-and-pen format, and the other group used an e-tutor consisting of an interactive version of the video with online exercises. Results showed that the interactive video group experienced a combined gain of 30 to 35 percent on word translation, sentence translation, and listening comprehension and a decrease in pronunciation errors. Conversely, the traditional video group experienced only negligible gains and "minimal improvement in pronunciation." These results must be interpreted with caution because of several caveats. For example, the use of a combined gain score makes it difficult to quantify L2 grammar gains in the sentence translation task; also, no specific grammatical forms were investigated.

Focusing specifically on a grammatical structure (Japanese particles), Nagata (1996) compared the effectiveness of an e-tutor versus workbook-mediated instruction. In her study, 26 English students of Japanese completed a preliminary grammar explanation session and four practice sessions including workbook

or online activities. Results showed that the e-tutor group significantly outperformed the workbook group in production (fill-in-the-blank and sentence production), both immediately after the treatment and three weeks later, but not in
comprehension (sentence translation into L1 English). Several limitations urge
caution in interpreting these results. First, the feedback received by the two conditions was qualitatively different. The e-tutor group received concurrent feedback that pinpointed and explained the nature of errors, and the workbook group
had access to an answer sheet with positive evidence only. Therefore, it is impossible to determine whether the observed differences were because of the use of
different instructional technologies or the quality of the feedback. Also, the study
did not control for timing and amount of pushed output. The students in the
e-tutor group were given three opportunities to modify their answers, but the
answer sheet approach of the workbook group precluded any opportunity for
modified output.

Switching the scope from poorly interactive workbooks to human instructors, Nutta (1998) compared the effects of an e-tutor against teacher-directed instruction for the acquisition of English past and conditional tenses. In her study,
53 participants were exposed to seven one-hour instructional sessions. Students
in the teacher-directed group used the *Focus on Grammar* textbook series and
engaged in a variety of communicative activities with their teacher. In contrast,
students in the e-tutor group followed a checklist to navigate through the *ELLIS
Mastery* multimedia system, completing online activities with feedback. For the
past tense, the students in the e-tutor group outperformed the teacher-directed
group in production posttests (fill-in-the-blank and open-ended sentence completion), but no differences were observed for recognition (multiple choice). These
results were partially maintained after two weeks, when again the e-tutor group
performed best for open-ended sentence production. The results for the English
conditional tense, on the other hand, were less differential. Both groups experienced similar gains on all tests except on the delayed open-ended sentence production test, in which the e-tutor group once again performed significantly better.
This study, however, did not specify whether both conditions received comparable
practice in terms of type and quantity; consequently, caution must be exerted
when interpreting its findings.

In a similar study, Torlaković and Deugo (2004) compared the effects of instruction with an e-tutor versus teacher-fronted instruction for English adverb
placement. Twenty-one college students were exposed to six hours of instruction over the course of two weeks and were divided into three groups. One group
completed a number of pedagogical activities with an e-tutor, *Adverbial Analyzer*;
another group completed similar activities in the context of teacher-directed instruction; and a control group was involved only in testing. Results showed that
the e-tutor group was the only one that experienced significant learning in the assessment tasks, a grammaticality judgment task (both immediately after the treatment and two weeks later), and written controlled production (in the immediate
posttest only). These results, however, must be interpreted with caution because
the feedback received by the two experimental conditions during practice was
qualitatively different. The e-tutor group had access to rules on adverb placement

with every practice item, but in the teacher-fronted group, students received positive feedback only when they made correct generalizations.

Building on previous studies, AbuSeileek and Rababah (2007) compared four different types of instructional settings, determined by the source (e-tutor vs. teacher) and the pedagogical approach (presentation of rules before or after practice activities). The targeted grammatical structures were five English verb tenses: simple present, simple past, present continuous, present perfect, and simple future. Participants were 128 male college students, and instruction took place over the course of four weeks. Results showed that although all conditions experienced significant learning gains, the combined e-tutor group outperformed the teacher-driven group in all verb tenses except for the present perfect, for which both groups experienced comparable learning. These results must be interpreted in light of the fact that during some parts of the experiment, students worked in groups rather than individually, which introduced a hybrid component in the e-tutor groups.

In a partial replication study, AbuSeileek (2009) again investigated the effects of learning grammar inductively or deductively with an e-tutor or a human teacher. The targeted structures this time were four types of English sentences: simple sentence, compound sentence, complex sentence, and compound complex sentence. Participants were 72 undergraduate male students, instruction time was four weeks, and assessment tests comprised a combination of multiple-choice recognition and written sentence production. Results showed that for the two easiest sentence structures (simple and compound sentences), the e-tutor and teacher-centered groups learned comparably; in contrast, for the more difficult sentence structures (complex sentence and compound complex sentence), the e-tutor groups performed significantly better. As in AbuSeileek and Rababah (2007), these results should be interpreted with caution because the e-tutor groups did include a hybrid component based on small group discussions.

Finally, Petersen (2010) compared the effects of instruction using oral recasts delivered by a teacher versus written recasts delivered by an intelligent e-tutor, *Sasha*. Participants were 56 high school students, and the targeted structure was English question formation. Results indicated that participation in recast-intensive interaction was a significant predictor of learning, in terms of both question development and morphosyntactic accuracy. However, the mode of the interaction did not have an effect on development—participants who received oral recasts from a teacher learned comparably to those who received written recasts from the e-tutor.

To sum up, then, accruing evidence suggests a positive answer to the *whether* question, that is, whether or not e-tutors can facilitate L2 grammar development. On the one hand, more than 20 empirical studies unanimously showed that e-tutors did facilitate L2 grammar development. On the other hand, incipient empirical research comparing the effectiveness of e-tutors versus other instructional technologies showed that under certain circumstances and for certain targeted grammatical structures, learners using e-tutors can at least parallel, and even supersede, the accuracy gains experienced by learners in instructional conditions with video, workbooks, and human teachers. However, this latter claim must be interpreted with caution given important limitations. For one, although there is a growing body of empirical research comparing the effectiveness of hybrid versus F2F instruction, there is a blatant need for more studies comparing the effectiveness of e-tutors against other instructional conditions. And second, some of the existing studies present serious methodological caveats, involving lack of control for targeted linguistic structure, pedagogical practice, or corrective feedback, in terms of quantity, quality, or both.

The "Why" Question: Why Can E-tutors Promote Second Language Grammar Development?

Arguably, at least three theoretical frameworks can be proposed to account for the success of e-tutors in promoting L2 grammar development: the dual coding theory (or the related theory of multimedia learning), the noticing hypothesis, and the interaction framework. Paivio's (1986) dual coding theory and Mayer's (2001) theory of multimedia learning contend that visual and verbal information are processed differently and separately, along distinct channels, and they can enhance processing and learning of information if displayed concurrently through a multimedia environment—as long as they do not compete with each other, causing working memory overload. These two theories could then explicate why e-tutors led to superior learning than workbook instruction in Nagata (1996) because computers have greater multimedia capabilities than printed workbooks. However, this does not seem to be the case because Nagata's e-tutor displayed written text only, yet it promoted higher learning gains than her workbook approach. Similarly, these theories would fail to explicate why e-tutors yielded better results than videos (Watts, 1989) and teacher-centered instruction (AbuSeileek, 2009; AbuSeileek & Rababah, 2007; Nutta, 1998; Petersen, 2010; Torlaković & Deugo, 2004) because both movies and teachers can concurrently display written, aural, and visual information in effective ways.

From a different standpoint, e-tutors can be argued to increase students' attention to L2 input, which according to Schmidt's noticing hypothesis is "the necessary and sufficient condition for the conversion of input into intake" (Schmidt, 1993). According to Watts (1989, pp. 19–20), one of the advantages of the e-tutor over the traditional video approach in her study was that it eliminated students' passivity toward the screen. For example, Watts reported that the vast majority of students in the e-tutor group (29 of 30) actually spoke aloud when instructed to do so, but only a minority in the video group (7 of 30 students) followed the instructions. Interestingly, some students in the traditional video group declared that they felt stupid talking to a TV because it did not give them "the same confidence that a computer gives you." Even the students who reported enjoying both instructional approaches demonstrated lower rates of attention in the video treatment, completing only half of the worksheets. This suggests that computers have a greater ability than other media (e.g., books or non-interactive videos) to direct students' attention to L2 input, perhaps because they increase students' motivation to learn. On this token, the participants in the e-tutor group in Nagata's

(1996) study reported significantly greater satisfaction in their Likert-scale ratings of the format, interest, and content of the practice exercises, "in spite of the fact that both groups received the same exercises in the same format" (p. 66). However, beyond this evidence, more research addressing the role of attention and motivation as independent variables (and their possible correlation) is certainly warranted.

Finally, from a third perspective, the better results of e-tutors over other instructional technologies may be because of their inherent "interactive features" (Nagata, 1996, p. 66). Interestingly, a number of early comparative studies (1960–1980s) reviewed by Pederson (1987) showed no significant advantages of the computer versus other learning technologies based on audiovisual labs, teachers, or paper and pencil. Notably, the computers used in these earlier studies were not capable of evaluating the students' responses; therefore, they were not e-tutors in the strict sense. As argued by Nagata (1996), when e-tutors "simply transfer printed textbooks to the computer screen, the computer is nothing more than an electronic page-turner, and we cannot expect better results" (p. 54). It appears, then, that the advantage of e-tutors versus other technologies may lie in their capability to interact with learners or to present them with large amounts of interactive practice. Interestingly, though, very few studies have empirically addressed this.

Drawing on the interaction hypothesis (Long, 1996), it can be argued that participation in interactive practice can promote SLA because it allows learners to notice, comprehend, and process input; produce output; form and revise hypotheses in response to feedback; and produce modified output, processes that have been shown to be developmentally helpful (Mackey, 2007). However, the interaction hypothesis does not specify whether the effects of these processes are determined by the type of *agency* of the learner, that is, whether it is necessary for learners to engage proactively in the aforementioned processes or whether mere exposure to interactive practice by others (e.g., watching a video in which different interlocutors engage in these processes) may suffice. To date, only two e-tutor studies have investigated the impact of practice versus exposure to practice on L2 grammar development. In a seminal study, Hsieh (2007) obtained mixed results for Spanish *gustar* constructions, with both conditions experiencing similar gains in written recognition and production and the practice condition outperforming the observers in oral production. In turn, using an e-tutor that allowed students to interact with prefilmed human avatars, Cerezo (2010) found that learners who had the chance to interact with the e-tutor significantly outperformed their observers in written and oral production of L2 Spanish grammar but only under more demanding conditions (with less explicit feedback as opposed to feedback with grammatical explanations) and for easier rather than complex structures (prepositional relative clauses as opposed to present subjunctive).

To sum up, then, incipient literature suggests that the reason why e-tutors may facilitate grammar development (per se or compared to other instructional technologies) lies in their ability to engage learners in greater amounts of proactive interaction. However, this advantage may arise only in conditions that impose higher cognitive demands on the part of the student (e.g., inferring a rule, producing rather than recognizing grammar) and for structures that are governed by simpler rather than complex rules (i.e., rules that learners can infer through repeated practice in line with their developmental level).

The "Which" Question: Which E-tutors Best Promote Second Language Grammar Development?

Arguably, e-tutors may differ in two main components: the type of pedagogical practice and the type of corrective feedback that they provide. Practice is typically thought of as a prerequisite for interaction (DeKeyser, 2007), and corrective feedback is the feature that distinguishes testing from learning tasks (Loschky & Bley-Vroman, 1993). The following two sections discuss the effects of these variables separately.

Type of Computerized Practice

Existing studies on the effects of type of practice in e-tutors can be classified into two groups: (a) type of practiced skill, such as comprehension, interpretation, recognition, or production (Morgan-Short & Wood Bowden, 2006; Nagata, 1998a, 1998b), and (b) type of task features, such as task essentialness or task complexity (Medina, 2008; Moreno, 2007). Studies addressing the effects of type of practiced skill have compared input- versus output-focused practice for Japanese honorifics (Nagata, 1998a), Japanese nominal modifiers (Nagata, 1998b), and Spanish preverbal direct object pronouns (Morgan-Short & Wood Bowden, 2006). In Nagata (1998a, 1998b), five types of exercises were used to elicit interpretation and production at the word, sentence, or paragraph level. Input-focused practice involved selecting, from three choices, the correct English interpretation for the Japanese targeted form. In contrast, output-focused practice involved using Japanese in translation, editing, or retelling activities. Similarly, in Morgan-Short and Wood Bowden (2006), referential and affective activities were included to elicit interpretation or production in the aural and written modes, although the focus was on the word and sentence levels rather than the paragraph level.

Taken together, these three studies found that both input- and output-focused practice led to comparable gains in the interpretation of the target grammatical structures, but for production, output-focused practice yielded the best results, both in the short term (Morgan-Short & Wood Bowden, 2006; Nagata, 1998a, 1998b) and weeks later (Nagata, 1998a, 1998b). Furthermore, the superior effectiveness of output-focused instruction manifested itself for both complex and easy structures (Nagata, 1998a, 1998b). When comparing these findings with the general SLA literature, the following conclusions can be drawn: (a) These findings lend support to the growing number of empirical studies showing the facilitative role of output in L2 grammar development (e.g., Izumi, Bigelow, Fujiwara, & Fearnow, 1999; Loewen, 2005; Mackey, 1999; McDonough, 2005); (b) they contradict some studies on processing instruction that found no significant differences in production and an advantage of input-focused practice for interpretation (e.g., Benati, 2005; Cadierno, 1995; Farley, 2001); and (c) they seem to contradict skill acquisition theory (Anderson, 1993), according to which both input- and output-focused practice develop comprehension and production skills, respectively (e.g., DeKeyser & Sokalski, 2001).

Focusing on task features rather than practiced skills, Medina (2008) compared the pedagogical effects of task complexity in input-focused tasks. In her experiment, participants were asked to read a text containing exemplars of the targeted structure, Spanish imperfect subjunctive. Participants in the more complex condition were asked to spot the structures and select them in the text, and those in the less complex condition were instructed to re-highlight the forms that were already underlined for them. Results showed that task complexity had a significant effect on the written production of the target structure, with participants in the more complex task group achieving significantly higher learning outcomes. Extrapolation of these findings to the general SLA literature yields the following two conclusions: (a) there is increasing support for the cognition hypothesis, according to which more complex tasks promote higher levels of accuracy (e.g., Iwashita, McNamara, & Elder, 2001; Kuiken, Mos, & Vedder, 2005), and (b) the observed lack of effects of task complexity for recognition confirms Flynn's (1986) hypothesis that comprehension precedes production, so the effects of more complex tasks are more likely to arise in production measures.

Also addressing task features, Moreno (2007) investigated the effects of task essentialness in input-focused practice on the development of Spanish preverbal direct object pronouns. Participants in her study were presented with a picture cue and had to compose or select a sentence that described it. In the more task-essential condition, students composed the sentence by navigating a tree that successively branched out with a set of object pronouns. In contrast, students in the less task-essential condition completed an interpretation task by selecting one of two fully composed sentences. Crucially, in this latter condition, attention to the targeted form was not enforced because the two sentences differed only in terms of their subjects rather than their objects. Results showed that both conditions performed statistically similarly. Notably, Moreno's (2007) findings are hard to extrapolate given the lull of empirical research on task essentialness.

In sum, existing literature on the effects of type of computerized practice on L2 grammar development suggests that output-focused practice yields better results than input-focused practice because it can promote comparable learning gains in interpretation and superior learning gains in production. In terms of task features, increased task complexity has been shown to have a positive effect on L2 grammar development (Medina, 2008), but task essentialness has not (Moreno, 2007). Clearly, however, the marked paucity of studies in this field of inquiry warrants further investigation to elucidate the role of these and other task features.

Type of Computerized Feedback

In contrast to the scant literature on the type of computerized practice, there is a considerably larger body of research investigating the effects of the type of computerized feedback. Interestingly, although existing studies all agree that feedback, regardless of its type, has a positive effect on L2 grammar development, the jury is still out as to the relative effectiveness of different types of feedback. Most studies to date have shown a significant advantage of more "explicit" types of feedback in which learners are given an explanation of the sources of their errors (Bowles, 2005; Cerezo, 2010; Lado, 2008; Lin, 2009; Nagata, 1993, also reported in Nagata & Swisher, 1995; Rosa & Leow, 2004; Sachs, 2011). However, counterevidence exists, with other studies finding no significant differences between more and less explicit types in which learners were merely informed that their responses were incorrect (Camblor, 2006; Hsieh, 2007; Moreno, 2007; Sanz & Morgan-Short, 2004). Additionally, one study showed significantly greater gains of less over more explicit feedback in oral delayed measures (Moreno, 2007). Notably, these mixed findings are in line with the longer established literature on feedback in classroom interaction, in which recent meta-analyses found that although corrective feedback has facilitative effects (Li, 2010; Lyster & Saito, 2010; Russell & Spada, 2006), it is still unclear which type of feedback yields the highest effect sizes. Russell and Spada (2006) and Mackey and Goo (2007) concluded that more studies are needed to decide whether implicit and explicit types of feedback are differently beneficial. In Li's (2010) meta-analysis, explicit feedback outperformed implicit types in the short to medium run, and in Lyster and Saito (2010), the developmental effects of recasts and explicit correction were comparable, and prompts yielded the best results.

Arguably, several external factors may explicate the conflicting findings in the literature on e-tutors (see, e.g., Nassaji, 2007, for a review of potentially mediating factors in classroom interaction research). One such factor is the type of computerized task at hand. Some studies used input-focused tasks, such as assembling sentence constituents (Bowles, 2005; Hsieh, 2007), matching pictures with sentences (Lado, 2008; Lin, 2009; Moreno, 2007; Sanz & Morgan-Short, 2004), matching the content of a text with its title (Sanz & Morgan-Short, 2004), truth-value judgments (Sachs, 2011), or filling in blanks using a list of possible forms (Rosa & Leow, 2004). In contrast, other studies used output-focused tasks, such as writing sentences to describe pictures (Camblor, 2006) or responding to context cues, both at the phrase level (Cerezo, 2010) and at the sentence level (Nagata, 1993). Another possibly mediating factor may have been the type of targeted grammatical structure, which included Japanese particles and passivization (Nagata, 1993), Japanese reflexive constructions (Sachs, 2011), Latin assignment of semantic functions (Lado, 2008; Lin, 2009), Spanish dative experiencer constructions with *gustar* (Bowles, 2005; Hsieh, 2007), Spanish noun–adjective gender and number agreement (Camblor, 2006), Spanish direct object pronouns (Moreno, 2007; Sanz & Morgan-Short, 2004), Spanish past counterfactual conditional sentences (Rosa & Leow, 2004), and Spanish present subjunctive and preposition pied-piping in adjectival relative clauses (Cerezo, 2010). Additionally, one study (Nagata, 1993) failed to isolate the role of corrective feedback from prior grammatical explanation, and only three studies (Lado, 2008; Lin, 2009; Sachs, 2011) addressed the role of learners' individual differences such as language aptitude or working memory to explicate within- and between-group variance.

In addition to external factors, the conflicting findings in the literature may also be explicated by a poor definition of the intrinsic nature of feedback. Specifically, most studies on types of computerized feedback have exclusively focused on the explicitness of negative evidence (i.e., explaining the rule or not), overlooking the fact that feedback moves can also encapsulate positive evidence (i.e., models of correct language) and prompt learners to repair their errors. For example, except for Camblor (2006) and Cerezo (2010), all studies included models of correct grammar either in the feedback message or implicitly in the task, so it is impossible to assess whether the observed learning gains resulted from processing positive or negative evidence. Similarly, all studies but Cerezo (2010) pushed learners to repair their errors at all times. On this token, the findings of seminal studies in the oral interaction literature by Leeman (2003) and McDonough (2005) suggest that under specific circumstances, the role of positive evidence and prompting for repair may outweigh the impact of negative evidence per se. Addressing this gap, Cerezo (2010) studied the separate contributions of prompts and negative evidence in the absence of positive evidence. In his study, participants interacted with an e-tutor to complete two different tasks, reporting a theft and finding an apartment. Some received grammatical explanations of their errors, but others were only informed about the place and nature of their errors and did not receive the rule. Some participants were asked to modify their output after an error, but others were not. Results showed that in the absence of positive evidence, more explicit negative evidence positively affected learning, but prompting did not. This provides additional support to the claim that prompting is only likely to have facilitative effects when learners have access to positive evidence, either concurrently in the ambient input or retrospectively by rescuing previously stored knowledge (see, e.g., VanPatten, 2004; but see Toth, 2006, for counter-arguments).

In sum, then, the growing body of literature on the effects of the type of computerized feedback on L2 grammar development has largely focused on comparing different degrees of explicitness of negative evidence (explaining the rule at play or not), with inconclusive findings. This may result from a lack of control over external and internal factors. At an external level, a variety of input- and output-focused tasks were used, different grammatical structures were targeted, and individual differences in language aptitude were controlled for only in a fraction of studies. At an internal level, studies have largely failed to isolate the relative and combined contributions of the three components of feedback (positive evidence, negative evidence, and prompting for repair). Specifically, most studies have neglected the role of positive evidence because they included models either in the feedback message or implicitly in the task. Similarly, they mostly did not control for the role of pushed repair, prompting learners to fix their errors at all times. On this token, incipient research showed that in the absence of positive evidence, the role of explicit negative evidence outweighed prompting, which was not beneficial.

Conclusion and Further Research

In the new millennium, the field of TELL is expanding its horizons to address ever more interesting research questions. Besides testing the pedagogical potential of technology per se and against other forms of instruction, researchers have also started to compare different technologies with each other to identify the most efficient ones. Also, premised on current theories of SLA and using hybrid designs that triangulate quantitative and qualitative analysis, researchers have started to explain why technologies can promote L2 development.

So far, however, the spotlight has been cast primarily on the use of technology as a medium of communication among tutors and peers in hybrid learning curricula. Yet given the increasing interest of university administrators in online learning curricula, language program administrators must turn to the incipient but steadily growing body of research on e-tutors to make better informed curricular decisions. So far, research has shown that under certain circumstances, e-tutors can successfully facilitate L2 grammar development per se and even better than other instructional technologies. Although several psycholinguistic and psychocognitive frameworks may explain this, it seems likely that the pedagogical potential of e-tutors lies in their ability to engage learners in large amounts of proactive practice, but not always—only under more demanding learning conditions (e.g., with output-focused tasks and less explicit feedback). Additionally, incipient research comparing different types of e-tutors tentatively suggests that the most efficient systems are those that use output-focused and complex tasks. As for the type of corrective feedback, the jury is still out. Although a growing body of studies suggests that, overall, more explicit feedback yields better results, a number of studies have shown that in some cases, minimally explicit feedback can work equally well, and learning outcomes may vary depending on several factors, including the complexity of the targeted structures.

In light of several methodological caveats and the overall paucity of studies on e-tutors, further research is certainly warranted. There is a blatant need for original and replication studies comparing the pedagogical effectiveness of e-tutors against other instructional technologies, including but not limited to F2F instruction. Also, researchers should compare different types of computerized features to contribute to the development of more sophisticated and efficient e-tutors. Specifically, further research should investigate how different types of computerized practice affect learning, comparing subtypes of input- and output-focused practice with varying degrees of complexity and task essentialness, at different levels (word, sentence, paragraph). Additionally, studies on computerized feedback should investigate the separate and combined contributions of different components of feedback (e.g., prompts, differently explicit positive and negative evidence). There is also a need for more studies addressing the role of modality (written, aural, visual, or a combination) in computerized instruction, in terms of both the L2 input and feedback. Finally, more studies should empirically address what kinds of learner external and internal variables may moderate the effects of computerized instruction.

Clearly, e-tutors still have a long way to go until they can effectively train language learners in all levels of communicative competence—grammatical, sociolinguistic, and strategic. Actually, the question of whether or not e-tutors might be able to ever replace human language instructors is a futile one: most learners study languages to communicate with other humans, not machines. But in a time when using technology for language learning is becoming the norm rather than the exception, when university administrators have identified online instruction as a critical goal, and given the many potential contributions of e-tutors to provide learners with additional access to language practice and corrective feedback, e-tutors should clearly occupy a more prominent position in our research agendas and language program administrators should remain informed.

References

Abraham, L. B. (2008). Computer-mediated glosses in second language reading comprehension and vocabulary learning: A meta-analysis. *Computer Assisted Language Learning, 21*(3), 199–226.

AbuSeileek, A. F. (2009). The effect of using an online-based course on the learning of grammar inductively and deductively. *ReCALL, 21*(3), 319–336.

AbuSeileek, A. F., & Rababah, G. A. (2007). The effect of computer-based grammar instruction on the acquisition of verb tenses in an EFL context. *The JALT CALL Journal, 3*(1-2), 59–80.

Allen, I. E., & Seaman, J. (2011). Going the distance: Online education in the United States, 2011. Retrieved March 25, 2012, from http://www.onlinelearningsurvey.com/reports/goingthedistance.pdf.

Anderson, J. R. (1993). *Rules of the mind.* Hillsdale, NJ: Erlbaum.

Benati, A. (2005). The effects of processing instruction, traditional instruction, and meaningful-based output instruction on the acquisition of English past simple tense. *Language Teaching Research, 5*, 95–127.

Blake, R. (2001). What language professionals need to know about technology. *ADFL Bulletin, 32*(3), 93–99.

Blake, R. (2007). New trends in using technology in the language curriculum. *Annual Review of Applied Linguistics, 27*, 76–97.

Blake, R. (2009). The use of technology for second language distance learning. *Modern Language Journal, 93*(Focus Issue), 822–835.

Bowles, M. A. (2005). Effects of verbalization condition and type of feedback on L2 development in a CALL task. (Unpublished doctoral dissertation). Georgetown University, Washington D.C.

Bowles, M. A. (2008). Task type and reactivity of verbal reports in SLA: A first look at a L2 task other than reading. *Studies in Second Language Acquisition, 30*(3), 359–387.

Cadierno, T. (1995). Formal instruction from a processing perspective: An investigation into the Spanish past tense. *Modern Language Journal, 79*(2), 179–193.

Camblor, M. (2006). *Type of written feedback, awareness, and L2 development: A computer-based study.* Unpublished doctoral dissertation, Georgetown University, Washington, DC.

Cerezo, L. (2010). *Talking to avatars: The computer as a tutor and the incidence of learner's agency, feedback, and grammatical form in SLA.* Unpublished doctoral dissertation, Georgetown University, Washington, DC.

Chapelle, C. A. (2010). The spread of computer-assisted language learning. *Language Teaching, 43*(1), 66–74.

Chen, L. (2006). The effect of the use of L1 in a multimedia tutorial on grammar learning: An error analysis of Taiwanese beginning EFL learners' English essays. *The Asian EFL Journal Quarterly, 8*(2), 76–110.

DeKeyser, R. M. (2007). Situating the concept of practice. In R. M. DeKeyser (Ed.), *Practice in a second language: Perspectives from applied linguistics and cognitive psychology* (pp. 1–18). New York: Cambridge University Press.

DeKeyser, R. M., & Sokalski, K. J. (2001). The differential role of comprehension and production practice. *Language Learning, 51*(supplement 1), 81–112.

Doughty, C. J. (1991). Second language instruction does make a difference: Evidence from an empirical study of SL relativization. *Studies in Second Language Acquisition, 13*(4), 431–469.

Egbert, J., Huff, L., McNeil, L., Preuss, C., & Sellen, J. (2009). Pedagogy, process, and classroom context: Integrating teacher voice and experience into research on technology-enhanced language learning. *The Modern Language Journal, 93,* 754–768.

Farley, A. P. (2001). Processing instruction and meaning-based output instruction: A comparative study. *Studies in Applied Linguistics, 5,* 57–93.

Felix, U. (2005a). Analysing recent CALL effectiveness research? Towards a common agenda. *Computer Assisted Language Learning, 18*(1-2), 1–32.

Felix, U. (2005b). What do meta-analyses tell us about CALL effectiveness? *ReCALL, 17*(2), 269–288.

Flynn, S. (1986). Production vs. comprehension: Differences in underlying competences. *Studies in Second Language Acquisition, 8,* 135–164.

Goertler, S. E. (2011). Blended and open/online learning: Adapting to a changing world of language teaching. In N. Arnold & L. Ducate (Eds.), *Present and future promises of CALL: From theory and research to new directions in language teaching* (pp. 471–502). San Marcos, TX: CALICO.

Grgurovic, M., Chapelle, C. A., & Shelley, M. (in preparation). Effectiveness of CALL: A meta-analysis and research synthesis.

Heift, T., & Schulze, M. (2007). *Parsers and pedagogues: Errors and intelligence in computer assisted language learning.* London: Routledge.

Hsieh, H. C. (2007). *Input-based practice, feedback, awareness and L2 development through a computerized task.* Unpublished doctoral dissertation, Georgetown University, Washington, DC.

Hubbard, P. (2005). A review of subject characteristics in CALL research. *Computer Assisted Language Learning, 18*(5), 351–368.

Hulstijn, J. H. (2000). The use of computer technology in experimental studies of second language acquisition: A survey of some techniques and some ongoing studies. *Language Learning & Technology, 3*(2), 32–43.

Iwashita, N., McNamara, T., & Elder, C. (2001). Can we predict task difficulty in an oral proficiency test? Exploring the potential of an information-processing approach to task design. *Language Learning, 51,* 401–436.

Izumi, S., Bigelow, M., Fujiwara, M., & Fearnow, S. (1999). Testing the output hypothesis: Effects of output on noticing and second language acquisition. *Studies in Second Language Acquisition, 21,* 421–452.

Kuiken, F., Mos, M., & Vedder, I. (2005). Cognitive task complexity and second language writing performance. In S. Foster-Cohen, M. P. García & J. Cenoz (Eds.), *EUROSLA Yearbook* (Vol. 5, pp. 195–222). Amsterdam: John Benjamins.

Lado, B. (2008). *The role of bilingualism, type of feedback and cognitive capacity in the acquisition of non-primary languages: A computer-based study.* Unpublished doctoral dissertation, Georgetown University, Washington, DC.

Leeman, J. (2003). Recasts and second language development: Beyond negative evidence. *Studies in Second Language Acquisition, 25,* 37–63.

Levy, M. (1997). *CALL: Context and conceptualisation.* Oxford: Oxford University Press.

Li, S. (2010). The effectiveness of corrective feedback in SLA: A meta-analysis. *Language Learning, 60*(2), 309–365.

Lin, H. J. (2009). *Bilingualism, feedback, cognitive capacity, and learning strategies in L3 development.* Unpublished doctoral dissertation, Georgetown University, Washington, DC.

Loewen, S. (2005). Incidental focus on form and second language learning. *Studies in Second Language Acquisition, 27*(3), 361–386.

Long, M. H. (1996). The role of the linguistic environment in second language acquisition. In W. C. Ritchie & T. K. Bhatia (Eds.), *Handbook of second language acquisition: Vol. 2. Second language acquisition* (pp. 413–468). New York: Academic Press.

Loschky, L., & Bley-Vroman, R. (1993). Grammar and task-based methodology. In G. Crookes & S. M. Gass (Eds.), *Tasks and language learning* (pp. 123–167). Clevedon, UK: Multilingual Matters.

Lyster, R., & Saito, K. (2010). Oral feedback in classroom SLA: A meta-analysis. *Studies in Second Language Acquisition, 32*, 265–302.

Mackey, A. (1999). Input, interaction, and second language development: An empirical study of question formation in ESL. *Studies in Second Language Acquisition, 21*, 557–587.

Mackey, A. (2007). Introduction: The role of conversational interaction in second language acquisition. In A. Mackey (Ed.), *Conversational interaction in second language acquisition: A collection of empirical studies* (pp. 1–26). Oxford: Oxford University Press.

Mackey, A., & Goo, J. (2007). Interaction research in SLA: A meta-analysis and research synthesis. In A. Mackey (Ed.), *Conversational interaction in second language acquisition: A collection of empirical studies* (pp. 407–452). Oxford: Oxford University Press.

Mayer, R. E. (2001). *Multimedia learning.* New York: Cambridge University Press.

McDonough, K. (2005). Identifying the contributions of negative feedback and learners' responses to L2 development. *Studies in Second Language Acquisition, 27*, 79–103.

Medina, A. D. (2008). *Concurrent verbalization, task complexity, and working memory: Effects on L2 learning in a computerized task.* Unpublished doctoral dissertation, Georgetown University, Washington, DC.

Moreno, N. (2007). *The effects of type of task and type of feedback on L2 development in CALL.* Unpublished doctoral dissertation, Georgetown University, Washington, DC.

Morgan-Short, K., & Wood Bowden, H. (2006). Processing instruction and meaningful output-based instruction: Effects on second language development. *Studies in Second Language Acquisition, 28*(1), 31–65.

Nagata, N. (1993). Intelligent computer feedback for second language instruction. *Modern Language Journal, 77*, 330–339.

Nagata, N. (1996). Computer vs. workbook instruction in second language acquisition. *CALICO Journal, 14*, 53–75.

Nagata, N. (1998a). Input vs. output practice in educational software for second language acquisition. *Language Learning & Technology, 1*, 23–40.

Nagata, N. (1998b). The relative effectiveness of production and comprehension practice in second language acquisition. *Computer Assisted Language Learning, 11*(2), 153–177.

Nagata, N., & Swisher, M. V. (1995). A study of consciousness-raising by computer: The effect of metalinguistic feedback on SLA. *Foreign Language Annals, 28*(3), 336–347.

Nassaji, H. (2007). Elicitation and reformulation and their relationship with learner repair in dyadic interaction. *Language Learning, 57*(4), 511–548.

Norris, J. M., & Ortega, L. (2010). Research timeline: Research synthesis. *Language Teaching, 43*(4), 461–479.

Nutta, J. W. (1998). Is computer-based grammar instruction as effective as teacher-directed grammar instruction for teaching L2 structures? *CALICO Journal, 16*, 49–62.

Paivio, A. (1986). *Mental representations: a dual coding approach.* Oxford: Oxford University Press.

Pederson, K. M. (1987). Research on CALL. In W. F. Smith (Ed.), *Modern media in foreign language education: Theory and implementation* (pp. 99–131). Lincolnwood, IL: National Textbook.

Petersen, K. A. (2010a). *Implicit corrective feedback in computer-guided interaction: Does mode matter?* Unpublished doctoral dissertation, Georgetown University, Washington, DC.

Peterson, M. (2010b). Computerized games and simulations in computer-assisted language learning: A meta-analysis of research. *Simulation & Gaming, 41*(1), 72–93.

Robinson, P. (1996). Learning simple and complex second language rules under implicit, incidental, rule-search, and instructed conditions. *Studies in Second Language Acquisition, 18*(1), 27–67.

Rosa, E. M., & Leow, R. P. (2004). Computerized task-based instruction in the L2 classroom: The effects of explicitness and type of feedback on L2 development. *Modern Language Journal, 88*(2), 192–216.

Russell, J., & Spada, N. (2006). The effectiveness of corrective feedback for the acquisition of L2 grammar. In J. M. Norris (Ed.), *Synthesizing research on language learning and teaching* (pp. 133–162). Philadelphia: John Benjamins.

Sachs, R. (2011). *Individual differences and the effectiveness of visual feedback on reflexive binding in L2 Japanese.* Unpublished doctoral dissertation, Georgetown University, Washington, DC.

Sagarra, N., & Zapata, G. (2008). Computer-assisted instruction and L2 grammar accuracy. *Hispania, 91*(1), 93–109.

Sanz, C. (2000). Implementing LIBRA for the design of experimental research in SLA. *Language Learning and Technology, 13*(2), 27–31.

Sanz, C., & Morgan-Short, K. (2004). Positive evidence versus explicit rule presentation and explicit negative feedback: A computer-assisted study. *Language Learning, 54*, 35–78.

Schmidt, R. W. (1993). Awareness and second language acquisition. *Annual Review of Applied Linguistics, 13*, 206–226.

Schulze, M. (2008). AI in CALL: Artificially inflated or almost imminent? *CALICO Journal, 25*(3).

Stockwell, G. (2007). A review of technology choice for teaching language skills and areas in the CALL literature. *ReCALL, 19*(2), 105–120.

Tang, H. W., Yin, M. S., & Lou, P. J. (2009). A meta-analytic review of current CALL research on second language learning. *IT in Medicine & Education, 1*, 677–684.

Taylor, A. M. (2009). CALL-based versus paper-based glosses: Is there a difference in reading comprehension? *CALICO Journal, 27*(1), 147–160.

Taylor, R. P. (Ed.). (1980). *The computer in the school: Tutor, tool, tutee.* New York: Teachers College Press.

Torlaković, E., & Deugo, D. (2004). Application of a CALL system in the acquisition of adverbs in English. *Computer Assisted Language Learning, 17*(2), 203–235.

Toth, P. D. (2006). Processing instruction and a role for output in second language acquisition. *Language Learning, 56*(2), 319–385.

Tsutsui, M. (2004). Multimedia as a means to enhance feedback. *Computer Assisted Language Learning, 17*(3), 377–402.

VanPatten, B. (2004). Input processing in second language acquisition. In B. VanPatten (Ed.), *Processing instruction: Theory, research, and commentary* (pp. 5–32). Mahwah, NJ: Lawrence Erlbaum Associates.

Watts, C. (1989). Interactive video: What the students say. *CALICO Journal, 7*(1), 17–20.

Zhao, Y. (2003). Recent developments in technology and language learning: A literature review and meta-analysis. *CALICO Journal, 21*(1), 7–27.

Chapter 5
Hybrid Learning Spaces: Re-envisioning Language Learning

Lara Ducate, Lara Lomicka, and Gillian Lord

The advent of hybrid learning is causing what some have termed a "paradigm shift in higher education" (Buzzetto-More & Sweat-Guy, 2006, p. 153; see also Allen & Seaman, 2003; Lorenzetti, 2005; Young, 2002). Various studies have asserted that enhancing course content through technology can support in-depth delivery and analysis of knowledge (Young, 2002) and increase student satisfaction (Dziuban & Moskal, 2001; Rivera, McAlister, & Rice, 2002; Wu & Hiltz, 2004). As institutions of higher education are encouraged to do more with fewer resources, educators and administrators are increasingly contemplating "hybrid" or "blended" learning, whether to redesign whole programs or simply offer more sections. This proliferation of online learning models necessitates a reexamination of various facets of teaching and learning, from delivery mode and contact hours to homework and activities for face-to-face (F2F) time. Language classes are no exception.

The publication of this volume is a testament to the fact that our profession is rethinking our vision of language classrooms, teachers, and students. Because of ongoing challenges, such as budget shortfalls, reduced staff, and increasing course enrollments, educators and administrators are seeking ways to alter traditional class formats and delivery systems for course content. This chapter addresses some of the primary theoretical issues at stake in this re-envisioning of our discipline while also providing case study examples of ways in which Web 2.0 technologies can be exploited to make the most of our new educational landscape.

In this first section, we define the term *hybrid* learning—specifically in the case of language classes—and we examine how different educators have implemented these new delivery methods. We also examine how Web 2.0 tools are relevant to the discussion of our changing classroom landscapes and the redefinition of the role of teachers, learners, and learning spaces. Furthermore, second language acquisition (SLA) theories are discussed with respect to their implementation in hybrid learning because a solid theoretical foundation is crucial as educators embark on the process of adopting and adapting technologies for their classes. The following section of the chapter then takes a critical look at tools that have been used in F2F contexts and adapted in blended or hybrid courses at undergraduate as well as graduate levels. These examples are provided to showcase the ways in which technological tools can enable the enrichment and extension of the classroom setting in both traditional and alternative settings.

Hybrid Learning

Hybrid or *blended learning*[1] can be defined in many ways (see, for example, Goertler, 2011; Graham, 2005; Nicolson, Murphy, & Southgate, 2011; or Osguthorpe & Graham, 2003). For the purposes of this chapter, we operationalize this mode of delivery as Heinze and Procter (2004) have: "Blended learning is learning that is facilitated by the effective combination of different modes of delivery, models of teaching and styles of learning, and is based on transparent communication amongst all parties involved with a course" (pp. 8–9). With respect to language classes, this definition generally implies a learning space where instruction takes place in a traditional classroom setting and is enhanced or supplemented—sometimes even replaced—by computer-based or online activities. Such activities can, but do not necessarily, replace classroom seat time, but the implementation of a hybrid approach implies that students interact with the instructor and other students both in person and virtually.

However, given the variation in how we define blended learning, one of the greatest challenges educators and program directors face when contemplating a move to hybrid platforms is knowing how, precisely, to structure these courses. A common approach is to reduce the number of weekly contact hours, usually from 4 or 5 down to 2 or 3, and make up those credits via online activities (e.g., Scida & Saury, 2006). Other institutions opt for different patterns, such as one lecture-type meeting and one small group tutoring session with the remainder of the contact occurring virtually (e.g., http://romlcourses.unc.edu/Spanish/spanhybrid/). At the same time, many instructors have managed to increase contact hours and content beyond the confines of the classroom by adding hybrid elements to their courses without officially changing the number of credits. The combinations and permutations are limitless and depend generally on external factors related to administrative issues, classroom space, personnel, and technological support (Goertler, 2011). Regardless of the variation in contact hours or delivery formats, though, hybrid programs rely on solid pedagogy and innovative technologies to make learning as effective as possible. The wealth of technology tools available to instructors has made these many formats possible and even successful.

Technological Tools for the Hybrid Class

Recent innovations in emerging technologies have brought change and excitement to the language classroom. For language learning, technology serves as a set of tools that allows teachers and students to communicate with other speakers of the language virtually (Belz, 2003; Belz & Müller-Hartmann, 2003; Furstenberg, Levet, English, & Maillet, 2001; Lomicka, 2009; Sadler, 2009), build classroom

---

[1]For the purposes of this chapter, we use the terms *hybrid* and *blended* learning interchangeably. Other terms such as *integrative learning* or *multimethod learning* have also been proposed; however, for the sake of simplicity, we prefer to use the most common terminology.

community (Comas-Quinn, Mardomingo, & Valentine, 2009; Lomicka & Lord, 2012; Rovai & Jordan, 2004), engage students in their learning (Comas-Quinn et al., 2009), and collaborate with others (Rovai & Jordan, 2004). As such, language learning extends beyond the classroom and continues to grow virtually by means of new and innovative technologies. In the earlier implementation of hybrid learning, technology was often thought of as a way to deliver instruction—only one aspect of online learning as we know it today. It is equally important to fully integrate technology into the course and to allow the course content to drive the technology, affording students opportunities to learn, interact, and communicate both in and out of the classroom. Although a growing number of tools are poised to revolutionize the way we teach, our focus in this chapter is on blogs, wikis, Facebook, and Twitter (see Appendix 5-1 for URLs and related tools). We chose these tools because of their popularity and availability, as well as their potential to connect learners and foster collaborative learning.

Two important considerations of hybrid learning are collaboration and community (see, for example, Rovai & Jordan, 2004). When learning expands beyond the classroom, technological tools can help students to apply lessons learned in class or to extend discussion beyond the walls of the classroom. Two tools we are focusing on in this chapter, blogs and wikis, lend themselves well to collaborative work and are user friendly. Blogs are often thought of as spaces for individual writing and reflection (Granberg, 2010; Miceli, Murray, & Kennedy, 2010), but followers can interact with the blogger through comments. Through this interaction, students can engage in knowledge sharing, reflection, and even debate. Blogs can also serve as an engaging way to build community (Comas-Quinn et al., 2009) because followers can now receive notifications when updates are made. It is also possible to create group blogs in which usernames and passwords are shared among members. Group or shared blogs are more collaborative, affording all followers a chance to participate and interact individually within a group.

Even more than blogs, wikis serve as a way to collaborate and share information with other learners; they also engage students in their learning. Members can edit text, and when revisions are made, the history page reveals the specific changes made. Collaboration is naturally built into wikis; they serve as unique tools that offer learners a powerful way to share and jointly construct knowledge.

As we have indicated already, another key aspect of successful hybrid learning is establishing a community of learners and creating a virtual presence. For learners, it is crucial to be active participants in learning both in and out of the classroom. In more traditional classroom contexts, students are physically visible, and even if their participation is low, they are still seen in the community. In online formats, the learner needs to establish a presence to be "seen" and must make concerted efforts to interact and communicate with others. Learners must participate and interact to help build and maintain an online community. Tools such as Facebook and Twitter may be well suited for establishing strong virtual presence and community and for building a social network among participants.

Inherently social, Facebook has as its goal to "create a richer, faster way for people to share information about what [is] happening around them" (Zuckerberg, 2009, p. 2). As one of the largest social networks, Facebook offers students more opportunities to develop personal relationships than F2F settings (Mazer, Murphy, & Simonds, 2007). It can also nurture student–teacher relationships if used effectively and appropriately (Mazer et al., 2007). Facebook is a useful tool for establishing connections, exchanging updates and information through the common wall, discussing or debating in the discussion forum, sharing information and pictures, and engaging in instant chat (including video chat), to name a few.

Similar to Facebook, the microblogging tool Twitter is aimed at connecting with others quickly; receiving instant updates from friends, businesses, and celebrities; and finding out what's going on in the world. Through Twitter, users can send, read, and repost messages of up to 140 characters, which are displayed on the author's profile page and delivered to the author's followers. Tweets are often short, unconnected, informal, and surface-level thoughts about what people are doing or what is going on at a particular moment in time. Twitter provides students with a quick and easy way to practice language out of the classroom, and its potential is great for connection, communication, and language exchange. Twitter can help teachers connect with students as well as help students connect with each other, thus building community and establishing a social presence (Antenos-Conforti, 2009; Borau, Ullrich, Feng, & Shen, 2009; Dunlap & Lowenthal, 2009; Messner, 2009; National Education Association, 2009; Parry, 2008; Walker, 2009). Both Twitter and Facebook hold great potential in education to help students and teachers to transform and bring new dimensions to learning. Having briefly introduced the tools that make up the focus of the chapter, the next section considers the implications that administrators, teachers, and students face as they work together to move toward more successful learning in hybrid contexts.

Implications

Although few would deny that human interaction remains essential in learning and using language, advances in technologies, such as those already described, have enabled us to reach a point in which students can accomplish a great deal by working independently, thus reserving class time for F2F communication and interactive learning. Administrators are also aware that today's learners, because of the increasing amounts of nontraditional students, often need more flexible learning opportunities. To address these needs, instructors must re-evaluate how they stimulate interaction and what tools they use to do so. In hybrid contexts, teachers must provide clear structure to online activities (e.g., outline the clarity of tasks and provide specific roles for students and teacher) but also need to allow learners to freely use technology to interact and respond with each other. Learning in virtual spaces takes place differently than classroom instruction, where learning tends to be more linear (Carroll, 2007). Online instruction provides learners with more dynamic and active ways of interacting, collaborating, and learning. Instructors must therefore find ways to interact and communicate with students that can supplement (or compensate for a lack of) F2F contact time. Furthermore, students need to feel both supported and connected in online contexts. McBride and Fägersten (2008) posit that students must maintain "a sense of connection with a learning community" (p. 43), which is achieved through allowing students to take on a greater responsibility for their own learning.

In addition to changes that teachers must face with instruction in hybrid contexts, students' roles shift as well. For example, Reynard (2007) mentions that hybrid contexts provide an opportunity for students to become more autonomous and more engaged in their learning. She also posits that through hybrid courses, students learn to drive the learning process in a more direct way, thus pointing toward a shift where students and instructors are equally active. If these changes are successfully implemented, hybrid learning can take on new dimensions and offer a different experience than in the physical classroom. Although traditional and virtual environments both offer valuable experiences and interaction for students, they are not mutually exclusive and can work well together. In fact, Grgurovic (2007) reviewed 25 comparative studies on blended or hybrid instruction and concluded that blended learning is just as effective as or even more effective than traditional classroom spaces.

However, even though hybrid learning is becoming more accepted as an instructional approach, it is important to consider its challenges. Stracke's (2007) research examines learners who leave hybrid language courses because of a lack of administrative support, lack of a paper medium, or rejection of the computer by the learner as a tool for language learning. Goertler and Winke (2008) point out that it is increasingly difficult to accommodate more students in language classes because of a lack of physical space and that administrators see technology as a possible solution to this challenge in that it can allow more students access to courses, although it cannot instantly solve these issues.

Regardless of the technology implemented, it is important to create a learning experience that is "as 'seamless' as possible for students, providing intentionality for each environment and the technology used" (Reynard, 2007, p. 1). In sum, hybrid learning should enable instructors to become "more connected and aware of each student, and students can become more aware of their own learning and take more responsibility for it" (Reynard, 2007, p. 3). In this chapter, we provide examples, based on SLA theory, of sound and effective use of technology in hybrid language learning.

Second Language Acquisition Theory and Hybrid Learning

Although there will always be new and interesting technologies for the second language (L2) classroom, deciding which tools to use for which purposes must be informed by SLA research (Chapelle, 2009). With this in mind, this section explores relevant theories and pedagogical principles in order to provide a framework for the use of the tools discussed in this chapter. As current research in SLA, L2 pedagogy, and technology demonstrates, teaching with technology has shifted from using computers for structural drills to a sociocultural or constructivist orientation, in which the computer serves more as a medium to facilitate communication rather than as a tutor (Kern, 2006). The following section discusses many of these elements in their theoretical context and as they relate to blogs, wikis, Facebook, and Twitter.

Sociocultural Theory

One of the key principles of sociocultural theory asserts that learning takes place through interaction or mediation (Lantolf, 2000; Lantolf & Thorne, 2006; Vygotsky, 1978) as "external socio-cultural activities are transformed into internal mental functioning" (Basharina, 2007, p. 84). Tools, including both physical tools, such as cultural products, and psychological tools, such as language, help to direct behavior and lead to higher mental processing (Basharina, 2007; Lantolf & Appel, 1994). In regard to language learning, for example, tools can include textbooks; authentic materials; classroom tasks; and interactions with teachers, other learners, or native speakers (Basharina, 2007). During a problem-solving task, learners use tools or scaffold with a peer or a more experienced learner or instructor to pass through the zone of proximal development and progress from being able to complete a task with help to being able to complete the task alone (Donato, 1994; Lantolf, 2000; Lantolf & Thorne, 2006). Collaborative learning then, depending on how it is structured, can help students to produce better final products. During collaboration, students are encouraged to reflect more deeply on their own ideas and course material (Arnold & Ducate, 2006; Lord, 2008; Lord & Lomicka, 2008), can telecollaborate with native speakers to improve linguistic or intercultural competence (Belz, 2003; Belz & Müller-Hartmann, 2003; Furstenberg et al., 2001; Lomicka, 2009; Sadler, 2007), and connect with others through blogging or social networking (Antenos-Conforti, 2009; Ducate & Lomicka, 2005, 2008; Lomicka & Lord, forthcoming, 2012; McBride, 2009). In addition, by working on wikis collaboratively, students are able to achieve more than they would be able to alone in terms of content, accuracy, organization, and research (Arnold, Ducate, & Kost, 2009, 2012; Arnold, Ducate, Lomicka, & Lord, 2009; Ducate, Lomicka, & Moreno, 2011; Elola & Oskoz, 2010; Kessler, 2009; Lee, 2010; Sykes, Oskoz, & Thorne, 2008). To take full advantage of these learner-to-learner interactions, instructors can design activities that engage students in problem-solving tasks in order to encourage them to maintain focused interactions with clear goals (Gánem Gutiérrez, 2003; Spodark, 2005, 2008).

In addition to mediation through tools and interaction, another important consideration of learning, especially relating to learners' goals, is activity theory. Activity theory was initially introduced by Vygotsky and Leont'ev and then expanded by Engeström and can help researchers to more deeply understand learner motivations because of its micro- and macro-analysis of student interactions and orientations toward tasks (Engeström, 1999). This theory investigates the different ways that learners progress through an activity by focusing on their goals, including physical needs, career aspirations, or personal goals, and how these aims help to mediate their actions (Blin & Appel, 2011; Lantolf & Thorne, 2006).

Three factors mediate actions according to activity theory: the available tools, the community, and the guidelines of the task and how the labor is divided (Lantolf & Thorne, 2006). When considering these factors, one can examine not just the outcome of the task but also how learners mediate their interactions and work on the task with others (Allen, 2010). Motivation, therefore, comes not only from an individual but also from the learning context and evolves with and is mediated by the co-participants through actions completed during the activity. Actions are thus motivated by one's goals and desire for specific outcomes. One can think of activities as more long-term endeavors and actions are focused on subgoals for that activity. For example, the activity might be to learn German for purposes of work, travel, or personal enrichment, but the actions associated with that activity could be completing blog postings, collaborating on a wiki, speaking with native speakers or classmates, or listening to authentic texts online (Blin & Appel, 2011).

Using activity theory as their theoretical framework, Blin and Appel (2011) were able to investigate what artifacts students used, how and why they used them, and where artifacts were used to encompass their potential development. The researchers examined how a computer-supported collaborative writing task exemplifies Lantolf and Appel's (1994) assertion of three factors that mediate activity and the influence of these mediating factors as the students worked toward completing their activity. In this case, the writing task was mediated by (1) tools such as the L2 and the computer-mediated communication (CMC) technologies; (2) guidelines, both for the task and for other wiki and forum postings; and (3) the other participants in the task and their degree of collaboration (community). Blin and Appel (2011) found that the instructors' guidelines and the messages on the forum "mediated the collective activity and sometimes triggered focus shifts by prompting students to question their emergent practice. Teacher interventions also helped redirect students' attention to the object and desired outcomes" (p. 493). Villamil and De Guerrero's study (1996) on peer revision in Spanish students' writing, for example, found that students mediated their actions with external resources, their first language (L1), scaffolding, interlanguage knowledge, and vocalizing private speech.

In a study in which student motivation during study abroad was investigated, students reported linguistic and career-oriented motives for learning French and that studying abroad was critical in achieving these goals (Allen, 2010). Students seemed to be more motivated if they were more personally interested in learning French rather than for merely practical goals such as a better career. Activity theory demonstrated in this study that "it is impossible to view motivation as a stable, internal characteristic of individuals or to see students as possessing either 'low' or 'high' motivation" (p. 45) because some students were more socially motivated and generally interested in learning something new but others were more focused on a tangible goal such as fulfilling a French minor, which did not lead to as many gains in language proficiency as those with more intrinsic goals. Computer-assisted language learning (CALL) studies have found similar results concerning students' use of a large variety of tools to mediate their learning (Basharina, 2007; Haneda, 1997; Lei, 2008), which allows researchers to gain more insight into students motivations and successes for using various tools when carrying out CALL tasks.

In terms of research, using the micro- and macro-analysis described by activity theory enables the researcher to analyze many different types of data such as chat transcripts, forum postings, and wiki pages to see how students communicate and use language and how they negotiate and renegotiate their actions. Activity theory therefore allows the instructor a view into students' interpretation of the guidelines and how they negotiate them within their learning community and can help instructors of hybrid courses to more fully understand their students' motivations toward tasks in order to organize instruction in a way that is most beneficial to everyone.

Communities of Practice

The importance of collaboration and interaction through community-building has been discussed earlier and relates directly to the formation of communities of practice (CoPs). CoPs were originally defined as all kinds of groups with shared interests or occupations, and, according to Wenger (1998), must include a community or "mutual engagement" (characterized by regular interactions and discussions with a common goal that bind the community together), a domain or "joint enterprise" (a shared topic of interest), and a practice or "shared repertoire" (the resources they produce while achieving their common goals) (pp. 72–73). In education, CoPs refer to groups of people who are all involved in learning or researching a similar topic and thereby help each other to learn more or complete the task more successfully through regular interactions (Wenger, 1998). CoP interactions are characterized by problem solving, requests for information, seeking experience, reusing assets, coordination and synergy, discussing developments, documentation projects, visits, and mapping knowledge and identifying gaps (Wenger, 1998). Richards (2010) found that some of the benefits of belonging to a CoP, especially for in-service teachers, include collaborating with other learners, teachers, and administrators; sharing ideas, lesson plans, and knowledge; forming reading groups, action research teams, and peer observation groups; and helping members feel part of a larger group to keep them from feeling isolated. Although these benefits were suggested for in-service teachers, many can also apply to students in an L2 hybrid class, where it is especially important that students feel part of a larger group with a common purpose or joint enterprise.

Research on CoPs also allows for a deeper analysis of learning behaviors, including both how and why they occur (He, 2009; Kiely, 2009; Wiltse, 2006). In the case of Kiely's study (2009), for example, although both L2 learners examined in the case study were successful, analyzing the data using the CoP framework demonstrated how one Chinese learner of English did not as easily take advantage of the interpersonal aspects of language learning and did not pay close attention to context and therefore felt that language learning was more of a solitary endeavor. Her strategy was to focus more on the fixed rules she had learned to help her progress in her language learning. Although she was just as successful and motivated as the other learner in the study, she ultimately had a harder time developing language awareness, the goal of the study, and did not take advantage of being a member of a CoP and stayed on the periphery of the group. Her classmate, on the other hand, was more aware of her language development in general and of the importance of interpersonal communication. She therefore also felt more integrated into the CoP and took advantage of the opportunities for language learning within the group.

In a study of the discourse of junior high students in a language arts class, Wiltse (2006) used CoPs to illustrate the importance of the relationship between the teacher and the learners in a CoP of learners. Wiltse points out, however, as Wenger (1998) also admitted, that the CoP framework was not designed for school contexts because "legitimate peripheral participation makes a fundamental distinction between learning and intentional instruction" (p. 217). Because students are required to be in their classes, they are not, at the beginning at least, voluntarily in their classroom CoP, and the framework is therefore not necessarily adequate to explain all aspects of a classroom setting. In agreement with Haneda (1997), Wiltse (2006) suggests that when the CoP framework is applied to classroom contexts, especially when there is explicit teaching involved, the concept of scaffolding should be included in the CoP framework to provide a larger role for that of the teacher and more proficient peers, as demonstrated in the next study.

In an analysis of in-service teachers' interactions with teacher trainers, He (2009) found that learning did not happen automatically but rather only when what was termed as a broker helped the participants to negotiate their roles within the CoP to reach the principals of a CoP: "mutual engagement, a joint enterprise, and a shared repertoire" (Wenger, 1998, pp. 72–73). Because each participant stemmed from different professional contexts and histories, the broker helped to mediate between the teacher trainers and the in-service teachers so that each had enough knowledge about the school or the subject knowledge to be able to cooperatively complete their task within the CoP.

Although CoPs may not originate spontaneously in hybrid learning contexts (Haneda, 1997), providing students with a common goal and a problem-solving task may help them to begin one on their own. A collaborative wiki project, for example, can provide a common goal, and the accompanying discussion board can supply a forum for learners to engage in the various characteristic behaviors of a CoP listed above. Given a specific task, members of a Facebook group can also form a CoP based around their common goal of improving their L2 skills and cultural knowledge. Foreign language (FL) methods graduate students, for example, exhibited characteristics of a CoP on a discussion board when conversing about FL pedagogy and teaching methods with experts in the field (Arnold, Ducate, & Lomicka, 2007).

Interactionist Theory

Each of the four tools we discuss also has a great potential for providing input from native speakers, other L2 learners, and instructors, as well as forcing L2 learners to produce output. Input is vital to language learning because it provides learners with a model for their output and encourages interaction (Gass & Mackey, 2006; Krashen, 1985; VanPatten, 2003). Through increased interaction, students produce output, which allows them to test hypotheses about their interlanguage (Gass & Mackey, 2006). Therefore, students must be given the opportunity to engage in negotiation of meaning, whereby they engage in comprehension checks, recasts, and paraphrasing to understand and be understood (Gass & Mackey, 2006; Long, 1996). Through the feedback students receive during this negotiation of meaning, they can make adjustments to their language and fill in any necessary gaps. Although Long's interaction hypothesis (1996), defined above, focused on speaking, interaction through writing in such applications as synchronous and asynchronous CMC have also been suggested to encourage more negotiation of meaning and even lead to gains in language proficiency (Baburhan, 2010; Beauvois, 1998; Bower & Kawaguchi, 2011; Payne & Whitney, 2002; Pelletieri, 2000; Sauro, 2009; among others). As Chun (2008) points out, though, there is also recent evidence that computer-mediated interactions between non-native speakers or between native and non-native speakers do not always lead to language gains in terms of "noticing linguistic errors, lexical or syntactic complexity, length of discourse produced, or equality of participation" (p. 24), reported by many of the above studies. Nonetheless, most of the research does point to a positive transfer from written CMC to oral proficiency. These conflicting results point to the need for continued research on these issues, including the role of the teacher within these learner-guided interactions because, as Chapelle (2009) points out, the teacher is necessary for planning and guiding successful tasks in CMC.

Although blogs, wikis, Facebook, and Twitter are not necessarily synchronous, they do provide learners with large amounts of input from their classmates, instructors, and native speaker interlocutors. In addition, they engage students in meaningful interactions, which can lead to the negotiation of meaning and thereby language learning. It has also been found, for example, that blogging leads to improved writing proficiency (Arslan & Sahin-Kizil, 2010). There are also certain pedagogical principles, including autonomy, motivation, and learning styles, that should be considered when integrating technology into a hybrid course; these are discussed in the following subsections.

Autonomy

Autonomy is defined as the process by which learners assume control and guidance of their own education and thereby make decisions involved in the learning process according to what they believe is most necessary for their learning (Benson, 2001; Dickinson, 1987, 1995; Little, 2000). In the context of wikis, blogs, Facebook, Twitter, and hybrid learning, it is possible to examine autonomy from a variety of perspectives, including where students are located when they engage in their L2 learning, what individual characteristics they bring to the learning, how they interact with other learners and tools, and how they manage to assert their own voice in the learning. The nature of Web 2.0 technologies promotes autonomy, which is also necessary in a hybrid-learning context. Such autonomy, though, may lead to isolation, and studies have shown that students must be prepared, trained, and provided with the appropriate tools to gradually take autonomy over their own learning in effective ways (Fischer, 2007; Murray, 1999, 2005; Ruschoff, 1998; Thang & Bidmeshki, 2010) and it can also be influenced by the supportiveness of their classmates or group members (Chang, 2007).

Few studies have specifically focused on autonomy and the tools we focus on here, although the concept has come up indirectly in several wiki projects. In a study by Kessler (2009), students were given complete autonomy over a wiki they wrote to define culture. However, the students seemed to pay more attention to content than form when left to their own devices. It has also been found that students are able to work collaboratively on a wiki and successfully revise both form and content autonomously (Arnold et al., 2009; Elola & Oskoz, 2010; Lee, 2010). The researchers of each of these wiki studies recommend that for students to successfully collaborate and revise their wikis, they need instructor guidance and training to set expectations, confirming previous research on autonomy in general.

Motivation

Motivation in L2 learning is often closely linked to learner autonomy in L2 research, and it has been suggested that one affects the other. According to Gardner (1991), there are two types of motivation: instrumental, which entails learning a language in order to achieve an external goal such as fulfilling a language requirement or getting a better job, and integrative, or learning a language because of a genuine love of the target language and culture. In Gardner's socioeducational model (2000), he suggests that motivation is supported by integrativeness and the learner's attitude toward the learning environment. Dörnyei (1994, 2001) agrees that the classroom experience can have an influence on students' motivation, including the teaching methods, the connection between the teacher and students, and the learning atmosphere and dynamics among students. Other factors that have been found to influence motivation are the level of difficulty of a task, meaningful learning objectives, feedback from the instructor, and minimal hindrances to learning (Good & Brophy, 1987).

As shown in this chapter, blogs, wikis, Facebook, and Twitter can tap into students' motivations by providing meaningful contexts for interaction, varied teaching methods, increased communication, and community building between teachers and students and among classmates. Although studies have not specifically examined motivation related to these specific tools, incidental evidence indicates that they increase motivation for the reasons mentioned above. Lee (2010), for example, found that students enjoyed the collaborative nature of a wiki to practice their writing, which led to increased motivation for writing. Kessler (2009) also found that his students appreciated the chance to work autonomously on a wiki.

Learning Styles and Multiple Intelligences

Learning styles and multiple intelligences can factor into motivation and success toward learning a language. Learning styles include visual, auditory, and kinesthetic in terms of different types of sensory learning styles, or analytic versus global, intuitive versus random, sensory versus sequential, orientation to closure, or competition versus cooperation (Scarcella & Oxford, 1992). According to James and Gardner (1995), there are nine types of intelligences: intrapersonal, interpersonal, logical/mathematical, verbal/linguistic, bodily/kinesthetic, visual/spatial, musical/rhythmic, naturalist, and existential. The versatility of blogs, wikis, Facebook, and Twitter allows learners to tap into many of these learning styles and intelligences with the guidance of an instructor. Each is visual and can include auditory material, and by engaging in projects using a variety of tools, students are engaging their kinesthetic, or active, sense. Audioblogging, vlogging (video blogging), and moblogging (uploading from a mobile device) allow for blogging through multimedia and can relate to various learning styles of both the producer and the audience.

As Spodark (2008) points out, students of the millennial generation need these varied activities even more than their predecessors, and instructors should take advantage of the telecollaborative tasks available using new technologies, such as collaborative work, peer review, and multimedia presentations. Van Deusen-Scholl (2008) also found that engaging beginning and advanced German learners in CMC allowed them to tap into their own learning styles to make learning more individualized and helped them use their strengths to their advantages while addressing their weaknesses. Hybrid learning also provides more opportunities for students to make use of their multiple intelligences and individualize instruction as long as teachers assess what students need to best fit their learning styles and intelligences and plan the use of technology accordingly (Chakraborty, 2010; Chisolm & Beckett, 2003).

Although there is not enough space to address them in depth, there are also cultural learning advantages to using blogs, wikis, Facebook, and Twitter. Reading native speaker blogs or wikis, for example, can provide a window into the target culture (Ducate & Lomicka, 2005, 2008) because they are easily accessible authentic materials, materials written by a native speaker for a native speaker. Engaging in what Thorne and Reinhardt (2008) term "bridging activities," advanced students can choose their own news blogs or wikis or personal L2 blogs and analyze various linguistic or cultural aspects. Allowing students to choose their own material helps them to see the relevance of reading these materials outside of the classroom and provides them with more ownership over the task, possibly leading to higher motivation and autonomy (Thorne & Reinhardt, 2008). Wikis can also be developed to serve as a reference about the target or home culture, language, or history (Arnold et al., 2009) and thereby possibly even advance their intercultural competence (Elola & Oskoz, 2008, 2010). As the chapter continues, examples will be shown that relate back to each of the theories and pedagogical principles discussed above.

Putting It into Practice: Case Studies and Examples

Keeping in mind the previous discussions of hybrid learning, technological innovations, and SLA theories, as well as best pedagogical practices, this section examines how certain tools (those introduced earlier) have been used in blended contexts to enhance and expand the language learning experience. The examples provided come from different language classes, at both undergraduate and graduate levels, and encompass a range of delivery formats. In all cases, though, the technology is used to its greatest advantage to offer the most in terms of linguistic and learning outcomes based on the theoretical considerations previously addressed. Although there is not enough space to discuss each tool and example in great detail, the purpose of this review is to begin to provide ideas for implementing these tools into hybrid learning and for further exploration.

Blogs

Within a hybrid-learning context, blogs can create a supportive environment; encourage reflection and sharing among students; provide greater access to the L2, including authentic materials; and facilitate linking to references and outside sources. The most productive way to use blogs in L2 learning is to take advantage of the opportunities they provide for reflection and community building. For example, students can post responses to readings, cultural questions, or class discussions, or current and future FL teachers can use blogs to reflect on their teaching experiences and get encouragement and advice from classmates. In relation to the SLA theories already mentioned, it will be evident in the descriptions here that using blogs in the classroom can provide students with a CoP in which to scaffold and learn about the target culture and language together; they can provide a variety of input from classmates or native speakers and encourage output from their authors. Because students work on blogs outside of class with differing amounts of guidance from the instructor, they promote autonomy and motivation, and because of their multimodality (images, sound, text), they appeal to different learning styles and intelligences. These advantages will be evident through the examples discussed below.

Weekly Blog Postings

In a blog study conducted by Ducate and Lomicka (2008), intermediate language students completed a weekly blog journal in which they responded to questions provided by the teacher based on in-class readings and discussions with a few open topics. Their classmates were then required to comment on two blog postings per week. At the end of the semester, the instructors found that writing a weekly blog encouraged a sense of community that may not have been possible without the blogs. The students learned many personal details about each other that most likely would not have come up during class discussions, and shier students were much more likely to write about themselves. The students appreciated the forum because it gave them the opportunity to practice their writing and learn more about each other.

Blogging as a Tool for Teacher Reflection

Another blog project takes place in a service-learning course in which intermediate and advanced German students teach German every week during an after-school program at an elementary school (Ducate, 2009). Students use the blogs to reflect on their teaching experiences and provide their classmates with encouragement and suggestions. Because students are writing in German, this is a chance for them to internalize pedagogical terms and issues in the L2. The blogs also add to the feeling of community within the classroom and give them an opportunity to express triumphs and frustrations. Blogs as a forum for reflecting on teaching have also been used for beginning graduate teaching assistants and K to 12 teacher candidates with similar benefits but without the added benefit of L2 practice for students whose native language was English (Arnold & Ducate, 2010). For both blog projects, students were graded on a combination of factors, including accuracy, content, and relevance to the topic. Although blogs tend to be a more solitary endeavor with the option for others to read posts and comment and thereby lead to more reflective thoughts, wikis are tools that, through their very nature, encourage collaboration.

Wikis

Outside of education, wikis can be used for project management, event planning, policies and FAQs, collaboration, and brainstorming (WebWorkerDaily, 2007). Many of these uses are also applicable in L2 education, including collaborative writing in which students use a wiki to compose, revise, and edit (Arnold et al., 2009; Kessler, 2009; Larusson & Alterman, 2009; Lee, 2010), to process information (Matthew, Felvegi, & Callaway, 2009), to engage in writing as a process (Gibbons, 2010), and to enhance group interaction (Bradley, Lindstrom, & Rystedt, 2010). In hybrid learning, wikis can promote collaboration, encourage revisions based on community or teacher feedback, provide an audience for final products, supply a log of what everyone contributed to make it easier to monitor contributions, and plan a project using the attached discussion board. In terms of SLA theory, wikis have many of the same advantages as blogs in terms of autonomy, motivation, learning styles, and input and output but provide even greater possibilities for scaffolding and co-constructing meaning to build new understandings because they are collaborative in nature. From a CoP perspective, a class or group wiki project provides learners with a "joint enterprise" (shared topic), "mutual engagement" (common goal that binds the community), and "shared repertoire" (resources) (Wenger, 1998, pp. 72-73), which hopefully allows them to profit from the benefits of a CoP, such as group problem solving and combining assets and experiences. As mentioned earlier, though, when building CoPs in fixed classes where students have not necessarily chosen to be a part of the CoP, one must also acknowledge the important role the instructor plays in encouraging scaffolding throughout the task (Haneda, 1997; Wiltse, 2006).

Foreign Language Teaching Wiki

In one example project, graduate students in four different methods classes collaborated to produce a wiki on an FL teaching topic such as feedback, culture, technology, or target versus native language use (Arnold et al., 2009). Students from the different universities worked together on one topic or page to provide a resource on important topics of FL teaching at the end of the semester. Students also used the discussion board to comment, plan, and provide peer feedback and were easily able to post links and pictures and edit content and format. The instructors found at the end of the project that each of the groups produced well-designed and informative pages, but how they produced them varied greatly depending on the group dynamics.

Historical and Cultural Wiki

In another study that took place in intermediate German classes, students were required to produce a wiki based on historical topics from a novel set before the fall of the Berlin Wall as a pre-reading task (Arnold et al., 2009). After writing the wiki, the students began reading the book and were able to consult the wiki if they had questions about, for example, the secret police in the former German Democratic Republic or the history of the Berlin Wall. Non–group members commented on the other groups' pages throughout the project, and each group was asked to collaboratively revise content and grammar. Most students appreciated being able to work together on a final product, but data analysis revealed that not all students contributed equally to the project, which was also a complaint made by some students (Arnold et al., 2012). Whereas in a blog it is easy to assess whether a student posted or commented because it is more of an individual project, wikis have the added challenge of ensuring that the work that students do is truly collaborative, where it is necessary for all students to work together to complete the final product, rather than merely cooperative, where students can each individually complete a part of the whole (Arnold et al., 2012). Assessment took place several times throughout the project and considered format, content, accuracy, relevance of pictures, and references and considered both individual contributions and group dynamics. After having discussed both blogs and wikis, which foster reflection and collaboration, among other things, we now look to more community-building tools such as Facebook and Twitter.

Facebook

Facebook can serve as a course organizer and community-building tool and as a way to further content knowledge; it can also be useful in helping learners to analyze native speaker language. In this section, examples are provided that give readers a sense of how to effectively use Facebook in different contexts for language classes. Time constraints often limit the amount of interaction and socialization during class time; however, social networking tools offer increased opportunities for students to easily connect with their classmates, peers, and instructors in ways that can be more personal and motivating (Blattner & Lomicka, 2012). Because of the high level of social interaction that is inherent in these tools, CoPs (Wenger, 1998) and sociocultural theory both lend themselves well to social networking tools. Sociocultural theory suggests that learning takes place through interaction or mediation (Lantolf, 2000; Lantolf & Thorne, 2006; Vygotsky, 1978), and thus social networking tools allow for both of those to take place. Facebook also brings together communities of people that share, interact, communicate, and dialogue on given topics. Thus, with respect to the creation of CoPs, forming groups to learn about or research a similar topic allows students to work together to complete their task more successfully by working with each other. Because social networking tools are relatively new to the language learning classroom, research has only begun to offer a glimpse into how these tools can be used in language teaching and in SLA.

Blattner and Lomicka (2012) provide a detailed analysis for using the discussion forum in Facebook to build community and exchange perspectives. A second example (Blattner & Fiori, 2011) discusses student use and analysis of Facebook groups and how it leads to the development of sociopragmatic competence and multiliteracy skills.

Facebook as a Discussion Forum

In a study by Blattner and Lomicka (2012), Facebook was used in an intermediate university-level French class to organize common discussions, exchange perspectives, and foster community among students in the United States and in France. Students expressed their opinion (50 words or less) on a given topic approximately twice a month using the Facebook discussion forum feature. For example, during election time, students were asked to respond to questions about their thoughts on the upcoming elections, how they choose candidates to vote for, and the role that politics plays in their daily lives. All students shared their ideas and perspectives, and many contributed follow-up responses. Because students were writing for a native speaker audience and their peers, they were graded on completion and not on grammatical accuracy.

The data reveal positive attitudes toward the use of Facebook but at the same very time limited use of social networking in language learning. The atmosphere of Facebook was considered by students as "casual" and "pressure free," making it both an attractive and comfortable place to engage in communication and interaction outside of the classroom. Learners saw Facebook as a new platform where they could practice their developing target language skills to use and naturally engage in authentic and meaningful exchanges, which are essential in order to develop communicative competence. Their personal and academic use of Facebook varied greatly, however. In personal contexts, students tended to use a wide variety of functions, but for academic purposes, students were much more limited in their ideas on how Facebook could be used.

Facebook Groups to Develop Sociopragmatic and Multiliteracy Skills

In a different context (Blattner & Fiori, 2011), intermediate-level students studying Spanish in a university setting were required to find and share three different content-related Facebook groups with their classmates and then post links to relevant content areas that they were studying. They then analyzed sites for specific linguistic information (e.g., greetings, abbreviations, leave takings) and shared this with their classmates. The study examined language that was part of different Facebook groups and students were able to identify or recognize certain norms at the site, such as those associated with greeting and leave taking. Although CoP formation was not a goal of this study, it would seem interesting to explore this in more detail.

Blattner and Fiori (2011) concluded that students have the potential to increase their sociopragmatic awareness and multiliteracy skills in an FL through such tasks. The authors also emphasize the importance of becoming familiar with the conventions of discussion forums and of target country cultural aspects and that those are crucial to making engaging and meaningful connections with native speakers. A relatively new tool like Facebook, Twitter also serves as a tool to help to foster community building, interaction, and communication among learners.

Twitter

As has been shown, microblogging can be an ideal way to supplement class time by enhancing social presence and building a sense of community among users. As a learning tool, one of Twitter's strengths is allowing for quick and easy communication with others. However, given the 140-character limit in posts, Twitter may not allow for as much reflection or detail in responses. Research in CMC has pointed to several interesting trends: F2F interaction can be replicated (Sotillo, 2000), negotiation of meaning can be enhanced (Pellettieri, 2000), and opportunities to increase learner output can be produced (de la Fuente, 2003). Interactionist theory lends itself well to Twitter because students, by engaging in increased amounts of interaction, produce more output. Given that Twitter posts are by nature short, students may be less intimidated to produce output and more motivated to interact frequently. This interaction can lead students to examine their own hypotheses about their interlanguage (Gass & Mackey, 2006).

The two examples discussed in this section illustrate how these tools can be used to engage lower level language students in interaction and communication and to build a network for pre-service FL teachers during their student teaching experiences to connect with other language teachers to create a CoP and support.

Undergraduate Language Class

In a study by Lomicka and Lord (2012), microblogging was used in an undergraduate, intermediate-level French class to encourage students to engage in language practice with their peers outside of class. After establishing their accounts and learning the basics of Twitter, students in the class were required to interact with each other and with native speakers of French in an English class (tweeting from France) at least three times a week (all Tweets consisted of short posts of 140 characters or less). Of those three interactions, two posts were in French and one post was in English for the U.S. students and two posts were in English and one in French for the native French speakers. Both languages were used so that reading and writing could be practiced and observed for both native and non-native speakers. In their Tweets, students were able to share information about themselves, their daily lives, and what they were doing at the time. It should be noted that the instructor did not overtly correct grammar or spelling or otherwise grade the tweets, which were evaluated only for effort and completion. In a medium such as this one, it was determined that communication should be the primary focus.

This study offers several insights into the use of microblogging. Students involved in the project created a stronger connection with each other and with their instructor beyond the classroom (which supports prior research by Antenos-Conforti, 2009), but this relationship also enhanced connections among U.S. students, creating an overall stronger and more dynamic community of learners. The students and the instructor built relationships over the course of the term and were thus more comfortable sharing more information with each other and in turn using more target language. Another advantage was the opportunity for interaction with native speakers, thus allowing for more realistic and meaningful exchanges among the students. In sum, the tweets were able to make the language come alive for the learners involved in the project.

Graduate Methodology Seminar

Microblogging can also be used at other levels of instruction. For example, in one project, more than 80 new language instructors across the United States and Canada used Twitter to connect with each other and share their learning experiences in the language classroom. Many of the participants in this study were involved as part of their teaching methodology course, but a number of instructors became involved on their own and used the opportunity to connect with language instructors that they otherwise would not have known or had access to. Participants tweeted three times weekly—two original posts and one response—and focused on the triumphs and challenges they faced as they developed into language educators. The Twitter community was used as a way to connect to others, learn from their peers, and develop a CoP that existed beyond the confines of their own institutional settings.

Although the use of the target language was not an issue in this case, the use of the microblogging service enabled these new instructors to share, reflect, and engage with a large group of peers that were going through similar experiences. The short and somewhat informal nature of the Twitter interactions may have precluded the more in-depth reflections that a blog project would promote, but the ease of posting to Twitter made the project an attractive one for these new teachers. Participants connected to peers around the world with whom they would have had no way to communicate otherwise. They were able to take more control of their own professional development by engaging in continual reactions, and their motivation to share and reflect helped them in their classrooms as well. The participants created a true CoP in which they were able to reinforce class content and continue their development as language instructors.

Conclusion

In an era in which more work is being carried out beyond class time and outside the four walls of the classroom, instructors must find new and creative ways to connect with students and to encourage ongoing learning in alternative settings. The tools described here all contribute to this goal and, if used appropriately, can extend our classrooms in theoretically and pedagogically sound ways.

As illustrated in this chapter, blogs can help learners to reflect, build a community within and beyond a class, engage in autonomous learning, access multiple learning styles and intelligences, and interact with authentic cultural materials. Wikis, in turn, are also useful for promoting autonomous learning and motivation as well as generating collaboration and scaffolding among learners, encouraging revision, and improving writing proficiency through increased output. Facebook and other social networking sites are ideal tools for creating learning communities and engaging students outside of class time to enhance the learning experience and to help students analyze sociolinguistic features (Blattner & Fiori, 2011).

Finally, Twitter (and microblogging) affords increased opportunities for interaction and thus output and allows students to connect with each other and with native speakers (Antenos-Conforti, 2009; Lomicka & Lord, 2012), to build relationships outside of class, and to reinforce content learned in class. Both Facebook and Twitter as relatively new tools to the language classroom merit additional research so that their full potential can be more carefully examined.

There are many advantages to using these tools, particularly in hybrid language learning contexts. Teachers are able to relinquish the "sage on the stage" control that is often prevalent in classrooms. Students learn in a self-directed way and can benefit from increased interaction with classmates and the instructor. Offering both flexibility and convenience, hybrid contexts afford more opportunities to all learners and open doors to learning anytime and anyplace, as well as tailor instruction based on student needs, considering different styles, skills, and abilities. Hybrid learning, one of the fastest growing sets of delivery modes, is indeed promoting a paradigm shift and with it an emphasis on technological tools that foster collaboration and community. This shift, coupled with a multitude of benefits and challenges, is fueling student engagement and effecting a potential transformation of learning.

References

Allen, H. W. (2010). Language-learning motivation during short-term study abroad: An activity theory perspective. *Foreign Language Annals, 43*(1), 27–49.

Allen, I., & Seaman, J. (2003). *Sizing the opportunity: The quality and extent of online education in the United States, 2002–2003.* Needham, MA: Sloan.

Antenos-Conforti, E. (2009). Microblogging on Twitter: Social networking in intermediate Italian classes. In L. Lomicka and G. Lord (Eds.), *The next generation: Social networking and online collaboration in foreign language learning* (pp. 59–90). San Marcos, TX: CALICO.

Arnold, N., & Ducate, L. (2006). Future foreign language teachers' social and cognitive collaboration in an online environment. *Language Learning & Technology, 10*(1), 42–66.

Arnold, N., & Ducate, L. (2010, November). *Using technology to promote enriched reflection in teacher education.* Paper presented at The American Council on the Teaching of Foreign Languages Annual Convention, Boston.

Arnold, N., Ducate, L., & Kost, C. (2009). Collaborative writing in wikis: Insights from culture projects in German classes. In Lomicka, L. and Lord, G. (Eds.), *The next generation: Social networking and online collaboration in foreign language learning* (pp. 115–144). San Marcos, TX: CALICO.

Arnold, N., Ducate, L. & Kost, C. (forthcoming, 2012). Collaboration or cooperation? Analyzing group dynamics and revision processes in wikis. *CALICO Journal, 29*(3).

Arnold, N., Ducate, L., & Lomicka, L. (2007). Virtual communities of practice in teacher education. In M. Kassen, R. Lavine, K. Murphy-Judy, & M. Peters (Eds.), *Preparing and developing technology-proficient L2 teachers* (pp. 103–132). San Marcos, TX: CALICO.

Arnold, N., Ducate, L., Lomicka, L., & Lord, G. (2009). Assessing online collaboration among language teachers: A cross-institutional case study. *Journal of Interactive Online Learning, 8*(2), 121–139.

Arslan, R., & Sahin-Kizil, A. (2010). How can the use of blog software facilitate the writing process of English language learners? *Computer Assisted Language Learning, 23*(3), 183–197.

Baburhan, U. (2010). An investigation of alignment in CMC from a sociocognitive perspective. *CALICO Journal, 28*(1), 135–155.

Basharina, O. (2007). An activity theory perspective on student-reported contradictions in international telecollaboration. *Language Learning & Technology, 11*(2), 82–103.

Beauvois, M. H. (1998). Conversations in slow motion: Computer-mediated communication in the foreign language classroom. *Canadian Modern Language Review, 54*(2), 198–217.

Belz, J. (2003). Linguistic perspectives on the development of intercultural competence in telecollaboration. *Language Learning and Technology, 7*(2), 68–99.

Belz, J. A., & Müller-Hartmann, A. (2003). Teachers as intercultural learners: Negotiating German-American telecollaboration along the institutional fault line. *The Modern Language Journal, 87*(1), 71–89.

Benson, P. (2001). *Teaching and researching autonomy in language learning.* Harlow, England: Longman/Pearson Education.

Blattner, G., & Fiori, M. (2011). Virtual social network communities: An investigation of language learners' development of sociopragmatic awareness and multiliteracy skills. *CALICO Journal, 29*(1), 24–43.

Blattner, G., & Lomicka, L. (2012). "Facebook: The Social Generation of Language Learners." Special issue of the *Alsic* (Apprentissage des Langues et Systèmes d'information et de communication) *journal* "social media and language learning: (r)evolution ?" 15 (1). Blin, B. & Appel, C. (2011). Computer supported collaborative writing in practice: An activity theoretical study. *CALICO Journal, 28*(2), 473–497.

Borau, K., Ullrich, C., Feng, J., & Shen, R. (2009). Microblogging for language learning: Using Twitter to train communicative and cultural competence. *Advances in Web Based Learning, 5686*, 78–87.

Bower, J. & Kawaguchi, S. (2011). Negotiation of meaning and corrective feedback in Japanese/English eTandem. *Language Learning and Technology, 15*(1), 47–71.

Bradley, L., Lindstrom, B., Rystedt, H. (2010). Rationalities of collaboration for language learning in a wiki. *ReCALL, 22*(2), 247–265.

Buzzetto-More, N.A., & Sweat-Guy, R. (2006). Hybrid learning defined. *Journal of Information Technology Education 5*, 153–156.

Carroll, K. (2007). *Linear and non-linear learning.* Retrieved February 10, 2012, from http://ken-carroll.com/2007/12/13/linear-and-non-linear-learning/.

Chakraborty, P. (2010). Multiple intelligences, blended learning and the English teacher. *Language in India, 10*(10), 546–555.

Chang, L. (2007). The influences of group processes on learners' autonomous beliefs and behaviors. *System, 35*(3), 322–337.

Chapelle, C. A. (2009). The relationship between second language acquisition theory and computer-assisted language learning. *The Modern Language Journal 93*, 741–753.

Chisolm, I. M., & Beckett, C. (2003). Teacher preparation for equitable access through the integration of TESOL standards, multiple intelligences and technology. *Technology, Pedagogy and Information, 12*(2), 249–275.

Chun, D. (2008). Computer-mediated discourse in instructed environments. In Magnan, S. (Ed.), *Mediating discourse online* (pp. 15–45). Amsterdam: John Benjamins.

Comas-Quinn, A., Mardomingo, R., & Valentine, C. (2009). Mobile blogs in language learning: making the most of informal and situated learning opportunities. *ReCALL, 21*(1), 96–112.

de la Fuente, M. J. (2003). Is SLA interactionist theory relevant to CALL? A study on the effects of computer-mediated interaction in L2 vocabulary acquisition. *Computer Assisted Language Learning 16*(1), 47–81.

Dickinson, L. (1987). *Self-instruction in language learning.* Cambridge: Cambridge University Press.

Dickinson, L. (1995). Autonomy and motivation: A literature review. *System, 23*(2), 165–174.

Donato, R. (1994). Collective scaffolding. In J. Lantolf & G. Appel (Eds.), *Vygotskian approaches to second language research* (pp. 33–56). Norwood, NJ: Ablex Publishers.

Dörnyei, Z. (1994). Understanding L2 motivation: On with the challenge! *The Modern Language Journal, 78*, 515–523.

Dörnyei, Z. (2001). *Teaching and researching motivation.* London: Longman.

Ducate, L. (2009). Service learning in Germany: A four-week summer teaching program in Saxony-Anhalt. *Die Unterrichtspraxis, 42*(1), 32–40.

Ducate, L., & Lomicka, L. (2005). Exploring the blogosphere: Use of web logs in the foreign language classroom. *Foreign Language Annals, 38*(3), 410–421.

Ducate, L., & Lomicka, L. (2008). Adventures in the blogosphere: From blog readers to blog writers. *Computer Assisted Language Learning, 21*(1), 9–28.

Ducate, L., Lomicka, L., & Moreno, N. (2011). Wading through the world of wikis: An analysis of three wiki projects. *Foreign Language Annals, 44*(3),495–524.

Dunlap, J. C., & Lowenthal, P. R. (2009). Tweeting the night away: Using Twitter to enhance social presence. *Journal of Information Systems Education 202*, 129–135.

Dziuban, C., & Moskal, P. (2001). Evaluating distributed learning at metropolitan universities. *Educause Quarterly, 24*(4), 60–61.

Elola, I., & Oskoz, A. (2008). Blogging: Fostering intercultural competence development in foreign language and study abroad contexts. *Foreign Language Annals, 41*(3), 454–477.

Elola, I., & Oskoz, A. (2010). Collaborative writing: Fostering foreign language and writing conventions development. *Language Learning & Technology, 14*(3), 30–49.

Engeström, Y. (1999). Activity theory and individual and social transformation. In Engeström, Y. Miettinen, R., & Punamäki, R. (Eds.), *Perspectives on activity theory* (pp. 19–38). Cambridge: Cambridge University Press.

Fischer, R. (2007). How do we know what students are actually doing? Monitoring students' behavior in CALL. *Computer Assisted Language Learning, 20*(5), 409–442.

Furstenberg, G., Levet, S., English, K., & Maillet, K. (2001). Giving the virtual voice to the silent language of culture: The CULTURA project. *Language Learning and Technology, 5*(1), 55–102.

Gánem Gutiérrez, G. (2003). Beyond interaction: The study of collaborative activity in computer-mediated tasks. *ReCALL, 15*(1), 230–251.

Gardner, R. C. (1991). Attitudes and motivation in second language learning. In A. J. Reynolds (Ed.), *Bilingualism, multiculturalism, and second language learning: The McGill Conference in Honour of Wallace E. Lambert* (pp. 43–63). Mahwah, NJ: Lawrence Erlbaum Associates.

Gardner, R. C. (2000). Correlation, causation, motivation and second language acquisition. *Canadian Psychology, 41*, 1–24.

Gass, S., & Mackey, A. (2006). Input, interaction and output: An overview. *AILA Review, 19*, 3–17.

Gibbons, S. (2010). Collaborating like never before: Reading and writing through a wiki. *English Journal, 99*(5), 35–39.

Goertler, S. (2011). Blended and open/online learning: Adapting to a changing world of language teaching. In Arnold, A. & Ducate, L. (Eds.), *Present and future promises of CALL: From theory and research to new directions in language teaching* (pp. 470–501). San Marcos, TX: CALICO.

Goertler, S., & Winke, P. (Eds.). (2008). *Opening doors through distance education: Principles, perspectives, and practices.* CALICO Monograph Series Volume 7. San Marcos, TX: CALICO.

Good, T. L., & Brophy, J. E. (1987). *Looking in classrooms* (4th ed.). New York: Harper & Row.

Graham, C. R. (2005). Blended learning systems: Definition, current trends, and future directions. In C. J. Bonk & C. R. Graham (Eds.), *Handbook of blended learning: Global perspectives, local designs* (pp. 3–21). San Francisco: Pfeiffer.

Granberg, C. (2010). Social software for reflective dialogue: Questions about reflection and dialogue in student teachers' blogs? *Technology, Pedagogy and Education, 19*(3), 345–361.

Grgurović, M. (2007). *Research synthesis: CALL comparison studies by language skills/knowledge.* Retrieved July 23, 2011, from http://tesl.engl.iastate.edu:591/comparison/main.htm.

Haneda, M. (1997). Second language learning in a "community of practice": A case study of adult Japanese learners. *The Canadian Modern Language Review/La Revue Canadienne des Langues Vivantes, 54*(1), 11–27.

He, A. (2009). Bridging the gap between teacher educator and teacher in a community of practice: A case of brokering. *System, 37*(1), 153–163.

Heinze, A., & Procter, C. (2004). *Reflections on the use of blended learning. Education in a changing environment.* University of Salford, Salford, UK, Education Development Unit. Retrieved July 23, 2011, from http://www.ece.salford.ac.uk/proceedings/papers/ah_04.rtf

James, W. B., & Gardner, D. L. (1995). Learning styles: Implications for distance learning. *New Directions for Adult and Continuing Education, 67*, 19–32.

Kern, R. (2006). Perspectives on technology in learning and teaching languages. *TESOL Quarterly, 40*(1), 183–210.

Kessler, G. (2009). Student-initiated attention to form in wiki-based collaborative writing. *Language Learning & Technology, 13*(1), 79–95.

Kiely, R. (2009). Observing, noticing, and understanding: Two case studies in language awareness in the development of academic literacy. *Language Awareness, 18*(3-4), 329–344.

Krashen, S. (1985). *The input hypothesis: Issues and implications.* London: Longman.

Lantolf, J. (2000). Introducing sociocultural theory. In J. Lantolf (Ed.), *Sociocultural theory and second language learning* (pp. 1–26). Oxford: Oxford University Press.

Lantolf, J., & Appel, G. (1994) Theoretical framework: An introduction to Vygotskian perspectives on second language research. In J. Lantolf & G. Appel (Eds.), *Vygotskian approaches to second language research,* (1–32) Norwood, CT: Ablex Publishing Corporation.

Lantolf, J., & Thorne, S. L. (2006). *Sociocultural theory and the genesis of second language development.* Oxford: Oxford University Press.

Larusson, J. A., & Alterman, R. (2009). Wikis to support the "collaborative" part of collaborative learning. *The International Journal of Computer Supported Collaborative Learning (ijCSCL) 4*(4), 371–402.

Lee, L. (2010). Exploring wiki-mediated collaborative writing: A case study in an elementary Spanish course. *CALICO Journal, 27*(2), 260–276.

Lei, X. (2008). Exploring a sociocultural approach to writing strategy research: Mediated actions in writing activities. *Journal of Second Language Writing 17,* 217–236.

Little, D. (2000). Learner autonomy: why foreign languages should occupy a central role in the curriculum. In S. Green (Ed.), *New perspectives on teaching and learning modern languages* (pp. 24–45). Clevedon, UK: Multilingual Matters.

Lomicka, L. (2009). An intercultural approach to teaching and learning French. *The French Review 82*(6), 1227–1243.

Lomicka, L. & Lord, G. (2012) "A tale of tweets: Analyzing microblogging among language learners." *System,* 40(1): 48–63.

Long, M. H. (1996). The role of the linguistic environment in second language acquisition. In W. R. Ritchie & T. J. Bathie (Eds.), *Handbook of second language acquisition* (pp. 412–68). San Diego: Academic Press.

Lord, G. (2008). Podcasting communities and second language pronunciation. *Foreign Language Annals, 41*(2), 364–379.

Lord, G., & Lomicka, L. (2008). Blended learning in teacher education: An investigation of classroom community across media. *Contemporary Issues in Technology and Teacher Education, 8*(2). Retrieved February 10, 2012, from http://www.citejournal.org/vol8/iss2/general/article1.cfm.

Lorenzetti, J. (2005). Lessons learned about student issues in online learning. *Distance Education Report, 9*(6), 1–4.

Matthew, K., Felvegi, E., & Callaway, R. (2009). Wiki as a collaborative learning tool in a language arts methods class. *Journal of Research on Technology in Education, 42*(1), 51–72.

Mazer, J. P., Murphy, R. E., & Simonds, C. J. (2007). I'll see you on "Facebook": The effect of computer-mediated teacher self-disclosure on student motivation, affective learning and classroom climate. *Communication Education, 56*(1), 1–17.

McBride, K. (2009). Social-networking sites in foreign language classes: Opportunities for re-creation. In L. Lomicka & G. Lord (Eds.), *The next generation: Social networking and online collaboration in foreign language learning* (pp. 35–58). San Marcos, TX: CALICO.

McBride, K., & Fägersten, K. B. (2008). Student's role in distance learning. In S. Goertler & P. Winke (Eds.), *Opening doors through distance language education: Principles, perspectives, and practices* (pp. 43–66). San Marcos, TX: CALICO.

Messner, K. (2009). Making a case for Twitter in the classroom. *School Library Journal.* Retrieved July 23, 2011, from http://www.schoollibraryjournal.com/article/CA6708199.html.

Miceli, T., Murray, S. V., & Kennedy, C. (2010). Using an L2 blog to enhance learners' participation and sense of community. *Computer Assisted Language Learning, 23*(4), 321–341.

Murray, D. (2005). Technologies for second language literacy. *Annual Review of Applied Linguistics, 25,* 188–201.

Murray, G. (1999). Autonomy and language learning in a simulated environment. *System, 27*(3), 295–308.

National Education Association. (2009). Can Tweeting help your teaching? *NEA Today Magazine.* Retrieved July 23, 2011, from http://www.nea.org/home/32641.htm.

Nicolson, M., Murphy, L., & Southgate, M. (Eds.). (2011). *Language teaching in blended contexts.* Edinburgh: DunedIn Academic Press.

Osguthorpe, R. T., & Graham, C. R. (2003). Blended learning environments: Definitions and directions. *The Quarterly Review of Distance Education, 4*(3), 227–233.

Parry, D. (2008). Teaching with Twitter. *The Chronicle of Higher Education.* Retrieved July 23, 2011, from http://casesblog.blogspot.com/2008/09/video-teaching-with-Twitter.html.

Payne, S., & Whitney, P.J. (2002). Developing L2 oral proficiency through synchronous CMC: Output, working memory, and interlanguage development. *CALICO Journal, 20*(1), 7–32.

Pellettieri, J.L. (2000). Negotiation in cyberspace: The role of chatting in the development of grammatical competence. In M. Warschauer & R. Kern (Eds.), *Network-based language teaching: Concepts and practice* (pp. 9–34). Clevedon, UK: Multilingual Matters.

Reynard, R (2007). Hybrid learning: Challenges for teachers. *T.H.E. Journal.* Retrieved February 9, 2012, from http://thejournal.com/Articles/2007/05/17/Hybrid-Learning-Challenges-for-Teachers.aspx?Page=2.

Richards, J. (2010). Competence and performance in language teaching. *RELC Journal, 41,* 101–122.

Rivera, J., McAlister, K., & Rice, M. (2002). A comparison of student outcomes and satisfaction between traditional and web-based course offerings. *Online Journal of Distance Learning Administration, 5*(3), 151–179.

Rovai, A. P., & Jordan, H. (2004). Blended learning and sense of community: A comparative analysis with traditional and fully online graduate courses. *The International Review of Research in Open and Distance Learning, 5*(2). Retrieved July 24, 2011, from http://www.irrodl.org/index.php/irrodl/article/viewArticle/192

Ruschoff, B. (1998). Neue Medien als Grundlage neuer Lernwelten für das fremdsprachliche Lernen. *Franzosisch heute, 1,* 21–33.

Sadler, R. (2007). Computer-mediated communication and a cautionary tale of two cities. *CALICO Journal, 25*(1), 12–30.

Sauro, S. (2009). Strategic use of modality during synchronous CMC. *CALICO Journal, 27*(1), 101–117.

Scarcella, R., & Oxford, R. L. (1992). *The tapestry of language learning.* Boston: Heinle and Heinle.

Scida, E., & Saury, R. (2006). Hybrid courses and their impact on classroom performance: A case study at the University of Virginia. *CALICO Journal, 23*(3), 517–531.

Sotillo, S. M. (2000). Discourse functions and syntactic complexity in synchronous and asynchronous communication. *Language Learning & Technology, 4*(1), 82–119. Retrieved February 14, 2012, from http://llt.msu.edu/vol4num1/sotillo/default.html.

Spodark, E. (2005). Technoconstructivism for the undergraduate foreign language classroom. *Foreign Language Annals, 38*(3), 428–435.

Spodark, E. (2008). Technoconstructivism and the millennial generation: Creative writing in the foreign language classroom. In C. M. Cherry, & C. Wilkerson (Eds.), *Languages for the nation: Dimension 2008* (pp. 27–38). Valdosta, GA: Southern Conference on Language Teaching.

Stracke, E. (2007). A road to understanding: A qualitative study into why learners drop out of a blended language learning (BLL) environment. *ReCALL, 19*(1), 57–78.

Sykes, J., Oskoz, A., & Thorne, S. (2008). Web 2.0, synthetic immersion environments, and mobile resources for language education. *CALICO Journal, 25*(3), 528–546.

Thang, S. M. & Bidmeshki, L. (2010). Investigating the perceptions of UKM undergraduates towards an English for science and technology online course. *Computer Assisted Language Learning, 23*(1), 1–20.

Thorne, S., & Reinhardt, J. (2008). Bridging activities, new media literacies and advanced foreign language proficiency. *CALICO Journal, 25*(3), 558–572.

Van Deusen-Scholl, N. (2008). Online discourse strategies: A longitudinal study of computer-mediated foreign language learning. In S. Magnan (Ed.), *Mediating discourse online* (pp. 191–217). Amsterdam: John Benjamins.

VanPatten, B. (2003). *From input to output: A teacher's guide to second language acquisition.* New York: McGraw-Hill.

Villamil, O. S. & De Guerrero, M. C. M. (1996). Peer revision in the L2 classroom: Social-cognitive activities, mediating strategies, and aspects of social behavior. *Journal of Second Language Writing, 5(1),* 51–75.

Vygotsky, L. S. (1978). *Mind and society: The development of higher psychological processes.* Cambridge, MA: Harvard University Press.

Walker, L. (2009). Nine reasons to Twitter in schools. *Tech & Learning.* Retrieved July 23, 2011, from http://www.techlearning.com/article/17340.

WebWorkerDaily. (2007). 15 productive uses for a wiki. Retrieved July 23, 2011, from http://gigaom.com/collaboration/15-productive-uses-for-a-wiki/.

Wenger, E. (1998). *Communities of practice: Learning, meaning, and identity.* Cambridge: Cambridge University Press.

Wiltse, L. (2006). "Like pulling teeth": Oral discourse practices in a culturally diverse language arts classroom. *The Canadian Modern Language Review/La Revue Canadienne des Langues Vivantes, 63*(2), 199–223.

Wu, D., & Hiltz, R. (2004). Predicting learning from asynchronous online discussions. *Journal of Asynchronous Learning Networks, 8*(2), 139–152.

Young, J. (2002). "Hybrid" teaching seeks to end the divide between traditional and online instruction. *Chronicle of Higher Education, 48*(28), A33.

Zuckerberg, M. (2009). The Facebook blog. Retrieved July 23, 2011, from http://blog.facebook.com/blog.php?post=72353897130.

Appendix 5-1. Additional Tools

Blogs

Blogger (www.blogger.com)
Edublogs (www.edublogs.org)
LiveJournal (www.livejournal.com)
Wordpress (www.wordpress.com)

Wikis

PBwiki (www.pbwiki.com)
Wikispaces (www.wikispaces.com)
Wikidot (www.wikidot.com)
Wetpaint Central (www.wetpaint.com)

Social Networking

Facebook (www.facebook.com)
Grou.ps (www.grou.ps)
Grouply (www.grouply.com)
Linked In (www.linkedin.com)
Ning (www.ning.com)
Spruz (www.spruz.org)
Webs (www.webs.com)

Microblogging

Beeing (http://www.beeing.com)
EdModo (www.edmodo.com)
Emote.in (http://www.emote.in)
identi.ca (http://identi.ca)
Jaiku (http://www.jaiku.com)
Plurk (http://www.plurk.com)
Tumblr (http://www.tumblr.com)

Chapter 6

Blended Learning in Large Multisection Foreign Language Programs: An Opportunity for Reflecting on Course Content, Pedagogy, Learning Outcomes, and Assessment Issues

Dolly Jesusita Young and Jason Lee Pettigrew

From the new millennium to the present, colleges and universities have experienced increased pressure to integrate technology into higher education for the purpose of reducing instructional costs (Twigg, 1999; see also Neumeier, 2005; Sagarra & Zapata, 2008; Young, 2008). In addition to pressure from academic administrators, universities experience pressure from government-funded agencies (Bober, 2002) and the technology industry (e.g., Blackboard Inc.) to compete with the potential of a profit-seeking private sector that believes higher education needs a makeover (Pittinsky, 2003) or pressure from within the field spurred by new demands on the foreign language (FL) profession (Garrett, 2009). Technology and instructional costs are forcing consideration of educational issues that are long overdue and that have not been widely addressed or overtly discussed for entirely too long, namely curriculum, pedagogy, and learning outcomes. The primary purpose of this chapter is to explore these issues more systematically. Their consideration is essential before we can realistically evaluate the effectiveness of blended learning (BL) programs. More specifically, we consider the discourse present in disseminating information about large multisection elementary and intermediate FL programs, which are typically targeted for redesign for BL instruction because of their significant potential for cost saving. Lastly, in an effort to illustrate the type of curricular and pedagogical considerations that are associated with these programs, we describe in greater detail, from the point of conception to implementation, one multisection FL program redesigned for BL instruction.

The definition and characteristics of BL have evolved over the years and range from being broadly based, such as defining it as any online and face-to-face (F2F) learning, to one that takes into account the percentage of the curriculum online compared with F2F. Others, such as Dziuban, Hartman, and Moskal (2004), argue that BL "should be viewed as a pedagogical approach that combines the effectiveness and socialization opportunities of the classroom with the technologically enhanced active learning possibilities of the online environment" (p. 3). Watson (2008) specifies that BL requires a thoughtful integration of F2F and online learning that implies a restructuring and replacement of traditional class contact hours by rethinking the course design to maximize active and interactive student engagement both online and F2F. He advocates increasing interaction between students, between students and the instructor, and between students and outside resources in BL instruction. This type of interaction is even more significant in FL instruction (Antón & Ewald, 2008; Brandl, 2007).

If we are to consider issues related to curriculum and pedagogy, we need to explain how we use them in the present chapter. The topic of a program's "curriculum" can take a macro-level approach and others a micro-level approach. At the national level, a curriculum might provide a set of overriding goals that guide the profession as a whole, such as in the curricular changes suggested in the 2007 Modern Language Association (MLA) report or the FL national standards, which were partly sponsored by the U.S. Department of Education. At the state level, it may set a curriculum for state certification of FL teachers, for example. At the local level, the school district may adopt a specific curriculum for grades K to 12. At the university level, it may establish a sequence of courses designed to achieve competencies in particular subject areas, such as for an FL major or minor. The reality in most large state universities and large community colleges is that the first two years of an FL are often treated as separate from the curriculum for the FL major or minor and occur without consideration of how these courses play into the FL curriculum (see MLA, 2007). As a result, the word "curriculum" in this chapter is used to refer to the courses, or a sequence of courses, that consist of a first-year FL program, a second-year FL program, or both (Barr-Harrison & Daugherty, 2000; Dorwick & Glass, 2003; Willis Allen, 2008). At this program level, the curriculum may provide the framework of its courses, such as setting the course's goals, specifying content and learner outcomes, and addressing issues of assessment. In addition, courses being redesigned for BL instruction may want to take into account the technological availability and reliability, as well as the technological support, required in these redesigns, particularly because of the large number of students that will rely on technology in this form of instruction.

In essence, a curriculum expresses desirable qualities at some level and then determines which experiences generate these qualities. *Pedagogy* can refer to the processes, strategies, focus, style, methods, approach, and philosophical or theoretical framework used in instruction. Pedagogies and curricular goals are tightly intertwined in that pedagogies can frame the "experiences" component of a curriculum (Barr-Harrison & Daugherty, 2000).

On the surface, the concept of BL may appear apparent, but the actual application is complex, particularly for large introductory and intermediate FL programs that offer multiple sections of their courses. In the following section, we provide some historical context to the movement toward BL for beginning and intermediate FL instruction at the university level to contextualize the discourse used in describing redesigned courses.

Evolution of Blended Learning Foreign Language Programs in Higher Education

Research on large-scale FL BL instruction was practically nonexistent until 1997 when Adair-Hauck, Willingham-McLain, and Youngs (2000) set out to evaluate the effectiveness of integrating technology into a second semester college-level French course at Carnegie Mellon University. Part of the rationale for the study was to address the paucity of research on replacing some F2F instruction with technology-enhanced language learning and to explore more cost-effective approaches to instruction. Two classes of second-semester French served as a control group ($n = 16$) and a treatment group ($n = 17$). The treatment group met three days per week and completed multimedia assignments, such as watching instructional videos and completing computerized grammar and vocabulary exercises created with the Dasher authoring system, outside of class. The control group met four days per week and one of those days consisted of completing the same multimedia assignments but on paper and in class or by group viewing of the instructional videos. Both groups were taught by the same instructor and used the same textbook and supplementary materials. Students in both groups took five achievement tests measuring listening, reading, and writing skills designed by the instructor and a quiz on knowledge about the Francophone culture. The findings of this research indicated "students in the treatment group performed equally well as the control group in listening and speaking and better on reading and writing achievement measures" (p. 269). Research subsequent to this initial study also suggests that there are no significant differences in language gains or that specific skills are positively and/or negatively affected by BL instruction[1] (e.g., Young, 2008).

At the end of the 20th century, the University of Illinois, funded by the Sloan Center for Asynchronous Learning Environment Efficiency Projects (1997), began a project to place the first FL workbook online using a homegrown course manager called Mallard (Arvan & Musumeci, 2000). An electronic version of what had been a hard copy of the workbook, also called activity manual (AM), that accompanied the Spanish program's textbook was to become the stepping-stone toward the creation of a hybrid course for its first-year Spanish program, subsequently resulting in significant cost savings for the University of Illinois. In addition to the online workbook, students completed writing assignments using online journals via FirstClass, a management system with a conferencing feature, and additional reading and listening activities. The first-year program, which originally met four days per week but in the hybrid format met only two days per week, allowed the graduate students to teach twice as many courses without increasing their workloads; an electronic workbook was a welcomed technological innovation at the time because it freed up instructors from grading the majority of the workbook exercises because they were automatically computer graded.

At the national level, the Center for Academic Transformation, what is today the National Center for Academic Transformation (NCAT), as early as 1998 began to engage higher education in some kind of virtual effort. One year later, the Pew Symposia in Learning and Technology was created to foment an ongoing national conversation about issues related to the intersection of learning and technology based on the redesign efforts of a few universities, including the University of Illinois. Subsequently, the Pew Charitable Trusts awarded the NCAT $6 million over three years (1999–2002) to explore ways to achieve cost-effective and quality learning environments in higher education via technology (Twigg, 1999, 2001, 2002).

---

[1]See Young (2008) for a review of research that examines the effects of language learning in elementary and intermediate FL programs in predesign and redesigned BL course formats.

The NCAT funded three rounds of course redesigns and later a variety of redesign initiatives, indicated below. We list only the redesigns related to FL learning.

Program in Course Redesign (PCR), Round 1, 1999–2001

No FL programs awarded

Program in Course Redesign (PCR), Round 2, 2000–2002

The University of Tennessee

Program in Course Redesign (PCR), Round 3, 2001–2003

Portland State University

Roadmap to Redesign (R2R), 2003–2006

The University of Alabama

Texas Tech University

Montclair State University

Colleagues Committed to Redesign (C²R), 2007–2008

The University of North Carolina, Chapel Hill

The University of North Carolina, Charlotte

SUNY Course Redesign Initiative (SCRI), 2007–2010

SUNY, Fredonia

Mississippi Course Redesign Initiative (MCRI), 2007–2010

The University of Southern Mississippi

The University of Tennessee was the first state university to receive one of the 30 to 35 $200,000 grants for the purpose of redesigning its first-year Spanish intensive review course, and a year later, Portland State University was the second. Both Spanish programs[2] were redesigned to achieve cost savings and maintain quality instruction and relied heavily on either Blackboard or WebCT for the online learning component. By the time the Portland State University redesigned course came online in 2003 (Sanders, 2005), publishing companies had begun providing commercialized electronic versions of their first-year Spanish workbook or AM. In these early redesigned courses, F2F time was replaced primarily with automated online assignments or homework that relied heavily on the electronic version of the workbook or AM. We suspect that without the subsequent advent of the electronic workbook, the BL format might not have evolved as quickly.

These events contributed significantly to a national trend gaining ground in FL instruction, the reduction of F2F time for online learning or homework in beginning- and intermediate-level FL programs in higher education. Table 6-1

---

[2]To underscore the significant challenges in time, effort, and funding to conducting empirically based research on BL programs, as well as the challenges inherent in developing sound research designs, we point out that the University of Tennessee and Portland State University are the only two NCAT networked redesigned FL programs with research findings published in refereed FL journals.

Table 6-1. National Center for Academic Transformation Initiatives in Blended Learning Foreign Language Programs

Predesign Format	Redesigned Format
University of Tennessee	
NCAT project abstract: http://www.thencat.org/PCR/R2/UTK/UTK_Home.htm. **Course(s) redesigned:** Intermediate Spanish Transition. **Redesign initiative:** PCR (1999–2003). **Students:** 1100. **Personnel:** Lecturers and GTAs only.	
Predesign Format	**Redesigned Format**
Met 3 days per week.	**F2F sessions:** Meets 2 days per week. **F2F pedagogy:** F2F time emphasizes interactive, collaborative oral and written communication. **Online assignments:** Online workbook was placed on Blackboard along with the input activities from *¿Sabías qué?* In addition, asynchronous interactive activities were designed to foster negotiation of meaning via emails.
Portland State University	
NCAT project abstract: http://www.thencat.org/PCR/R3/PoSU/PoSU_Home.htm. **Course(s) redesigned:** Introductory Spanish I and II. **Redesign initiative:** PCR (1999–2003). **Students:** 690. **Personnel:** One faculty member and TAs.	
Predesign Format	**Redesigned Format**
Met 3 days per week. In-class instruction mimicked older teaching practices focusing on language structure (grammar) rather than functional language acquisition, practice, and proficiency.	**F2F sessions:** Meets 2 days per week. **F2F pedagogy:** F2F time spent in the crucial area of interactive speaking. Reduced in-class time for students clearly performing above standards (with remediation in class for others). Increased class time spent in oral communication; increased small group communication and oral practice in assigned study groups; directed low-achieving students to small group sessions for additional oral practice to address the most common issue driving low achievement. **Online assignments:** The primary instructional material is a multimedia version of the comprehensive proficiency-oriented introductory Spanish program *¿Cómo?* produced at Portland State University. Moved testing, writing and grammar instruction, and partner and group activities outside the classroom using the multimedia materials (see above) composed of reading, writing, and listening materials. Used WebCT chat (synchronous) and discussion board (asynchronous) features.
Texas Tech University	
NCAT project abstract: http://www.thencat.org/R2R/Abstracts/TT_Home.htm. **Course(s) redesigned:** Comprehensive Spanish Review First Year. **Redesign initiative:** R2R (2003–2006). **Students:** 1595. **Personnel:** Graduate students.	

96

Predesign Format	Redesigned Format
Met 5 days per week. Comprehensive Spanish Review First Year is a five-credit course with two in class (30–32 students) and two nontraditional versions of the course composed of two large (110 students) lecture and discussion and one online and TV version (90 students).	**F2F sessions:** Meets three times a week with a reduced class size of 20. Graduate students teach two sections (40 students). The large lecture and TV versions of the course were eliminated. **F2F pedagogy:** F2F class time devoted to communicative exercises emphasizing oral skill development. Studio sessions taught by GTAs are held for students scoring less than 80% on the first exam. **Online assignments:** Workbook, grammar, and writing components moved online. Students spend 2 hours of online practice in grammar with automated immediate diagnostic feedback and write weekly compositions that are semiautomatically graded with diagnostic feedback. Students participate in one hour of language lab weekly.

University of Alabama

NCAT project abstract: http://www.thencat.org/R2R/Abstracts/UA_Home.htm. **Course(s) redesigned:** Introductory Spanish I and II and Intensive Review of Elementary Spanish. **Redesign initiative:** R2R (2003–2006). **Students:** 1,046 students in 45 sections. **Personnel:** Lecturers and GTAs.

Predesign Format	Redesigned Format
Each course met 5 hours per week.	**F2F sessions:** Redesign replaces 1 class hour per week for Introductory Spanish I and II and 2 hours per week for the Intensive Review of Elementary Spanish (two semesters in one). Free tutoring online and in Language Resource Center. **F2F pedagogy:** Shift to more innovative methodologies and communicative methodologies. Communicative and interactive activities in class reinforce online learning. Students take an oral test three times per semester. **Online assignments:** Students practice vocabulary and grammar via computer with automated feedback activities from online workbook. Videos corresponding to textbook assigned at home instead of viewing in class. Students complete self-tests online. Online portfolio assignments (cyber journals and web searches), related to students' individual interests, discussed and evaluated in class by peers and content recycled in oral interviews throughout semester.

Montclair State University

NCAT project abstract: http://www.thencat.org/R2R/Abstracts/MSU_Abstract.htm. **Course(s) redesigned:** Introductory Spanish. **Redesign initiative:** R2R (2003–2006). **Students:** 700. **Personnel:** Adjunct faculty, senior students, GTAs teach.

(continued)

Predesign Format	Redesigned Format
Met 2 days per week for two 75-minute periods or once a week for 150 minutes rather than 3 days per week. Most in-class time is used by faculty to explain grammar and vocabulary, limiting student opportunities to develop their communicative skills.	**F2F sessions:** Meets 2 days per week for 50 minutes. **F2F pedagogy:** F2F sessions are primarily devoted to communicative "real-life" tasks and to raising cultural awareness. Students practice and enhance their listening, speaking, and reading skills. **Online assignments:** F2F sessions supplemented with a 50-minute online session. In the online sessions, students study the grammatical and lexical information and concentrate on the more mechanical aspects of language through homework assignments, online workbook exercises, and other web-based materials (not specified). These assignments are necessary to perform in class activities.

NCAT project abstract: http://www.thencat.org/RedesignAlliance/C2R/R1/Abstracts/UNCCH_Abstract.htm. **Course(s) redesigned:** Elementary Spanish. **Redesign initiative:** C²R (2007–2008). **Students:** 380 students annually. **Personnel:** Taught mostly by GTAs.

University of North Carolina—Chapel Hill

Predesign Format	Redesigned Format
Met 4 days per week.	**F2F sessions:** Meets 2 days per week, one day with instructor and the other day with undergraduate student assistants in small discussion groups. **F2F pedagogy:** F2F instructor-led sessions emphasize communicative language learning. Small group conversation sessions led by undergraduate student assistants. **Online assignments:** Interactive, feedback-rich program via Vista Higher Learning's *En línea* online workbook or e-book.

NCAT project abstract: http://www.thencat.org/RedesignAlliance/C2R/R3/UNCC_Abstract.htm. **Course(s) redesigned:** Elementary Spanish I, four-credit course. **Redesign initiative:** C²R (2007–2008). **Students:** 800 students in 28 sections each fall term. **Personnel:** A mix of instructors (typically one full-time faculty member, nine adjuncts, and four GTAs) teaches the course each semester.

University of North Carolina—Charlotte

Predesign Format	Redesigned Format
Met twice a week for 75 minutes with an online workbook component. The online textbook system, *Centro*, provided diverse types of interactive learning activities as well as presentations of grammar and vocabulary. Instructors used some of the online materials in class sessions and gave online homework assignments, which was 10% of the grade.	**F2F sessions:** Meets once a week. All students have the same course materials and lesson plans. Class size increased from 30 to 60 students. Part-time faculty reduced from 19 to 5, and the number of GTAs increased from 7 to 15. **F2F pedagogy:** Classroom time focuses on facilitating proficiency-oriented communicative learning activities such as role-plays, dialogs, and writing assignments. Students are able to practice every skill area of language proficiency. Instructors provide counseling meetings with students who are not keeping up with assignments. **Online assignments:** Online workbook continued to be used. Assignments, exams, and class announcements are handled electronically. Instructors provide individual assistance to students through e-mail feedback.

SUNY Fredonia

NCAT project abstract: http://www.thencat.org/States/NY/Abstracts/Fredonia Spanish_Abstract.htm. **Course(s) redesigned:** Introductory Spanish I and II. **Redesign initiative:** SCRI (2007–2010). **Students:** 450. **Personnel:** No information provided.

Predesign Format	Redesigned Format
Met 3 days per week. Two three-credit courses of first-year Spanish.	**F2F sessions:** Condensed two three-credit courses into one intensive, five-credit Spanish course. One section of the traditional course continues to be offered for true beginners (i.e., students who have no previous language experience). Section size is reduced from 30 to 22 students, which allows for a greater level of student active participation. **F2F pedagogy:** The instructor can focus on meaningful communication activities such as conversation and oral practice during class. Students' progress is monitored to identify specific problems, which the instructor addresses either in class or with the individual student. **Online assignments:** Online workbook. Practice of grammar, vocabulary, listening, reading, and writing takes place online with assignments completed before each class. Students are able to repeat online exercises as often as necessary, receiving automatic feedback and references to material for further study. Language lab staff is available to provide assistance in grammar and vocabulary.

University of Southern Mississippi

NCAT project abstract: http://www.thencat.org/States/MS/Abstracts/USM Spanish_Abstract.htm. **Course(s) redesigned:** Introductory Spanish sequence (Spanish 101 and 102). **Redesign initiative:** MCRI (2007–2010). **Students:** Averages 1,620 students per year. **Personnel:** Instructors supported by GTAs and undergraduate assistants.

Predesign Format	Redesigned Format
Met three times per week. Twelve minimally coordinated sections of 30 students each semester.	**F2F sessions:** Meets two times per week with an increased number of students. Redesigned to six coherent sections of 60 students each semester. All sections are taught by a coordination team of two faculty instructors of record, supported by graduate and undergraduate assistants. **F2F pedagogy:** Biweekly class meetings emphasize oral communication. **Online assignments:** Direct student interactions with course concepts via online learning (online workbook and e-book) replace one traditional lecture per week.

C²R, Colleagues Committed to Redesign; F2F, face-to-face; GTA, graduate teaching assistant; MCRI, Mississippi Course Redesign Initiative; NCAT, National Center for Academic Transformation; PCR, Program in Course Redesign; R2R, Roadmap to Redesign; SCRI, SUNY Course Redesign Initiative; TA, teaching assistant.

summarizes the FL BL programs of the various universities that participated in the Pew Charitable Trust grant or the subsequent NCAT-driven redesign initiatives, which was an outgrowth of the Pew Learning and Technology Program but without the same level of funding. The data in Table 6-1 are based on reports submitted to the NCAT by each university, which NCAT then summarized and published in its online publication called *The Learning Marketspace* under the title *The Redesign Alliance*, "a member organization of institutions, organizations and companies committed to and experienced with large-scale course redesign" (see http://www.thencat.org/subscribe.htm). An analysis of the type of information about BL in these publications falls into specific categories and affords some insight into the discourse that has been used to talk about FL BL. By discourse, we refer to the language, as well as content, used to describe BL programs at this level.

Although the NCAT had its finger on the national pulse, research and implementation of FL BL programs were occurring across the nation. With the advent of the new millennium, an upsurge of FL BL programs surfaced, often supported by university grants or national foundations. The list of programs in Table 6-2 is not meant to be exhaustive but is intended to be representative of FL BL programs across the nation. The information about them in Table 6-2 was obtained from published journal articles, professional presentations, and personal contacts. As in Table 6-1, the data available in published research-based articles or presentations were limited, but even so, we can glean much about the discourse used to talk about BL in FL programs.

Absent from Tables 6-1 and 6-2 is information related to the FL curriculum, the pedagogy used to support it, the learner outcomes that drive it, and the assessment instruments used to measure program objectives because Table 6-1 data were based on the NCAT Initiative program reports from the *Redesign Alliance* publication (see earlier), and that type of information was not provided. Understandably, the discourse used in describing these programs orbits around characteristics of the program that are linked to cost savings and addresses the delivery and instructional components of the courses, such as the pre- and postdesign meeting times in number of days per week, course delivery (graduate teaching assistants, adjuncts, lecturers, faculty), what students do in-class and for homework online, and so on. The discourse used in describing FL BL programs for first- and second-year FL courses was rooted in the NCAT redesign initiatives, and information related to curricular or pedagogical issues was not the focus of the publications. These initiatives challenged large multisection programs to maintain course quality and show cost savings. To illustrate how they arrive at reduced instructional costs, the discourse focused on issues related to where the savings occur (e.g., reduced contact time, increased class sizes, personnel). Subsequently, universities used these initiatives as models and continued to frame the discourse related to BL in those terms. In addition, the data obtained from the majority of BL programs in Table 6-2 were collected later via personal contacts[3] and were based on the same

---

[3]We contacted schools that had redesigned programs for which we could not find information (University of Utah and Florida State University) and requested the same type of information. We, too, fell into giving the highest priority to the operations component of the programs.

Table 6-2. Blended Learning Foreign Language Programs

Predesign Format	Redesigned Format
	Carnegie Mellon University Language Online Project
	Course(s) redesigned: Elementary Spanish I and II; Intermediate Spanish I and II. **Implementation:** Chenoweth, Ushida, and Murray (2006). **Students:** Research sample—354 students across 34 sections. **Personnel:** 11 "teachers" (no additional specific information provided.)
Predesign Format	**Redesigned Format**
Met 4 days per week at introductory level (Spanish and French I) and 3 days per week at intermediate level (Spanish and French II).	**F2F sessions:** Meets 2 days per week for both introductory and intermediate level; 1 hour per week is F2F with instructor and the second F2F session meets with a FL major or native undergraduate for 20-minute chats. **F2F pedagogy:** No information provided in article. **Online assignments:** Completed online exercises, quizzes, chats, and discussion board postings managed via WebCT.
	University of Virginia
	Course(s) redesigned: Elementary Spanish I and II and Accelerated Elementary Spanish. **Implementation:** Emily Scida (2006). **Students:** Research sample varied based on semester. **Personnel:** Primarily GTAs.
Predesign Format	**Redesigned Format**
Met 5 days per week (Elementary Spanish). GTAs teach one section with 25 students.	**F2F sessions:** Meets 3 days per week, and GTAs teach two sections with 22 students. **F2F pedagogy:** F2F sessions emphasize communicative activities. **Online assignments:** Using Mallard course management system, students complete approximately 2 hours of web-based assignments and quizzes per week. Online activities focus on grammar and vocabulary practice in listening, reading, and writing to prepare students for F2F sessions. Other homework not online is assigned, such as written homework for in-class discussion, readings, and preparation of oral presentations and informal journal assignments.
	Penn State University
	Course(s) redesigned: Elementary Spanish I and II. **Implementation:** Nuria Sagarra (2008). **Students:** Program size—5000 students. **Personnel:** Primarily GTAs.

(continued)

Predesign Format	Redesigned Format
Met 5 days per week.	**F2F sessions:** Meets 4 days per week. **F2F pedagogy:** Classroom instruction emphasizes communicative activities, group discussion, instruction with multimedia (video and audio), and cultural readings. **Online assignments:** Online customized workbook using Angel, a course management system. Online workbook focuses on input and output grammar and vocabulary activities, listening tasks, and content-based reading tasks.

University of Florida

Course(s) redesigned: Beginning Spanish 1 and 2. **Personnel:** Primarily GTAs.

Predesign Format	Redesigned Format
Met 5 days per week.	**F2F sessions:** Meets 3 days per week. **F2F pedagogy:** F2F stress communication skills in Spanish. Students engage in a variety of activities and assignments, such as using vocabulary and grammar learned to communicate in oral and written modes, reading activities and exercises (e.g., pre-and postreading), intensive and extensive reading, sociolinguistic practice, and functions through communicative activities (pair and group work). Writing activities range from short paragraphs to developed compositions. Integration of skills in projects and tasks in small groups or as a class. **Online assignments:** Online homework exercises that are assigned appear in MySpanishLab, Pearson's electronic platform and system.

University of Utah

Students: 700-student first-year program. **Personnel:** Adjunct instructors and GTAs.

Predesign Format	Redesigned Format
Met 4 days per week.	**F2F sessions:** Meets 2 days per week F2F plus two virtual days. Not all sections were converted to the blended learning model; a number of traditional sections were maintained. **F2F pedagogy:** F2F meetings emphasize interactive oral communication. Instruction based on tasks that are completed partially during virtual days (individual components) and partially in class (group components). Redesign added an LA to the classroom. LAs help facilitate communication and provide feedback in the classroom. They also monitor much of the online work. **Online assignments:** Grammar may be introduced and reviewed in class, but most is dealt with during the virtual days. Online learning focuses on written communication (mostly in the form of blogs), interpretive communication, and individual (as opposed to pair or group) activities. In general, online learning emphasizes preparation work to be ready to communicate in class. Cengage's iLrn is the main platform for online learning.

Florida State University	
Course(s) redesigned: Elementary Spanish I and II and Intermediate Spanish I and II. **Implementation:** 2004. **Personnel:** Primarily GTAs.	
Predesign Format	**Redesigned Format**
Met 5 days per week for first through third semester Spanish. Meets 4 days per week for fourth semester Spanish.	**F2F sessions:** All four semesters meet 3 days per week. **F2F pedagogy:** F2F time emphasizes interactive, collaborative oral and written communication. **Online assignments:** Both the *Sol y viento* (used for Spanish 1 through 3) workbook and textbook are online and are accessed through McGraw-Hill's Centro online learning platform. Automated feedback and computer grading of most activities are provided. For Spanish 4, only the workbook for *Así lo veo* is used online, also through Centro.

University of X	
Course(s) redesigned: Intensive Elementary Spanish and Intermediate Spanish Transition. **Implementation:** 2011. **Students:** 700. **Personnel:** 50% lecturers and 50% GTAs.	
Predesign Format	**Redesigned Format**
Met 3 days per week.	**F2F sessions:** Meets 2 days per week. **F2F pedagogy:** F2F time emphasizes content and task-based learning where students use Spanish in pairs or small groups for a specific purpose. Emphasis is on building a Spanish learning community in class and cross-cultural perspectives. **Online assignments:** In addition to the online AM or workbook, which was already used, aural and written input from the textbook was moved to the e-book and linked to AM grade book for automated grading and feedback. In addition, students complete interactive tasks requiring them to obtain or exchange information with each other using voice recordings (podcasts) or wikis (charts with which students answer questions and read each others' answers). Using the podcast or wiki information, students blog about what they learn about individual students or about the whole class. Students also complete two ePortfolio tasks (collaboratively or individually) and post them in their Personal Learning Space, which houses artifacts about their language development throughout their undergraduate progress in Spanish at the university. The podcast, wiki, blog, and personal learning space tools are included in Learning Objects' Campus Pack tool suite. Assessments include student self-tests, a checklist of self-assessment items (using Linguafolio), online exams with in-class compositions, and oral interviews. Extra support material was developed, such as Prezis and PowerPoints made available to students.

AM, activities manual; F2F, face-to-face; GTA, graduate teaching assistant; LA, learning assistant.

type of information modeled in Table 6-1, which gives priority to the operations component of the programs. In short, we failed to request information related to curricular issues. This explains why references are absent in Tables 6-1 and 6-2 to redesigning courses on the basis of curricular issues, paradigm shifts (Swaffar & Arens, 2005), or for pedagogically based reasons. References to the curricula of the course or course objectives, learner outcomes, assessment, and pedagogy most likely exist; we simply did not ask for it. To demonstrate how at least one BL program addressed curricular and pedagogical issues, we describe one in detail later. We do not mean to insinuate here that the information that is available in Tables 6-1 and 6-2 is not important. In fact, before we turn to issues of curriculum, pedagogy, and learner outcomes, we will address what we can learn about BL based on the information that *is* provided in the tables.

Characteristics of Blended Learning Based on Tables 6-1 and 6-2

Tables 6-1 and 6-2 suggest that a variety of BL formats were adopted, but all reduced the number of F2F sessions either in days (i.e., five to three), or in number of contact hours over specific semesters (i.e., two semesters at three days per week replaced by one course at five days per week), or in time (i.e., 75-minute sessions to 50-minute sessions), or in class size (increased or reduced class sizes), and most targeted introductory Spanish I (first semester) and II (second semester) or Intensive Introductory Spanish courses (two semesters in one). In some cases, the F2F time is reduced by 50 percent and in others by 20 or 30 percent. In some cases, replacing F2F sessions with online learning led to cost savings by serving growing numbers of FL students with the same resources; increasing the number of students that could be taught without increasing personnel; or using cost-effective personnel, such as upper-level FL students.

Graduate students, followed by lecturers, taught a majority of the BL courses and then tenure-track faculty, but a few redesigned courses used upper-level undergraduate students (The University of Utah; The University of North Carolina, Chapel Hill; The University of Southern Mississippi; Carnegie Mellon Language Online Project). Next to upper-level undergraduates, graduate students are the most cost-saving form of instruction over lecturers, adjuncts, and faculty.

References to the pedagogical and content objectives of the F2F sessions were common. In many cases, for example, the F2F sessions emphasized an oral and interactive communicative approach to FL instruction. These were expressed in various ways, such as communicative "real-life" tasks, small group communication, the development of speaking, conversation or meaningful communication, collaborative oral communication, and using grammar and vocabulary to communicate orally. In addition, some programs also included written communication and cultural awareness or readings. Other programs integrated cultural content into the F2F sessions.

Online Assignments and Homework

The electronic workbook has become a staple in FL programs and was used in most predesign formats, but because of the limited documentation of how the electronic workbooks were used or how much was used from them in their pre- and redesigned format, it is difficult to know how much of the reduction in contact time, if the program had some, was replaced with additional electronic workbook homework or other supplementary material provided by the textbook. Publishing companies increasingly offer electronic workbook platforms in rich multimedia formats with interpersonal tools (e.g., Wimba and other types of voice boards), and these may have been used in the programs summarized, except that there were few references to these tools. The characterization of the online assignments, practices, and tasks ran the gamut from delivery of writing, listening, and reading practices to grammar explanations or mechanical aspects of language learning to participating in meaningful vocabulary exercises to class announcements and some were characterized as meaningful input-based learning. A few courses indicated that the online work emphasized practice with vocabulary and grammar in listening, reading, and writing for the purpose of preparing students for the interactive tasks in the F2F sessions and for developing their language skills. We suspect most references to such practices were based on the electronic workbook provided through the publishers' electronic platforms, such as Centro, WileyPLUS, MySpanishLab, and iLrn, but some may be in addition to it.

A number of BL programs appeared to have created some additional online assignments via their school's course management system, such as Mallard, WebCT, Angel, or Blackboard. Some programs offered interactive or interpersonal online assignments (e.g., using discussion boards, chat tools, computer-mediated communication, or journaling software). No reference was made to synchronous uses of online tools; most tools used for interpersonal communication were used asynchronously.

In the descriptions of online learning that replaced F2F sessions, we found no BL programs using mobile technologies or social media, such as Tweets, text messaging, or Facebook. In addition, few of them used Web 2.0 technologies for developing interpersonal communication via student voice recordings (e.g., via Wimba, Audacity, or Podcast tools). In fact, there were limited references to using web-based tools to achieve interpersonal oral exchanges online or for completing online communicative or collaborative language tasks. For programs that experienced a decrease in contact time, we wonder whether marshaling technology to meet course goals of interpersonal communication online and outside of F2F instruction could have been considered. Perhaps these programs made deliberate decisions to focus on communicative and collaborative tasks only during F2F sessions or maybe the lack of online interactive activities may have more to do with university-wide technological constraints related to large multisection programs; issues of instructor workload; or the hesitation to rely on the technology that would promote interaction online, such as wikis, blogs, Facebooking, chatting, and so on. Indeed, the greatest challenge in using the potential of technologies is when theory and practice are constrained by reality. In large programs in which multiple sections of elementary and intermediate courses must be coordinated to use the same syllabus, materials, quizzes, exams, and so on, the challenge is more grave, even within their predesign formats. The need for consistency in quizzes, absence policies, number and type of exams, grading rubrics, and so on is necessary to reduce disparities in grades based on individual instructor practices and policies. In addition, most large multisection programs use graduate students who usually enter the MA and PhD programs with little to no teaching experience or time to write their own assessment instruments. Last, a sense of fairness prevails among students when all are held to the same standards across sections.

Implications

On the basis of the description of the BL programs in Tables 6-1 and 6-2, we can generate some general implications of these redesigned courses. In emphasizing interactive oral communication in the F2F sessions and moving more "mechanical" practices and input-based practice to online formats, we should see a reduction in teacher-led, teacher-fronted instruction and an increase in communicative and interpersonal activities in F2F sessions. The findings by Young (2008) indicate that providing introductory Spanish students in a BL format with opportunities for interactive and interpersonal activities in F2F classes can positively affect students' speaking skills. Garrett (2009) warns, however, that "many students from lower-level language courses that devote most of the class work on oral communication skills tend to have an inadequate foundation in grammar, reading, and writing to support the work required of them. . ." (pp. 730–731). If the F2F sessions emphasize written and oral communication, the online activities or tasks should ensure that students still obtain the foundation in vocabulary and grammar they need to develop their FL.

Whether class sizes increased or contact time was reduced, the resigned courses put the onus of learning on the students to a greater degree. For students to be able to communicate in the FL in F2F sessions, they have to prepare even more for the F2F sessions, which means reading about and working through the grammar in question via exercises before class. In addition, students need to study new vocabulary at home to be able to understand it or use it in class. In short, students are required to become independent learners and take control of their own learning, whether they like it or not. Even though research suggests that autonomous learning can be more effective than learning characterized by a reliance on the teacher (Benson, 2001), students accustomed to a traditional teacher-centered approach may resent and resist this shift and need time to adjust. Learners may need to be sensitized to shifting the locus of control for learning from external to internal forces. In addition, instructors whose educational orientation is framed by a culture of authority also need to adjust to this approach to the learning process. For students to buy into autonomous learning, we may also want to give some thought to how BL programs can build in motivations for independent learning, particularly if an increase in independent learning determines a portion of the program's effectiveness.

For students to be independent learners, they must be provided with the appropriate support to facilitate independent learning, such as links to technological online support and training; online self-tests; clear grammar explanations (from both a structural perspective as well as a functional perspective) (Garrett, 2009); animated grammar tutorials; pre- and postreading activities to assess comprehension; engrossing interactive ways to engage students in learning vocabulary; and a process approach (as opposed to a product approach) to writing, for example. A place online, such as in a discussion board, where students could ask each other technology-related questions could be another type of "support" tool for students.

Two BL programs built in F2F support opportunities for students, beyond office hours or email. The University of North Carolina at Charlotte provided separate meetings for students who got behind on assignments, and Texas Tech University offered study sessions for students who scored less than 80 percent on the first exam. BL instruction at the University of Alabama included free tutoring online and in the Language Resource Center.

We delimit here only a few of the numerous ways BL programs are constrained and the implications that even slight changes in a program can produce. These constraints will influence how these types of BL programs are designed and the ease with which students and instructors will adapt to them.

In summary, in the published and public documents on these courses redesigned for BL instruction, we found some information related to the pedagogical emphasis of the F2F classes and information related to which components of a curriculum were included or moved to online formats. We cannot, however, determine much about a course's content, objectives, pedagogy, learner outcomes, or forms of assessment on the basis of the information that was made public or that we collected. In an effort to move beyond the current discourse used to describe large multisection elementary and intermediate FL programs for BL instruction and for insights into the reflections, processes, and considerations that can go into redesigning a large multisection course, we will examine in greater detail one redesigned program from Table 6-2. Before we do this, however, it behooves us to take into account the constellation of issues in which these programs exist.

As stated in the MLA report (2007), the standard configuration of university FL curricula consists of a two- or three-year language sequence followed by the FL curriculum required for majors and minors. This configuration ". . . impedes the development of a unified language-and-content curriculum. . . ." (MLA, 2007, p. 3). Until the two-tiered language-literature structure can be replaced "with a broader and more coherent curriculum in which language, culture, and literature are taught as a continuous whole" (MLA, 2007, p. 2), we cannot address how these large multisection FL BL courses might affect the university or departmental FL curriculum. In addition, the curricula of large FL programs are constrained by their size. The need to reduce the variability across multiple classes to ensure quality of instruction means that the courses share the same syllabus, textbook, and assessments. Variation in the classes is based on individual differences in the instructors' personalities, style of teaching, pedagogical prowess, FL proficiency, and cultural experiences.

The following describes from beginning to implementation the way curricular and pedagogical issues were considered in the processes one program under-
went in redesigning a beginning Spanish program for BL instruction. This is not
to say we believe it to be the best model, just a typical model. We share this in an
effort to reveal how most of these FL multisection programs approach curricular
and pedagogical issues in redesigning courses for BL instruction.

Case Study

To meet a College of Liberal Arts and Sciences mandate to reduce instructional de-
pendence on lecturers, the head of the Modern Foreign Languages & Literatures
department proposed developing BL language courses. The head commissioned a
committee to investigate the possibility of shifting instructional time from classroom to online delivery, which would reduce the number of contact hours for lecturers. A committee of French and Spanish language program coordinators and
linguistics faculty, the department head, the coordinator of the Language Learning
Resource Center, and lecturers who served as course coordinators met throughout
the 2010 spring semester. The committee surveyed BL course redesigns of numerous multisection large university FL programs (see Tables 6-1 and 6-2) and from this
survey questioned whether redesigns approached the courses as primarily the product of shifting homework from non–class time to virtual class time. The committee conferred with two consultants, a director of a large Spanish language program
at a comparable institution that had recently experienced a redesign of its first-year
Spanish program and a recommended expert instructional designer (ID) from an
institution in California that has been a pioneer in shifting to online BL courses at
her institution. The ID expert conducted a two-day workshop with the committee in
May 2010. Under her guidance, the committee considered models for more produc-
tively using online time for students, such as through active learning opportunities both
online and F2F, as suggested by Watson (2008) and Dziuban et al. (2004), and decided to
implement alternative assessments for the program (Cummins & Davesne, 2009).

Curricular and Pedagogical Considerations

The first step in designing the first-year Spanish courses for BL instruction consisted
of establishing the philosophical framework[4] or goals of the program. A framework
loosely informed by work based on the American Council on the Teaching of Foreign
Languages (ACTFL) Proficiency Guidelines[5] and closely aligned to the National FL

---

[4]Our philosophical approach was further influenced by research in processing instruction (VanPatten,
2002), interactionist research (Gass, 2003; Long, 1996; Swain, 2000), task-based instruction (Lee,
2000; Long, 2003), and content-based language instruction (Brinton, 2003).

[5]Input from instructors indicated that a great deal of instructional effort and time was being spent on
structures that learners were not "ready" to acquire, and we cross-referenced this instructor input to the
references to grammar functions in the ACTFL Guidelines. To examine this issue in depth, a committee
of Spanish professors and instructors in the Department of Foreign Languages and Literatures was
charged with establishing a general grammar curriculum for first- through third-year language classes.

Standards[6] was embraced. It was also influenced by the university's Ready for the World[7] goals. The ACTFL Proficiency Guidelines were used to establish realistic minimum level and achievable language program goals. The FL Standards are content standards based on what FL learners should know and be able to do, and the Ready for the World goals were designed to promote intercultural knowledge that would prepare university students for a culturally diverse world. Last, the pedagogical framework of the program emphasized a balance between input-based practices followed by an active and interactive approach to instruction. After these were loosely established, the committee set out to examine textbooks that most closely matched them. Some of the most salient features of the textbook sought included integrating culture into every aspect of the material, reflecting a cross-cultural approach to culture instruction, and providing opportunities for students to give and get information and recognize that more than one viewpoint (Standard 3.2) exists. A textbook evaluation questionnaire that reflected these features—and more—was designed (Appendix 6-A). In addition, a checklist of items was created to document the many factors that would need to be considered as the redesign went forward (Appendix 6-B).

Foundation of the Foreign Language Curriculum

A fact that cannot be disputed is that for large institutions with multiple sections of beginning and intermediate courses, the curricula of these programs are fundamentally linked to the textbooks (Dorwick & Glass, 2003), whether we like it or not. The description that best characterizes FL textbooks at this level is that because they are driven by a business model, they "are written for everyone and no one" (Willis Allen, 2008, p. 6). Textbooks provide consistent material and sequencing of material to ensure standardization of the courses, a necessity for large first- and second-year Spanish programs. The textbook may not be used in the same way by all instructors, and some "use textbook materials extensively as a common point of reference orienting instruction and students' acquisition of FL vocabulary and grammar as well as a source of certain types of activities or potential transformation of activities" (Willis Allen, p. 17). However the textbook is used, it provides the scope and sequence of the courses, which are ultimately linked to the learner outcomes for the course. To deviate from the scope and sequence of the textbook would require a substantial amount of work and coordination.

A careful selection of the first-year textbook is essential to successfully implement BL instruction. The committee targeted three textbooks, and publishers were invited to provide presentations of their electronic platforms. The ePlatform plays an important role in large multisection courses, whether via BL instruction or not.

---

[6]Adhering to a national curriculum at the university level may not be as common as in K to 12, but the FL National Standards capture the content and pedagogical approach that we found most appropriate for adult FL learning and the goals of our program.

[7]More specifically, Ready for the World is an ambitious university-wide program designed for "undergraduates to gain a worldview that recognizes, understands and celebrates the complexity of cultures and people," to advance "competence in cross-cultural communication, both domestic and international; the capacity to think critically about international and intercultural issues; the understanding that knowledge is global; and a passion for life-long engagement with global learning" (http://www.utk.edu/readyfortheworld).

After the appropriate textbook was identified[8] and substantive evidence supplied that the textbook reflected the general program goals (Appendix 6-C), specific learner outcomes were established (Appendix 6-D) on the basis of the scope and sequence of the textbook. In addition, assessments that would take into account curricular and pedagogical goals, as well as technological constraints linked to these, were discussed.

Curricular and Pedagogical Interface of Face-to-Face Sessions and Online Assignments

Online assignments cannot be addressed without first referring to F2F sessions because they are tightly interconnected. An interactionist approach to instruction for the F2F sessions was embraced because of the role it played in the predesign program and the need for learners to be able to use the FL in F2F sessions in addition to efforts to help students internalize grammar and get and give information. The program is not based on a skills approach, but consideration was given to textbook content to ensure that learner outcomes could be achieved through the appropriate amount of practice and in ways in which students would be prepared for using Spanish in the F2F sessions. Toward this end, most of the input-based activities in the textbook (mostly related to vocabulary and grammar practice and cultural content) were transformed into an electronic format, called electronic textbook (eTB) practices, within the publisher's electronic platform and, similar to the practices in the online AM, were computer graded, thereby providing feedback to students. Students complete the eTB practices or do the readings before coming to class in preparation for the interpersonal activities that are emphasized in the F2F sessions. To successfully complete the preparatory practice before class, students must also read grammar explanations in the book, which are provided in English, and view video tutorials on specific grammar points; the latter are provided by the publishing company. Listening comprehension that corresponds to the same vocabulary and grammar, as well as pronunciation practice, are also part of the preparatory assignments. In this way, they are preparing students to engage in all aspects of the interpersonal activities in the F2F class. After the F2F class, online homework from the AM recycles the same material (vocabulary, grammar, and cultural content) as a way to reinforce what learners did the night before and in the F2F session. In short, learners have two purposes for completing online homework from the textbook and the AM. First, comprehension-based activities taken directly from the textbook are used to introduce new material. Second, the online AM assignments are for the purpose of recycling and reinforcing previous material (Table 6-3).

---

[8]The selected textbook was designed to promote language learning through cultural content. Sentences used in pronunciation, grammar, and vocabulary sections reflect aspects of Hispanic culture. Culturally related readings are integrated throughout the chapters, and cultural content culminates in a *Contextos* and *Perspectivas* section (a total of 18 for nine chapters) in which students are pushed to synthesize the chapter's cultural content, think critically, and experience distinctive viewpoints by first becoming aware of viewpoints based on their native culture and bridging these with the foreign culture or being sensitized to viewpoints of the foreign culture and then bridging them with awareness of perspectives in their native culture.

Table 6-3. Relationship between Online Assignments and Face-to-Face Sessions

A	B	C
Preparatory assignments from the textbook or eTB	F2F sessions	Homework assignments from AM
Introduction of new material, i.e., reading of grammar explanations and cultural content in book, viewing grammar tutorials, and doing eTB practices grammar converted to an electronic format and computer graded.	Emphasis on using new material in interpersonal communications, such as interviews, information gaps, and signature searches. Review of cultural content, written work, and grammar-related clarifications are also provided.	Computer-graded practice on material and content from A and B. Introduction of new material (i.e., reading of explanations, viewing of grammar video tutorials, reading of cultural content, and doing eTB practices)

AM, activities manual; eTB, electronic textbook; F2F, face-to-face.

Interactive Online Assignments in Blackboard

An effort was made to maintain student opportunities for interpersonal or presentational tasks in some online assignments because in the course redesign, contact time was reduced from 150 minutes per week, spread equally over three days, to 100 minutes per week, spread equally over two days. The loss of 50 minutes per week meant the loss of opportunities for students to engage in interpersonal tasks. An effort was made to identify the user-friendliest technological tools that fomented interpersonal communication in Blackboard, the course management system used at the university. Three tools were selected—wikis, podcasts, and blogs—and interpersonal and presentational tasks were designed that promoted the content and learner outcomes and pedagogical objectives of the program.

Wikis

The online Wiki tasks consist of a chart created on a wiki page; students insert their names in the first column and then answers to personalized questions (Fig. 6-1).

After the chart is mostly completed, students read their classmates' responses and make some general conclusions about the class and individual students. Linguistic support is provided as a form of structured output, as in the model below. This summary or synthesis of information was then posted on the *Retratos de la clase blog* (see below).

> ***Modelo***: Hay _____ personas en la clase que tienen amigos extranjeros. La mayoría es de _____. Hay _____ estudiantes que hablan otra lengua. _____ habla italiano y ____ habla francés. Los parientes de ____ son de Italia. La persona más popular de la actividad 3A.6 es _____. _____ y yo somos muy parecidos porque. . . .

"Retratos de la clase" Blog

These blogs are open to the instructor only (Fig. 6-2). The instructor is encouraged to use the information in these blogs in class as a way to develop a sense of

Figure 6-1. Sample online wiki assignment.

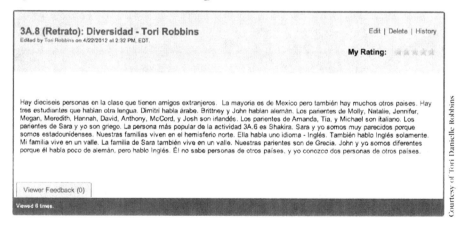

Nombre	1. ¿Cuántas personas conoces que no son estadounidenses? ¿De dónde son?	2. ¿Cuántas lenguas hablas? ¿Cuáles son?	3. ¿En qué hemisferio vive tu familia?	4. ¿Cuál es tu nacionalidad?	5. ¿Cuál es la nacionalidad de algunos de tus parientes (relatives)?	6. ¿Vive tu familia cerca (near) del océano, en una península o en un valle?	7. ¿Cuál es tu persona favorita de la lista de personas que hay en Actividad 3A.6 en p. 112?	8. ¿Cuáles son las nacionalidad amigos más cercanos (close)?
Modelo: JLP	Conozco a muchas personas de otros países. Tengo amigos de México, España, Argentina, Colombia, Brasil e Israel.	Hablo dos lenguas - inglés y español.	Mi familia vive en el hemisferio norte.	Soy estadouni-dense.	Mi esposa es mexicana. Mis otros parientes son estadounidenses.	Mi familia vive en un valle.	Mi persona favorita es Pau Gasol.	Mis amigos son estadounidenses.
Tori Robbins	Conozco dos personas de otros países. Tengo el amigo de Grecia, y tengo la amiga de Wales.	Hablo una lengua - inglés	Mi familia vive en el hemisferio norte.	Soy estadounid-ense.	Mi familia extendido es griegos, india cherokee, y estadounid-enses.	Mi familia vive en un valle.	Mi persona favorita es Penélope Cruz porque ella es una actriz muy bien. Tambien ella es mucha bonita.	Mis amigos mayoria son estadounidenses.

Figure 6-2. *Retrato de la clase* blog.

3A.8 (Retrato): Diversidad - Tori Robbins   Edit | Delete | History
Edited by Tori Robbins on 4/22/2012 at 2:32 PM, EDT.

My Rating: ★★★★★

Hay dieciseis personas en la clase que tienen amigos extranjeros. La mayoria es de Mexico pero también hay muchos otros paises. Hay tres estudiantes que hablan otra lengua. Dimitri habla árabe. Brittney y John hablan alemán. Los parientes de Molly, Natalie, Jennifer, Megan, Meredith, Hannah, David, Anthony, McCord, y Josh son irlandés. Los parientes de Amanda, Tia, y Michael son italiano. Los parientes de Sara y yo son griego. La persona más popular de la actividad 3A.6 es Shakira. Sara y yo somos muy parecidos porque somos estadounidenses. Nuestras familias viven en el hemisferio norte. Ella habla uno idioma - Inglés. También hablo Inglés solamente. Mi familia vive en un valle. La familia de Sara también vive en un valle. Nuestras parientes son de Grecia. John y yo somos diferentes porque él habla poco de alemán, pero hablo Inglés. Él no sabe personas de otros países, y yo conozco dos personas de otros países.

Viewer Feedback (0)

Viewed 6 times.

class community and foment personalization, especially important when instructors see students only twice a week. Instructors do not correct students' writing mistakes but may provide comments and often extract some of the students' interlanguage to edit with students in class as a form of positive feedback.

Podcast Assignments

The podcasts are asynchronous, presentational, and interactive tasks that ask students to record certain information based on a specific task or specific questions and then post the podcast (or mp3 file) (Standards 1.1 and 1.2). Students listen to a certain number of these class podcasts, and most of the time they make some conclusions about their classmates based on the content. In these cases, a writing framework is again provided because students are not fully capable of conveying some of the information without it. Below is an example of a type of information-gap podcast assignment that does not require writing in the *Retrato de la clase* blog but requires students to compare drawings and turn them in to their instructor (Fig. 6-3).

Figure 6-3. Podcast online assignment.

IB.15 ¿Cuantos hay?
Tool- Wimba Podcast
Location: Online Assignments
Record by 8/27; Due date is 8/30
Location: Online Assignments

Paso 1: Draw a fictitious classroom and include as many objects as possible (using IB vocabulary for class objects). Be prepared to turn in this drawing to your instructor.

Paso 2: Then, click the Assignments buttom in our Bb course site and record a description of your drawing using the following model.
"*Hay 10 sillas en la close.*" "*Hay 11 estudiantes en la close,*" etc.

To record your responses, click "New." Type in activity number (IB.15) followed by your Initials (in my case this would be djy). Click the red button to record and square button to stop recording. To listen to your recording, click the green arrow. If you are satisfied with your recording, scoll to the bottom and click "Post." Your recording should now be listed.

Paso 3: Listen to two of your classmates' recordings and draw the classrooms based on their descriptions. Turn in your original drawing and the other two drawings to your instructor.

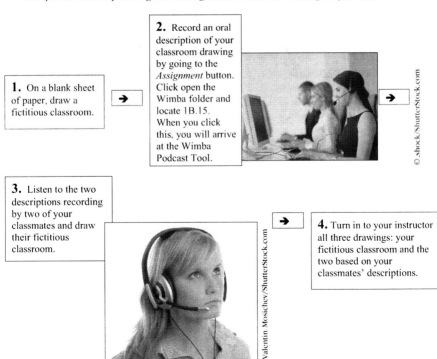

Again, most of the time podcast assignments require that students post a summary of what they glean about fellow classmates on the *Retrato de la clase* blog for the instructor to read.

Hablando de mí mismo

This is another blog but has a journal-like feel. Students write about themselves and provide only information they are willing to share. The blog is open to all classmates. Topics (see sample in Fig. 6-4) are tailored to promote learner outcomes and correspond to the textbook content. These writing tasks are good examples of Standard 1.3.

As the above examples illustrate, online interactive tasks are used in which students engage in writing or speaking assignments with each other to develop their interpersonal language skills but also to promote a sense of community in their class as they learn about each other or as they profile the class as a whole. In the process of doing these various assignments, students also end up reflecting on their own cultures or on the class as a microcosm of society.

Proyecto Cultural

This online assignment carries more weight than the other online assignments because it is designed to promote various aspects of the FL Standards, such as the degree to which students can communicate effectively in Spanish, how well they understand and make comparisons of language and culture (Standards 2.1, 2.2, and 3.1), how well they can think critically and illustrate competence in cross-cultural communication, and how well they use Spanish beyond the school setting (Standard 5.1). This is a semester-long assignment that includes checkpoints at various times in the semester. It requires some type of "presentation" task (Standard 1.3). See Appendix 6-E for the eight projects from which students select one or two to develop.

To some degree, the evidence above suggests that this program, and perhaps others in Tables 6-1 and 6-2, attempts to marshal technologies' potential to promote a complementary approach to F2F and online learning. Other technologies could be used, such as social media and handheld technologies that might motivate students even more and may be more relevant to students' lives, depending on the program goals, curriculum, and pedagogy.

Figure 6-4. Online *Hablando de mí mismo* blog assignments.

❏ **Blog Entry 1. Mi vida universitaria** (minimum range of words: 75–100)

Investigatión 2A: If you are communicating with other (Spanish-speaking) college students, they may be interested in what your university life is like. How would you describe it to them? Discuss things such as what you like to do, what your major is, what classes you like/don't like.

❏ **Blog Entry 2. Mi familia** (minimum range of words: 100–125)

Investigatión 2B: What can you tell your online acquaintances about your family? Describe them. Include their ages, gender, profession, personalities, and any additional information you are able to express in Spanish.

Table 6-4. Grade Distribution for Blended Learning Programs

Component	Grade (%)
F2F participation	15
WileyPlus assignements	15
Exams	30
Quizzes	15
Spanish ePortfolio (includes to ePortfolio tasks, self-assessment, one podcast, and three best blogs)	10
Online assignments and *Hablando de mí mismo*	10
Oral performance	5

F2F, face-to-face.

Finally, Table 6-4 illustrates the grading categories and weights for the various components of the BL program. In addition to the Proyecto cultural assignment, cultural content formed approximately one-third of the items on the online exam, alongside vocabulary and grammar.

Assessments

Rubrics were designed for all online assignments, from wikis, podcasts, *Retrato de la clase* blogs, and *Hablando de mí mismo* blogs, to the cultural projects, and oral interview exams. These rubrics can be found at http://web.utk.edu/~djyoung/ Rubrics-BL Program.docx.

Oral Interviews

Face-to-face sessions and podcast assignments promote oral interpersonal skills using vocabulary and grammar from the scope and sequence of the textbook (Standards 1.1 and 1.2) and provide opportunities to discuss cultural content in class (Standards 2.1 and 2.2). In addition, in the *Contextos & Perspectivas* section of the textbook, students compare two cultures from distinct perspectives (Standards 4.1 and 4.2). To assess students' ability to use Spanish in interpersonal ways, they participate in a paired oral interview with each other and their instructor at the end of the courses (usually during the two-hour final exam block). In addition to verifying learner outcomes, these oral interviews also provide instructors with an opportunity to inform and adjust expectations of students' proficiency and ensure that students are ready for the second-year courses.

Online Exams

The eTB and AM assignments emphasize vocabulary and grammar acquisition and encompass knowledge of cultural products and practices and are assessed primarily by exams at the Learning Resource Center on campus through a lock-down browser (Respondus). The exam formats parallel the online practices that correspond to the textbook. The exams are made available over a five-day period and are computer-graded.

ePortfolio

Students are required to create an ePortfolio to set and gauge their personal language learning goals and monitor their progress in Spanish. The ePortfolio allows students to develop and showcase their ability to communicate in Spanish based on individual interests, strengths, and motivations and to promote realistic self-expression in Spanish and encourage reflective learning. The student ePortfolios house the items shown in Table 6-5.

Self-assessment of Language Development

Using the LinguaFolio self-assessment, designed by the Center for Applied Lingustics, students "collect evidence demonstrating their communicative abilities to themselves and others" and "document intercultural experiences and reflections that enhance language learning and cultural understanding" (see the LinguaFolio website).

The level of detail we provide here on curricular and pedagogical considerations may provide insights into how large multisection programs can reflect on curricular and pedagogical issues in redesigning a course or a program for BL instruction. We do not claim to model the best practices, but we believe this one program may represent, to varying degrees and for better or for worse, many other redesigned courses in Tables 6-1 and 6-2. In addition, we are relatively certain that this is one of the first universities to integrate alternative assessment efforts as well as "technologically enhanced active learning possibilities." As such, we fill a void because little information related to curriculum and pedagogy are provided in published accounts of BL at this level of instruction and no other programs appear to use an ePortfolio to the extent used here.

Table 6-5. Content of student ePortfolios.

Retratos	Podcast	Proyecto Cultural	Self-Assessment of Spanish Proficiency
Choose your three best samples from the following: IP. 13 Retrato 3A. 8 Retrato 4B.21 Retrato 6A.12 Retrato 9A.12 Retrato	Re-upload one of the two MP3s you created during the semester (the one you believe that represents your best work).	Must be done in Spanish at a level that reflects first-year competence.	You will upload four self-assessment checklists.

Discussion

The curriculum implemented in the case study above is heavily influenced by the FL National Standards, but what if these are not considered appropriate for a particular program? According to Dorwick and Glass, "the single most important determining factor in adoption decisions at the college level is the grammar sequence around which a given textbook is constructed" and professors state outright that they "never cover the culture; there's just no time for it" (2003, p. 593). They also claim that the profession has not made as many changes as we might like to claim because the textbooks published have only been slightly altered. They have not really changed in significant ways except to include more partner and group tasks. In short, Dorwick and Glass have not seen the kind of changes where policies actually filter down to practices despite the calls for change. Professors and instructors dictate which books get adopted, so although it can be argued that textbooks drive the national FL curriculum, it can also be argued that the practitioners do. To understand the complexity of this issue even better, we have to ask, Who are the majority of instructors teaching at the beginning and intermediate levels in this country? Although the Language Program Director of large multisection elementary and intermediate programs might have a background in applied linguistics or FL education or be well informed by these two fields, the majority of the actual instructors are graduate students or adjuncts and lecturers with MAs and PhDs who have had one, maybe two, courses on FL instruction, SLA, or applied linguistics.

In a discussion about the curriculum and pedagogy of large multisection beginning and intermediate programs, we cannot lose sight of the confounding variables and constraints that program directors and supervisors face as we address curricular and pedagogical issues of BL instruction. They are just as relevant to non-BL instruction, however.

Even within the professional structure discussed above, we can still ask whether BL instruction affects the established curriculum and pedagogy of a program. We use the case study above to address this question.

In the above BL program, course content was reduced by one textbook chapter. Instead of the pencil-and-paper exams reflecting the way the classes were taught, online exams limited the format to multiple choice, short answer, true or false, and fill-in-the blank items. Computer-graded formats are not the best way to test FL learning if the mantra is "Test how you teach." Thus, content, learner outcomes, and assessments were affected by BL instruction. At the same time, alternative assessments were added to address the limitations of the online exam format and articulation between the elementary and intermediate programs discussed to allow for a smoother content-related transition to the intermediate Spanish courses.

We posit that the greatest effect of BL instruction rests with the change in learner and instructor roles. F2F sessions require less teacher-centered instruction and more independent learning on the part of the students. We believe these are positive changes, however. Nonetheless, if students are not independent learners actually reading the homework assignments in the textbook and completing the online textbook and AM assignments, this will lead to the "inadequate foundation in grammar" that Garrett (2009) mentions. Moreover, it is difficult to know whether instructors are concentrating on interpersonal tasks in F2F sessions and not devoting a major portion of the 50-minute F2F sessions to grammar explanations.[9] We do know that students are completing the wiki, blog, and podcast tasks online and doing the cultural projects because there is verifiable evidence of this. These concerns were also relevant for the predesigned course but have become intensified in BL instruction.

Lastly, as in non-BL programs, if students are motivated, are independent learners, and do their homework; if instructors adhere to the F2F pedagogy they were trained to use;[10] and above all else, if the technology is dependable,[11] then BL instruction may be a viable approach to cost savings, and the effects of BL instruction on the curriculum and pedagogy need not be negative. In the case study above, the component of the program that depends on Blackboard was not as reliable in the second semester of implementation as in the first semester, creating ripple effects that have influenced instructor workload, pedagogy, and assessment issues.

Conclusion

We set out to investigate BL instruction at large multisection elementary and intermediate FL programs and realized that publications on them were limited, and intentionally or unintentionally, what was available provided information relevant to their evolution, operations, and cost savings. In an effort to fill a void on the topic of curricular and pedagogical issues related to BL instruction, we described in detail how one university approached these issues while redesigning its intensive elementary Spanish courses for BL instruction. Our purpose was not to provide a model for curricular and pedagogical decision making in BL instruction at the elementary or intermediate level but to reflect on the unique contexts

---

[9]At the end of the first academic year of the BL Spanish first-year program, we administered a questionnaire to all students in our BL programs, Spanish 150 and 123. A general analysis of the open-ended comments indicated that instructors were indeed promoting interactive activities in the F2F sessions because students commonly sited this as a "strength" of the program.

[10]All instructors slated to teach in the redesigned courses were provided extensive pedagogical training related to the F2F sessions.

[11]The Office of Instructional Technology worked closely and extensively on the technological aspects of the redesigned course. Issues that surfaced on the technological end were related to outages, Blackboard's Campus Pack tool suite, and Respondus updates. Significant problems surfaced throughout the fall and spring semesters because students procrastinated in taking the online exams until the last day. Even when we extended the exam availability, students waited until the last day to take the exam, resulting in the inability to accommodate all students in the testing center.

in which curricular and pedagogical issues are considered. The context is not unique to BL instruction, however. Even so, we cannot adjudicate whether and how BL instruction should or can be judged positively without careful curricular planning and careful consideration of pedagogies. Without reflection on learning goals, programs will be reacting to outer circumstances rather than reflecting deeply on issues pertaining to adult instructed language learning.

References

Adair-Hauck, B., Willingham-McLain, L., & Youngs, B. E. (2000). Evaluating the integration of technology and second language learning. *CALICO Journal, 17*, 269–306.

Antón, M., & Ewald, J. D. (2008). No me gusta hablar con mis compañeros de clase porque cometen tantos errores como yo. ¿Por qué tenemos que trabajar en grupos? In J. D. Ewald & A. Edstrom (Eds.), *El español a través de la lingüística: Preguntas y respuestas* (pp. 262–273). Somerville, MA: Cascadilla Press.

Arvan, L., & Musumeci, D. (2000). Instructor attitudes within the SCALE efficiency projects. *Journal of Asynchronous Learning Networks, 4* (3), 196–215.

Barr-Harrison, P., & Daugherty, C. P. (2000). Multiple realities of the classroom. In R. M. Terry (Ed.), *Agents of change in a changing age* (pp. 79–105). *Northeast Conference on the Teaching of Foreign Languages Reports*. Lincolnwood, IL: National Textbook Company.

Benson, P. (2001). *Teaching and researching autonomy in language learning*. Essex, England: Pearson Education.

Bober, M. J. (2002). Technology integration: The difficulties inherent in measuring pedagogical change. *TechTrends, 46* (1), 21–24.

Brandl, K. (2008). *Communicative language teaching in action: Putting principles to work*. Upper Saddle River, NJ: Prentice Hall.

Brinton, D. (2003). Content-based instruction. In D. Nunan (Ed.), *Practical English language teaching* (pp. 199–224). New York: McGraw-Hill.

Cummins, P. W., & Davesne, C. (2009). Using electronic portfolios for second language assessment. *The Modern Language Journal, 93*, 848–867.

Dorwick, T. &, Glass W. R. (2003). Language education policies: One publisher's perspective. *The Modern Language Journal, 87*, 592–594.

Dziuban, C. D., Hartman, J. L., & Moskal, P. D. (2004, March 30). *Blended learning* (ECAR Research Bulletin, 2004, Issue 7). Boulder, CO: The EDUCAUSE Center for Applied Research. Retrieved June 25, 2011, from http://net.educause.edu/ir/library/pdf/ERB0407.pdf.

Garrett, N. (2009). Computer-assisted language learning trends and issues revisited: Integrating innovation. *The Modern Language Journal, 93*, 719–740.

Gass, S. M. (2003). Input and interaction. In C. J. Doughty & M. H. Long (Eds.), *The handbook of second language acquisition* (pp. 224–255). Oxford: Blackwell.

Lee, J. F. (2000). *Tasks and communicating in language classrooms*. San Francisco: McGraw-Hill.

Long, M. H. (1996). The role of the linguistic environment in second language acquisition. In W. C. Ritchie & T. K. Bhatia (Eds.), *Handbook of second language acquisition: Vol 2* (pp. 413–468). New York Academic Press.

Long, M. H. (2003). Español para fines específicos: ¿Textos o tareas? [Spanish for specific purposes: Texts or tasks?]. In V. de Antonio, R. Cuesta, A. van Hooft, et al. (Eds.), *Español para fines específicos. Actas del II CIEFE* (pp. 15–39). Madrid: Ministerio de Educación y Ciencia del Reino de España.

Modern Language Association. (2007, May). *Foreign languages and higher education: New structures for a changed world.* Retrieved February 25, 2012, from http://www.mla.org/pdf/forlang_news_pdf.pdf.

Neumeier, P. (2005). A closer look at blended learning: Parameters for designing a blended learning environment for language teaching and learning. *ReCALL, 17,* 163–178.

Pittinsky, M. S. (Ed.). (2003). *The wired tower: Perspectives on the impact of the Internet on higher education.* Upper Saddle River, NJ: Prentice Hall.

Sagarra, N., & Zapata G. (2008). Blending classroom instruction with online homework: A study of student perceptions of computer-assisted L2 learning. *ReCALL, 20,* 208–224.

Sanders, R. F. (2005). Redesigning Introductory Spanish: Increased enrollment, online management, cost reduction, and effects on students learning. *Foreign Language Annals, 38,* 523–532.

Swaffar, J., & Arens, K. (2005). *Remapping the foreign language curriculum: An approach through multiple literacies.* New York: Modern Language Association.

Swain, M. (2000). The output hypothesis and beyond: Mediating acquisition through collaborative dialogue. In J. P. Lantolf (Ed.), *Sociocultural theory and second language learning* (pp. 97–114). Oxford: Oxford University Press.

Twigg, C. A. (1999). *Improving learning & reducing costs: Redesigning large-enrollment courses.* New York: Center for Academic Transformation at Rensselaer Polytechnic Institute. Retrieved June 25, 2011, from http://www.thencat.org/Monographs/mono1.pdf.

Twigg, C. A. (2001). *Innovations in online learning: Moving beyond no significant difference.* New York: Center for Academic Transformation at Rensselaer Polytechnic Institute. Retrieved June 27, 2011, from http://www.thencat.org/Monographs/Mono4.pdf.

Twigg, C. A. (2002). *Redefining community: Small colleges in the information age.* New York: Center for Academic Transformation at Rensselaer Polytechnic Institute. Retrieved June 25, 2011, from http://www.thencat.org/Monographs/Mono5.pdf.

VanPatten, B. (2002). Processing instruction: An update. *Language Learning 52,* 755–803.

Watson, J. (2008). *Blended learning: The convergence of online and face-to-face education.* North American Council for Online Learning. Retrieved June 25, 2011, from http://www.inacol.org/research/promisingpractices/NACOL_PP-BlendedLearning-lr.pdf.

Willis Allen, H. (2008). Textbook materials and foreign language teaching: Perspectives from the classroom. *NECTFL Review, 62,* 5–28.

Young, D. (2008). An empirical investigation of the effects of blended learning on student outcomes in a redesigned intensive Spanish course. *CALICO Journal, 26,* 160–181.

Appendix 6-A. First-Year Spanish Textbook Questionnaire for Blended Learning Instruction

Textbook title: _____   Online platform: _____

Textbook

Conceptual/theoretical considerations:

1. In general, does the author's approach match the first-year program's conceptual framework? Consider the following as practical and theoretical guidelines:

   • Activities that move from input (comprehension) to output (production), as opposed to beginning with production activities.

- Sufficient culture integrated into material, as opposed to stand-alone boxes that might get dropped.
- Cultural content that promotes higher order thinking.
- Promotion of using language for a purpose, as opposed to merely the "show and tell" of language use (activities designed for students to "practice" the language but not necessarily for a real purpose).
- Interactive activities that promote several language skills: speaking, listening, reading, writing.
- Grammar with clear grammar explanations (students will study these online/outside of class).
- Meaningful and communicative exercises using vocabulary and grammar, as opposed to mechanical exercises in which students do not need to attend to meaning.

2. Are learner outcomes specified via the content and scope and sequence of the textbook? Are these appropriate for our program? On what basis do you make this evaluation?
3. What are the salient features that represent the general pedagogical approach of the textbook?
4. How is culture covered in this text? Keep in mind that we would like to have sufficient culture integrated into the textbook material, as opposed to stand-alone boxes that might get dropped. We would also like to have cultural content and tasks that promotes higher order thinking.
5. Does the material seem appropriately gauged for our first-year Spanish students?
6. Does the textbook include a reasonable approach to grammar instruction?
7. Is the vocabulary common to first-year programs? Does it use "high frequency" words? Is there sufficient and appropriate vocabulary covered to prepare students for second-year courses?

Practical considerations:

8. How are the chapters structured in this textbook and is the structure logical/ user friendly?
9. In your opinion, would this text work well in the proposed blended learning model? Face-to-face sessions will emphasize communicative activities, although not exclusively.
   a. Does the textbook offer enough communicative activities and task-based activities to use in class, such as interviews, surveys, and information-gap activities?
   b. Could the majority of the interpersonal tasks be used "as is," or would many require instructors to modify them to meet our needs?
   c. Does the textbook offer purposeful comprehension-based practice for vocabulary, pronunciation, and clear and concise grammar explanations, as well as comprehension-based grammar practices that students can do independently and that will prepare them to use Spanish for interpersonal tasks in F2F sessions?

10. What types of things might we need to supplement if we use this text? For example, would we need to develop more input activities to use online, comprehension activities to go along with readings in the text?
11. Does the textbook provide sufficient opportunities to promotes the development of reading, writing, and listening comprehension in Spanish?
12. Are there authentic texts used to promote authentic language uses?
13. Does the textbook offer instructional resources, such as additional activities, PowerPoints, a video component, a testing program? If so, what are these like?

Online Platform: e-Book, Online Workbook, Grammar Tutorials

14. Is the design and navigation of the e-book platform easy to follow for students and instructors?
15. In your opinion, is the online material, i.e., content, organization, practice activities, etc. well synchronized with the textbook material?
16. Does the online platform offer communicative activities online or activities that could easily be adapted for online communicative and interpersonal tasks?
17. What can this online platform offer in terms of input, grammar explanation, etc. Keep in mind that some of the tasks we currently do in class will need to be completed by students independently as homework?
18. In general, what portion of online activities are computer graded versus instructor graded?
19. What features does the grading component of the online platform offer and how user friendly is it?
20. Are there aspects of the online program that this textbook offers that the others do not or vice versa? (opportunity here to make comparisons with other texts)
21. Are there sufficient listening exercises online (these also serve as input for vocabulary and grammar)?
22. How easy are the instructions for the activities, particularly if students will be doing these on their own?
23. Does the textbook program offer good grammar tutorials?
24. How easy would it be to design additional activities or tasks and integrate them into this specific online platform, if necessary?
25. On a scale from 1 (best) to 5 (worst), how would you rank this textbook in general?

Explain why. 1   2   3   4   5

General evaluation and impressions:

Pros/strengths of this text and online platform:
Cons/weaknesses of this text and online platform:

Appendix 6-B. Course Redesign for Blended Learning Instruction in Multiple-Section Foreign Language Courses

Checklist of Considerations for Programs That Are Reducing Face-to-Face Sessions

Program Goals

❑ What are the various goals for first-year Spanish?
❑ Will these goals stay the same or will they need to be modified to accommodate the BL format?
❑ How will you reconfigure material, content, activities, pedagogy, etc., to achieve these goals?
❑ How can you use technologies to achieve them?

Learner Outcomes

❑ What are the learner outcomes for your program?
❑ Will these outcomes need to be modified for the BL format? If so, how?
❑ What material, content, activities, pedagogy will help you achieve these learner outcomes?
❑ Are course expectations and learner outcomes clear and accessible to learners?

F2F Sessions

❑ What are the objectives of the F2F sessions in the traditional program format?
❑ Will these objectives be modified for the F2F sessions in the blended learning format?
❑ Have the pedagogical goals for the F2F sessions changed/been modified?
❑ Will lesson plans or pedagogical guidelines be provided for the F2F sessions?
❑ Are there physical qualities to consider for the BL F2F classrooms? If so, what are they?

Beyond the Physical Classroom: Online Learning/Activities/Tasks/ Homework

❑ What curricular goals do the online materials (i.e., e-book, online activities manual, learning management system course site, e-Portfolio) serve?

❏ How do the various technologies in the blended learning course format support the curricular and pedagogical goals of the course?

❏ Are task instructions clear, consistent, and scaffolded (if necessary)?

❏ Are the activities/tasks gauged at the right level?

❏ Is the purpose of each activity/task clear and expectations well established?

❏ Do learners have the right amount of opportunities to obtain written and aural input online to engage successfully in F2F interpersonal activities/tasks?

❏ Do learners have the right amount of opportunities to express themselves orally online in the BL format?

❏ Do learners have the right amount of opportunities to express themselves in writing in the BL format?

❏ Do learners have an appropriate number of interactive/collaborative activities/tasks in the BL format?

❏ Is there an appropriate amount of online homework (whether via activities manual, book, interactive tasks, e-Portfolio assignments)?

❏ How much time will online activities/tasks take?

Assessments

❏ What forms of assessment will the blended learning format include and how often?

❏ What assessment formats will the blended learning format include?

❏ What alternative assessment formats will the blended learning format include?

❏ Will students have opportunities to "self-assess" their language proficiency and cultural knowledge?

❏ Are the criteria for all forms of assessment available to students?

❏ Will F2F assessments have a different purpose than online assessments?

❏ How many assessments will be made available online?

❏ Has student accountability for online assessments been accounted for?

❏ How do assessment measures parallel course goals, objectives, and learner outcomes?

Practical Considerations

Instructors

❏ Who are the personnel for your first-year courses?

❏ How will their workload be redistributed?

❏ What new training will they need (pedagogical and technological)?
❏ When will this training take place? How often? Who will lead the training?
❏ How is the role of the instructor changed (if at all)?
❏ What responsibilities will instructors have outside of F2F sessions?
❏ How is workload made equitable for instructors?

Course Management

❏ How will BL instruction be configured in the program?
❏ How will the syllabus be organized (what information and where)?
❏ How detailed is the syllabus (are the due dates indicated)?
❏ How will the interface of the various components of the course be configured? (Blackboard, Angel, or D2L course site, e-book/online workbook [such as Centro, WileyPlus, MySpanishLab, etc.], e-Portfolio tool, such as Campus Pack ePortfolio.)
❏ Is there sufficient time between F2F sessions to manage out-of-class and online homework?
❏ How will you set up the pairs and groups for online interaction?
❏ What default mechanisms are in place for students when a group member does not participate?
❏ Who will maintain the master course site for the program (whether via Blackboard or another Learning Management System)?
❏ What will each instructor need to add/adjust/change to his or her individual course sites?
❏ Where will online tasks be stored and how will they be set up?
❏ Will there be a location online for students to offer feedback about the hybrid course?
❏ Will student guides to technological tools be provided and where?
❏ How are the various grading components and tools interfaced?
❏ How might you reduce the ripple effect caused by new editions of the program textbook?
❏ What technologies will students be required to own/use in the hybrid format that are not currently required in your introductory Spanish program?
❏ Will there be additional student support, such as drop-in tutoring, online office hours, etc. in the BL format?
❏ What type of long-term personnel will be required to maintain technological components of the hybrid course?

Appendix 6-C. Foreign Language Standards and the First-Year Spanish Program

Communication: Communicate in Languages Other Than English

Standard 1.1

Standard 1.1 states that students should engage in conversation, provide and obtain information, express feelings and emotions, and exchange opinions. The textbook that was adopted for the first-year Spanish program using blended learning instruction contains a wide range of pair and group activities which encourage and develop oral communication skills.

Opportunities to provide and obtain information.

See activities such as: IP.4, IP.10, 1A.1, 1A.19, 1B.10, *En vivo* Chapter 1, 2A.3, 2A.23, 2B.14, 2B.26, *En vivo* Chapter 2, 3A.8, 3A.21, 3B.15, 3B.19, *En vivo* Chapter 3, 4A.5, 4A.23, 4B.16, 4B.24, *En vivo* Chapter 4, 5A.5, 5A.12, 5B.12, 5B.23, *En vivo* Chapter 5, 6A.3, 6A.12, 6B.27, 6B.31, *En vivo* Chapter 6, 7A.4, 7A.26, 7B.12, 7B.17, *En vivo* Chapter 7, 8A.1, 8A.18, 8B.11, 9A.8, 9A.23, 9B.17, 9B.22, 10A.13, 10A.15, 10B.13, 10B.18, 11A.9, 11A.22, 11B.4, 12A.12, 12A.19, 12B.22

Opportunities to express feelings and emotions.

See activities such as: 2A.15, 3A.17, 8A.2, 8A.4, 8A.10, 8A.25, 11A.10, 12B.9

This objective is particularly appropriate in *Investigación* 8A where expressions relating to emotion are presented as vocabulary and students are discussing their emotional reactions to various works of art and situations.

Opportunities to exchange opinions.

See activities such as: 2B.24, 3A.27, 3A.35, 3B.25, 4A.11, 4A.20, 4B.25, 5A.34, 5B.10, 5B.20, 6A.13, 6A.19, 6B.13, 6B.15, 7A.12, 7B.7, 7B.23-27, 8A.20, 8A.28, 8B.9, 8B.19, 9A.11, 9B.11, 9B.26-27, *En vivo* Chapter 9, 10A.14, 10A.27, 10B.10, *En vivo* Chapter 10, 11A.19, 11A.31, 11B.12, 11B.22, 12A.23-25, 12B.14, *En vivo* Chapter 12.

Students engage in the material in a deeper way by analyzing, sharing, and comparing opinions.

Standard 1.2

Standard 1.2 states that students should understand and interpret written and spoken language on a variety of topics.

Written language (reading development).

Reading is developed through:

- Readings in the *Adelante* section of each *Investigación* (exclusively in Spanish as of *Investigación* 3A). (See pp. 113, 138, 160, 184, 206)
- *Vívelo: Cultura* sections, generally one to four per *Investigación* (exclusively in Spanish as of *Investigación* 4A). (See pp. 116, 124, 171, 261, 288, 441, 562)

- Additional readings associated with specific activities (e.g., 1A.11, p. 22; 2B.4, pp. 84–85; 11A.21, p. 497; 11B.13, p. 515)
- Realia and falsealia-based activities (e.g., 2A.4, p. 62; 2A.16, p. 72; 3A.15 and 3A.17, pp. 118–119, 5A.27, p. 220)
- *Contextos* and *Perspectivas* activities, one of each per *Investigación* (exclusively in Spanish as of *Investigación* 3A). See pp. 150–152, 222–223, 342–344, 430–432, 456–458, 476–478, 546–547

Topics vary widely and include profiles of prominent Hispanics, both contemporary and historical; cultural and religious practices and values (e.g., meal times, *compadrazgo*, family ties, work–life balance, bullfighting, 24-hour clock); education and study abroad; Native American civilizations; art and artists; sports and leisure; geography; Hispanics in the United States and the concept of hispanismo/hispanidad.

Spoken language (comprehension).

- Listening activities throughout each *Investigación* in both the textbook and the Activities Manual are indicated by a headphones icon (e.g., *Investigación* 2B: 2B.2, 2B.4, 2B.7, 2B.11, 2B.16, 2B.21, 2B.27; *Investigación* 5A: 5A.4, 5A.6, 5A.11, 5A.19; *Investigación* 9A: 9A.1, 9A.3, 9A.4, 9A.15; *Investigación* 11B: 11B.1, 11B.3, 11B.9).
- *Bien dicho* activities in both the textbook and the Activities Manual often focus on sound/word discrimination (e.g., 2A.6, p. 63; 3A.11, p. 115; 3B.7, p. 139; 4A.7, p. 161; 4B.8, p. 185; 5A.7, p. 207; 5B.5, p. 229; 6A.6, p. 255; 7A.7, p. 307; 7B.5, p. 329; 8A.5, p. 353; 8B.6, p. 375; 9A.5, p. 400; 10A.8, p. 443; 10B.4, p. 463; 11A.5, p. 487; 11B.6, p. 511; 12A.7, p. 533; 12B.5, p. 555).
- Each chapter test includes from two to three listening comprehension tasks.

Standard 1.3

Standard 1.3 states that students should present information, concepts, and ideas to an audience of listeners or readers on a variety of topics.

One-way writing.

"Hablando de mí mismo" online writing activities (like open journaling)

Wiki pages and *"Retratos"* (Blogs or follow-up writing assignments)

- Mini-writing activities are found throughout the textbook (e.g., 5B.16, p. 237; 5B.17, p. 237; 6B.16, p. 287; 6B.21, p. 290; 6B.26, p. 293; 8B.21, p. 384; 10A.22, p. 455).

One-way speaking.

- Students engage in a number of activities where individuals or groups report to the class, carry out a debate, or present information/skits to the class (e.g., IP.4, p. 6; 1A.5, p. 18; 1B.23, p. 52; 2B.25, p. 96; 3A.27, p. 128; 3B.3, p. 137; 5A.17, p. 212; 5A.22, p. 215; 5B.13, p. 235; 6A.15, p. 261; 6B.22, p. 291; 7B.17, p. 339; 7B.24-25, p. 343; 8A.26, p. 367; 8B.4,

p. 372; 8B.28, p. 389; 9A.10, p. 403; 9A.23, p. 412; 9B.22, p. 428; 9B.27, pp. 431–432; *En vivo* Chapter 9, p. 434; 10A.26, p. 458; 10B.10, p. 466; 10B.15, p. 470; 10B.18, p. 473; 11A.20, p. 496; 11B.4, p. 510; *En vivo* Chapter 11, p. 526; 12A.4, p. 531; *En vivo* Chapter 12, p. 570).

- As of Chapter 7, activities encourage students to present their findings to the class (e.g., pp. 314, 335, 337, 339, 359, 361, 379, 416, 423, 442, 453, 472, 475, 489, 499, 511, 524, 533, 537, 561).
- There is an oral component included in each of the exams.
- For a sampling of other two-way or small group speaking activities, see 1P. 5, p. 7; 1B.15, p. 45; 2B.6, p. 85; 3A.21, p. 123; 3A.26, p. 128; 3B.16, pp.146–7; 4A.27, p. 174; 4B.16, p. 190; 6A.10, p. 258; 7A.11, p. 309; 8A.22, p. 351; 8A.10, p. 356; 8B.17, p. 383; 9A.8, p. 402; 9B.10, p. 420; 9B.16, p. 425; 10A.14, p. 447; 10B.14, p. 470; 11A.22, p. 498; 11A.25, p. 501; 12A.13, p. 537.
- *Retrato de la clase* activities and *En vivo* activities also involve speaking with one or more classmates.

Cultures: Gain knowledge and Understanding of Other Cultures.

Standard 2.1

Standard 2.1 states that students should demonstrate an understanding of the relationship between the practices and perspectives of the culture studied. Students explore *el compadrazgo* from a historical and social perspective (pp. 100–101); understand how weather conditions and geography help shape what a culture eats (p. 214), and when, (pp. 222–223); how explicit social practices, such as the celebration of saints and the celebration of *días feriados* offer insight into the evolution of cultures, i.e., that much of the Hispanic population was Catholic (pp. 61, 405, 410); how Spain's cultural practices were fused with practices of indigenous peoples of the New World (pp. 398, 456–457); how even sports (soccer) is much more than what it appears to be (p. 416) and how it is tied into the social fabric of a country; and how media and communication effect and shape cultural practices (pp. 504–505, 523, 552, 562, 563).

Standard 2.2

Standard 2.2 states that students should demonstrate an understanding of the relationship between the products and perspectives of the culture studied. Students examine why the small *tienditas* are characteristic of small and large cities in Latin America (p. 294); how what people wear (hats) can give insight into their culture (p. 233); how something as benign as the design of the Spanish patio can reveal a great deal about the values of Hispanic cultures (p. 274); what art has in common across cultures and why (pp. 389, 313, 322–324); how the perception of historical figures/cultural heroes can change within and across cultures (pp. 476–478).

Connections: Connect with Other Disciplines and Acquire Information.

Standard 3.1

Standard 3.1 states that students should reinforce and further their knowledge of other disciplines through the foreign language. Students learn the geography of the

Spanish-speaking world (pp. 113, 114, 118, 124, 133, 134, 154). Students further their knowledge about American art and artists, as well as Hispanic art and artists, in chapter 7 and 8. They explore historical events and peoples of Hispanic countries in chapter 9, as well as issues in globalization and technology in chapter 12.

Standard 3.2

Standard 3.2 states that students should acquire information and recognize the distinctive viewpoints that are only available through the foreign language and its cultures. Chapter content in the textbook culminates in the *Contextos* and *Perspectivas* sections at the end of each *Investigación*. In these sections, students experience distinctive viewpoints by first becoming aware of viewpoints based on their native culture and bridging these with the foreign culture, or by being sensitized to viewpoints of the foreign culture and then bridging them with awareness of perspectives in their native culture.

Comparisons: Develop Insight into the Nature of Language and Culture.

Standard 4.1

Standard 4.1 states that students should demonstrate understanding of the nature of language through comparisons of the language studied and their own.

- *Adelante* sections encourage students to use their knowledge of cognates to comprehend and use the Spanish equivalents. Use of cognates is reinforced constantly throughout the text in tasks, direction lines, and readings.
- *¡Atención!* sections heighten students' awareness of the fact that not every Spanish word that looks/sounds like an English word is a cognate.
- *Bien dicho* sections often make direct comparisons between English and Spanish pronunciation (e.g., pp. 36, 63, 85, 115, 161, 207, 307, 375, 400, 463, 487).
- *Estructuras clave* sections often make direct comparisons between English and Spanish grammars (e.g., pp. 25, 46, 74, 97, 145, 168, 217–218, 265, 289, 338, 360, 382).
- *Investigación* 1A points out how variations in non-verbal communication across cultures (i.e., gestures and greetings) can lead to misunderstandings.
- An effort is made to point out differences in the Spanish spoken across the Spanish-speaking world (e.g., pp. 12; 143; 5A.13, p. 210; 214; 228; 443; 463; 533).

Standard 4.2

Standard 4.2 states that students should demonstrate understanding of the concept of culture through comparisons of the cultures studied and their own. The central purpose of the *Contextos* and *Perspectivas* sections at the end of each *Investigación* is to make comparisons between Hispanic cultures and their own. The *Contextos y perspectivas* section explores the *Investigación* topic in a Hispanic context through an examination of both the Hispanic perspective and the students' home culture perspective. In some *Investigaciones*, the order is reversed, with students focusing on themselves or their own culture in the *Contextos* activities and then examining that same issue from a Hispanic cultural perspective in the *Perspectivas* activities. The cultural comparisons that are the focus of the *Contextos y perspectivas* sections are further explored in the corresponding *Contextos y perspectivas* activities in the Activities Manual.

The topics explored in *Contextos y perspectivas* vary widely and are intended to spark student interest. In *Investigación* 1A, students are asked to explore the notion of personal space and greeting behaviors, first in Hispanic cultures and then in their home culture. Similarly, in *Investigación* 1B students are asked to compare the Mexican education system to that of their home country. In *Investigación* 2B, students are asked to compare the notion of *compadrazgo* with similar family and social network in their own culture. *Investigación* 3A asks students to compare Latin American geography with that of their native country. *Investigación* 4A asks students to compare Hispanic influences in U.S. culture and U.S. influences in Hispanic cultures. *Investigación* 6B asks students to explore issues relating to work-life balance, first on a personal level, and then among Hispanics in their community. *Investigaciones* 7A and 7B ask students to analyze and compare the work of U.S. artists such as Norman Rockwell and Edward Hopper with that of Hispanic artists such as Carmen Lomas Garza, Fernando Botero, and Pablo Picasso. *Investigación* 10B asks students to explore the ambiguous legacy of Che Guevara and then apply that to a more familiar figure in U.S. culture, Christopher Columbus. *Investigación* 11B asks students to compare the role/influence of technology in their own lives with how the role/influence of technology is viewed through the work of the Argentine cartoonist Maitena and then draw some conclusions about cross-cultural perspectives on the role/influence of technology in people's lives. *Investigación* 12B asks students to compare the level of contact they and four classmates have had with other cultures with the contact that five individuals born outside of the U.S. had with U.S. culture in their native countries and draw some general conclusions about the role of technology in fostering communication among individuals from different countries/cultures. From this partial list, it should be evident that fostering these types of cross-cultural comparisons is truly one of the guiding principles behind the *Textbook Name* program.

Communities: Participate in Multilingual Communities at Home and Around the World.

Standard 5.1

Standard 5.1 states that students should use the language both within and beyond the school setting. With regard to using the language within the school setting, many of the activities encourage students to use the language to communicate with classmates. On the one hand, there are numerous activities that require students to obtain and give information, principally the *Retrato de la clase* activities (e.g., IP.6, p. 8; 1A.12, p. 23; 1B.14, p. 45; 2A.3, p. 60; 2B.14–15, pp. 90–91; 3A.8, p. 113; 3B.19, p. 148; 4A.10, p. 163; 4B.21, p. 193; 5A.5, p. 206; 5B.12, p. 234; 6A.22, p. 268; 6B.15, p. 287; 7A.26, p. 321; 7B.14, p. 336; 8A.17–18, p. 363; 8B.3, p. 371; 9A.11–12,

p. 404; 9B.11, p. 420; 10A.15, p. 449; 10B.13, p. 469; 11A.9–12, pp. 490–1; 11B.11–12, p. 514; 12A.12, p.536; 12B.14, p. 561). On the other hand, there are numerous activities that require students to work with classmates to share opinions or carry out a particular task in Spanish. In terms of using the language beyond the school setting, there are several activities that encourage students to interview Spanish speakers or individuals from other countries to get information (e.g., 4B.15, p. 189; 5A.13, p. 210; 6A.16, p. 262, 6A.32, p. 298; 6B.32, p. 298; *En vivo*, p. 392; 12.32, p. 566). There are other cases where annotations in the Instructor's Edition provide suggestions for expanding/adapting an activity to include getting information from individuals in the wider community (e.g., pp. 42, 51, 219, 228, 268, 382, 421, 463).

Standard 5.2

Standard 5.2 states that students should show evidence of becoming life-long learners by using the language for personal enjoyment and enrichment. Personal enrichment is also a goal. Students are not only exposed to personal (e.g., family, favorite pastimes, classes) or concrete topics (e.g., foods, clothing, home, sports, holidays, transportation, technology), but they are also exposed to topics with which they may be less familiar or are more abstract (art, globalization, work-life balance, *la hispanidad*, and looking at history from different perspectives). This pushes students beyond exploring what they know to exploring more complex, less easily defined topics, thereby making them both more well-rounded and more culturally aware, which in turn makes them better prepared to live and work in an increasingly multicultural society and an increasingly interconnected world. Students are able to immediately apply the Spanish they are learning, thereby gaining confidence in their abilities to communicate and experience the satisfaction of being able to communicate, albeit at an elementary level, with Spanish speakers from across the Hispanic world.

Summary of Textbook as It Relates to FL Standards and Ready for the World Goals

The first-year Spanish program embraces the synergy between language and culture. Students understand other cultures by understanding how practices (linguistic, social, etc.) reflect culture and how culture influences practices. This has been achieved by carefully embedding and connecting language and cultural content throughout the material, from the sentences used to model grammatical concepts, to statements that are used for pronunciation, to activities in and out of class. More noticeably, cultural content is embedded in authentic and literary readings, in the explorations on the Internet, and ultimately in the experiential learning tasks that lead students to think critically about the origin of cultural practices as a way to understand their native culture, as well as other cultures (to encourage cross-cultural perspectives).

The goals of the first-year program include moving beyond superficial descriptions to explorations about how a diversity of variables influence and form cultures, such as social, geographical, creative and historical conditions, and how, taken as a whole, these influence one's perspectives about a native culture as well as other cultures. For example, students learn how what people wear can give insight into their culture; how something as benign as the design of the Spanish patio can reveal a great deal about family values; what art has in common across cultures and why; how the perception of historical figures/cultural heroes can change within and across cultures.

Appendix 6-D. The University of X First-Year Spanish Program

Conceptual Framework of the First-Year Spanish Program

Learner Outcomes for the First-Year Spanish Program

After successfully completing Spanish 111-112, 150, or 123, students will be able to manage successfully a number of uncomplicated communicative tasks in straightforward social situations and on specific topics.

You will be able to talk and write about:

- your weekly schedule
- activities and objects in the classroom
- places around the university
- professions and careers
- various activities and preferences regarding those activities (*me gusta . . .*)
- personality traits/characteristics
- family relationships
- what you do
- what someone else does
- a variety of foods
- various forms of entertainment
- what you wear and when
- likes and dislikes of others
- weather conditions
- clothing and accessories
- the scenery and figures in artwork
- the customs or traditions associated with holidays
- sports

In addition, you will be able to:

- express nationalities of Spanish-speaking countries
- express the location of Spanish-speaking countries and capitals
- express years in Spanish
- make and comprehend comparisons in Spanish
- express how you get somewhere
- avoid repetition when talking about something already mentioned

- interpret who does what for whom in a statement
- order food at a restaurant
- indicate your preferences with regard to food
- indicate what you have eaten for breakfast, where you have eaten, what you have or have never eaten
- express reasons for going somewhere
- talk about shopping for others
- express the names of holidays
- describe what is happening at a specific moment in the present
- describe persons, places, locations, objects, characteristics, and amounts, and contextualize these (when appropriate) in terms of times (days, hours, months, and times such as today and tomorrow), frequency of occurrence, order, and quality

The following learner outcomes are specifically related to narration in the past:

- recognize references to actions completed in the past
- recognize references to routine practices in the past
- recognize descriptions referring to the past
- recognize references to repeated actions in the past
- indicate references to past emotions
- recognize references to a sequence of actions in the past
- recognize references to what someone was doing in a work of art
- recognize references to what happened in a piece of art
- recognize references to actions that have occurred up to the present moment

Using authentic texts, you will be able to:

- fill out an order form for a magazine
- interpret an airplane ticket
- interpret ads for housing
- interpret some public signs in Spanish
- complete forms requesting personal data
- interpret a table of contents
- fill out a university schedule
- interpret online ads and forms related to studying abroad
- restate the main ideas in brief magazine articles
- interpret and create horoscopes
- interpret wedding invitations
- interpret maps reflecting climate patterns and physical typology
- create movie advertisements
- follow recipes
- read and write email messages
- interpret weather reports as reported in newspapers
- listen to and take telephone messages
- interpret art exhibition announcements

The following are learner outcomes related to cultural content for the Spanish 111–112, 150, or 123 courses.

You will be able to:

- recognize socially appropriate ways of greeting and addressing people in the Spanish-speaking world
- infer cross-cultural misunderstanding based on different social practices
- justify some social customs and cultural celebrations particular to Spanish-speaking cultures, such as *"el compadrazgo"* and *"la quinceañera"*
- compare characteristics of soap operas in Spanish-speaking and U.S. cultures
- compare the educational system in Mexico and the U.S.
- analyze the relationship between the Catholic Church, university education, and cultural practices in South America and make comparisons between the history and function of the Church across two cultures
- analyze the values behind social behaviors and how these can lead to cross-cultural misunderstandings within the education system (between non-English-speaking Hispanic students and their teachers)
- examine the diversity of ethnic and racial groups that form the Spanish-speaking world
- review the importance and influence of indigenous languages of South America
- examine how Spanish-speaking cultures influence U.S. society and how U.S. cultures influence Spanish-speaking countries
- understand how food products and practices are connected to cultures within and across languages
- justify the dining practices in two cultures (U.S. and Spain or Latin America) based on social and historical contexts
- infer how dining practices of two cultures can lead to cross-cultural misunderstandings
- analyze culture's influence to dictate what we wear
- recognize how some celebrations originated and analyze what they have in common across cultures
- analyze how a country's holidays and celebrations offer insight into its culture
- identify well-known Hispanic directors, artists, writers, and singers
- compare characteristics of Hispanic artists and U.S. artists
- predict how interpersonal relationships and behaviors in business practices reflect cultural values

Conceptual Framework of the Second-Year Spanish Program

The second-year Spanish program focuses on teaching students to interpret, express, and negotiate meaning in context. The textbook and the second-year program aim to develop students' linguistic fluency and accuracy while fostering their ability to function within Hispanic cultures. Communicative activities used to facilitate learning are based on authentic materials and cultural information. These activities are designed to either increase cultural awareness or help students personalize and relate the material to their own experiences and cultures, again encouraging cross-cultural perspectives. Topics addressed in the second-year textbook move beyond the here-and-now of students' daily lives to more abstract concepts and ideas, for example, multiculturalism, immigration, health, the environment, human rights, art, technology, and globalization.

Appendix 6-E. Summary of ePortfolio Tasks

Task Name	Goals	Task Summary	Potential Audience	MEDIA USED
Task # 1: *Estudiar en el extranjero*	Explore study abroad possibilities and empower students to set their own study abroad goals.	Propose a study abroad plan. What is involved? What is the where, how, and how much to study abroad?	Self and classmates	Internet search and Google Earth
Task # 2: *Paisajes Lingüísticos*	Encourage reflective learning and create awareness of local Hispanic community.	Explore local community to find Spanish language images. Is there a Spanish presence in your community, and what can you say about it?	Students in other Spanish classes	Camera
Task # 3: *Orientación para/de. . .*	Encourage self-expression in Spanish and experience collaborative learning and teamwork.	Create an orientation video on a topic of interest. Will your audience have a detailed idea of topic or content of orientation?	Students in other Spanish classes	Video camera with audio
Task # 4: *Festival de cine (useful vocabulary for film can be found in Investigación 4A)*	Create multicultural understanding via cinema. Publicize, inform about, and recommend Hispanic films.	Recommend Hispanic films (movie reviews). Which films are flops, and which are highly recommended?	Students in other Spanish classes	Movies in Spanish (on commercial sites, in the library, or streamed)

(*continued*)

Task Name	Goals	Task Summary	Potential Audience	MEDIA USED
Task # 5: *Mi galería de arte (useful vocabulary for film can be found in Investigaciones 7A and 7B)*	Create multicultural understanding via art. Illustrate ability to design and present in Spanish.	Design a personalized online gallery.	Self and classmates	Internet
Task # 6: *Mis preferencias de música hispana (useful vocabulary for music can be found in Investigación 4A)*	Create multicultural understanding via music. Explore variety of Hispanic music.	Showcase your preferences in Hispanic music.	Self and classmates	Internet and Pandora
Task # 7: *Anuncio de interés público*	Reflect on social or global issues and create public awareness of them (e.g., environment, education, family issues).	Develop a public service announcement to promote global awareness. What is your fundamental message to the world?	UT students	Video camera with audio
Task # 8: *Un documental de un día feriado /reflexiones culturales(useful vocabulary for holidays can be found in Investigación 9A)*	Explore Hispanic traditions and practices related to cultural celebrations.	Document a holiday or celebration celebrated by an Hispanic culture. How does this culture celebrate the holiday?	Students in other Spanish classes	Video camera with audio

Chapter 7

The Effects of Blended Learning on Second Language Fluency and Proficiency

Fernando Rubio

In foreign language classrooms, technology has allowed us to change the way we teach. By facilitating quick and easy access to target language communities, technology makes it possible for language professionals to move from a focus on language as a subject of study to a focus on its value as a tool for intercultural communication. The relative ubiquity of course management systems on campuses across the country and the improvements in textbook design, which increasingly include online components, enable a shift in the way we design language courses by allowing us to rely on technology to deliver some of the components that were traditionally part of the classroom. This is pushing many programs to re-evaluate their goals and the delivery system that will most effectively allow them to achieve those goals. Alongside this growth in the presence of technology in the language classroom, programs across the country have been under increased pressure to reduce per-student costs while maintaining the quality of instruction. Many administrations, based on the experience gained in other disciplines, encourage language departments to look at technology-enhanced courses as the logical way to address those pressures and become more fiscally efficient (Chenoweth, Ushida, & Murday, 2006; Scida & Saury, 2006). However, the relative paucity of studies that look at the effects of technology-enhanced courses on language proficiency and the somewhat inconclusive results that stem from the few studies that exist to date result in a certain degree of resistance on the part of some faculty who still believe that face-to-face (F2F) contact with students is a necessary ingredient for successful language acquisition. A common way to address this situation has been to redesign courses by reducing, without eliminating, F2F time to complement it with interactive online materials as well as student–instructor and student–student interaction in an online environment (Scida & Saury, 2006). This model that combines traditional F2F instruction with computer-mediated instruction has been termed *hybrid* or *blended* teaching and learning (BL). A widely accepted definition is the one presented in the introduction to this volume and proposed by Laster, Otte, Picciano, and Sorg (2005).

An additional justification for BL may come from Marc Prensky's 2001 article *Digital Natives, Digital Immigrants.* Prensky coined the term *digital natives* to refer to today's students, who have grown up with digital technology as an integral part of their lives. Using an analogy that resonates with language professionals, Prensky suggests that "our Digital Immigrant instructors, who speak an outdated language (that of the pre-digital age), are struggling to teach a population that speaks an entirely new language" (p. 2). However, to be fair, recent research shows that language students may not be as ready for online learning as we might think (e.g., Goertler, Bollen, & Gaff, 2012; Winke & Goertler, 2008). In any case, in an effort to address the changing landscape and remain fiscally efficient, many departments have decided to move some components of their language programs to the online or blended formats.

Following many of the same motivations already mentioned, the University of Utah decided to redesign its first-year Spanish program (Beginning Spanish I and II) in 2007 by converting some sections of the traditional F2F course to a blended model that reduced F2F time by 50 percent: from four hours per week to two hours. During the first two years, we progressively added blended sections and reduced the number of F2F options until we reached the current balance in which one-third of the sections are taught in the traditional model and two-thirds are blended. This chapter presents the results of a study comparing the proficiency and fluency gains of two groups of first-year Spanish students in our program. One of the groups completed two consecutive semesters of F2F classroom instruction in the traditional format, meeting four days a week. The second group enrolled in two consecutive semesters of beginning Spanish in a BL format that combines two F2F sessions per week with two "virtual days." The study measures speaking and writing proficiency levels according to the American Council on the Teaching of Foreign Languages (ACTFL) scale and provides a more fine-grained, quantitative analysis of a number of features typically associated with fluency.

Research on the Effects of Blended Teaching and Learning

A number of studies published since the beginning of the century have documented the impact of BL courses on a variety of outcomes, from student achievement and satisfaction to financial implications and student retention (Adair-Hauck, Willingham-McLain, & Youngs, 2000; Chenoweth et al., 2006; Kraemer, 2008; Sagarra & Zapata, 2008; Scida & Saury, 2006; Stracke, 2007; Young, 2008). Additionally, the National Center for Academic Transformation (NCAT) has published the results of eight projects that the Center sponsored between 1999 and 2010 to redesign Spanish beginning and intermediate courses to the blended model.[1] Both the published research and the NCAT reports detail a number of positive effects of the blended model. Often cited among the beneficial outcomes of the blended courses are improved completion and retention rates, better pedagogy, higher student satisfaction, and reduced costs, as well as practical advantages such as reduction in physical space demands, grading time, or preparation time needed. Additionally, the added flexibility of the blended courses makes it possible for more students to complete the lower-level language courses, which results in increased enrollments at the upper levels. However, most of the few empirical studies available

---

[1]Between 1999 and 2010, the NCAT received funding from the Pew Charitable Trust and the Fund for the Improvement of Postsecondary Education (FIPSE) to conduct three rounds of course redesigns in a variety of disciplines, eight of them in Spanish. Program descriptions, progress reports, and some final reports are available on the NCAT's website at http://www.thencat.org/PCR/Proj_Discipline_all.html.

to date that have looked at the effects of BL on students' second language (L2) proficiency show inconclusive or nonsignificant results (Adair-Hauck et al., 2000; Sanders, 2005; Young, 2008). These findings stand in stark contrast to a recent meta-analysis conducted by the U.S. Department of Education (U.S. Department of Education, 2010) that reviews research in a variety of disciplines published between 1996 and 2008. The report indicates that when comparing F2F, fully online, and BL modes of instruction, "Instruction combining online and face-to-face elements had a larger advantage relative to purely face-to-face instruction than did purely online instruction" (p. XV). Perhaps the lack of similarly conclusive evidence in the case of BL language courses results from the fact that most of these studies were done with beginning-level learners and measured the effects of the learning context after a short period of exposure (between one semester and one academic year). This temporal limitation, coupled with the fact that proficiency was measured using holistic assessments (Simulated Oral Proficiency Interview in Young's case; Oral Proficiency Interview and ACTFL's Writing Proficiency Test in Sanders' study; instructor-designed achievement tests in Adair-Hauck et al., 2000), may explain why it is difficult to find significant differences in overall proficiency or achievement between the traditional F2F and BL models: the assessment instruments are not subtle enough, and the time elapsed does not allow for significant differences to appear. In fact, when finer-grained and more easily quantifiable aspects of proficiency and fluency were taken into account in Young's study, they showed that "the language of the students in the redesigned course format with online activities demonstrated broader and more varied language use and completed more of the oral tasks than the students in the traditional instructional format" (p. 173).

Fluency and Proficiency

Fluency and proficiency are two aspects of learner language that have been shown to be sensitive to the learning context in which they develop (Brecht, Davidson, & Ginsberg, 1995; Freed, 1995; Freed, Segalowitz, & Dewey, 2004; Lafford, 1995; Segalowitz & Freed, 2004). The present study compares the effects of a BL and an F2F course on these two aspects of the L2.

In this study, we refer to oral and written proficiency as defined by the ACTFL Proficiency Guidelines—Speaking (Breiner-Sanders, Lowe, Miles, & Swender, 2000) and ACTFL Proficiency Guidelines—Writing (Breiner-Sanders, Swender, & Terry, 2002). The guidelines measure proficiency based on four criteria: accuracy, content/context, functions, and text type. We used the Proficiency Guidelines as a baseline indication of whether any significant overall proficiency differences between the two groups were evident after exposure to the two learning conditions. However, as stated above, two limitations inherent to the guidelines made it necessary to use additional quantitative measures. The holistic nature of the guidelines, which are based on broadly defined descriptors of proficiency, prevents them from picking up fine-grained differences between speakers at the same level. ACTFL, in fact, underscores the fact that different proficiency profiles are to be expected within the same proficiency level. Additionally, the fact that this study looks at proficiency after only two semesters of language study implies that the overall differences between students will be necessarily small. The application of a holistic form of assessment exclusively would therefore only provide statistically significant results in the case of considerably larger samples than the one used in this study. Therefore, for the study reported in this chapter, we decided to supplement standard measures of speaking and writing proficiency with a number of quantitative measures of fluency.

The concept of fluency has been the object of much discussion in the profession. The past four decades have seen repeated efforts to come up with coherent definitions of what it means to be fluent both in a first language (L1) and in a second language (L2) (see Fillmore, 1979, for a good description of the requirements that a fluent native speaker should meet). Early on, Möhle (1984) identified several aspects of speech that could show an empirical correlation with fluency: length, type and placement of pauses, length of pause-free runs, speech rate, and frequency of repetitions and retracings. Lennon (1990), now dealing with L2 speakers, distinguishes two main senses in which the term *fluency* can be used. The "broad" sense is a subjective term that is often equated with oral proficiency. It is in this sense that people are described as being "fluent" speakers of a language, roughly meaning that they approximate native-speaker norms. In its "narrow" sense, *fluency* is often used to refer to the speed of performance. In this sense, native speakers (and fluent L2 speakers) are able to produce speech that flows at a faster pace without excessive or unnecessary pauses, repetitions, self-corrections, and so on. This narrow sense is a common feature in oral exam rubrics in which instructors have to rate the learners' fluency together with their grammatical accuracy, vocabulary, and so on. The narrow definition is also implied in some standardized proficiency guidelines. For example, the ACTFL speaking guidelines state that learners at the novice high level, because they often rely on memorized chunks of language, "may sometimes appear surprisingly *fluent* and accurate" (emphasis added). Similarly, the Council of Europe (2011) in its Common European Framework of Reference (CEFR) states that a speaker at the C1 level "can express him/herself *fluently* and spontaneously without much obvious searching for expressions" (emphasis added). Although distinct, Lennon agrees that these two interpretations of fluency are related, the narrow sense being perhaps the most easily perceivable feature of the broad proficiency connotation. This connection is articulated in a later study (Lennon, 2000) in which he defines fluency as "the rapid, smooth, accurate, lucid, and efficient translation of thought or communicative intention into language under the temporal constraints of on-line processing" (p. 26).

The relationship between fluency and proficiency, both in speaking and in writing, has also received considerable attention. There is general agreement that growth in fluency parallels other aspects of L2 interlanguage development. Schmidt (1992) provides an excellent review of how different theories may explain the psychological mechanisms that promote increased fluency. An aspect of his conclusions that is crucial for our study—because we are concerned with lower-level L2 learners—is his argument that "fluency improvement is more easily observable in the early stages of L2 use, with a gradual slowing of improvement over time until asymptote is reached" (p. 376). What is less clear after a review of relevant literature is which features of fluency can be directly correlated to the development of proficiency. A number of studies have dealt with the relationship between quantifiable measures of fluency and native speaker judgments of fluency (Dubiner, Freed, & Segalowitz 2007; Freed, 2000; Kormos & Dénes, 2004; Lennon, 1990). In his seminal study of the linguistic gains of 10 advanced English as a foreign language learners after a six-month stay in Britain, Lennon (1990) found that "speech-pause relationships in performance and frequency of occurrence of *dysfluency markers* such as filled pauses and repetitions" (p. 388, emphasis in the original) correlated strongly with the subjective assessment of the learners' proficiency as determined by expert judges. Dubiner et al. (2007) studied native speakers' judgments of fluency based on samples of speech of two groups of L2 learners: students who had been abroad for a semester and a control group who had taken courses on campus. They found that when asked, their judges tended to define fluency in broad terms, typically mentioning grammatical accuracy as one of its features. However, when asked to judge the learners' levels of fluency, their judgments were "based on more narrow definitions of fluency, which included a set of circumscribed features such as the presence or lack of filled and silent pauses, and the rate and amount of speech" (p. 14).

Others (Iwashita, Brown, McNamara, & O'Hagan, 2008; Osborne, 2008) have tried to determine or compare the correlation between measures of fluency and standardized language proficiency ratings. Osborne studied the relationship between specific features of oral fluency and the ratings that learners received on the CEFR scale. He concludes that the relationship between quantitative fluency measures and proficiency scales is strongest when fluency is measured as a group of features, rather than as individual, independent features. Iwashita et al. (2008) studied the correlation of a set of oral features in the language produced by learners and the proficiency level that trained raters assigned to them. They found that certain vocabulary and fluency features showed the strongest correlation with proficiency levels.

Similar findings have been made in the case of writing that prove a significant correlation between various types of proficiency measures and features of developmental fluency and grammatical and lexical complexity. In a review of 39 studies conducted between 1974 and 1995, Wolfe-Quintero, Inagaki, & Kim (1998) found that the best measures of fluency were minimally terminal unit (T-unit) length, error-free T-unit length, and clause length. According to their findings, "these three measures consistently increased in a linear relationship to proficiency level across studies, regardless of task, target language, significance of the results, or how proficiency was defined" (p. 29).

What can be inferred from the above-mentioned studies is that a number of identifiable features of fluency in speech and writing correlate strongly with assessed levels of proficiency. Kormos and Dénes (2004) differentiate between what they term low-order features of fluency, mainly temporal measures, and high-order features such as accuracy and lexical diversity. For the purpose of this study and based on the results of the research mentioned above, we decided to look at what Kormos and Dénes would consider two low-order features of oral fluency: rate of speech measured in words per minute (WPM) and fluent runs. We also looked at two higher-order features that reflect complexity–lexical diversity and mean length of utterance (MLU)–and a third feature that indicates accuracy: the percentage of error-free clauses (EFCs) to the total number of clauses. In the case of writing fluency, we computed four measures. We counted the total number of words produced by the students as a baseline, low-order measure, and then three high-order ones: the length of minimally terminal units (T-unit), error-free T-unit length, and lexical diversity. Previous research demonstrates that these features show good correlations with proficiency and with one another and can provide a good picture of a learner's ability in the L2. More detailed description of these features is included in a later section.

Research Questions

This study seeks to answer the following questions:

1. Is there a significant difference in the level of proficiency achieved by students who learn the language in a traditional format compared with those enrolled in a blended course?
2. Is there a significant difference in the type of fluency developed by students who learn the language in a traditional format compared with those enrolled in a blended course?
3. Is there a significant correlation between overall oral and writing proficiency and certain features of fluency that are facilitated by each of the two teaching contexts?

One of the goals of this study is to give language program directors the necessary empirical data to make informed decisions as to the effects of BL courses on students' overall language proficiency. Therefore, the first research question attempts to test the validity of the conclusion drawn by a number of recent studies on BL language courses that there is no significant difference in students' achievement when compared with traditional courses. Regardless of the answer to the first question, the second and third questions seek to determine whether the differences or similarities between the two groups can be expressed in terms of fluency and whether those differences, if any, correlate with differences in proficiency.

Method

Contexts and Participants

The subjects in this study were 78 students enrolled in Beginning Spanish II, second semester in a two-semester sequence, at the University of Utah. All students had completed Beginning Spanish I the previous semester. To enroll in Spanish I, students have to come with no previous academic experience in the language. The control group was made up of two sections (a total of 37 students) who had completed the two semesters in a traditional F2F format in which they met four days a week for 50 minutes a day. The experimental group consisted of two sections (a total of 41 students) that had taken both semesters in a BL format. The latter group had two 50-minute sessions of contact time in the classroom plus two "virtual" days that included computer-mediated individual and collaborative work. Pretests given at the beginning of the first semester of study showed no significant differences between the groups in level of proficiency, average age, or gender. The format of the pretest is described in the *Procedure* section below.

Both models use the same textbook (Spaine Long, Carreira, Madrigal Velasco, & Swanson, 2010) and its associated online components. The syllabus, calendar, course requirements, and tests are also the same. Both teaching formats follow the communicative language teaching approach. The main difference lies in the type and amount of work that students have to do online and the focus of the F2F sessions. Some of the preliminary work necessary to prepare for communicative activities (form-focused practice, vocabulary presentations, visual and written input, and so on) is done by F2F students in class with direct instructor guidance. BL students, on the other hand, do most preparation work by interacting with the material and with classmates—synchronously and asynchronously—in the online environment. They interact with other classmates frequently in writing and respond to input (visual, aural, or written) by making frequent blog posts, mostly written but occasionally oral. They receive frequent written feedback both from the instructor and from classmates on their postings and written reactions. Although both course formats require students to do a certain amount of work outside of class, the message is stronger in the BL classes where, from the beginning (and in the syllabus), it is made very clear that classroom time will be spent almost exclusively on communicative practice with very limited time devoted to grammar explanations and reviews or presentation of new vocabulary.

The BL students in our study completed the two-course sequence under two different instructors, a graduate teaching assistant (GTA) and an adjunct instructor. Those in the F2F format had two different GTAs. Although the ideal situation would have involved the same instructor for all four classes to control for the potential effect of different teaching styles, this was not an option in our case. The instructor and the GTAs were all experienced and had taught the class before and all met weekly to review lesson plans, exams and quizzes, and so on. Class sizes ranged between 18 and 26 students. Although our initial intent was to try to maintain the groups intact, there was some degree of transfer between sections within each model. That is, some of the students who had taken the first semester of the BL course with the GTA changed to the section taught by the instructor in the spring and vice versa. The same thing happened in the F2F courses. However, as stated earlier, only those students who completed the two-course sequence under the same learning context were included in this study.

Procedure

Students were administered an oral and a writing test at the beginning and then at the end of their two-semester sequence. Both tests were administered electronically in one of the university's computer labs and were proctored by the instructors.

The oral exam was a computer-based assessment that was designed in house and had been used in our program for several years with minor modifications. It consists of nine prompts that range in difficulty from basic novice-level functions (introducing yourself or describing your room) to advanced-level past narration. For the lower-level questions, students have 15 seconds to think about their answers before the program starts recording and then one minute to complete their recording. The more advanced prompts allow 30 seconds of thinking time and 90 seconds to respond. The prompts are delivered in English both as audio recordings and as text. During the recording, the students can see the prompt text on the screen and an indication of how much recording time is left. They can stop the recording if they finish before the allotted time runs out, but they cannot pause while recording. When a question is complete, the program moves automatically to the next one.

When they completed the oral part, students then moved on to the writing test. This test is also part of the computerized assessment tool described above. Students had 30 minutes to complete three writing prompts. The first prompt, which elicits novice-level language, asks the students to provide basic information about themselves. In prompt 2, they describe why they think they are qualified to perform a certain job that they want to apply for. The third prompt assumes that the student got the job and completed it and elicits past narration by asking for a description of the experience. Again, all prompts are delivered in English. We chose these prompts following Wolfe-Quintero et al. (1998), who suggest that language development be measured "as it is manifest in written acts of communication, not form-focused exercises" (p. 1)

Both groups were given the computerized proficiency test as a pretest during the second week of their first semester of study and as a posttest during the last week of classes in their second semester. The pretest differed from the posttest in that it contained only oral and written prompts targeting the novice level with one prompt in each test targeting the intermediate level. The pretest was used also as a placement test to weed out any students whose level was advanced enough to go directly into the second-semester course: Beginning Spanish II. To determine proficiency levels, oral and written samples were double rated according to the ACTFL scale by a group of experienced instructors of Spanish who had received ACTFL training. None of the instructors were rating their own students. The interrater reliability for the raters was found to be kappa = 0.72 ($p < .001$), which is considered to be a substantial level of agreement. Samples in which the ratings differed were assigned a final rating by a certified ACTFL tester. Following the system used by Sanders (2005), we assigned a numerical value to each proficiency level as follows: 1 = novice low; 2 = novice mid; 3 = novice high; 4 = intermediate low; 5 = intermediate mid; and 6 = intermediate high. As expected, there were no proficiency scores higher than intermediate high.

For the fluency component of the analysis, we transcribed the students' answers to four of the oral questions: one at the novice level, two at the intermediate level, and one at the advanced level. The maximum combined recording time for the three questions was 5 minutes and 30 seconds per student, but not all students used the entire allotted time. The average recording time was 5 minutes and 22 seconds, so the total amount of audio transcribed was approximately seven hours. For the analysis of writing proficiency and fluency, we used the entire writing sample produced by the students. Both the written and oral parts of the test were segmented and transcribed following the system described below.

Data Transcription and Analysis

The transcription of the oral and written data was done by the author and a research assistant. Data were transcribed, segmented, coded, and annotated using the Codes for the Human Analysis of Transcripts (CHAT) and then analyzed using the tools available through the Computerized Language Analysis (CLAN) set of computer programs. CHAT and CLAN are components of the Child Language Data Exchange System (CHILDES) developed originally by MacWhinney and Snow. For a description of the CHILDES system and its application, see MacWhinney (2000). All of the tools referred to in this chapter are available for free at the CHILDES website at http://childes.psy.cmu.edu. These tools were originally designed to do research on first language acquisition, although a number of recent second language acquisition studies have used them (Marsden, Myles, Rule, & Mitchell, 2002; Myles, 2007, 2008). CHAT provides specific guidelines for coding features such as pauses (filled and unfilled, fluent and disfluent), repetitions, self-corrections, retracings, incomprehensible speech, neologisms, L1 items, and so on. In addition to the transcription codes already available in CHAT, the system also allows new codes developed by the researcher to deal with specific needs of a project.

After the transcription process is complete, the transcripts have to be run through CLAN for analysis. The first step is to run them through the CHECK program to make sure that the files meet all the requirements to be read by CLAN. After the files have been checked, CLAN can perform lexical, syntactic, morphological, discourse, and phonological analyses, among others. The following sections discuss and describe the specific features of fluency that we analyzed using CHAT and CLAN.

Measures of Oral Fluency

We analyzed the following dimensions of fluency in the oral data: rate of speech, fluent runs, MLU, EFCs, and lexical diversity.

Rate of speech, measured as WPM, has been used as a measure of fluency in a number of previous studies (Freed, 1995, 2000; Lennon, 1990). Included in the count for our study were all Spanish words and English proper nouns, but we excluded all repetitions, false starts, and incomprehensible words.

The coding of pauses in the transcripts was necessary to calculate fluent runs, defined as the number of words in the longest run of speech without a silent disfluent pause or filled pause (Freed et al., 2004). To that end, we distinguished between filled and unfilled pauses and between fluent and disfluent ones. Filled pauses include fillers (e.g., *uh, mmm*) and filler words or phrases both in English (e.g., *like, you know*) and in Spanish (*este, bueno*). Following MacWhinney (2000), we distinguished between fluent and disfluent pauses. Fluent pauses are the ones that occur naturally as determined by discourse rules or where commas would indicate them in writing. Drawing on work by Freed (1995), Riggenbach (1991), and Freed et al. (2004), a pause was considered fluent only if it occurred at the expected juncture and it lasted no more than 400 msec. Any other pauses were considered disfluent. In CHAT, pauses are marked with the # symbol. Longer pauses, depending on their length, are indicated as ## or ###;

incomplete utterances are followed by +. . . . Disfluent pauses are marked with #d and filled pauses with @fp. Pause phenomena have received a good degree of attention in the relevant literature and have frequently been associated with L1 and L2 fluency (Freed, 1995; Riggenbach, 1991). Below is a transcribed excerpt that shows different types of pauses in one of our speech samples (the code *STU identifies the speaker as a student and has to be entered at the beginning of each utterance).

*STU: durante la semana ahh@fp estudio mucho.

*STU: tengo ahh@fp tres clases ahhh@fp ##.

*STU: asisto #d.

*STU: tres clases.

*STU: y ahhh@fp ##.

*STU: voluntario +. . .

Mean length of utterance has been identified as one of the strongest indicators of language development. In L1, it has been found to be as good a predictor of language development as age and sometimes even better (Brown, 1973; Garton & Pratt, 1998). MLU or other similar measures such as mean length of T-unit have also been found to be good predictors of L2 development (Iwashita et al., 2008; Ortega, 2003; Wolfe-Quintero et al., 1998). In our corpora, MLU was calculated by counting the total number of morphemes per utterance. As in the calculation of speech rate, repetitions, false starts, and incomprehensible words were excluded.

To include a component of accuracy as part of the analysis, we decided to measure the ratio of EFCs to the total number of clauses produced, which has proved to be a valid measure in previous studies (e.g., Kanno, Hasegawa, Ikeda, & Ito, 2005; Llanes & Muñoz, 2009). Measuring EFCs obviously requires a working definition of what is going to be counted as an error. In our study, we included all morphosyntactic errors and lexical choice errors but did not count other errors related to style or register. Additionally, we did not distinguish between clauses that had one error and clauses that included several errors.

The last feature of oral fluency that we studied was lexical diversity. Lexical diversity has been shown to exhibit a positive correlation with overall writing and speaking proficiency (Malvern, Richards, Chipere, & Durán, 2004; Yu, 2009; Zareva, Schwanenflugel, & Nikolova, 2005). We used a measure of lexical diversity called D that was first described by Malvern and Richards (1997). The measure is roughly based on the ratio of different words to the total number of words. The main advantage of this measure as opposed to others previously used—namely TTR (type-to-token ratio)—is that D is independent of the sample size. This makes it more applicable to smaller samples of speech like the ones that we worked with in this study.

Measures of Writing Fluency

In the analysis of writing fluency, we used one low-order measure, total number of words, and three high-order features (T-units, error-free T-units, and lexical diversity).

The term *T-unit* was first coined and defined by Hunt (1965). A T-unit consists of a main clause and all its dependent clauses. In our study, we measured the average length of the T-unit as an indicator of complexity that parallels MLU in oral fluency. The length of T-units has been widely used in both first and L2 research as a reliable measure of syntactic development (Gaies, 1980). There is some degree of disagreement as to whether T-units are good indicators of overall language proficiency or fluency because they simply take one aspect of it into account, namely syntactic complexity. However, because our analysis looks at a variety of aspects of fluency in addition to syntactic complexity, we decided to keep T-units as part of the analysis.

The second measure was the number of error-free T-units produced by our subjects on the writing test. Error-free T-units have also been widely used in studies of fluency and proficiency and have been identified as a more reliable measure than length of T-units (Gaies, 1980; see Polio, 1997, for an excellent review). We applied the same system described in the oral fluency section to code errors, that is, a strong version of the definition of error that counts all instances of morphological, syntactic, and lexical choice mistakes. We did not count spelling errors (including diacritics) unless they involved grammatical markers. We did not count punctuation errors, either. As in the case of speaking, we did not discriminate between T-units with only one error and those with several.

Lexical diversity was measured following the procedure described in the previous section.

Results

Pretest Results

As mentioned earlier, the pretest was used as a way to eliminate from the first-semester course and hence from the study, any student whose proficiency score was higher than novice mid. As a result, those students who stayed in Beginning Spanish I, both F2F and BL, were all rated novice low or mid in the ACTFL scale. The mean for the oral proficiency test, measured according to the system employed by Sanders (2005), was 1.19 for the F2F group and 1.15 for the BL group. A *t*-test showed no significant difference between the two groups. On the writing test, the F2F group had a mean score of 1.24, and the BL group's mean was 1.22. Again, a *t*-test showed no significant difference between the two means. As the pretest results show, the mean scores for both groups placed them at the novice low level at the beginning of their first semester of study. Because of the limited language that students are able to produce at that level of proficiency, we decided not to analyze the pretests for fluency features.

Posttest Results

Proficiency

The two groups show highly significant ($p < .01$) proficiency gains between the pretest and the posttest, both in speaking and writing. However, as was the case on the pretest, there were still no significant differences between the groups at the time of the posttest (Table 7-1).

Oral Fluency

We analyzed the fluency features discussed earlier in an effort to determine whether they would allow us to identify more fine-grained differences between the groups. We first looked at the two features of oral fluency that we had classified as low order: rate of speech (WPM) and fluent runs. Table 7-2 shows the results of the analysis, which indicate no significant differences between the two groups on either variable.

However, the results were different when we analyzed the high-order features of fluency. There was a significant difference in terms of MLU, in which the F2F group outperformed students in the BL format. The BL group showed a significant advantage in the ratio of EFCs and in their degree of lexical diversity (D). Table 7-3 shows the results of the analysis for each of these variables.

Writing Fluency

Table 7-4 shows a comparison of the four measures of writing fluency that we examined. The statistical analysis indicates that only T-unit length showed a slightly significant difference between the groups ($p = .048$), with an advantage for the students in the BL format. The differences in total number of words, lexical diversity, and error-free T-units were not significant.

Table 7-1. Results of t-Test for Speaking and Writing Proficiency Posttest

	Group	n	Mean	SD	t	p
Oral	F2F	37	3.54	.96	−1.63	.108
	BL	41	3.88	.87		
Writing	F2F	37	3.19	.81	3.73	.710
	BL	41	3.12	.78		

BL, blended learning; F2F, face-to-face; SD, standard deviation.

Table 7-2. Comparison of Oral Fluency Measures: Fluent Runs and Rate of Speech (Words per Minute)

	Group	n	Mean	SD	t	p
Fluent runs	F2F	37	15.78	4.51	1.43	.158
	BL	41	14.34	4.41		
WPM	F2F	37	50.27	10.38	8.27	.411
	BL	41	47.85	14.86		

BL, blended learning; F2F, face-to-face; SD, standard deviation; WPM, words per minute.

Table 7-3. Comparison of Oral Fluency Measures: Mean Length
of Utterance, Error-Free Clauses, and Lexical Diversity

	Group	n	Mean	SD	t	p
MLU	F2F	37	5.54	1.63	3.36	.001
	BL	41	4.39	1.38		
Error-free clauses	F2F	37	.64	.071	−2.77	.007
	BL	41	.69	.102		
D	F2F	37	47.65	11.94	−2.838	.006
	BL	41	55.22	11.61		

BL, blended learning; D, degree of lexical diversity; F2F, face-to-face; SD, standard deviation;
MLU, mean length of utterance.

Table 7-4. Comparison of Writing Fluency Measures

	Group	n	Mean	SD	t	p
T-unit length	F2F	37	9.05	1.24	−2.009	.048
	BL	41	9.70	1.57		
Number of words	F2F	37	229.1	35.2	.584	.561
	BL	41	224	42.7		
D	F2F	37	67.4	17.7	−.382	.704
	BL	41	69	17.6		
Error-free T-units	F2F	37	10.7	1.85	−.618	.538
	BL	41	11	1.93		

BL, blended learning; D, degree of lexical diversity; F2F, face-to-face; SD, standard deviation.

Fluency–Proficiency Correlation: Oral

For the second part of the analysis, we wanted to measure the possible correlation
between overall level of proficiency of each group and the specific features of fluency under consideration in our study. Table 7-5 shows the result of the analysis
of the correlation between oral proficiency and oral fluency for the BL group. The
results indicate that overall proficiency correlates most strongly with a low-order
feature of fluency: the length of fluent runs. They also show that fluent runs is the
feature of fluency that shows the highest correlation with other fluency measures,
particularly WPM and MLU.

The results are similar in the case of the F2F group (Table 7-6). In this case,
fluent runs and lexical diversity (D) both correlate—although not as strongly—
with level of proficiency. Again, fluent runs appears to be the feature that most
clearly correlates with other aspects of fluency.

Table 7-5. Fluency–Proficiency Correlations in Speaking: Blended Learning Group

		Proficiency Level	WPM	MLU	D	Error-Free MLU	Fluent Runs
Proficiency level	Pearson correlation	1	.193	.230	.085	.229	.407†
	Significance (two-tailed)		.227	.149	.596	.150	.008
	n	41	41	41	41	41	41
WPM	Pearson correlation	.193	1	.803†	.317*	.237	.523†
	Significance (two-tailed)	.227		.000	.044	.136	.000
	n	41	41	41	41	41	41
MLU	Pearson correlation	.230	.803†	1	.439†	.115	.601†
	Significance (two-tailed)	.149	.000		.004	.473	.000
	n	41	41	41	41	41	41
D	Pearson correlation	.085	.317*	.439†	1	.048	.133
	Significance (two-tailed)	.596	.044	.004		.766	.409
	n	41	41	41	41	41	41
Error-free MLU	Pearson correlation	.229	.237	.115	.048	1	−.078
	Significance (two-tailed)	.150	.136	.473	.766		.629
	n	41	41	41	41	41	41
Fluent runs	Pearson correlation	.407†	.523†	.601†	.133	−.078	1
	Significance (two-tailed)	.008	.000	.000	.409	.629	
	n	41	41	41	41	41	41

*$p < .05$.
†$p < .01$.
D, degree of lexical diversity; F2F, face-to-face; WPM, words per minute.

Table 7-6. Fluency–Proficiency Correlations in Speaking: Face-to-Face Group

		Proficiency	WPM	MLU	D	Error-Free MLU	Fluent Runs
Proficiency. level	Pearson correlation	1	.084	.312	.415*	.155	.361*
	Significance (two-tailed)		.620	.060	.011	.360	.028
	n	37	37	37	37	37	37
WPM	Pearson correlation	.084	1	.687†	.263	.137	.547†
	Significance (two-tailed)	.620		.000	.115	.418	.000
	n	37	37	37	37	37	37
MLU	Pearson correlation	.312	.687†	1	.244	.050	.639†
	Significance (two-tailed)	.060	.000		.145	.767	.000
	n	37	37	37	37	37	37
D	Pearson correlation	.415*	.263	.244	1	.040	.372*
	significance (two-tailed)	.011	.115	.145		.816	.023
	n	37	37	37	37	37	37
Error-free MLU	Pearson correlation	.155	.137	.050	.040	1	.107
	significance (two-tailed)	.360	.418	.767	.816		.529
	n	37	37	37	37	37	37
Fluent runs	Pearson correlation	.361*	.547†	.639†	.372*	.107	1
	significance (two-tailed)	.028	.000	.000	.023	.529	
	n	37	37	37	37	37	37

*$p < .05$.
†$p < .01$.
D, degree of lexical diversity; F2F, face-to-face; WPM, words per minute.

Fluency–Proficiency Correlation: Writing

The picture that emerges from the written data is not as homogeneous. As Tables 7-7 and 7-8 show, proficiency level appears to correlate well in both groups with number of words produced (again, a low-order feature) and T-unit length. However, there are some clear differences between the groups, particularly the strong correlation that appears to be between number of words, T-unit length, and lexical diversity for the BL group.

Discussion

The results of the analysis clearly indicate that students in both learning contexts experienced significant gains in proficiency throughout the course of the year. Furthermore, the answer to our first research question is that based on the results

Table 7-7. Fluency–Proficiency Correlations in Writing Blended Learning Group

		Proficiency Level	No. of Words	T-unit Length	D	Error-Free T-unit
Proficiency level	Pearson correlation	1	.617[†]	.326[*]	.263	.173
	significance (two-tailed)		.000	.038	.097	.279
	n	41	41	41	41	41
No. of words	Pearson correlation	.617[†]	1	.588[†]	.388[*]	.289
	significance (two-tailed)	.000		.000	.012	.067
	n	41	41	41	41	41
T-unit length	Pearson correlation	.326[*]	.588[†]	1	.291	.236
	significance (two-tailed)	.038	.000		.065	.138
	n	41	41	41	41	41
D	Pearson correlation	.263	.388[*]	.291	1	.402[†]
	significance (two-tailed)	.097	.012	.065		.009
	n	41	41	41	41	41
Error-free T	Pearson correlation	.173	.289	.236	.402[†]	1
	significance (two-tailed)	.279	.067	.138	.009	
	n	41	41	41	41	41

[*]$p < .05$.
[†]$p < .01$.
D, degree of lexical diversity.

Table 7-8. Fluency–Proficiency Correlations in Writing: Face-to-Face Group

		Proficiency Level	No. of Words	T-unit Length	D	Error-Free T-unit
Proficiency level	Pearson correlation	1	.457[‡]	.469[‡]	.225	.202
	significance (two-tailed)		.004	.003	.181	.232
	n	37	37	37	37	37
No. of words	Pearson correlation	.457[‡]	1	.188	.226	.257
	Significance (two-tailed)	.004		.266	.178	.125
	n	37	37	37	37	37
T-unit length	Pearson correlation	.469[‡]	.188	1	.175	.206
	Significance (two-tailed)	.003	.266		.301	.221
	n	37	37	37	37	37
D	Pearson correlation	.225	.226	.175	1	.267
	Significance (two-tailed)	.181	.178	.301		.110
	n	37	37	37	37	37
Error-free T	Pearson correlation	.202	.257	.206	.267	1
	Significance (two-tailed)	.232	.125	.221	.110	
	n	37	37	37	37	37

*$p < .05$.
[‡]$p < .01$.
D, degree of lexical diversity.

of our study, exposure to a traditional F2F format or a BL format has no significant effect on the level of proficiency attained after two semesters of instruction. A variety of reasons could explain why eliminating F2F time from a traditional class has no detrimental effect on proficiency. The U.S. Department of Education's meta-analysis cited above (U.S. Department of Education, 2010) points out that increased gains in language proficiency are explained not by the presence or absence of technology itself but also by the positive effects that the integration of technology has in the course structure, particularly when the online component involves collaborative or instructor-directed work as opposed to individual work (p. XV). The lack of significant differences may be attributable to the fact that students self-select—they choose which version of the course they want to register for. There is a chance that more independent learners may gravitate toward the BL because they know they will be comfortable in that model, and less autonomous learners may prefer the F2F version. If that is the case, the possible effects of context may be confounded by the interaction with learner-specific characteristics and with input delivery.

The results of the fluency analysis do not provide a conclusive picture either, although the BL seems to come out ahead. Out of the nine features of fluency that we analyzed, the BL group had a significant advantage over the F2F in three; the opposite was true in only one case. The different results also show interesting parallels with the different characteristics of the two contexts. It is probably safe to assume that students in the F2F context had more opportunities for interactive oral communication with other students and with their instructor, which perhaps explains why they show an advantage in the level of syntactic complexity (measured by MLU) of their oral performance. In contrast, the nature of the BL course is such that students engage in more written interaction with peers and instructors, which may be the cause of the advantage they show in length of T-units, a measure of written syntactic complexity.

More interesting is the fact that BL students show more vocabulary complexity and better accuracy and syntactic complexity (ratio of EFCs) in speaking than their F2F counterparts. That is, even though high-order features are still too weak to play a role in the overall level of proficiency of either group (more on this later), the truth is that BL students show an advantage when it comes to high-order features of oral fluency. This perceived advantage may have something to do with the different types of input to which the two groups are exposed and how they interact with it. There is a chance that the higher amounts of written input and more individualized feedback that are common in the BL format, as well as the added responsibility placed on the student to actively engage with the input, may result in higher levels of attention and deeper processing. This would, in turn, result in increased chances of the input being turned into intake and entering the learner's developing system. To put it simply, BL courses require learners to be more active participants in the learning process, which seems to result in better acquisition. Of course, such a claim could be made only after studying the effects of a BL context over a longer period of time. As the results of our study show, one academic year does not seem to make any clearly significant differences.

The third part of our analysis looks at correlations between fluency and proficiency and among different features of fluency to answer our third research question, namely whether any correlations can be established between proficiency and different aspects of fluency and among fluency measures themselves. The data show that fluent runs are a good predictor of overall oral proficiency in both groups, with vocabulary diversity (D) also showing a significant correlation to proficiency for the F2F group. The fact that a low-order feature (fluent runs) may be the best predictor of oral proficiency is noteworthy and is consistent with findings of previous studies that show a strong correlation between fluent runs and other measures (e.g., Freed et al., 2004). It seems reasonable to think that, at low levels of proficiency, learners may not have the attentional resources needed to activate more complex cognitive processes that would allow them to exhibit more high-order features, and thus the length of speech without pauses becomes the most salient feature of their fluency as assessed by the raters. In fact, the data also show that fluent runs exhibit the strongest correlation with other features of fluency.

The writing data also provide a positive answer to our third research question because both groups show significant correlations between overall level of proficiency and two fluency features: total number of words and length of T-unit. In contrast to what happened in the oral task, now a high-order feature, T-unit length, is a strong predictor of proficiency. In fact, as discussed earlier, text type, a category under which we would place T-unit length, is one of the benchmarks used to distinguish different levels of proficiency in the ACTFL scale. According to the scale, whereas speakers at the novice level function at the word level, a trademark of the intermediate level is the ability to produce sentence-length text. There is, therefore, an expected correlation between proficiency and text type (in this case, T-unit length). This finding is consistent with the review of previous research conducted by Wolfe-Quintero and her colleagues (1998) and discussed earlier. As in the case of speaking, we believe that the nature of the task has something to do with the type of fluency features that are relevant. Writing allows the learner time to access their explicit knowledge, to plan and revise, and to engage in more complex cognitive processes, which probably explains why a high-order feature of fluency can now discriminate between different levels of L2 sophistication.

If, as the data imply, T-unit length is a crucial feature of writing proficiency, the results of our study would give an advantage to the BL context because this is one aspect of fluency in which BL students showed a significant advantage over their F2F counterparts.

A review of the results of the analysis reveals a surprising lack of correlation between accuracy measures and overall proficiency. Several studies have pointed out the advantages of accuracy measures (error-free T-unit length and EFCs) over temporal measures (T-unit length and MLU) as an indicator of development (Ishikawa, 1995; Larsen-Freeman, & Strom, 1977; Robb, Ross, & Shortreed, 1986). Therefore, it is worth discussing a possible explanation for why the opposite was true in our study. As explained earlier, we adopted a strong definition of error that excluded from the count of error-free T-units and clauses any instance that included any type of lexical and morphosyntactic error and most types of spelling errors. There was no differentiation between different levels of seriousness of the error or between clauses that included only one as opposed to several errors. At the lower end of proficiency errors are a frequent and natural occurrence and it is often the type rather than the frequency of errors that discriminate between different levels of development. As a consequence, the way we counted errors rendered accuracy an irrelevant factor. Future studies will have to take this limitation into account and devise a more accurate way to account for number as well as type of error.

Conclusions

Often, programs that have undergone redesigns to implement technology-enhanced courses cite purely practical reasons (e.g., cost and space savings, increased retention rates). When those are the main motivations, the "no significant difference"—the common thread that unites most research on BL to date—is seen as justification in and of itself but, as Twigg (2001) and later Young (2008) suggest, we are at a point where we need to move beyond being content with getting the job done.

Although the results of our study still show the two groups as being statistically indistinguishable when it comes to levels of proficiency, there are indications of significant differences when proficiency is not considered holistically but in a more componential and quantitative way that looks at specific aspects of fluency. As we indicated in our introduction, there is a chance that the very nature of the ACTFL proficiency guidelines prevents them from picking up differences that would otherwise be more prominent.[2] Future studies should consider using a componential analysis of fluency, rather than overall proficiency, as a measure of L2 development when comparing the effects of different learning contexts at the lower levels of proficiency. Additionally, more studies are needed that look at long-term effects of exposure to the BL context. All of the relevant research to date looks at the effects of BL after a maximum of one academic year. Most, if not all, currently existing blended programs cover one or two semesters only. As a result, students who are exposed to the BL format are typically also exposed to traditional F2F teaching during the course of their language learning experience, which makes it difficult to draw any long-term conclusions. If it is true that exposure to a BL model results in improved fluency at the lower levels of proficiency and, as Schmidt (1992) suggests, most fluency growth happens at that early stage, we could hypothesize that those early gains will have a beneficial effect on the ultimate level of proficiency achieved. With blended courses becoming more common for both pedagogical and practical reasons, there is a good chance that more programs will redesign longer course sequences, which will make it possible to study the effects of longer-term exposure to this learning context.

The present study focuses on a limited set of quantifiable measures of fluency and does not take into consideration other areas such pragmatic competence or nonverbal communication, in which participants in a F2F may potentially make greater gains than those in a BL context. In addition, a limitation of the design of this study is the impossibility of controlling for instructor effect. Although, ideally, all students would have been exposed to the same instructor, the context in which the study was conducted made it impossible. Again, with access to higher numbers of students enrolled in BL courses, some of these limitations should be addressed in future studies.

References

Adair-Hauck, B., Willingham-McLain, L., & Youngs, B. E. (2000). Evaluating the integration of technology and second language learning. *CALICO Journal, 17*, 269–306.

Breiner-Sanders, K., Lowe, P., Miles, J., & Swender, E. (2000). ACTFL proficiency guidelines: Speaking, revised 1999. *Foreign Language Annals, 33*, 13–18.

Breiner-Sanders, K., Swender, E., Terry, R. (2002). Preliminary proficiency guidelines—writing revised 2001. *Foreign Language Annals, 35*(1), 9–15.

Brecht, R., Davidson, D. E., & Ginsberg, R. B. (1995). Predictors of foreign language gain during study abroad. In B. F. Freed (Ed.), *Second language acquisition in a study abroad context* (pp. 37–66). Amsterdam: Benjamins.

Brown, R. (1973). *A first language*. London: Allen and Unwin.

---

[2]The ACTFL published a new revised version of its Proficiency Guidelines in 2012. The online version, available at http://actflproficiencyguidelines2012.org, includes annotated multimedia samples of performance for each level of proficiency.

Chenoweth, A. N., Ushida, E., & Murday, K. (2006). Student learning in hybrid French and Spanish courses: An overview of language online. *CALICO Journal, 24*(1), 115–145.

Council of Europe. (2011). *Common European framework of reference for languages: Learning, teaching, assessment.* Retrieved August 21, 2011, from http://www.coe.int/t/dg4/linguistic/CADRE_EN.asp.

Dubiner, D, Freed, B. F., & Segalowitz, N. (2007). Native speakers' perceptions of fluency acquired by study abroad students and their implications for the classroom at home. In Wilkinson, S. (Ed.) *Insights from study abroad for language programs* (pp. 2–21). Boston: Thomson Heinle.

Fillmore, C. J. (1979). On fluency. In Fillmore, C., Kempler, D. & Wang, W. S. Y. (Eds.), *Individual differences in language ability and language behavior* (pp. 85–101). New York: Academic.

Freed, B. F. (1995). What makes us think that students who study abroad become fluent? In B. F. Freed (Ed.), *Second language acquisition in a study abroad context* (pp. 123–148). Amsterdam: Benjamins.

Freed, B. F. (2000). Is fluency, like beauty, in the eyes (and ears) of the beholder? In H. Riggenbach (Ed.), *Perspectives on fluency* (pp. 243–65). Ann Arbor, MI: The University of Michigan Press.

Freed, B. F., Segalowitz, N., & Dewey, D. P. (2004). Context of learning and second language fluency in French: Comparing regular classroom study abroad, and intensive domestic immersion programs. *Studies in Second Language Acquisition, 26,* 275–301.

Gaies, S. J. (1980). T-unit analysis in second language research: Applications, problems and limitations. *TESOL Quarterly, 14*(1), 53–60.

Garton, A. F., & Pratt, C. (1998). *Learning to be literate* (2nd ed.). Oxford: Blackwell.

Goertler, S., Bollen, M., & Gaff, J. (2012). Students' readiness for and attitudes toward hybrid FL instruction. *CALICO Journal, 29*(2), 297–320.

Hunt, K. W. (1965). *Grammatical structures written at three grade levels.* Champaign, IL: National Council of Teachers of English.

Ishikawa, S. (1995). Objective measurement of low-proficiency ESL narrative writing. *Journal of Second Language Writing, 4,* 51–70.

Iwashita, N., Brown, N., McNamara, T., & O'Hagan, S. (2008). Assessed levels of second language speaking proficiency: How distinct? *Applied Linguistics, 29*(1), 24–49.

Kanno, K., Hasegawa, T., Ikeda, K., & Ito, Y. (2005). Linguistic profiles of heritage bilingual learners of Japanese. In Cohen, J., McAllister, K. T., Rolstad, K. & McSwan, J. (Eds.), *Proceedings of the 4th International Symposium on Bilingualism* (pp. 1139–1151). Somerville, MA: Cascadilla Press.

Kormos, J., & Dénes, M. (2004). Exploring measures and perceptions of fluency in the speech of second language learners. *System, 32,* 145–164.

Kraemer, A. N. (2008). *Engaging the foreign language learner: Using hybrid instruction to bridge the language-literature gap.* Unpublished Doctoral Dissertation, Michigan State University. Retrieved August 1, 2011, from http://ezproxy.lib.utah.edu/?http://search.proquest.com/docview/304576528?accountid=14677.

Lafford, B. (1995). Getting into, through, and out of a survival situation: A comparison of communicative strategies used by students studying Spanish abroad and "at home." In B. F. Freed (Ed.), *Second language acquisition in a study abroad context* (pp. 97–121). Amsterdam: Benjamins.

Larsen-Freeman, D., & Strom, V. (1977). The construction of a second language acquisition index of development. *Language Learning, 27,* 123–34.

Laster, S., Otte, G., Picciano, A. G., & Sorg, S. (2005, April). *Redefining blended learning.* Paper presented at the 2005 Sloan-C workshop on blended learning, Chicago.

Llanes, A., & Muñoz, C. (2009). A short stay abroad: Does it make a difference? *System, 37*(3), 353–365.

Lennon, P. (1990). Investigating fluency in EFL: A quantitative approach. *Language Learning, 40,* 387–417.

Lennon, P. (2000). The lexical element in spoken second language fluency. In H. Riggenbach (Ed.), *Perspectives on fluency* (pp. 25–42). Ann Arbor, MI: The University of Michigan Press.

MacWhinney, B. (2000). *The CHILDES project: Tools for analyzing talk.* (3rd ed., Vols. 1–2). Mahwah, NJ: Lawrence Erlbaum Associates.

Malvern, D., & Richards, B. (1997). A new measure of lexical diversity. In A. Ryan and A. Wray (Eds.), *Evolving models of language: Papers from the annual meeting of the British Association for Applied Linguistics held at the University of Wales* (pp. 58–71). Clevedon, UK: Multilingual Matters.

Malvern, D., Richards, B., Chipere N., & Durán P. (2004). *Lexical diversity and language development: Quantification and assessment.* New York: Palgrave Macmillan.

Marsden, E., Myles, F., Rule, S., & Mitchell, R. (2002). *Oral French interlanguage corpora: Tools for data management and analysis.* Southampton, England: University of Southampton, Center for Language in Education.

Möhle, D. (1984). A comparison of the second language speech production of different native speakers. In H. W. Dechert, D. Möhle, & M. Raupach (Eds.), *Second language introduction* (pp. 26–49). Tübingen, Germany: Narr.

Myles, F. (2007). Using electronic corpora in SLA research. In D. Ayoun (Ed.), *Handbook of French applied linguistics* (pp. 377–400). Amsterdam: John Benjamins.

Myles, F. (2008). Investigating learner language development with electronic longitudinal corpora: Theoretical and methodological issues. In L. Ortega & H. Byrnes (Eds.), *The longitudinal study of advanced L2 capacities* (pp. 58–72). Hillsdale, NJ: Lawrence Erlbaum.

Ortega, L. (2003). Syntactic complexity measures and their relationship to l2 proficiency: A research synthesis of college-level L2 writing. *Applied Linguistics, 24*(4), 492–518.

Osborne, J. (2008, July). *Oral learner corpora and assessment of speaking skills.* Paper presented at the 8th Teaching and Language Corpora Conference, ISLA Lisbon, Portugal.

Polio, C. G. (1997). Measures of linguistic accuracy in second language writing research. *Language Learning, 47*(1), 101–143.

Prensky, M. (2001). Digital natives, digital immigrants. *On the horizon, 9*(5), 1–6. Retrieved May 20, 2011, from http://www.marcprensky.com/writing/prensky%20-%20digital%20natives,%20digital%20immigrants%20-%20part1.pdf.

Riggenbach, H. (1991). Towards an understanding of fluency: A microanalysis of nonnative speaker conversations. *Discourse Processes, 14,* 423–441.

Robb, S., Ross, T., & Shortreed, I. (1986). Salience of feedback on error and its effect on ESL writing quality. *TESOL Quarterly, 20,* 83–96.

Sagarra, N., & Zapata, G. C. (2008). Blending classroom instruction with online homework: A study of student perceptions of computer-assisted L2 learning. *ReCALL, 2008, 20*(2), 208–224.

Sanders, R. (2005). Redesigning introductory Spanish: Increased enrollment, online management, cost reduction and effects on student learning. *Foreign Language Annals, 38,* 523–532.

Schmidt, R. (1992). Psychological mechanisms underlying second language fluency. *Studies in Second Language Acquisition, 14,* 357–385.

Scida, E., & Saury, R. (2006). Hybrid courses and their impact on student and classroom performance: A case study at the University of Virginia. *CALICO Journal, 23*(3), 517–531.

Segalowitz, N., & Freed, B. F. (2004). Context, contact and cognition in oral fluency acquisition: Learning Spanish in at home and study abroad contexts. *Studies in Second Language Acquisition, 26,* 173–199.

Spaine Long, S., Carreira, M., Madrigal Velasco, S., & Swanson, K. (2010). *Nexos* (2nd ed.). Boston: Heinle.

Stracke, E. (2007). A road to understanding: A qualitative study into why learners drop out of a blended language learning (BLL) environment. *ReCALL, 19*(1), 57–78.

Twigg, C. A. (2001). *Innovations in online learning: Moving beyond no significant difference.* New York: Center for Academic Transformation at Rensselaer Polytechnic Institute. Retrieved June 27, 2011, from http://www.thencat.org/Monographs/Mono4.pdf.

U.S. Department of Education, Office of Planning, Evaluation, and Policy Development (2010). *Evaluation of evidence-based practices in online learning: A meta-analysis and review of online learning studies.* Washington, D.C: Author.

Winke, P., & Goertler, S. (2008). Did we forget someone? Students' computer access and literacy for CALL. *CALICO Journal, 25*(3), 482–509.

Wolfe-Quintero, K., Inagaki, S., & Kim, H. (1998). *Second language development in writing: Measures of fluency, accuracy, and complexity.* Honolulu: University of Hawai'i Press.

Young, D. J. (2008). An empirical investigation of the effects of blended learning on student outcomes in a redesigned intensive Spanish course. *CALICO Journal, 26*(1), 160–181.

Yu, G. (2009). Lexical diversity in writing and speaking task performances. *Applied Linguistics, 31*(2), 236–259.

Zareva, A., Schwanenflugel, P., & Nikolova. Y. (2005). Relationship between lexical competence and language proficiency–variable sensitivity. *Studies in Second Language Acquisition, 27,* 567–595.

Chapter 8

Complementary Functions of Face-to-Face and Online Oral Achievement Tests in a Hybrid Learning Program

Susanne Rott

The recent evolution in audio-based social networking technologies has provided many opportunities for language learners to improve their speaking abilities. A multitude of easy-to-use online voice recording tools allows students to share their research, ideas, opinions, and other types of narratives either asynchronously (e.g., podcasts, voiceblogs) or synchronously (e.g., chat tools). Although many of these tools are integrated into the publishers' websites accompanying textbooks and classroom management systems, they can also be found as shareware on the Internet.

Consequently, speaking prompts can extend the content discussed during class time and complement the use of discourse functions of face-to-face (F2F) class interactions. Partner, group, or whole-class assignments can emulate real-life F2F interactions and, to that extent, constitute meaningful exchanges among students (Abrams, 2011). The advantages for language development are many. The additional time needed to interact synchronously during which learners need to access and retrieve vocabulary and grammar on the fly may further the development of oral fluency (e.g., Hewett, 2000; Sun, 2009). Moreover, asynchronous assignments allow students to plan their output, pushing them to use the target language at the sentence and discourse levels. These assignments thus provide a practice opportunity that is often not available during class time for all students. Likewise, the option to re-record a response encourages students to monitor their language use (e.g., Sun, 2009) as well as their knowledge of the content. As a result, students are more likely to notice their knowledge gaps. They can then fill these gaps by looking up information in the course materials, dictionary, or a grammar reference guide. Additionally, if online assignments provide examples as speaking prompts, they have the potential to increase students' awareness of the sociopragmatic aspects of speech acts and the genre-specific uses of lexico-grammatical phrases (Sykes, 2005).

A natural extension of such online homework assignments is online oral tests. Students generally perceive homework and in-class activities as important if the relationship between these activities and what is being tested is apparent to them. This positive link has generally been described as a beneficial washback effect for learning (Shohamy, Reves, & Bejarano, 1986). That is, learners recognize the relevance of their oral homework to their ability to perform well on exams. In addition, technology can simplify the administration and grading of tests. The class can meet in a computer lab and take about 10 minutes to complete the recording of a three- to five-minute oral test. Thus, students' performance is not ephemeral, as is the case in F2F oral exams when the instructor needs to assess multiple students at the same time (e.g., role-plays) or when the teacher is the interviewer and evaluator at the same time (e.g., one-on-one interview).[1] The simplicity of conducting online oral exams may allow for the administration of multiple oral assessments during a single semester. As a result, online oral exams may result in a "more well-rounded and accurate picture of student abilities than a single oral interview" (Dykstra-Pruim, 1997, p. 16).

Most of the test banks accompanying textbooks, as well as the pedagogical literature (e.g., Bachman & Palmer, 1996; Dykstra-Pruim, 1997), provide a variety of example materials for oral achievement tests. These range from narratives and teacher–student and student–student interviews to role-play situations. And yet, these pedagogical resources tell little about which aspects of oral language abilities can be elicited from a specific test format or individual tasks. Obviously, one criterion for a successful oral test is whether the learner has accomplished the task (e.g., ordering a meal, describing a trip). At the same time, however, each test format or task requires a number of competencies that may vary from task to task. For example, although a narrative requires a genre-specific discourse structure and the use of cohesiveness markers (i.e., discourse competence), role-plays and interviews require context-specific turn-taking behaviors and possibly repair strategies (i.e., pragmatic and interactional competencies). Additionally, each task requires specific linguistic tools to accomplish the task (e.g., to convince, explain, or describe). That is, learners need to demonstrate grammatical competence by choosing and producing the grammatical structures that best encode their ideas and the conventionalized phrases that most clearly express their intended meaning (lexical competence).

Research on oral language assessment has mostly focused on the validity and reliability of standardized proficiency tests (e.g., Kenyon & Tschirner, 2000) or learners' language development across proficiency levels (e.g., Martinsen, Baker, Bown, & Johnson, 2011). Conversely, research on task-based language assessment has explored the question of whether examinees can accomplish a given task (e.g., Norris, Brown, Hudson, & Yoshioka, 1998) and how the manipulation of task characteristics affects the complexity and accuracy of student production (e.g., Gilabert, 2007b; Robinson, 2001).

In the past 30 years, many aspects of oral tasks and exams have been researched to explain variability in student performance. Yet no generalizable findings that can be applied to a wide variety of teaching and testing settings have emerged. Robinson (e.g., 2001) and Skehan (e.g., 1998) have attempted to establish a framework that predicts the effect of task complexity on fluency and accuracy. Although Skehan assumes that complexity and accuracy of language use are in competition because attentional resources are limited, Robinson argues that

---

[1]It is certainly possible to record one-on-one exams. However, it is a very time-consuming process to first conduct the exam and then listen to the recording to evaluate it. Moreover, it is possible to record role-plays. Yet it is challenging to recognize individual voices of students throughout a recording in order to assign a grade.

increasing cognitive demands may improve accuracy and complexity simultane-
ously. He suggests that tasks can be set up in a way that completion does not draw
on the same cognitive resources. Although empirical findings have been mixed for
both positions (e.g., Gilabert, 2007a; Mehnert, 1998; Yuan & Ellis, 2003), studies
have been able to show that planning time, for example, can be a mitigating factor.
Mehnert found that students who had planning time before engaging in a speaking task performed better than students with no planning time. Moreover, whereas
learners who had one minute to prepare focused more on accuracy, learners
who had 10 minutes tried to produce more complex speech. Likewise, Yuan and
Ellis showed that pre-task planning time promoted higher complexity and
lexical variety but not necessarily accuracy. However, when learners had unlim-
ited time for speaking, they performed less fluently yet more accurately because
they engaged in reformulation and self-correction. Addressing the correct use of
collocations during exam tasks, Wang and Shih (2011) found that students'
language for thinking, as they work on a task, affects collocational language use.
Test takers who reported that they thought in both the first language (L1) and
the second language (L2) produced more accurate collocations than learners who
reported that they were thinking either in the L1 or the L2.

Many studies have explored the social dynamics in interview and paired tests
and group-based tests. Brooks (2009) summarizes research findings emphasizing
what Lazaraton (1996) calls a wild-card effect. Performances among multiple test
takers are intricately linked and therefore can vary tremendously. Outlining effects of extraversion, personality, and gender, among other variables, Nakatsuhara
(2011) questioned how scores can be assigned for individual performances. Likewise, issues of authority and dominance affect student performance during paired
tasks and, in particular, teacher–student interviews. Brooks pointed out that student performance depends on whether the examiners simplify their language or
use display questions in order to accommodate students. In fact, based on the
discourse analysis of two different tester–student interactions, Brown (2003)
suggested that a student's performance strongly depends on the examiner's goal
orientation and the way of asking questions, as well as the type of interactional
feedback a learner receives.

Other studies have examined how a conversation task triggers negotiation
moves. Nakahama, Tyler, and Van Lier (2001), for example, found that information gap activities resulted in more negotiation of meaning than conversational
situations in which learners interacted with native speakers. Interestingly, they
also observed that in the conversational situation, learners paid more attention to
the entire discourse, but in the information gap activity, they attended mostly to
individual lexical items.

Few studies have directly compared the use of F2F and different modalities
of computer-mediated communication tools. Comparing negotiation patterns
of a jigsaw task through video-conferencing, audio-conferencing, or F2F chats,
Yanguas (2010) revealed that the group using audio-conferencing engaged in the
most negotiation moves. Yanguas suggested that this was because of the lack of
visual information. Further investigating the acquisition of speech acts, Sykes
(2005) compared the effectiveness of group discussions in written and oral chat as

well as in a F2F format. She discovered that the written and oral chat resulted in better learning than the F2F format. Moreover, the two online modalities demonstrated differences in interaction strategies. Although the written chat led to more complex interactions, the oral chat produced more diverse strategies for managing interactions.

Recent research has attended to various aspects of oral tasks. Yet there has been very little analysis of how different test tasks and formats are complementary in terms of the skills they elicit. One of the challenges facing practitioners who are interested in integrating multiple oral assessments into their language curriculum is determining which oral language competencies are elicited by a specific assessment task and, conversely, which tasks should be used to test the wide spectrum of oral competencies. That is, which oral assessment tasks would complement each other by eliciting the use of different strategies by the test taker? In particular, it is of interest to curriculum designers to better understand which test format lends itself best to assess a certain competence. The current investigation sought to compare students' performances on oral tests to determine whether a particular assessment task provided a good snapshot of their language abilities. Moreover, to align instruction and assessment, oral tests should be an integral part of the language curriculum. Accordingly, in a hybrid language program, the integration of oral assessments would mean the use of both F2F and online oral tests. Therefore, this study sought to shed light on the role of online oral tests compared with F2F tests. The three oral tests compared were a monologue narrative performed online, a role-play among three students who performed F2F, and a teacher–student F2F interview.

Research Questions

1. Do assessment tasks (monologue, interview, and role-play) elicit different aspects of oral competence in students' performance?
2. If the tasks elicit different aspects of oral competence, can the tasks be considered complementary?
3. Is there a relationship between the test task and students' perception of their ability to demonstrate their speaking abilities?

Method

Participants

Forty-five learners of German participated in this investigation. Students were enrolled in the third-semester course of the basic language sequence because they either had earned a passing grade in the previous two semesters or had placed into the course by taking a placement test. The basic language courses are delivered in a blended learning (BL) format. Students meet F2F in class three days each week. They also complete online learning materials outside of class in place of a fourth F2F class session. Online materials engage learners either in input-based preparatory work (e.g., learning vocabulary and its pronunciation as well as reading texts with the support of audio, cultural information, and an online dictionary) or in communication-focused output tasks. The latter tasks expand on the content covered in class mostly at the sentence level to written and oral language use at the discourse level (e.g., written blogs, oral voice blogs).

Procedure

Students were assigned to three treatment conditions. Two of the conditions took place F2F: one-on-one oral interviews and small-group role-plays. The third condition, monologue, took place in the computer lab, where students recorded their responses with an online recording tool. Students from three sections of third-semester classes participated in the study. Each condition presented an intact class. Random assignment of students from each class to the different treatment conditions was not possible. The three classes took place at different times during the day, and logistically it was not possible to administer the three different types of exams within one class section. In each treatment condition, students received the speaking prompt (see below) and had about two minutes to think about the topic and take some notes on the sheet with the prompt. They were not allowed to write complete sentences or read from their notes while they engaged in the oral exam. Notes were collected after the exam to verify that the participants had complied with the instruction to not write complete sentences. The instructor monitored students and intervened if students read from their notes as they were speaking during the exam. After completing the test, the participants were asked to complete a questionnaire about their learning and motivational background as well as their perception of the types of oral exams. For all three conditions, the data collection took place during a single 50-minute regular class session.

Materials

The oral achievement exam was based on a textbook chapter (Augustyn & Euba, 2008) that covered visiting the German city of Leipzig. Participants were asked to respond to the following prompt:

> During Spring Break you are going to visit the city of Leipzig with your classmates. You are going to fly from Chicago to Berlin and then take the train from Berlin to Leipzig. Plan your stay in Leipzig. You may want to address the following topics: How long do you want to stay in Leipzig; how to get from the train station to the hotel; what do you want to visit in Leipzig and why; where are you planning to eat; and whether you would like to visit the book fair. (translated from German)

Students were not limited to these questions. Rather, the questions served as a prompt reminding students of what they had discussed and learned in class. At the same time, the questions served as a guide for what was expected of them. All students were familiar with all three test tasks in their respective format (interview and role-play in the F2F and monologue in the online format) because they had been used as achievement tests in previous chapters and semesters. Privacy settings were available only for podcasting in the password-protected classroom management system. Therefore, the monologue task was chosen for the online format. For any of the software that allows recording synchronous interactions, a privacy setting was not an option. Consequently, all students had access to each other's exam recordings.

Test Tasks

Students were informed about the format of the oral exam in which they would participate (interview, role-play, or monologue) one week in advance of the study. Likewise, they received information about the general topic (the city of Leipzig), the length of the oral exam (see below), and the grading criteria. Grading criteria were the following: content/task completion (35%), appropriate use of vocabulary (20%) and grammar (15%), pronunciation (15%), and fluency (15%). Additionally, the researcher visited the three classes, informed the instructor and the students that the exam was used for a research study, and asked the students for their consent of participation. The researcher emphasized that the format of the exam would not deviate from the format of previous exams.

One-on-One Oral Interview. The course instructor met with each participant individually F2F for about three to five minutes. The role of the instructor was to listen to each student's report, ask questions if he did not comprehend what the student was saying, and function as an interlocutor. He encouraged students to continue their explanations by stating something to the effect that the plan sounds interesting and whether there would be any other items on the itinerary. The entire interaction was recorded with a digital voice recorder.

All instructors in the program received training on how to administer oral interviews. Emphasis is placed on the procedure, including how to make students feel comfortable (warm-up), how to encourage students to provide more details if the speech sample is too short to evaluate, how to request clarification if students' production is unclear, and how to finish the interview (wind-down).

Role-play. Three students were randomly assigned to each group to discuss their trip to Leipzig F2F. In the two-minute preparation and note-taking phase, students worked as a group. During the exam, the instructor did not intervene in the dialogue among the students. He observed students' interactions and took notes to assign a grade later. Only in two instances when a student did not participate sufficiently to award a grade, the instructor asked follow-up questions. The role-plays took about three to five minutes and were recorded with a digital voice recorder. When the group of students entered the classroom, the instructor made them feel comfortable by asking them, in German, how they were doing and talking about the weather (warm-up).

Monologue. Students were sitting at individual computer stations recording their monologues with an online voice recorder integrated into the classroom management system. Students were told that the monologue should be about three minutes long and that the maximum recording time was five minutes. The recordings were completed with a microphone that was attached to a headset. The use of the headset prevented students from overhearing what other students were recording. Before the recording of the exam monologue, students were required to complete a 10-second test recording to ensure that their microphone and recording devices were working.

Questionnaire. The purpose of the questionnaire was to determine the participants' attitudinal reactions to the test format and test tasks. The questionnaire was adapted from Kenyon and Malabonga (2001). The questionnaire sought to shed light on whether students had a preference for one of the formats and whether they perceived one test format as a better measure of their ability. Students were asked to respond to the following three statements on a four-point scale: (a) I feel I had the opportunity to adequately demonstrate both my strengths and my weaknesses in speaking on the test; (b) I feel the test was difficult; and (c) I feel someone listening to my test responses would get an accurate picture of my current ability to speak in real-life situations outside the classroom.

Analysis

The recordings of all three treatment conditions were transcribed by research assistants. Transcriptions included false starts, repetitions, hesitations, and self-corrections. The recordings were analyzed for the following aspects:

Communication

C-units. Following Abrams (2003), C-units were used as the unit of analysis comparing the amount of content that learners produced in each condition. C-units are "isolated phrases not [necessarily] accompanied by a verb, but they have a communicative value" (Crookes, 1990, p. 184). For example, in the following interactional exchange, the question and the response are counted as a c-unit: "Q: Where is my hat? A: On the table" (Crookes, 1990, p. 184). C-units were used because they capture phrases not accompanied by a verb, which is a natural phenomenon in oral interaction. The commonly used utterance as a unit of analysis for spoken discourse was not adopted for the study because the analysis relies on intonation contour and pauses. Participants in the study were intermediate learners who cannot be assumed to have full control over intonation contours. The transcriptions were coded by two research assistants and the researcher. Interrater reliability reached 94.3 percent. Discrepancies were resolved by the principal investigator. Discrepancies mostly occurred with single-word responses in the role-play and the interview condition. Single-word responses referring to time, such as *afternoon* (*Nachmittag*) or *Monday* (*Montag*), counted as c-units even if the preposition was missing. In turn, single-word contributions, such as *opera* (*Oper*), were not counted as a c-unit because they did not specify whether the speaker suggested to visit the building, watch a performance, or walk by the opera building.

Number of Words Produced. The number of words produced by each student provided an additional measure to determine the size of the language sample obtained. The count included false starts, reformulations, self-corrections, and repetitions.

Interactional Competence.

Editing Features. Editing features, such as self-corrections, false starts, and reformulations, generally demonstrate that learners monitor their output. The use of editing features was considered an indicator of the students' concern about being understood and getting their meaning across clearly. Therefore, only linguistic edits (vocabulary and grammar) were counted. For example, self-corrections happened when learners corrected verb endings; false starts happened mostly when learners changed verbs (*Dann stehen wir drei . . . dann bleiben wir drei Tage in Leipzig; Then we stand three . . . then we stay for three days in Leipzig*); reformulations mostly happened when participants attempted to improve their pronunciation. For the analysis, no strict distinction between the three editing features needed to be made. Each attempt to use any of these three features counted as one point even if the editing did not result in a more comprehensible utterance. The attempt to edit one's output is obviously higher on the interactional competence continuum (no attempt to a successful attempt) than no attempt at all.

Negotiation of Meaning. Any clarification request or comprehension check initiated by a learner was awarded one point. Negotiation moves were initiated when miscomprehension occurred because of lexical, grammatical, or pronunciation issues. This comparison was conducted only between the role-play and the interview conditions. The online monologue condition did not require the use of this aspect of interactional competence.

Questions

Content questions asked in order to solicit further information or an opinion from interlocutors were awarded one point. Again, this comparison was conducted only between the role-play and the interview conditions. The online monologue condition did not require the use of this aspect of interactional competence.

Discourse Competence

Word-to-Clause Ratio. Discourse competence describes learners' ability to speak at the sentence and multi-sentence level as compared with the multi-word level. A higher level of discourse competence indicates that learners support and provide details for their statements. This aspect of discourse competence was calculated by the ratio of words per total number of clauses (main and subclauses combined).

Discourse Markers. Participants' use of discourse markers was used as a measure of discourse competence. Discourse markers included but were not limited to adding (e.g., and, besides, in addition), structuring (e.g., first of all, finally, then), and logical consequence (e.g., as a result, consequently, then) markers. The use of discourse markers demonstrated that participants were able to produce cohesive discourse at the multi-sentence level. Participants earned one point for each attempt to use any discourse marker. Instances of partial or incorrect use of discourse markers were also awarded one point because it indicated the emerging development of discourse competence.[2]

---

[2]No explicit difference was made between correct use and emergence of discourse markers.

Lexical Competence

Collocations. Participants' data were analyzed for the correct use of conventionalized multi-word chunks. The use of collocations is considered an important factor in one's ability to express ideas concisely as well as an indicator of the development of advanced language abilities (e.g., Schmitt & Carter, 2004; Wray, 2001). The use of native-like (Pawley & Syder, 1983) expressions demonstrated that students did not need to use L1 transfer as a crutch to express their ideas. Noun–verb combinations, such as *stay in a hotel* (*im Hotel übernachten* compared with **im Hotel stehen*, which translates as *stand in a hotel*), or expressions, such as *I go to Leipzig* (*ich fahre nach Leipzig* compared with **ich gehe nach Leipig*," which translates as *I walk to Leipzig*) were counted as multi-word chunks. The transcripts were coded by two research assistants and the principal investigator. Interrater reliability was 92 percent.

Lexical Richness. Lexical richness is an indicator of learners' breadth of the lexicon. It was measured by means of Giraud's Index (Vermeer, 2000), according to which the total number of word types is divided by the square root of the total number of word tokens. The square root is included to eliminate the effect of differences in text length.

Grammatical Competence

Syntactic Complexity. Syntactic complexity was calculated in order to determine which task pushed learners to produce more complex language as a measure of grammatical competence. Complex language use is generally marked by using subordinate clause structures. Therefore, complexity was measured by determining each learner's subordinate-to-clause ratio. Following previous studies (e.g., Foster & Skehan, 1996; Michel, Kuiken, & Vedder, 2007; VanDaele et al., 2006), complexity was computed by dividing the total number of subordinate clauses by the total number of clauses. Previous research has shown that students produced syntactically simpler structures in dialogues than in monologues (Michel et al., 2007).

Results

The first research question sought to determine whether different types of oral assessment tasks elicit similar or different oral competencies. Table 8-1 presents descriptive statistics from the three treatment conditions tasks—monologue, interview, and role-play—for all aspects of the production data that were compared. For all comparisons, one-way ANOVAs (analyses of variance) were conducted. Post hoc contrasts between the three different treatment conditions were submitted to Tukey's HSD (honestly significant difference) test because the three sample sizes were equal and homogeneity of variance was met.

Communication

The first objective of the study was to determine whether the three treatment tasks led to the same amount of information exchange and whether the tasks produced the same amount of language from each participant. Although the

Table 8-1. Descriptive Statistics (Means and Standard Deviations) of All
Measures for All Three Conditions

Measure	Interview ($n = 15$)	Role-Play ($n = 15$)	Monologue ($n = 15$)	Results
Communication				
content units	32.00 (13.40)	24.40 (11.61)	29.60 (17.04)	NS
Number of words	178.00 (43.80)	138.13 (41.68)	203.60 (58.41)	Monologue > role-play Interview > role-play
Interactional competence				
Editing features	0	0	0.44 (0.73)	
Negotiation of meaning	0.20 (0.41)	0.40 (0.63)	0	NS
Questions	0.87 (0.91)	3.4 (2.41)	0	Role-play > interview
Discourse competence				
Clause-to-word ratio	0.09 (0.05)	0.05 (0.03)	0.11 (0.04)	Monologue > role-play Interview > role-play
Discourse markers	4.87 (3.24)	4.40 (2.89)	4.93 (3.01)	NS
Lexical competence				
collocations	3.60 (3.52)	1.8 (2.68)	3.73 (2.46)	Monologue > role-play Interview > role-play
Lexical richness Giraud's index	9.02 (1.50)	7.67 (1.87)	10.87 (1.47)	Monologue > role-play Monologue > interview
Grammatical competence				
Syntactic complexity Subclause-to-clause ratio	0.08 (0.12)	0.1 (0.05)	0.21 (0.12)	Monologue > role-play Monologue > interview

NS, not significant.

quantity of content exchanged in each condition was indeed the same ($F[2, 42] = 1.12$; not significant [NS]), the size of students' speaking samples varied significantly ($F[2, 42] = 6.93$; $p < .05$). The post hoc comparison revealed that the overall production of words was not significantly different when participants engaged in the monologue or the interview tasks. Not surprisingly, the role-play condition resulted in a significantly smaller language sample of each student's speech than the interview (mean difference = 65.47; 95% confidence interval [CI] = 22.41, 108.52; $p < .05$) and the monologue (mean difference = 39.87; 95% CI = -75.63, -4.1, $p < .05$) conditions.

Interactional Competence

Student production data were further analyzed for their use of interactional language characteristics, such as using editing features and posing questions, and the negotiation of meaning. None of these features was used much in any condition. Few participants self-corrected and reformulated their speech when they produced the monologue online ($\bar{x} = 0.44$), and none of the participants in the two other tasks used these features. By contrast, some students who participated in the role-play or the interview initiated clarification requests and confirmation checks to negotiate meaning ($F[2, 42] = 1.05$, NS). Naturally, this was not possible in the monologue task in which students sat individually at computer stations. Also, these students were unable to ask questions. However, participants in the role-play condition used the interactional feature of asking questions significantly more than students in the interview condition ($F[2, 42] = 21.07; p < .05$).

Discourse Competence

Participants' level of discourse competence was measured by the clause-to-word ratio and the use of discourse markers. The production data showed that the assessment task affected whether participants spoke more at the sentence and multi-sentence level than at the word or multi-word level ($F[2, 42] = 10.51; p < .05$). The post hoc comparison revealed that participants produced significantly more discourse-level language when they engaged in the monologue and the interview tasks as compared with the role-play (mean difference = .06; 95% CI = .03, .09; $p < .05$ and mean difference = .04; 95% CI = $-.07, -.01; p < .05$, respectively). Discourse markers were used with equal frequency in all three conditions ($F[2, 42] = .09$, NS).

Lexical Competence

Two aspects of lexical competence were compared: the correct use of conventionalized collocations as well as lexical richness. The treatment condition did have an impact on the number of correctly used collocations ($F[2, 42] = 8.6; p < .05$). Students who participated in the role-play used significantly fewer collocations than students in the interview (mean difference = 5.67; 95% CI = 2.85, 8.48; $p < .05$) and students in the monologue (mean difference = 3.87; 95% CI = 1.05, 6.68; $p < .05$) conditions. Likewise, the treatment condition had an impact on the students' ability to demonstrate the depth of their mental lexicon ($F[2, 42] = 14.66; p < .05$). In the monologue condition, participants used more varied vocabulary than in the interview (mean difference = 1.85; 95% CI = 1.73, 4.67; $p < .05$) and in the role-play (mean difference = 3.20; 95% CI = .38, 3.33; $p < .05$) conditions. The interview and role-play tasks resulted in the same level of lexical richness.

Grammatical Competence

Grammatical competence was determined by assessing participants' ability to use syntactic subordination. Similar to the lexical richness, the assessment task affected syntactic complexity ($F[2, 24] = 14.47, p < .05$). The monologue task

Table 8-2. Descriptive Statistics for the Questionnaire for All Three Conditions*

	Condition		
	Interview	**Role-Play**	**Monologue**
I feel I had the opportunity to ade-quately demonstrate both my strengths and my weaknesses in speaking on the *test*.	3.15 (.55)	3.33 (.48)	2.33 (.72)
I feel the *test* was difficult.	2.15 (.55)	2.39 (.78)	2.30 (.77)
I feel someone listening to my *test* re-sponses would get an accurate picture of my current ability to speak in real-life situations outside the classroom.	3.08 (.90)	2.72 (.26)	2.13 (.92)

*$n = 45$
4 = strongly agree, 3 = agree, 2 = disagree, 1 = strongly disagree.

led participants to use more syntactically complex sentences than the interview (mean difference = .20; 95% CI = .11, .29; $p < .05$) and role-play (mean differ-ence = .13; 95% CI = .04, .22; $p < .05$) conditions.

Student Perception

Table 8-2 reports the means and standard deviations of the questionnaire that as-sessed the participants' perception of the test. Participants in each of the three treatment conditions ranked the three assessment tasks as equally difficult. They thought that the test was not very difficult. However, when participants were asked whether they thought that they had the opportunity to demonstrate their strengths and weaknesses (question 1), students who participated in the online monologue task mostly disagreed (xM = 2.33), but learners in the role-play (xM = 3.33) and interview (xM = 3.15) conditions thought that they had been able to demonstrate their abilities adequately. Likewise, participants who had completed the monologue task online (xM = 2.13) thought that they had not been able to demonstrate their ability to speak German in real-life situations outside the class-room. In contrast, when students engaged in the role-play (xM = 2.72) or the interview task (xM = 3.08), they thought that they had had the opportunity to demonstrate speaking abilities similar to those needed in real-life situations.

Discussion

This study is of particular relevance to language program directors who are in-volved in pedagogical decisions and the design of BL courses. The reduction of F2F time in BL courses often results in a prevalence of online speaking tasks. Thus, an understanding of what types of online and F2F tasks provide opportunities to practice specific competencies, and thereby have a direct impact on students' linguistic development, is essential. Because assessment tasks should be a natural extension of classroom tasks and homework assignments, the main goal of this investigation was to determine whether different oral assessment tasks trigger and consequently allow to measure different language competencies. Understanding which language competencies can be elicited with a single test task is vital for program directors in order to make informed pedagogical decisions regarding the oral assessment component for a language program. The assessment tasks used in this investigation were three commonly used exam tasks: role-play, a teacher–student interview, and a monologue. The study showed that each task elicited a combination of different competencies.

The first aim of the analysis was to establish that participants in all three conditions accomplished the task of planning a trip to Leipzig. Although students' responses as to which sites they wanted to visit and which means of transportation they were planning to take varied, the overall number of ideas produced was similar in each task condition. This quantitative measure served to establish a content baseline for further qualitative analyses of oral competencies. A second quantitative baseline measure assessed the amount of language produced in each condition. The rationale for this analysis was to ensure that the production data collected from each student provided a large enough sample to determine students' current language abilities. Because the role-play condition required the co-construction of content by the three participants, student samples were significantly shorter than in the interview and monologue conditions. That is, these students had fewer opportunities to demonstrate their competencies.

In fact, students in the role-play condition were not able to demonstrate their competencies to talk at the multi-sentence discourse level, their depth of lexical knowledge, or their syntactic abilities as well as participants in the other two conditions. The role-play task led students to talk in multi-word strings, with a smaller variety of words, and with little subordinate sentence structure. The need to interact with multiple task participants and under time constraints may have depleted the resources necessary for using more complex language. Nevertheless, the role-play task required students to demonstrate interaction skills that participants in the other two conditions did not need to show. Role-play participants had to comprehend and immediately respond to their peers' statements and questions without much time to plan their responses. That is, they needed to adhere to the talk patterns and dynamics of a group conversation. Consequently, it is vital that evaluation criteria for role-plays reflect this evidence. Moreover, future research needs to analyze more closely turn-taking and talk patterns. Some students' performances seemed very short and demonstrated parallel structures of turn taking. These students' participation was marked by contributing sentences or multi-word chunks without a clear reference to what was said in the previous turn, an issue outlined by Dimitrova-Galaczi (in Gan, 2010). In turn, one may require students in the role-play tasks to perform twice as long in order to provide them with more opportunities to demonstrate their language abilities. However, intermediate learners may not have more content knowledge to talk about to fill an additional three to five minutes.

Besides asking questions, the role-play condition nevertheless did not result in much use of interactional competencies. Although group interaction depended on the students' successfully comprehending each other, they did not seem to monitor their comprehensibility by correcting themselves or reformulating their ideas. Likewise, not many of the role-play participants initiated the clarification of other participants' statements. Of course, one reason could have been that participants did not feel the need to request clarification. Even though their output had lexical and grammatical errors, they may have comprehended each other's utterances—or at least they comprehended each other's utterances well enough to continue the dialogue. After all, the context and goal of the role-play dialogue was clear to all of the participants because they had had pre-task planning time before the exam. That is, planning time before engaging in a role-play may limit the need to understand precisely the interlocutor's message. It may be interesting to explore in future research whether eliminating planning time will lead to more clarification and negotiation moves because students will not know the outcome of the interaction from the outset of the task. Future research should further examine which types of errors specifically trigger learners to self-correct or to initiate negotiation of meaning. Likewise, a more in-depth analysis of students' interaction data could illustrate whether their interaction was indeed logical and coherent.

Participants in the monologue and interview conditions were equally successful in showing their level of discourse competence by using discourse markers and producing multi-sentence stretches of speech. However, neither of these two tasks elicited many instances during which students used language demonstrating their interactional competence. Although students in the monologue task showed a tendency to focus on lexical and grammatical form by correcting themselves, students in the interview demonstrated a tendency to initiate clarification requests. Considering that in the role-play situation, learners did not produce many clarification moves, it seems safe to say that the unplanned interaction with the instructor required students to engage in clarification moves in order to avoid communication breakdown.

In many ways, the online monologue and the interview tasks were similar: in both tasks, students provided responses to the question prompts on the instruction sheets. But whereas students in the online environment were completely left to their own devices, students in the interview situation received support through nonverbal cues, such as encouraging facial expressions as well as guiding questions from the instructor. Still, learners who completed the monologue task online produced lexically richer and syntactically more complex language than learners who engaged in the interview with the instructor. One could argue that the combination of the monologue task and the online environment pushed learners to produce oral competencies at a linguistically (lexically and syntactically) more sophisticated level. Future research should make direct comparisons between a monologue performed online and a presentation performed in front of an instructor to further tease out the effect of the online environment.

Interestingly, even though participants in the online monologue condition were able to demonstrate the highest level of linguistic complexity (lexical richness and grammatical competence) compared with the two other test tasks, the participants themselves did not think that they had been able to most adequately demonstrate their language abilities.[3] This may have been an artifact of the monologue task itself in which they did not have the teacher's or their peers' encouraging nonverbal cues or may have been attributable to the online test format. Even though these students had experience with online speaking activities, the online environment may have made them feel self-conscious because they may have noticed their linguistic limitations more than in a F2F speaking situation. Future investigations should tease apart the online factor and the monologue task factor to determine how they affect the level of comfort students experience in the assessment situation. Moreover, it would be interesting to see whether students considered the task to emulate a real-life speaking opportunity. To gain further insights into students' perception about online speaking prompts, future questionnaires could ask a question to the effect of whether they think that what they recorded is similar to what they would have said in front of a group of people.

Although the limitations of the current investigation prevent drawing definitive conclusions, the study suggests that a better understanding of which aspects of linguistic and interactional competencies a specific assessment task elicits is essential to test task design and the evaluation of student performance. Analyses of student production data revealed that the role-play task was distinctive in that the participants had to co-construct the content. Although the role-play task did not give learners the opportunity to display their linguistic competencies to the fullest extent, they were able to display and interpret nonverbal aspects of interactional competence. By contrast, participants who performed the monologue task in the online environment were able to demonstrate complementary competencies that demonstrated more sophisticated and complex language use. It seems too early to discard teacher–student interviews as a valuable oral assessment task. Nonetheless, the current findings revealed that learners neither demonstrated a higher level of interactive features compared with the role-play task nor elicited the same level of linguistic complexity as the monologue performed online. Moreover, considering that one-on-one interviews are time consuming and cumbersome to administer, monologue tasks recorded online may be an effective alternative. That is, a hybrid solution to oral testing seems to be a natural extension of the curricular design to the testing situation.

Limitations

The current study has a number of limitations that should be addressed in future investigations. Future studies should assess each student's performance on multiple test tasks and formats to gain more generalizable insights from a larger data set. Likewise, obtaining student performances across a variety of

---

[3]It may be possible that students may have interpreted the questions differently. They may have thought that what they do in front of a computer is not related to what happens in real life. That is, they may be assessing the comparability of the task rather than comparing the language produced.

different topics will help to determine whether the speech and interaction patterns identified in this study hold across different topics. Moreover, instead of using intact classes for each treatment, students should be assigned randomly to a condition. Additionally, it would be interesting to make a direct comparison of online and F2F testing formats. As collaborative technology tools become available for testing purposes, they may be a valuable alternative to time-consuming and difficult-to-administer F2F exams and may allow for multiple oral exams that test complementary competencies. Finally, students' self-evaluation of performance may be more valuable if the evaluation took place after several different exams. Other factors could have intervened to affect a student's perceptions besides the test task or mode of delivery, such as testing conditions (e.g., temperature, noise in the testing site, nervousness, composition of the small group, topic).

References

Abrams, Z. (2003). The effect of synchronous and asynchronous CMC on oral performance in German. *Modern Language Journal, 87,* 157–167.

Abrams, Z. (2011). Interpersonal communication in intracultural CMC. In N. Arnold, & L. Ducate (Eds.), *Present and future promises of CALL: From theory and research to new directions in language teaching* (pp. 61–92). Texas: CALICO.

Augustyn, P., & Euba, N. (2008). *Stationen: Ein Kursbuch für die Mittelstufe.* Boston: Thompson/Heinle.

Bachman, L., & Palmer, A. (1996). *Language testing in practice.* Oxford: Oxford University Press.

Brooks, L. (2009). Interacting in pairs in a test of oral proficiency: Co-constructing a better performance. *Language Testing, 26,* 341–366.

Brown, A. (2003). Interviewer variation and the co-construction of speaking proficiency. *Language Testing, 20,* 1–25.

Crookes, G. (1990). The utterance, and other basic units for second language discourse analysis. *Applied Linguistics, 11,* 183–199.

Dimitrova-Galaczi, E. (2004) *Peer-peer interaction in a paired speaking test: The case of the First Certificate in English.* Unpublished PhD dissertation, Teachers College, Columbia University.

Dykstra-Pruim, P. (1997). Integrating a series of oral assessments: Quick, low-stress options for the idealist. *Unterrichtspraxis, 30,* 16–29.

Foster, P., & Skehan, P. (1996). The influence of planning and task type on second language performance. *Studies in Second Language Acquisition, 18,* 299–323.

Gan, Z. (2010). Interaction in group oral assessment: A case study of higher- and lower-scoring students. *Language Testing, 27,* 585–602.

Gilabert, R. (2007a). The simultaneous manipulation of task complexity along planning and +/- Here-and-Now: Effects on L2 oral production. In M. P. García-Mayo (Ed.), *Investigating tasks in formal language learning* (pp. 44–68). Clevedon, UK: Multilingual Matters.

Gilabert, R. (2007b). Effects of manipulating task complexity on self-repairs during L2 oral production. *IRAL, 45,* 215–240.

Hewett, B. (2000). Characteristics of interactive oral and computer-mediated peer group talk and its influence on revision. *Computers and Composition, 17,* 265–288.

Kenyon, D., & Malabonga, V. (2001). Comparing examinee attitudes toward computer-assisted and other oral proficiency assessments. *Language Learning & Technology, 5,* 60–83.

Kenyon, D., & Tschirner, E. (2000). The rating of direct and semi-direct oral proficiency interviews: Comparing performance at lower proficiency levels. *Modern Language Journal, 84,* 85–101.

Lazaraton, A. (1996). Interlocutor support in oral proficiency interviews: The case of CASE. *Language Testing, 13,* 151–72.

Martinsen, R., Baker, W., Bown, J., & Johnson, C. (2011). The benefits of living in foreign language housing: The effect of language use and second-language type on oral proficiency gains. *Modern Language Journal, 95,* 274–290.

Mehnert, U. (1998). The effect of different lengths of time for planning on second language performance. *Studies in Second Language Acquisition, 20,* 83–108.

Michel, M. C., Kuiken, F., & Vedder, I. (2007). The influence of complexity in monologic versus dialogic tasks in Dutch L2. *Language Acquisition, 45,* 241–259.

Nakahama, Y., Tyler, A., & Van Lier, L. (2001). Negotiation of meaning in conversational and information gap activities: A comparative discourse analysis. *TESOL Quarterly, 35,* 377–405.

Nakatsuhara, F. (2011). Effects of test-taker characteristics and the number of participants in group oral tests. *Language Testing, 28,* 483–508.

Norris, J. M., Brown, J. D., Hudson, T., & Yoshioka, J. (1998). Designing second language performance assessments. *Technical report 18, Second Language Teaching and Curriculum Center, University of Hawaii at Manoa.* Honolulu: University of Hawaii Press.

Pawly, A., & Syder, F. H. (1983). Two puzzles for linguistic theory: Native like selection and native like fluency. In J. Richards & R. Schmidt (Eds.), *Language and communication* (pp. 191–226). London: Longman.

Robinson, P. (2001). Task complexity, task difficulty and task production: Exploring interactions in a componential framework. *Applied Linguistics, 21,* 27–57.

Schmitt, N., & Carter, R. (2004). Formulaic sequences in action. In N. Schmitt (Ed.), *Formulaic Sequences* (pp. 1-22). Amsterdam: John Benjamins.

Shohamy, E., Reves, T., & Bejarano, T. (1986). Introducing a new comprehensive test of oral proficiency. *ELT Journal, 40,* 212–20.

Skehan, P. (1998). *A cognitive approach to language learning.* Oxford: Oxford University Press.

Sun, Y. (2009). Voice blog: An exploratory study of language learning. *Language Learning & Technology, 13,* 88–103.

Sykes, J. M. (2005). Synchronous CMC and pragmatic development: Effects of oral and written chat. *CALICO Journal, 22,* 399–431.

Vermeer, A. (2000). Coming to grips with lexical richness in spontaneous speech data. *Language Testing, 17,* 65–83.

Wang, H., & Shih, S. (2011). The role of language for thinking and task selection in EFL learners' oral collocational production. *Foreign Language Annals, 44,* 399–416.

Wray, A. (2001). *Formulaic language and the lexicon.* Cambridge: Cambridge University Press.

Yanguas, Í. (2010). Oral computer-mediated interaction between L2 learners: It's about time! *Language Learning & Technology, 14,* 72–93.

Yuan, F., & Ellis R. (2003). The effects of pretask planning and on- line planning on fluency, complexity, and accuracy in L2 monologic oral production. *Applied Linguistics, 24,* 1–27.

Chapter 9

Analyzing Linguistic Outcomes of Second Language Learners: Hybrid Versus Traditional Course Contexts

Joshua J. Thoms

Hybrid models of teaching and learning continue to emerge in a number of foreign language (FL) programs at several universities and colleges across the United States (Allen & Seaman, 2010; Goertler & Winke, 2008; National Center for Education Statistics, 2011). A hybrid approach is one in which a traditional FL course, such as one that meets four days each week in a regular, face-to-face (F2F) format, is redesigned so that students meet only two days each week in a regular classroom, and the other two days are carried out via online work. As such, students do not come to class as frequently and instead rely on technological tools and tasks built into the course syllabus that allow them to do part of their coursework outside of the physical classroom (for additional definitions of hybrid and other models of learning with technology, see Allen & Seaman, 2010; Goertler, 2011; Goertler & Winke, 2008).

Given the growing number of FL programs that are incorporating more hybrid and fully online options in their course offerings (Parry, 2011; Thoms, 2011), much more work is needed to understand the positive and negative effects of the hybrid format on learners' linguistic abilities in the FL. Although a small number of studies have attempted to demonstrate differences in linguistic gains between students enrolled in traditional FL courses versus hybrid FL courses (Adair-Hauck, Willingham-Mclain, & Youngs, 2000; Blake, Wilson, Cetto, & Pardo-Ballester, 2008; Chenoweth, Ushida, & Murday, 2006; Echávez-Solano, 2003; Sagarra & Zapata, 2008; Sanders, 2006; Scida & Saury, 2006; Young, 2008), much more work is needed.

This chapter reports on a small-scale empirical study that analyzes the speaking and writing gains of students enrolled in a Spanish language course taught in a traditional, F2F context versus students studying the same content in a hybrid course format. The chapter begins with a review of the literature that (a) highlights reasons as to why the number of hybrid FL courses are increasing in universities in the United States, (b) reviews past empirical work that has looked at linguistic outcomes of students in both contexts, and (c) describes some technological tools and applications that are becoming more commonly used in both hybrid and traditional FL courses. The chapter then describes the methodology of the study and reports on its results. The overarching research question investigated in this project is the following: what are the differences in speaking and writing gains of students enrolled in a hybrid Spanish language course compared with a traditional F2F Spanish language course? The chapter concludes with a summary of the implications of the project and suggestions for future avenues of research in this area.

Reasons for Increasing the Number of Hybrid Courses

A confluence of factors has resulted in the increased demand for hybrid models of teaching and learning in the United States (Goertler, 2011). One important factor is the economy. The recent economic decline has significantly impacted the budgets of many universities. University budget cuts and spending freezes have adversely affected FL departments across the country and, as a result, individual FL programs have suffered. Some examples of these effects include the termination of several fixed-term lecturers and the elimination of Russian, Portuguese, Swahili, and Japanese, as well as the elimination of German and Latin majors in the Department of Foreign Languages and Literatures at Louisiana State University in January 2011 (Foderaro, 2010); proposed elimination of French, Italian, Russian, and Classics at the State University of New York at Albany (Jaschik, 2011); proposed elimination of course offerings in several "priority" FLs (e.g., Pashto, Turkish, Arabic); and reductions in funding for other FLs such as Arabic, Chinese, and Russian at many universities across the United States (Nelson, 2011). Current economic conditions have therefore made it more difficult for academic administrators such as deans and department chairs to justify supporting FL programs that typically have low enrollment numbers (e.g., Classics in many institutions), while at the same time having to deal with the insatiable demand for more widely studied FLs (e.g., Spanish).

Although the aforementioned examples might be considered extreme negative effects of the economic downturn, other consequences of a sluggish economy have also been felt by FL programs. That is, many programs have had to do more with less. Instead of terminating entire programs, some FL departments have increased class sizes or increased the teaching loads of graduate student teaching assistants (TAs) and lecturers to deal with the economic shortfall. In the case of Spanish, where many institutions find it hard to meet student demand, many programs have implemented hybrid or online courses (Thoms, 2011).

Another reason why the number of hybrid and online course offerings has risen in recent years is because of an increase in the overall number of students who are enrolling in higher education. According to the National Center for Education Statistics (2011), the total enrollment of students in degree-granting institutions in the United States (i.e., public and private postsecondary institutions that offer an associate's, baccalaureate, or higher degree) will increase 13 percent between 2009 and 2020. Although a number of factors between now and 2020 may affect the accuracy of this projection, it is still worrisome for many regarding how institutions will be able to meet the demand, particularly in the case of FL programs. Some have suggested that unless the way in which courses are structured and delivered significantly changes over the next decade, it will be hard to accommodate student demand at the postsecondary level (Blake, 2008).

Recent figures indicate that more than a quarter of university students enroll in at least one online course during their four years at their institution (Allen & Seaman, 2010). Despite some anxiety and hesitancy by practitioners and students alike, the particular trend of more hybrid and online courses will become a permanent part of undergraduate students' experience in U.S. institutions in the future.

Because of the increasing number of hybrid and online courses along with the overall projected increase in student population at the postsecondary level, publishers have begun to craft FL textbooks in such a way that the content can be easily delivered in a number of different formats. Specifically, many FL textbook packages now come with a much more fully developed online component that allows teachers the ability to assign more of the content online via electronic workbooks and other ancillary materials such as podcasts, interactive online games, virtual vocabulary flashcards, and so on. Furthermore, many publishers now routinely offer students both paper and electronic copies (i.e., an e-text version) of the FL textbook. In addition, more interactive applications accompany many current FL textbooks. Tools such as Wimba Pronto, Elluminate, blogs, and wikis allow for more teacher–student and student–student interactions to take place outside of the physical classroom. Thus, creating syllabi for and assigning work to be carried out in hybrid and online courses via the numerous tools and activities that are included in many contemporary FL textbooks can also be considered an indirect factor that has helped to facilitate the development and proliferation of hybrid and online FL courses in the United States. However, although the number of hybrid and online FL course offerings continues to increase, many researchers and practitioners remain skeptical about the effects of these learning contexts on learners' second language (L2) linguistic competence. Some initial research efforts have shed light on the effects of hybrid learning contexts on learners' linguistic development. We now review some of the comparison studies that have been carried out to date.

Effect(s) of Hybrid Model on Linguistic Outcomes: Empirical Evidence

Recent empirical work related to the effects of hybrid FL courses on students' L2 learning has focused on a variety of linguistic aspects across different languages. Chenoweth and Murday (2003) carried out a small-scale research project that looked at differences and similarities in linguistic gains between learners of French enrolled in an online course and those in a traditional course. The traditional course met four times per week, and each class meeting lasted 50 minutes. Twelve students were enrolled in the traditional course. Eight students were enrolled in the online version of the course and met in class once each week for 50 minutes. However, the online group participated in an hour-long online chat session each week and also interacted with classmates via email and a class discussion board. The researchers compared the two groups via a number of measures and found that there were no statistically significant differences between the two groups with respect to listening, reading, and speaking abilities. However, the online group did achieve higher median scores on writing compared with the traditional group.

Chenoweth et al. (2006) carried out a large-scale study that analyzed the linguistic outcomes of students enrolled in traditional and hybrid French and Spanish courses. The study was carried out over five semesters and involved both F2F and hybrid elementary (i.e., first and second semester) and intermediate (i.e., third semester) French language courses and elementary (i.e., first and second semester) Spanish language courses. A total of 354 students participated in the study; 13 of the courses across the two languages were offered in a hybrid format, and 21 of the sections made up the traditional, F2F group. The elementary F2F courses for both languages met for four days per week, and the traditional French Intermediate course met three days per week; each in-class meeting lasted for 50 minutes. The hybrid sections across both languages had a one-hour class meeting each week. In addition, students in the hybrid sections had to meet F2F with their instructor or a TA 20 minutes each week on a rotating basis and had to carry out an online chat with classmates, which, on average, lasted 20 minutes. The hybrid sections also carried out a number of tasks each week via their online course management system (WebCT).

The researchers assessed differences between the two groups of learners (i.e., those enrolled in the hybrid vs. traditional sections) via a combination of speaking and writing assessments throughout each semester along with performance data from the final exams in each course. In all, they measured speaking, listening, reading, and writing abilities and assessed for grammatical accuracy and lexical richness in the various measures. Findings indicated that there were no significant differences between the two groups of learners among the majority of the components of the final exams and the speaking and writing assessments. Among all of the sections, two of the hybrid sections did not perform as well as their traditional counterparts. Nonetheless, the researchers concluded that overall, there were few significant differences between the two formats across the various courses in both languages.

Scida and Saury (2006) report on a pilot study originally carried out in 2003 at the University of Virginia that analyzed differences in student achievement between a traditional and a hybrid Spanish elementary (i.e., second semester) language course. The traditional course met five days per week and was composed of 22 students. In contrast, the hybrid course met three days per week in a regular F2F format. However, students also carried out several online activities (i.e., approximately two hours of work outside of class each week) via a course learning system originally created at the University of Illinois at Urbana-Champaign called *Mallard*. The program is essentially an early version of current learning management systems (e.g., Blackboard, Moodle), which allowed teachers to create a variety of language-learning tasks that were completed online. The researchers compared the final grades of the two groups of learners and discovered that 84 percent of the learners in the hybrid course earned a B or above compared with 73 percent of learners in the traditional course. Although the researchers admit that their study lacked more rigorous assessment measures, they conclude by indicating that it appeared that the hybrid model was as effective (or more effective) for the learners who participated in their project.

To provide a more thorough understanding of the effects of a hybrid format on students' linguistic outcomes, Young (2008) carried out an in-depth study at the University of Tennessee. The study involved 10 sections of an intensive elementary Spanish course. The course covered two semesters of beginning Spanish in one semester and was designed for students who had taken some Spanish in high school but needed a review of the basics of the language before enrolling in upper-level Spanish language courses. In all, 209 students participated, and approximately half of them took the hybrid version of the course, which met two days per week, and carried out various workbook activities online. The other half took the traditional version of the course and therefore met three days per week and carried out their workbook activities via a hard copy of the workbook. All students were subjected to a variety of assessment measures both at the beginning and at the end of the semester (i.e., all students took a version of the placement exam both at the beginning and at the end of the semester, and all students took a battery of proficiency tests to assess for speaking, reading, listening, and writing competencies as well as a SOPI, a tape-mediated oral proficiency exam). The results of the study indicated that there were no statistically significant differences between the two groups of learners across the aforementioned variables or measures (i.e., no significant difference in speaking, reading, writing, or listening ability). The researcher concludes her study by indicating that a possible factor regarding the insignificant differences between the two groups may be partly attributable to the fact that more experienced instructors and TAs were assigned to the hybrid sections.

When implementing a hybrid course in a FL program, many instructors and coordinators often worry about the effect of the hybrid format on students' developing speaking ability in the L2. Blake et al. (2008) focused their efforts on determining the differences in oral proficiency gains between students enrolled in traditional, hybrid, and fully online (termed *distance learning* in the study) Spanish language courses at the University of California—Davis. In all, 233 students enrolled in a traditional Spanish language course, 64 students took the hybrid version, and 21 enrolled in the fully online Spanish language course. The traditional sections met five days per week and were expected to invest an additional five hours per week outside of class to their studies (bringing their total number of hours to 10). The hybrid sections met three hours per week in a F2F format with their instructor and were also required to dedicate seven hours of additional work online (for a total of 10 hours per week dedicated to their coursework). Finally, the students taking the same course as a fully online course were expected to put in 10 hours of work each week. The researchers administered an automated oral proficiency exam (called *Versant for Spanish*) in all three course formats at the end of the semester. The results of the study indicated that there were no statistically significant differences regarding oral proficiency ability across all three formats. Although the findings confirmed what the researchers hypothesized about the differences and similarities of oral ability of learners across all three contexts (i.e., that there would be few differences), the authors conclude stating that more work is needed in this area.

In sum, the handful of studies that have been carried out to date indicate that there is little to no difference in the linguistic outcomes of learners who enroll in a F2F L2 course compared with those enrolled in a hybrid or online course. Some have indicated that because of the variety of ways in which hybrid courses are configured, coupled with the distinct data collection and analysis procedures across the various studies, caution is necessary when understanding the results of the comparative studies (Blake, 2011). However, it is clear that there is little empirical evidence to date that indicates that students in a hybrid L2 course will perform worse than students in a similar, F2F course. Nevertheless, more work is needed, especially as the nature of the technological tools used in all L2 courses continues to evolve. It is now necessary to briefly review some of the more interactive tools and applications that are available to both teachers and students in traditional and hybrid L2 learning contexts.

Computer-Assisted Language Learning and Web 2.0 Tools

The field of computer-assisted language learning in the past few years has turned its attention to a number of technologies that are finding their way into the social and academic lives of students and teachers alike (Arnold & Ducate, 2011). Specifically, many new technologies—termed Web 2.0 tools—allow teachers to be more creative and flexible when planning courses and determining what can be taught in and outside of the classroom. The omnipresence of Web 2.0 tools in the lives of many students has influenced how teachers, publishers, and so on create and deliver content in the L2 classroom. Web 2.0 tools include applications such as micro-blogging (e.g., Twitter), video-based online chats (e.g., Skype), wikis (i.e., web pages where one or more learners can edit the content on the page), text-based chats, among various other applications. These applications allow users to create and interact more with content and other users (e.g., classmates) in an online environment. In other words, Web 2.0 tools allow learners to move from being consumers of information in online environments to producers of content in those contexts.

In addition to the interactive characteristics of Web 2.0 tools, others have suggested that the term *Web 2.0* involves an attitude about technology and specifically about one's relationship with respect to others. "This Web 2.0 attitude revolves not so much around the individual as it does around the individual as an integral part of the collective whole" (Lomicka & Lord, 2009, p. 4). Whether one views the advent of Web 2.0 tools as a kind of attitudinal change on behalf of students or sees it as applications that allow for students to interact more freely outside of the physical classroom, the L2 classroom—both traditional and hybrid courses—will include the use of these tools for the foreseeable future. As such, this study hopes to add to the hybrid–traditional L2 course discussion while also reporting on the inclusion of Web 2.0 tools in both contexts.

Some researchers have looked at the use of specific technological tools in both traditional and hybrid L2 courses. Sanders (2006) analyzed two separate text-based chats of students in a traditional and in a hybrid Spanish language course. The traditional section met for just over three hours each week, and the hybrid section met for just over two hours each week. Both groups had similar online activities that accompanied their in-class coursework. However, the hybrid course had one additional online listening comprehension activity and quiz as well as one additional vocabulary exercise and quiz each week compared with the traditional course. Students in the traditional Spanish language course carried out the two online chats analyzed in the study in groups of three students (on average); students in the hybrid section carried out the two online chats on their own outside of class and also averaged three students per chat. The hybrid group was simply told to form and organize a time outside of class to carry out the two chats. It is important to note here that the two chats in both the traditional and hybrid sections were used in order for students to exchange information with each other that would later be used in a written composition that described another person in class. Therefore, collaboration was encouraged for both groups of learners in order to complete the written task after the chats were completed.

The researcher analyzed the chat logs for every learner in the traditional and hybrid groups and measured aspects such as time on task, total number of turns, number of Spanish words used, spelling accuracy, and social and off-task comments; he did not look at grammatical accuracy. Sanders found that both groups of students were attentive to the goals of the task and generally stayed on topic. However, the hybrid group spent more time on the task and overall produced more language during the chats compared with the traditional group. The researcher concludes that the hybrid group "engaged electronically in more social communication" (p. 67) and therefore maintained more student–student interaction outside of class versus the traditional group.

Although there are limitations related to Sanders's (2006) study, it does represent an initial attempt to understand how a specific type of Web 2.0 tool (i.e., text-based chats) can be used in hybrid L2 courses. Although this current study does not follow in the same vein as the study by Sanders (2006), it does report on differences in language production (i.e., speaking and writing) of students enrolled in a traditional and hybrid Spanish language class. Web 2.0 tools were incorporated in the study given the interactive nature of the tools themselves and because few hybrid-based studies to date include tasks that are carried out by learners via Web 2.0 tools.

Methodological Challenges of Comparative Research

Before moving on to the details of the current study, it is necessary to note here that there are inherent methodological challenges that are shared by many of the comparative studies described above. Specifically, the main caveat is that many of the studies that attempt to compare the effects of traditional versus hybrid FL courses on student learning do not control for potential differences in the amount of instruction or learning between the two conditions. Controlling this variable is necessary when carrying out this kind of research to ensure the validity of the study's results.

Research Questions

The following research questions were investigated:

1. What are the differences in speaking gains of students enrolled in a hybrid course compared with a traditional F2F course?
2. What are the differences in writing gains of students enrolled in a hybrid course compared with a traditional F2F course?

Methodology

Participants, Setting, and Course Information

This project was carried out in two sections of an Elementary (i.e., second semester) Spanish II language course at a large research institution in the southern United States during the spring 2011 semester. One section of the course was defined as a traditional Spanish language course in that it met four days each week in a F2F format. The other section was defined as hybrid. Instead of meeting four days each week F2F in a classroom, students met three days each week and in lieu of the fourth day carried out work outside of class via a variety of online activities. It is worth mentioning here that both classes were assigned the same amount of work. Each class took the same amount of reading, grammar, and vocabulary quizzes; carried out the same number of speaking and writing activities; took the same exams; and so on. In addition, both courses were taught by the same instructor to eliminate any possible teacher effects. The instructor was unaware of the main goal of the research project. The researcher intentionally did not inform the instructor about the specifics of data analysis. This was done so as to avoid any potential research bias on behalf of the instructor when she went about teaching the two different sections.

In all, 24 students were enrolled in the traditional section of the course, and 26 were enrolled in the hybrid course. Fourteen of the students in the traditional course were female, and 10 of them were male. Eighteen of the students in the hybrid course were male, and eight of them were female. Students' ages in both sections ranged from 18 to 22 years old. It is important to note that students who take the Elementary Spanish II course at the university where this project was carried out do not directly place into the course via a placement exam. For this particular course, all students had first completed Elementary Spanish I before being allowed to enroll in Elementary Spanish II. As such, all students were familiar with the textbook and its online tools because the first part of the book is covered in Elementary Spanish I and the latter half of the book is covered in

Elementary Spanish II. The textbook used in both courses was a custom edition of *Temas* (Cubillos & Lamboy, 2008).

It should be noted here that students had the opportunity to choose whether or not they wanted to take Elementary Spanish II in a traditional or hybrid format. Specifically, a description of the hybrid course was posted on the registrar's website during the course enrollment period during the fall 2010 semester. Therefore, students knew that the hybrid met only three days each week and included a heavy technology component.

The instructor for both sections of the course was 47 years old and had more than 10 years of experience teaching college-level Spanish language courses at the university where this project took place. She was familiar with teaching hybrid Spanish language courses at the university, and the course that she taught from which data was collected represented the third time that she had taught a hybrid section of the course. She was also very familiar with the technologies used in the course and with the online components that accompanied the Spanish language textbook.

The semester in which data collection took place was the last semester in a three-year Spanish language hybrid course pilot program that was initiated by an academic dean. The program provided some initial funding in the form of course releases for two instructors to redesign course syllabi in three lower-level Spanish language courses in order to convert them to hybrid courses. Other than the course releases, no other funding was provided to the instructors or the researcher to collect data for the project. The pilot program was implemented by the dean to see whether or not costs related to course offerings in Spanish could be reduced via a hybrid model and to understand any potential negative or positive effects of a hybrid course on students' ongoing linguistic development in Spanish (see Discussion and Conclusion for more on this aspect of the project).

As previously stated, the same number of graded assignments, quizzes, and exams were offered in both the traditional and the hybrid sections of the course. However, to make up for the fewer in-class days each week, students in the hybrid sections were often assigned two or three additional online workbook activities and grammar tutorials each week that were made available to them by the textbook's publisher. Students in the hybrid section also carried out four 30-minute audio or video-based chats with their classmates via Wimba during the course of the semester. The chats allowed them to interact with fellow classmates outside of the classroom to practice their speaking ability in Spanish. Finally, the hybrid students also maintained biweekly journals (for a total of eight entries) via personal blogs in addition to the regularly assigned written homework and in-class writing activities that were also done by the students in the traditional course. In sum, this study made use of the following Web 2.0 tools: blogs and audio- and video-based web chats.

Data Collection

To understand the differences in speaking and writing gains among students in the two course formats, speaking and writing measures were collected from students in both classes during weeks 2 and 15 of the spring 2011 semester. Each of the speaking diagnostics was composed of five questions (see Appendix 9-A for both diagnostics). Students were not given any preliminary information about the nature of the speaking exams. They were advised to go to a computer lab on a specific day during weeks 2 and 15 to do speaking activities and practice. On the day of the speaking diagnostics, students were assigned to their own computer and headsets in the lab. They were then given instructions about the nature of the task and directions as to how to hear the questions and how to record their answers.

Each of the five questions for every diagnostic was prerecorded and delivered to students via the *conversations* application from the Center for Language Education and Research housed at Michigan State University (CLEAR, 2011). The conversations application is free and allows teachers the ability to record questions via audio or video prompts. The application was also chosen because it allows the ability to build in timing restrictions for students' responses and creates an archived audio file that can be easily accessed by teachers after administering the exam. Students heard each question asked twice and then were prompted to respond. In addition to hearing the questions being posed to them on the computer, students also received a printed copy of the questions. This was done to ensure that the speaking diagnostic focused on students' speaking abilities and not on their listening comprehension skills. It should also be noted that students were instructed to respond to each question by speaking for 35 seconds. The timing feature in the application therefore stopped recording students' responses after 35 seconds and moved students on to the next question.

Similar to the speaking diagnostics, students in both the traditional and hybrid groups were asked to report to a computer lab during weeks 2 and 15. There was no information given to them before the two writing diagnostics were carried out. That is, students were told before the day of the diagnostics that they would be doing some additional practice with writing in the lab and nothing more. On the day of the diagnostics, each student was assigned to a computer. The researcher and cooperating instructor described the writing activity and answered any questions students had before they began to do the writing diagnostic. Each writing diagnostic was similar in that every one provided some structure for students and asked them to do similar things. In diagnostic 1, each student described him- or herself and his or her family in the United States to a future host family in Spain. In diagnostic 2, each student described his or her university or university life to a pen pal in Chile (see Appendices 9-B and 9-C for both writing prompts). For both diagnostics, students in each class had 25 minutes to write and composed their work electronically in a Word document. Students were not allowed to use any resources while they wrote (i.e., no hard copy or electronic dictionaries or translators, and they were not allowed to use their textbooks). After completing each writing diagnostic, the files were saved and collected by the researcher.

Data Analysis

Data analysis involved the rating of the speaking and writing samples collected in both the traditional and hybrid classes. Both diagnostics for speaking and writing were rated and compared to discover any differences in gains between students in each class format. The ratings for the speaking samples were based on a rubric that assessed students' answers to each of the five questions. Embedded in the rubric were the following five criteria: thoroughness, ease of expression, use of appropriate vocabulary, grammatical accuracy, and correct pronunciation (see Appendix 9-D for speaking rubric). Each answer for each question was therefore rated individually. Each of the five scores was totaled, and an average speaking score for each diagnostic was determined for every student.

The ratings for the writing samples were based on a rubric whose criteria consisted of two sub-areas: one score for content, organization, and coherence and another score for the quality of language or grammatical accuracy (see Appendix 9-E for writing rubric). The scores for each sub-area were combined to calculate a final written score for each writing sample for every student across both classes. The final scores for each writing diagnostic for each student were compared to determine which class format (i.e., traditional or hybrid) has more gains in writing ability over the course of the semester.

It is important to note here that two raters were used to carry out the ratings for both the speaking and writing samples. The raters were experienced full-time lecturers who were familiar with the course in which this project took place. Before carrying out their ratings, the researcher met with each rater individually and provided some basic training for them by answering their questions about how to interpret and apply both of the rubrics used in the study. Sample ratings for both writing and speaking samples were also carried out during the mini training sessions. After each of the two raters finished rating the speaking and writing samples, the researcher compared the results. Interrater reliability was determined to be 0.93. There were some discrepancies with some of the student samples between ratings. However, in those cases, the researcher consulted with the raters and came to an agreement about each rating in question.

Results

The results are presented based on each research question investigated in this project.

RQ1. What are the Differences in Speaking Gains of Students Enrolled in a Hybrid Course Compared with a Traditional F2F Course?

A Shapiro-Wilk normality test was first used to determine whether the variability or variation of the differences between speaking diagnostic 1 and 2 were normally distributed between the traditional and hybrid classes. The test determined that for both classes, differences in variation did not adhere to acceptable patterns of variability. Thus, a Wilcoxon rank sum test was used to more accurately understand differences between speaking diagnostic 1 and 2 in each of the classes. As can be seen in Table 9-1, there were no statistically significant differences between the traditional and hybrid courses with respect to speaking gains over the course of the semester. In other words, the hybrid students performed as well as their traditional counterparts with respect to the development of their oral proficiency over the course of the semester.

Table 9-1. Differences in Speaking and Writing Gains Across Traditional and Hybrid Courses

Wilcoxon Rank Sum Test Results				
Hybrid	**Traditional**	**_t_-Statistic**	**_p_**	**Significance***
Writing	Writing	−4.1627	.001	Yes
Speaking	Speaking	−1.4771	.152	No

*$p < .05$.

RQ2. What are the Differences in Writing Gains of Students Enrolled in a Hybrid Course Compared with a Traditional F2F Course?

Similar to research question 1, a Shapiro-Wilk normality test was first used to determine how the distribution of scores varied between both of the two writing diagnostics and across both types of classes. Similar to the speaking diagnostics, the normality test determined that the variation of scores did not follow a normal distribution. Therefore, a Wilcoxon rank sum test was run to determine any differences in writing gains between diagnostics 1 and 2 across both classes. Table 9-1 indicates that in the case of writing, there was a statistically significant difference between the traditional and hybrid courses. Specifically, students in the hybrid group improved their writing ability more than the students in the traditional course. Reasons as to why these differences appeared are explored below.

Discussion and Conclusion

This small-scale study has attempted to contribute to the ongoing discussion about the linguistic benefits and challenges for students enrolled in a hybrid language course. As we have seen, the results of the various diagnostic measures indicate that for the students participating in this study, those who were enrolled in the hybrid section experienced comparable gains as those enrolled in the traditional section of the same course with respect to their speaking development. These results are similar to previous comparative studies that have also looked at speaking ability (Blake et al., 2008; Chenoweth & Murday, 2006; Chenoweth et al., 2006; Echávez-Solano, 2003; Young, 2008). Although care must be taken when comparing the aforementioned comparative-oriented studies because of a number of different variables inherent in each project, a growing number of empirically based studies have indicated that less F2F class time does not translate into students in hybrid courses not being able to develop their L2 speaking ability.

Anecdotally, many practitioners and researchers in the fields of FL education and instructed L2 acquisition are skeptical about the possibility of learners in hybrid courses fully developing their oral skills compared with students in traditional L2 classrooms. However, as more interactive technology continues to evolve and more empirical work is carried out and established over time, fears of students not being able to fully develop their L2 speaking skills will be mitigated.

We have also seen how the learners in the hybrid section made more improvements in their writing ability over the course of the semester compared with the students enrolled in the traditional section. Again, these results are similar to those of previous studies that have looked at writing ability of students in hybrid and traditional L2 course contexts. Although it is uncertain as to why the learners in the hybrid section had more gains in their writing ability when compared to their counterparts in the traditional section, one can hypothesize that the learners possibly produced more written language doing the biweekly journals in their personal blogs and therefore simply had more time on task with practicing writing in Spanish. Again, the biweekly journal assignments in the hybrid sections were intended to compensate for the writing that might take place during the one day per week away from the classroom. This reason is merely speculative, and more investigation is needed to clearly determine why the hybrid students improved their writing more than the traditional students.

Although this study did not specifically focus on the effects of the Web 2.0 tools that were incorporated in the hybrid section in this study (i.e., blogs and the conferencing tool Wimba), it is worth noting that these new tools will only allow for greater interaction and the building of a community of learners for both traditional and hybrid L2 courses. In the case of hybrid courses, these tools will connect learners in a more meaningful way and will also allow for teachers to interact with their students even when they are not in a physical classroom space. Given the increased number of interactions afforded to learners in hybrid courses via an ever-evolving array of Web 2.0 tools, linguistic gains by learners in hybrid courses may likely increase compared with learners in traditional courses. However, future research efforts will need to confirm this.

Limitations

As previously mentioned, this study involved a small number of students. More students enrolled in additional sections of each of the two course formats would have increased the validity of the study's findings. The researcher recognized this limitation when conceptualizing the project. However, scheduling issues and the availability of adequate instructors to teach additional hybrid sections of the course during the semester in which this study took place made it impossible to add more hybrid courses and students to the project. A related limitation involves the lack of control for gender in both classes. However, given the ecological or naturalistic nature of the study, this gender difference could not be controlled.

The study would have also benefitted from a closer examination of each of the components that made up spoken and written discourse as defined in it. Specifically, the rubrics used included a variety of categories (e.g., quantity, fluency, grammar, vocabulary, and pronunciation made up the oral rubric). A more fine-grained linguistic analysis of each of these features for speaking and those that defined written discourse in the writing rubric would have shed more light on the differences in students' writing and speaking gains in both classes. This is a clear limitation that needs to be addressed in a follow-up study.

Future Avenues of Research

Future work in this area should focus more on a variety of aspects. One area of research that has currently received some attention looks at characteristics of learners that may indicate why they are successful in hybrid learning contexts. Specifically, a number of learner variables that are not related to the linguistic and technological competencies of learners, such as personality traits (e.g., conscientiousness, being open to new experiences), may indeed help determine whether or not learners are able to learn and further develop their L2 abilities in a hybrid context. Blake and Bilinski Arispe (forthcoming) are currently working on this issue, and it is likely that more research in this area will be carried out in the near future.

A second area of research related to hybrid language courses has to do with computer literacy itself. Given the fact that many undergraduate students arrive to L2 courses having been immersed in and grown up with technology since they were born may indeed facilitate their learning experience in a hybrid course context. Many hybrid–traditional comparative studies do not include this kind of information when looking at differences in student outcomes in the two contexts. Future work should attempt to describe what level of computer literacy one needs to have in order to be successful in a L2 hybrid course.

Finally, much more work is needed to understand how the proliferation of Web 2.0 tools is changing the ways in which students learn the L2 (in both hybrid and traditional contexts) and how these are affecting how L2 teachers approach their jobs in hybrid language learning contexts. Specifically, what training do teachers need to have in order to create a rich learning environment in hybrid and online contexts? What L2 teaching methods can successfully be transferred from traditional to hybrid and online learning contexts? Does the experience of teaching a hybrid language course have a reverse effect—that is, can anything (e.g., tools, tasks, concepts) that works well in a hybrid environment be applied to and improve teaching in traditional contexts? These are just some of the questions and research areas that still need to be addressed regarding L2 teaching and learning in hybrid environments. Hopefully, more research will soon answer these questions.

References

Adair-Hauck, B., Willingham-Mclain, L., & Youngs, B. (2000). Evaluating the integration of technology and second language learning. *CALICO Journal, 17,* 269–306.

Allen, I., & Seaman, J. (2010). *Learning on demand: Online education in the United States, 2009.* Retrieved June 10, 2011, from http://www.sloanconsortium.org/publications/survey/pdf/learningondemand.pdf.

Arnold, N., & Ducate, L. (Eds.). (2011). *Present and future promises of CALL: From theory and research to new directions in language teaching.* San Marcos, TX: CALICO.

Blake, R. (2011). Current trends in online language learning. *Annual Review of Applied Linguistics, 31,* 19–35.

Blake, R. (2008). *Brave new digital classroom technology and foreign language learning.* Washington, DC: Georgetown University Press.

Blake, R., & Bilinski Arispe, K. (forthcoming). Individual factors and successful learning in a hybrid course. *System*.

Blake, R., Wilson, N., Cetto, M., & Pardo-Ballester, C. (2008). Measuring oral proficiency in distance, face-to-face, and blended classrooms. *Language Learning & Technology, 12*, 114–127.

Chenoweth, A., & Murday, K. (2003). Measuring student learning in an online French course. *CALICO Journal, 20*, 285–314.

Chenoweth, A., Ushida, E., & Murday, K. (2006). Student learning in hybrid French and Spanish courses: An overview of language online. *CALICO Journal, 24*, 115–145.

CLEAR. (2011). Rich internet applications for language learning. Retrieved August 12, 2011, from http://clear.msu.edu/teaching/online/ria/.

Cubillos, J., & Lamboy, E. (2008). *Temas: Spanish for the global community* (Custom ed.). Mason, OH: Cengage Learning.

Echávez-Solano, N. (2003). *A comparison of student outcomes and attitudes in technology-enhanced vs. traditional second-semester Spanish language courses*. Unpublished doctoral dissertation, University of Minnesota, Minneapolis.

Foderaro, L. (2010). *Budget-cutting colleges bid some languages adieu*. Retrieved June 10, 2011, from http://www.nytimes.com/2010/12/05/education/05languages.html?_r=1&pagewanted=1.

Goertler, S. (2011). Blended and open/online learning: Adapting to a changing world of language teaching. In Arnold, N., & Ducate, L. (Eds.), *Present and future promises of CALL: From theory and research to new directions in language teaching* (pp. 471–502). San Marcos, TX: CALICO.

Goertler, S., & Winke, P. (Eds.). (2008). *Opening doors through distance education: Principles, perspectives, and practices*. San Marcos, TX: CALICO.

Jaschik, S. (2011). *Disappearing languages at Albany*. Retrieved June 10, 2011, from http://www.insidehighered.com/news/2010/10/04/albany.

Lomicka, L., & Lord, G. (2009). (Eds.). (2009). *The next generation: Social networking and online collaboration in foreign language learning*. San Marcos, TX: CALICO.

National Center for Education Statistics. (2011). *Section 5. Enrollment in postsecondary degree-granting institutions: Introduction*. Retrieved on August 18, 2011, from http://nces.ed.gov/programs/projections/projections2020/sec5a.asp.

Nelson, L. (2011). *Cutting back on Kazakh*. Retrieved September 4, 2011, from http://www.insidehighered.com/news/2011/09/02/foreign_language_programs_face_deep_cuts.

Parry, M. (2011). *Foreign-language instruction, digitally speaking*. Retrieved May 27, 2012, from http://chronicle.com/article/Foreign-Language-Instruction/129604/.

Sagarra, N., & Zapata, G. (2008). Computer-assisted instruction and L2 grammar accuracy *Hispania, 91*, 93–109.

Sanders, R. (2006). A comparison of chat room productivity: In-class versus out-of-class. *CALICO Journal, 24*, 59–76.

Scida, E., & Saury, R. (2006). Hybrid courses and their impact on student and classroom performance: A case study at the University of Virginia. *CALICO Journal, 23*, 517–531.

Thoms, J. (2011). Hybrid language teaching and learning: Assessing pedagogical and curricular issues. In C. Wilkerson & P. Swanson (Eds.), *Dimension 2011* (pp. 21–34). Valdosta, GA: SCOLT Publications (selected proceedings from Southern Conference on Language Teaching).

Young, D. (2008). An empirical investigation of the effects of blended learning on student outcomes in a redesigned intensive Spanish course. *CALICO Journal, 26*, 160–181.

Appendix 9-A. Speaking Diagnostics 1 and 2

Diagnostic #1

(Week 2)
NOTE: Students were given 35 seconds to respond to each question.

Pregunta #1: ¿Quién es tu mejor amigo o amiga? ¿Por qué es tu mejor amigo o amiga? Descríbelo/la.
Pregunta #2: Describe tu rutina diaria desde la mañana hasta la noche.
Pregunta #3: ¿Qué hiciste durante las vacaciones de Navidad (*Christmas*)?
Pregunta #4: ¿Qué te gusta hacer en tu tiempo libre?
Pregunta #5: ¿Qué quieres hacer después de graduarte de la universidad?

Diagnostic #2

(Week 15)
NOTE: Students were given 35 seconds to respond to each question.

Pregunta #1: ¿Cuál es tu programa de televisión favorito? ¿Por qué es tu programa favorito? Descríbelo.
Pregunta #2: Describe lo que haces normalmente cada día después de tu clase de español.
Pregunta #3: ¿Qué hiciste durante las vacaciones de Spring Break?
Pregunta #4: ¿Qué te gusta hacer los fines de semana?
Pregunta #5: ¿Qué tipo de trabajo quieres después de graduarte de la universidad? ¿Por qué?

Appendix 9-B. Writing Diagnostic #1

Week 2

Un semestre en España
Instructions. You have recently been accepted to participate in a study abroad experience in Madrid, Spain during this upcoming summer. While in Spain, you will be living with a host family. The study abroad program has asked you to write a letter to your host family in order to introduce and describe a bit more about yourself. Follow these steps:

1. Introduction

- Introduce yourself. You may want to include a physical description of yourself along with information about why you chose to study in Spain and/or why you are interested in learning Spanish.

2. Body of the text

- Describe your family (where they live, how many brothers and sisters you have, their ages, possible physical descriptions of each member of your family, their occupations, etc.)
- Indicate what you know about Spanish culture. Then describe some of your family's customs/traditions that are also part of American culture.
- You can include any other information in this section that you think your host family should know about you.

3. Conclusion

- Write a conclusion where you pose a few questions to your host family (either about the family itself or about Spanish culture) and then indicate that you are looking forward to your time in Spain.

Appendix 9-C. Writing Diagnostic #2

Week 15

Una descripción de tu universidad

Instructions. You have recently started communicating with a Chilean pen pal (Sofía) who attends the University of Santiago. In the last letter that you received from her, Sofía indicated that she would like to learn more about what it is like being a student at your university. Write a response to her where you do the following:

1. Introduction

- Begin by telling her why you chose to come to University X.

2. Body of the text

- Describe the kinds of classes that you are currently taking along with information about the professors who teach those courses (e.g., which course is your favorite, which is your least favorite and why)
- Indicate what kinds of social activities are available to students at University X.
- You can include any other information in this section that you think helps describe University X to Sofía.

3. Conclusion

- Write a conclusion where you pose a few questions to Sofía about her university/her university experience in Chile.

Appendix 9-D. Rubric for Speaking Diagnostics 1 and 2

NOTE: The rubric below was used for each response to each question on each of the diagnostics for every student. An average speaking score (i.e., the average score on all five questions) for each diagnostic was calculated for every student.

<u>Excellent</u> (Score of 5)
Response answers question thoroughly.
Considerable ease of expression and high level of fluency.
Wide range of vocabulary.
Virtually free of errors in structure.
Very good pronunciation.

<u>Very Good</u> (Score of 4)
Response answers question well.
Ease of expression and good fluency.
Good range of vocabulary.
Few errors in structure.
Good pronunciation.

<u>Good</u> (Score of 3)
Response addresses or answers question adequately.
Some fluency with occasional hesitancy; may self-correct.
Adequate vocabulary; few Anglicisms.
Some errors in structure.
Pronunciation that may interfere with communication.

<u>Fair</u> (Score of 2)
Response addresses question inadequately; may be unfinished due to lack of resources.
Labored expression, halting; limited to no fluency.
Few vocabulary resources.
Limited control of structures; fragmented Spanish.
Pronunciation that interferes with communication.

<u>Poor</u> (Score of 1)
Response clearly does not address the question.
Clearly does not understand the question.
"No sé" or "No entendí la pregunta."
No attempt made (although microphone is open and recording).
Mere sighs or nonsense utterances.

*If a student speaks less than half the time for a question, deduct 1 pt. from score for that question.

Appendix 9-E. Rubric for Writing Diagnostics 1 and 2

Content, Organization, Coherence

8-10: Writer has followed instructions and has written a coherent and convincing composition/letter. Length is sufficient given the time parameters and covers almost all of the points presented in the guide (introduction, body, conclusion). Writing is comprehensible throughout. Overall impression is one of coherence and completeness.

6-7: Structure of composition is clearly evident, but not all sections are fully developed. Use of surface-level translation strategy causes meaning to break down in places. Length is adequate or marginally adequate. Provides some details, but not enough to create an excellent composition/letter. Some attention to coherence is needed.

3-5: Weak organization and coherence. Shows evidence of "stream-of-consciousness" writing, rather than thoughtful organization. Considerable use of surface-level translation strategy causes frequent breakdowns of meaning. Clearly too short to do justice to the topic. Details may be seriously lacking.

1-2: Virtually no coherence or organization. Meaning may frequently be hard to decipher. Very poor in terms of content and length.

Quality of Language/Grammar

8-10: Accuracy in vocabulary and grammar is quite good, although there may be some errors, particularly in structures beyond the student's level. No systematic errors in agreement (e.g., subject-verb, noun-adjective) are present. Use and control of the present tense is apparent. To get a 9 or 10, there should be few errors in the basic structures that students at this level are expected to know well.

6-7: Accuracy in vocabulary and structure is acceptable, but there will be a good number of errors in structures that the student should know. Student may make errors in use of some familiar structures.

3-5: Accuracy in vocabulary and structure is weak, with errors in almost every sentence.

1-2: Very poor in all ways. Error-ridden and difficult to understand.

Chapter 10

Opening Up Foreign Language Education with Open Educational Resources: The Case of *Français interactif*

Carl S. Blyth

In his recent book on the global impact of open education, instructional technologist Curtis Bonk makes the bold claim that anyone can now learn anything from anyone at anytime thanks to the Internet. Following the lead of the Pulitzer prize–winning columnist Thomas Friedman, who argued that social "flatteners" had irrevocably changed the global marketplace (Friedman, 2005), Bonk (2009) argues that technological "openers" are currently transforming global education:

> At its hub, this book and its corresponding framework address how Web technology offers new hope for educating the citizens of this planet. It is the opening up of education that ultimately makes a flatter or more robust economic world possible. In the twenty-first century, education trumps economy as the key card to participation in the world. It is education, after all, from which robust economies are built. So when there are momentous shifts or megatrends occurring in education, they must be explored, documented, grasped and exploited ethically as well as thoughtfully (p. 8).

The goal of this chapter is to examine the "megatrend" known as open education in order to understand its potential impact on foreign language (FL) education in American colleges and universities. More specifically, this chapter explores the intersection between hybrid or blended FL learning and open educational resources (OERs). According to Plotkin (2010, p. 1), OERs refer to "teaching, learning, and research resources that reside in the public domain or have been released under an intellectual property license that permits sharing, accessing, repurposing—including for commercial purposes—and collaborating with others." First coined in 2002 during a UNESCO (United Nations Educational, Scientific and Cultural Organization) forum on the use of digitized materials and tools for global education, the term *open educational resources* was meant to emphasize knowledge construction as an ongoing process requiring dynamic pedagogical materials.

The terms *hybrid learning* and *blended learning* (BL) commonly refer to a combination of face-to-face (F2F) classroom methods with some form of computer-mediated instruction. Despite a lack of consensus among FL educators about the best way to blend offline and online learning, interest in blended language learning and computer-mediated communication is growing rapidly (Blake, 2008; Blyth, 2008; Chun, 2008; Thorne, 2008). Most discussions of BL focus on the mixture of F2F and online environments. However, what often goes unmentioned in these discussions is the mixture of open and closed materials and practices. Moreover, many educators continue to underestimate the disruptive effects of blending "closed" FL classrooms with "OERs" and their accompanying communities of practices (Baraniuk, 2012). But what exactly are closed and open forms of instruction, and what does it mean to blend them?

David Wiley (2009), a well-known leader in open education, argues that the terms "closed" and "open" index two opposing systems of educational beliefs and practices. Closed educational systems are defined by a heavy reliance on analogue materials such as printed textbooks, a static meeting place such as a classroom that is "tethered" to the physical world, the isolation of knowledge into discrete units, a single path of learning institutionalized in syllabi and pedagogical best practices, and a conception of learning as the transmission of ready-made knowledge from a producer (the teacher) to a consumer (the learner). In contrast, open educational systems emphasize the use of digital materials that are easily edited and customizable, a virtual or mobile learning environment, the integration of knowledge with social networks that connect people to ideas, an effort to personalize instruction as much as possible, and a belief that knowledge is best understood as a creative process of co-constructed meaning within a community of practice. According to Wiley, these opposing knowledge ecologies are at the heart of what he calls the "daily divide," that is, the growing disconnect between the relatively closed environment of formal education and the more open environment of everyday learning. Thorne (2008) raises similar concerns about traditional academic genres that risk appearing anachronistic to FL learners who are increasingly drawn to computer-mediated genres found in open Internet environments.

Although the "daily divide" between formal learning as traditionally conceived in higher education and informal learning associated with the Internet is profound, such differences do not necessarily fall into a neat dichotomy labeled "closed" and "open." In fact, many learners and teachers are currently seeking to bridge their own "daily divides" through BL. A good illustration of this new kind of personalized BL comes from the life of Timothy Doner, a 16-year-old polyglot whose love for FL learning was featured in *The New York Times* (Leland, 2012). A sophomore enrolled in French, Latin, and Mandarin classes at a private high school in New York City, Timothy discovered an online fellowship of autodidacts that "changed the metabolism of his language learning." Today, in addition to his formal language courses, Timothy studies an incredible number of languages online: Arabic, Croatian, Dutch, German, Hausa, Hindi, Italian, Indonesian, Kurdish, Objibwe, Pashto, Persian, Russian, Swahili, Turkish, and Yiddish. Although Timothy's "hyperpolyglottism" (2012) demonstrates a unique disposition to learn multiple languages, his story exemplifies the well-documented rise of informal learning made possible by a vast array of OERs. For example, before Timothy contacts speakers of a given language, he routinely avails himself of a host of language-related OERs to learn the basics, including reference grammars, closed captioned music videos, flash card applications, and online machine translators. As soon as he is able to form rudimentary messages in a new language, he then turns to Web 2.0 communication tools to connect with intellectual kindred spirits:

> In his family's apartment in the East Village, he made a video of himself speaking in Arabic and uploaded it onto YouTube, with subtitles in English. The response was sparse but enthusiastic, mainly from people in the Middle East: Way to go, Tim! He followed with more videos, each adding viewers, until his Pashto video, posted on December 21, had 10,000 views in two days. Suddenly, Timothy had people to talk to in all his languages—not just native speakers, but also people like himself, who were interested in language for its own sake, a small but vibrant subculture of language geeks, one made possible only by the Internet (Leland, 2012, p. 22).

I will suggest that students like Timothy represent the future of FL education. More and more, students enrolled in FL courses are taking the responsibility to create their own hybrid learning environments by blending their formal education with FL OERs. It bears repeating that "closed" and "open" are not meant to index two dichotomous categories, but rather two poles of a continuum. Therefore, it makes more sense to conceptualize FL educational practices in terms of degrees of openness. I will argue that FL program directors would do well to join forces with students like Timothy Doner and open up their curricula and praxis by incorporating elements of open Internet environments into their language programs.

This chapter is divided into four parts. The first part is devoted to a summary of the open education movement and, in particular, a description of open-access and open-source OERs. OERs are gaining in scope and quality and are supported by an increasingly robust community that includes many distinguished scholars and educators. Still in their infancy, OERs have been shown to improve learning outcomes, reduce costs, and improve the quality of teaching and learning (Plotkin, 2010). Although the term *OERs* is commonly used to refer to the pedagogical end products, it also represents the open and collaborative process that enables continuous improvement in materials. The second part responds to the questions that are frequently raised by skeptical faculty members. Can user-generated materials achieve the same level of quality as commercial materials? Do open materials violate copyright and intellectual property laws? The third part is a case study of *Français interactif*, an OER developed at the University of Texas at Austin as part of a hybrid French course for beginners (Kelton, Guilloteau, & Blyth, 2004). *Français interactif* illustrates openness in many of its unique features, including an open development process based on feedback from a community of users, a modular design, and an open license. The essay concludes with a few brief suggestions for FL program directors about how to participate in the open education movement.

The Open Education Movement

Open education refers to forms of education in which knowledge, ideas, or important aspects of teaching methodology or infrastructure are shared freely over the Internet. Richard Baraniuk, a professor of computer engineering at Rice University and a leading figure in the open education movement, describes the values and goals behind this paradigm shift:

> The open education (OE) movement is based on a set of intuitions shared by a remarkably wide range of academics: that knowledge should be free and open to use and re-use; that collaboration should be easier, not harder; that people should receive credit and kudos for contributing to education and research; and that concepts and ideas are linked in unusual and surprising ways and not the simple linear forms that today's textbook present. OE promises to fundamentally change the way authors, instructors, and students interact worldwide (Baraniuk, 2007, p. 229).

Similar to applied linguists who have increasingly adopted an ecological metaphor to understand language learning in relation to its contextual variables (Blyth, 2008; Kramsch, 2003; Levine 2011; Van Lier, 2004), open educators frequently invoke the concept of "knowledge ecosystem" to describe the relations between the various stakeholders in educational systems, including students, teachers, parents, administrators, textbook publishers, and other businesses such as testing services. Baraniuk (2007) contends that academic publishing constitutes a "closed knowledge ecosystem" because it shuts out "talented K-12 teachers, community college instructors, scientists and engineers out in industry, and the world majority who do not read and write English" (p. 230). Baraniuk's main point is that educational publishing is largely controlled by a small group of people in developed countries—publishers, editors, and academics—who are highly resistant to sharing control with the majority of end users. For example, open educators often note that commercial textbook publishers fundamentally differ from software companies in how they develop and test their products. Educational publishers overwhelmingly privilege the opinions of a minority of instructors over the majority of students for an obvious reason—instructors, not students, adopt textbooks. Given how textbook adoption drives product development, it is not surprising that publishers lavish attention on faculty focus groups and instructor surveys while largely ignoring student opinion. In contrast, the software industry focuses directly on end users who make their own purchasing decisions. As a consequence, software companies invest heavily in usability testing as part of their process of research and development. What would FL textbooks look like if they were the products of an equally rigorous process of usability testing?

Blyth and Davis (2007) argue that the textbook adoption model results in materials that are instructor friendly rather than student friendly. In addition, they argue that textbook publishers are often averse to any pedagogical innovation that might reduce potential adoptions, even innovations that are grounded in empirical research. To open up the system, Blyth and Davis (2007) call for publishers to conduct serious formative evaluation of FL materials as part of the developmental process, something similar to usability studies in software development. Formative evaluation of FL materials would require publishers to include the opinions of a much wider range of end users and to accord their opinions a greater weight. However, commercial publishers are not the only ones who must make changes to their practices. Rather than blame the dysfunctional system on commercial publishers alone, Blyth and Davis (2007) view it as the result of complicity among stakeholders in the system, including commercial publishers, textbook writers, reviewers, and language program directors.

Fortunately, this state of affairs is changing, thanks to the rise of *open content*, a term commonly used to refer to any kind of published digital content that may be freely used. Open pedagogical content comes in two basic forms: *open access* and *open source*. *Open access* refers to content made available to the Internet public without explicit permission to modify. In other words, the end user has the right to access the content but does not have the right to make derivative works based on the content. In contrast, open-source content allows users to reuse and repurpose the content to make original works. Open-source content has its roots in the open-software movement (Perens, 1999; Raymond, 2001). The revolutionary idea of this movement was to give end users free and open access to a software's source code by relaxing copyright restrictions, hence the term *open source*. Perens (1999, pp. 171–172) likens open source to a "bill of rights" that ensures computer users three basic rights:

1. The right to make copies of the computer program and distribute those copies
2. The right to have access to the software's source code, a necessary preliminary before you can change it
3. The right to make improvements to the program

One of the Internet's largest repositories of open-source educational materials is Connexions, a nonprofit publishing project founded at Rice University in 1999 by Richard Baraniuk (Baraniuk, 2006, 2007; Cohen, 2008; Guttenplan, 2012). Baraniuk (2012) reports usage statistics for Connexions that are mind boggling— more than 100 million hits from 190 countries per month. As long as students and teachers have Internet access, they may freely download any of Connexions' more than 1,100 open textbooks translated in more than 40 languages (Baraniuk, 2012). Baraniuk (2007, p. 230) also encourages authors, teachers, and learners to "create, rip, mix, and burn" the open content housed in Connexions to make their own pedagogical materials:

> In Connexions, anyone can create "modules of information"— smallish, Lego block documents that communicate a concept, a procedure, or a set of questions. Connect some modules together and you have a web course or textbook, or build a curriculum entirely of your choosing. All content is open-licensed under the Creative Commons attribution license; all tools are free and open-source.

In addition to letting "shut outs" play a major role in the development process, open education aims to drastically reduce the cost of materials as well as the time it takes to get materials into the hands of end users. Traditionally, academic publishers have used a careful prepublication review process before allowing access to the finished textbook. Such a slow review process makes sense when the publication medium is expensive and scarce (e.g., the paper and ink for book printing). However, publication practices used for printed textbooks are poorly suited to the fast pace of editorial change required by online digital materials.

There is also growing consensus on American college campuses that textbooks have simply become too expensive (Cohen, 2008; Guttenplan, 2012). The price of textbooks has actually risen more quickly than any other expense at two-year public colleges and at four-year colleges and universities, with the exception of room and board (Cohen, 2008). For some Americans, textbooks constitute the final barrier to college, particularly for low- and moderate-income students enrolled in community colleges where annual textbook costs are often equivalent to the price of tuition (Henderson, 2011). In a recent survey conducted by the Florida state legislature of 14,000 students enrolled in state-supported colleges and universities, roughly 50 percent of the students reported not buying a course textbook because of the price, and 24 percent said that they had not registered for a course because they could not afford the textbook (Open Access Textbook Task Force Final Report, 2010). Although these statistics may shock American educators, the problem is actually much worse in developing countries, where the price of textbooks is well beyond the means of the majority of students and teachers. In summary, there are four major goals of the open education movement: (a) to democratize education and thereby bring more people into the "knowledge ecosystem," (b) to reduce the high costs of pedagogical materials, (c) to reduce the time it takes to produce materials, and (d) to enable students and teachers to adapt materials to make them more appropriate for local contexts.

Challenges to Open Education

Despite an enthusiastic reception from instructors and administrators at community colleges (Plotkin, 2010), open education is still an unfamiliar concept to many faculty members in American higher education, including FL program directors. A recent study of more than 2,000 tenure and tenure-track faculty members at Florida public colleges indicated that just over 10 percent of instructors had actually used OERs, mainly as a supplement to traditional materials (Henderson, 2011). Although the Florida survey found widespread support for efforts to reduce the cost of textbooks, it also showed deep concern about the quality of OERs. If open education is to realize its promise, it must address concerns that fall into three related categories: quality control, copyright, and sustainability.

Quality Control

Concern about the quality of open content is best exemplified by the ongoing controversy surrounding Wikipedia. To some academics, the perceived deficiencies of Wikipedia's user-generated content simply outweigh potential virtues. Despite growing popularity among Internet users, Wikipedia is often criticized by faculty and educational administrators for including inaccurate and unreliable information. Nevertheless, Fallis (2008) cites several empirical studies that find the accuracy of Wikipedia comparable to that of traditional print encyclopedias. Furthermore, the reliability of Wikipedia compares even more favorably to the information sources that students would likely use *if Wikipedia did not exist*. In other words, comparing Wikipedia to a printed encyclopedia is simply beside the point because students rarely use printed encyclopedias anymore.

Critics of user-generated content would be surprised to learn that in addition to accuracy, epistemologists routinely cite other qualities for evaluating information: verifiability (are the sources trustworthy?), speed (how fast can knowledge be acquired?), power (how much knowledge can be acquired?), and fecundity (how many people can acquire the knowledge?) (Fallis, 2008). It appears that digital beats print by a wide margin if one cares about the epistemic virtues of speed, power, and fecundity. Apparently convinced that such virtues are important, *Encyclopedia Britannica*, arguably the world's most prestigious encyclopedia, announced that it was abandoning publication of its printed editions and would continue with digital versions available online (Kearney, 2012). Still, the questions of accuracy persist. Can user-generated content ever be as accurate and authoritative as commercial materials? Is it possible to allow end users to become producers of pedagogical materials and still maintain quality? These questions raise another question: who decides?

According to Plotkin (2010, p. 6), two primary methods are currently used to ensure the quality of OERs:

> The first replicates traditional academic practices by using a carefully vetted, top-down authoring system in which an institution places educational learning resources that carry its brand into an open format for free use, re-mixing or adaptation by others. In this instance, the institutions are responsible for the quality of the materials. The second methodology relies on the same basic procedures used in the open source software community. In this model, an unlimited number of authors collaborate on the creation of OER.

The first process described by Plotkin is relatively closed, given that it is restricted to an institution's faculty. For instance, the 15 Title VI National Foreign Language Resource Centers host a common web portal that constitutes one of the largest Internet archives of free FL materials (http://nflrc.msu.edu/lrcs.php). The quality of these materials is ensured by their host universities as well as by the U.S. Department of Education. Another well-known example is MIT OpenCourseWare, an initiative that relies entirely on MIT's faculty members. In the second approach, the so-called Wikipedia or "crowdsourcing" approach, the responsibility for creating and maintaining quality is shared among end users, typically a large crowd of heterogeneous contributors from different parts of the "knowledge ecosystem" (Howe, 2008; Johnson, 2010; Shirky, 2008, 2010a, 2010b; Tapscott & Williams, 2006). Taking inspiration from the open-source movement, this approach to quality control maintains that poor quality work will eventually gain notice and be improved upon by the crowd.

Connexions uses an approach to quality control that combines elements of traditional peer review and the newer crowdsourcing approach. According to the Connexions' website, the metaphor of a *lens* describes three groups of end users whose different perspectives and foci are represented in a self-organizing process:

> First, organizations, such as professional societies, can create *endorsement lenses* containing content they have carefully reviewed and deem to be of high quality. Second, organizations can also create *affiliation lenses* identifying content created by members of that organization (but not necessarily reviewed). Finally, anyone with a Connexions account can create *member list lenses*, identifying and describing content they deem to be of particular interest in the repository. All Connexions lenses can either be made privately viewable for personal use only or publicly viewable for anyone to see.

In addition to Connexions, many professional societies and organizations, such as OER Commons, Community College Open Textbook Collaborative, and WikiEducator, to name just a few, are explicitly concerned with vetting open content on the Internet. Another good example is Multimedia Educational Resource of Learning and Online Teaching (MERLOT), an online community of faculty and instructional technologists (http://www.merlot.org). According to its website, "MERLOT is a leading edge, user-centered, searchable collection of peer reviewed, higher education, online learning materials created by registered users and a set of faculty development support services." Materials in the MERLOT collection are divided into eight content areas: arts, business, education, humanities, mathematics/statistics, science/technology, social sciences, and workforce development. Humanities is further divided into various subdisciplines (e.g., American studies, classics, English, history, women and gender studies, world languages, and so on). Searchable by language and resource type, MERLOT's World Languages collection contains more than 2,000 peer-reviewed items, including assessment tools, online courses, journal articles, open textbooks, simulations, and tutorials.

MERLOT's process for evaluating pedagogical resources follows the standard academic model of peer review. MERLOT's editorial review board meets on a regular basis to identify Internet resources worthy of review. After materials have been deemed worthy of review, they are sent out to three faculty reviewers, who evaluate the quality of the materials according to established criteria. The reviews are then compiled into a single review and posted on the website along with a score based on a five-star rating system. In addition to these "expert" evaluations, reviews from ordinary teachers and learners are also posted.

The effectiveness of quality control via lenses is made possible by Web 2.0 social software that allows people to form online communities of practice where they share digital content and best practices. For example, Connexions and MERLOT both represent communities of users who collaboratively curate archives of open content. These online communities amplify and enrich the standard peer-review process based on expert reviews with informal comments, ratings, and tags from a wide variety of end users. A tag is a keyword descriptor created by an end user and assigned to a given online resource or OER. Tags automatically link content in a repository based on end users' personal interests and organizational schemes. Thus, an FL program director could go to MERLOT and conduct a keyword search that would yield many relevant OERs accompanied by reviews from end users. In summary, OER developers are exploring new ways to ensure the quality of their materials, blending traditional peer-review processes with promising, new methodologies native to the Internet.

Copyright

Many language program directors are unfamiliar with the open copyright license, an innovation that supports the sharing of intellectual property. They, like most academics, associate the concept of copyright with an approach to intellectual property summed up by their commercial textbooks' restrictive phrase "all rights reserved." Such an approach to copyright inhibits the sharing of ideas and scholarly materials, making collaboration among language program directors difficult if not downright illegal. Creative Commons (http://creativecommons.org), a nonprofit organization of legal experts, seeks to change the copyright situation by providing open licenses to any content creator. In essence, open licenses allow creators to disaggregate the rights bundled together in the phrase "all rights reserved" and to share those rights with end users:

> Copyright was created long before the emergence of the Internet, and can make it hard to legally perform actions we take for granted on the network: copy, paste, edit and post to the Web. The default setting of copyright law requires all of these actions to have explicit permission, granted in advance, whether you're an artist, teacher, scientist, librarian, policymaker or just a regular user. To achieve the vision of universal access, someone needed to provide a free, public and standardized infrastructure that creates a balance between the reality of the Internet and the reality of copyright laws (*The Power of Open*, 2011, p. 5).

Creative Commons' open licenses are legally solid, globally applicable, and responsive to user needs. A unique feature of Creative Commons licenses is their three-layer design. The first layer is the "legal code," consisting of traditional legal tools applicable around the world. This is supplemented with a "human-readable" explanation in more user-friendly language accessible to most creators (Figs. 10-1 and 10-2). The final layer is a "machine-readable" description that software systems, search engines, and other technology can understand and use to make searching for open-licensed works more convenient. In other words, after being tagged with an open license, all sorts of open content (e.g., text, music, images, video) can be located by end users using Internet tools such as Google, Flikr, Jamendo, and SpinXpress.

Creative Commons licenses are arrayed on a continuum of openness—from the most open to the least open. The most open license, the CC-BY license, is

Figure 10-1. CC-BY license.   Figure 10-2. CC-BY-NC-ND license.

shown in Figure 10-1. If a textbook carries a CC-BY license, end users are free to copy and change the textbook any way they want as long as they obey attribution, that is, as long as they indicate whom the original work was "by," hence the name "CC-BY." The most restrictive license, shown in Figure 10-2, does not allow users to sell the original work for profit or to change the original in any way. The terms of all Creative Commons licenses are spelled out by simple icons and acronyms: BY for attribution, NC for noncommercial works, SA for share alike, and ND for nonderivative works.

Sustainability

The issue of sustainability is closely related to the issues of quality and copyright. The old adage—"there is no such thing as a free lunch"—sums up the stance adopted by many who are unfamiliar with the open education movement. Language program directors responsible for dealing with the practical realities of pedagogical materials are likely to view free textbooks as a utopian concept, too good to be true. How can "free" be a viable, economic model for textbooks? The traditional economic models associated with printed educational materials do not directly apply to OERs because digital content and software platforms are often available on the Internet at no cost. For example, MIT incurred no significant additional costs when it made the MIT OpenCourseWare initiative available to the general Internet public.

Dissemination is not the same thing as development, however. Open materials may be free to disseminate and use, but they are not free to develop. For example, many of the "free" pedagogical materials produced by the National Foreign Language Resource Centers are actually subsidized by federal grant money via the U.S. Department of Education. In other words, American taxpayers have already paid for these "free" materials. Given the economic crisis in public education, proponents of open education are asking themselves how they can acquire the financial resources to sustain the production of OERs. As with quality control and copyright, open educators have developed alternatives to traditional economic models. One of the most promising models for OER publication is the "freemium model" pioneered by Chris Anderson, the editor of *Wired* magazine (Anderson, 2006, 2009). The freemium business model works by offering core services or products for free while charging a premium for advanced or special features. Anderson notes that Google, the most profitable and powerful Internet company, bases its entire economic model on giving its tools and services away for free to Internet users. In the case of pedagogical materials, an OER developer would provide free downloads of all its digital materials but require a small fee for the premium of printing, collating, and binding the digital materials into a printed textbook or workbook. But would students and teachers pay for materials that they could download for free? According to recent surveys (Henderson, 2011), college students and instructors overwhelmingly want materials in both digital and print formats and are willing to pay for printed materials as long as they consider the prices to be reasonable. In practical terms, this means that the freemium model works best when it can leverage the massive scale of the Internet to keep prices "reasonable."

Open Education Meets Hybrid Language Learning: The Case of *Français interactif*

This section focuses on how *Français interactif*, an OER in development at the University of Texas at Austin, blends hybrid learning and open education. In particular, four key features of the curriculum are discussed: (a) the open developmental process, (b) the print-on-demand technology and modular design that facilitate BL, (c) the Facebook community of practice, and (d) the open license that permits remixing and repurposing of content for derivative works.

Developing *Français interactif*

More than 10 years ago, the lower division French program at the University of Texas at Austin began conducting routine usability tests and attitudinal surveys to assess the efficacy of various elements of online learning environments. Surveyed students repeatedly expressed a desire for a clearer pedagogical sequence that began with decontextualized practice of vocabulary and grammar and led progressively to contextualized discourse (Blyth & Davis, 2007). With this feedback in mind, the developmental team of faculty and graduate students set out to design a BL environment based on the lexical approach as described by Lewis (1993). As its name implies, the lexical approach is characterized by a greater emphasis on vocabulary development, including lexical phrases. Lewis (1993) notes that language teaching has traditionally been organized around the grammatical system. In the lexical approach, students first learn to collocate words and then to grammaticalize meaning in a deliberate sequence: from word to sentence to discourse.

Although the methodological changes requested by the students were a significant departure from the materials used at the time, the most profound impact of allowing student feedback to drive curriculum development was a shift in focus—from the native speaker as a role model to the non-native speaker as a language learner (see Blyth, 2009b, for a complete narrative of the process). Many FL educators have questioned the exclusive use of monolingual native speakers as role models for learners trying to overcome their own monolingualism (Belz, 2003; Blyth, 1995, 2009a, 2009b; Kramsch, 1997; Levine, 2011). According to these scholars, the reliance on the idealized monolingual native speaker leads students to see themselves as deficient. And yet, for the most part, publishers continue to base their pedagogical materials on the native speaker norm. Seeking to reframe the curriculum in terms of multilingualism, *Français interactif* documents the subjective language learning experiences of a group of American students during their study abroad program in France. In essence, the study abroad students act as virtual tour guides who assist learners in a vicarious exploration of the French language and culture.

Français interactif accords a place of privilege to the non-native speaker (Kramsch, 1997), in this case, French–English bilinguals who exhibit a wide range of proficiencies from balanced bilingualism to the incipient bilingualism of the students who communicate as best they can in a mixture of French and English. Because the goal of the videos was to document authentic speech, both native and non-native, no attempt was made to remove grammatical and lexical errors. Moreover, by juxtaposing videos of fluent and incipient bilinguals, the developers hoped to raise learners' awareness about the nature of bilingualism and second language (L2) learning. More specifically, the developers wanted learners to understand that bilinguals use their languages according to situational need and that the use of the L1 is not an aberration signaling deficiency but a natural part of the learning process (Levine, 2011).

In a recent qualitative study using think-aloud data from 11 students who performed various pedagogical tasks while watching the *Français interactif* videos, Blyth (2009a) found that students attended to native and non-native input in quantitatively and qualitatively different ways. Students produced twice as many comments while watching their peers than while watching native speakers. For example, students routinely noticed and commented on the lexical and grammatical errors made by their peers. The errors made by the non-natives in the videos prompted students to project themselves into the communicative event they were watching and, as a consequence, to reflect on their own proficiency ("I wonder if I would do as well communicating in that situation"). Students frequently mentioned that they gained a greater awareness of communication strategies and strategies for self-correction by watching non-native speakers. Participants also mentioned that the videos gave them a more realistic picture of L2 acquisition and helped them to gauge their own language development. Based on these data, Blyth (2009a) claims that beginning FL learners are more likely to construct their projective linguistic identities (Gee, 2003) on proficient non-native speakers than on native speakers.

In addition to the inclusion of students in the ongoing developmental process of *Français interactif*, the participation of graduate student instructors (GSIs) is also a key feature. GSIs contribute to the curriculum as part of their professional training by updating old materials, designing new materials, and testing materials in their classrooms. The professional development of GSIs is thus tightly woven into the development of the curriculum itself (Rossomondo, 2011). GSIs not only gain marketable skills in developing digital materials, but they also gain a deeper understanding of how the materials relate to classroom practice. In short, because they play an active role in helping to develop the materials, GSIs become more proficient users of the materials and are more committed to the success of the materials.

Modular Design and Print-on-demand Technology

Designed for use in a variety of educational contexts (e.g., formal, instructed environments vs. informal, self-taught environments; secondary education vs. higher education), OERs are typically more modular than traditional textbooks.

The modular design of OERs presents significant challenges for instructors who are used to the textbook's traditional linear format and integration of vocabulary, grammar, and thematics. To overcome this problem, all learning objects in each chapter are labeled either by media type (e.g., video, audio, print, Internet link) or by pedagogical category (e.g., vocabulary, phonetics, grammar, culture). In addition to several hours of multimedia content, *Français interactif* features a printed "textbook" of activities for the classroom. The textbook is available as a free, downloadable PDF or as a print-on-demand textbook that may be purchased for less than $30. The term "print-on-demand" refers to a growing movement in the publishing industry in which new copies of a book are not printed until an order has been received. Open, print-on-demand textbooks avoid the publishing, printing, and inventory costs associated with traditional textbooks. The use of a printed textbook option in the digital age may strike some as a step backward. However, the usage statistics of *Français interactif* corroborate recent reports that students and teachers still demand hard copies of pedagogical materials. To purchase a print-on-demand textbook, users simply click on a link that takes them to Qoop.com, a print-on-demand company, where they may choose what kind of copy they wish to purchase (black and white or color). After purchasing their copy, students can expect the textbook to be delivered within five business days.

The flexible design of *Français interactif* facilitates the movement between online and offline environments that is the hallmark of BL. Students prepare online content as homework that is recycled and expanded upon in subsequent classroom activities. For example, students begin each chapter online by viewing a brief introductory video that previews the chapter's theme. In Chapter 5, *Bon appétit*, the introductory video features a student who comments on the different foods he has tasted during his study abroad experience in Lyon. Next, learners are led through a multistep activity titled *Préparation du vocabulaire* in which they must listen to recorded vocabulary items, noting the words they find difficult to pronounce. Students are then asked to identify "word families" of related vocabulary items such as *goûter* (to taste), *un goûter* (a snack), and *du bon goût* (good taste, tasteful) and to invent several examples of a French word game called *Chassez l'intrus* ("Find the Intruder"). To play the game, students must make a list of four words in which three words are semantically related and one word is not related (the intruder). The *préparation du vocabulaire* activities focus students on the meaning and pronunciation of each word without having them use the words in a grammatical frame, an activity inspired by the lexical approach. After the students have finished working with the vocabulary in decontextualized lists, they watch a series of videos in which native speakers employ the vocabulary in a natural context. Students are asked to identify which vocabulary items they hear, a rather difficult listening task given the rapid rate of speech.

The next day in class, students compare which words they found difficult to pronounce and which word families they identified. They also play the *Chassez l'intrus* game that helps them bind vocabulary forms to their meaning. These word games are followed by a series of group activities in their textbook, including a structured input activity that focuses on the use of definite articles with verbs of preference (e.g., *J'aime le café*—I like coffee), a dictogloss that recycles vocabulary, and a discovery grammar activity in which students induce the rules for the partitive articles (*du, de la, de l'*—some, any).

The following evening, students go to the online grammar module, where they read a grammatical explanation of the partitive articles, listen to dialogues that demonstrate usage, and complete several form-focused exercises. Immediate feedback is available for all online grammar drills. Students post their completed grammar exercises to Blackboard, where their instructors verify their progress. In addition to the online grammar exercises, students prepare homework activities that require them to watch a video and respond in a meaningful way. The students' written production for every online assignment becomes the point of departure for subsequent classroom activities, which in turn lead back to another sequence of online activities. In this manner, all online homework is recycled and expanded in the classroom. As the chapter progresses, the video and audio content becomes more challenging and varied (interviews, television reports, songs) and forms the basis of extended activities that may last several days. For example, every chapter ends with a two-minute video produced by Rhône-Alpes television. Students prepare previewing questions at home about the topic, and then they view the video in class and perform pair and whole-class activities that help them comprehend the content. For homework, the students view the video by themselves and do a follow-up reading from a highlighted website. Thus, the progression of activities for one video is spread over several days.

Social Media and Communities of Practice

Since its launch in 2004, *Français interactif* has gained an international following of users from all walks of life—high school students preparing for final exams, tourists brushing up on French before a holiday, teachers looking for additional materials. To curate its online community of users, the developers launched a Facebook page in early 2011. Moderated by a community college French instructor who teaches with *Français interactif*, the community has grown rapidly. Although the community includes instructors who join the discussion from time to time, it is essentially composed of language enthusiasts who learn from each other, an example of peer-to-peer learning. The moderator posts a variety of questions that follow the thematics of the *Français interactif* curriculum. This allows learners to experience the "textbook" language in a real context and to practice what they are learning in class in an open Internet environment (Thorne, 2008). The moderator periodically posts a provocative or funny image and asks learners to share their comments in French. Some prompts generate more than 100 comments. Inevitably, students begin by responding to the instructor but end up engaging each other. In addition to practicing French with speakers from around the world, members of the Facebook community benefit from sharing their language learning tips with each other ("To learn vocabulary, I write words on Post-it notes and put them around my apartment."). Learners frequently share their favorite websites and tools for language learning and discuss how they like to use these resources.

Open Licenses for Remixing and Repurposing

As noted, one of the biggest differences between OERs and commercial textbooks is copyright. *Français interactif* carries the most open Creative Commons license currently available that allows the end user to "create, rip, mix, and burn." Although it is true that textbook companies provide custom publishing services that allow adopters some flexibility regarding layout and content, such services should not be confused with the rights afforded to the users of open-licensed content. In other words, anybody is free to take any of the content in *Français interactif*—text, audio, video, images—and repurpose it according to their needs and desires as long as the derivative work carries attribution of the original work. This means that an instructor may rewrite a grammar explanation or replace an image with a personal photo. Or she may choose to personalize communicative activities by substituting the names of her students for the names in the textbook. Two short anecdotes suffice to illustrate the potential benefits of repurposing open materials.

Two years ago, a French professor who taught francophone African literature at an American university contacted the developers of *Français interactif* to inquire about using the program to teach French in a Nigerian university where she was a visiting faculty member. The professor explained that she was primarily interested in the curriculum because it would be free for her African students to access and use. After teaching with the materials for a few weeks, she noted that the book's premise of understanding French culture and language as filtered through the subjectivity of American college students did not suit her Nigerian context. However, rather than discontinue using the book because it was deemed culturally inappropriate, she embraced the concept of open-source materials and told her students that it was their job to repurpose the textbook for an African audience. She reported that her students felt a new sense of ownership of the program when they were empowered to make editorial decisions about how to include an African perspective.

Another example comes from a French professor at a small liberal arts university who was inspired to create videos of her own students during their study abroad program in France. The professor commented that her students benefitted from comparing the experiences of the *Français interactif* students with the experiences of students from their own university. Similar to the Nigerian students who gathered images and texts that represented and validated their own language learning experiences, these American students were able to construct their own projective identities based on locally created materials.

Both of these anecdotes demonstrate an important lesson: it is ultimately the task of the instructor (and perhaps the students as well) to adapt materials to the local context. Therefore, instructors should see OERs more like templates rather than textbooks. Currently, *Français interactif's* textbook and printed activities are in the form of PDFs that do not lend themselves to customization. Retrofitting the materials will require the adoption of an open-source technology platform to facilitate the publication of newly developed content as a "Flexbook"—defined simply as an adaptive, web-based set of instructional materials with a print-on-demand option. One simple and low-cost solution under review is Google Docs, a secure, online word processing platform that allows users to create, store, and share documents in real time.

Conclusion

For language program directors to produce open pedagogical materials, they should first become a member of the open education community of practice. New members of communities of practice are typically viewed as apprentices whose "legitimate peripheral participation" includes observing the practices of the more expert members and gradually learning to perform in similar ways (Lave & Wenger, 1991). Here, then, are a few suggestions of peripheral practices for newcomers to the OER community:

1. *Learn how to locate OERs.* There are many places to go on the Internet to locate top-quality OERs. A few suggested places to start your search are noted in the Appendix under "Learning Objects." Another excellent resource is CC Search (see http://search.creativecommons.org). From this web page, users can find just about any open content in a variety of formats, including images, videos, music, texts, and courses. The Department of Education's National Foreign Language Resource Centers portal is another treasure trove of free FL materials (http://nflrc.msu. edu/lrcs.php).
2. *Join the World Languages Community at MERLOT.* MERLOT is a non-profit project of California State University that offers peer-reviewed online teaching and learning materials. Create your own personal collection of materials and write a review for the community (see http://www. merlot.org/merlot/index.htm).
3. *Become an informal language learner.* Most language program directors have forgotten what it was like to be a beginning language learner. There is no better way to understand the power of openness than by learning a new language online with the aid of OERs and an online community.

As long as FL program directors continue to see themselves as consumers rather than as producers of pedagogical materials, they will remain on the margins of the open education movement. Fortunately, many FL instructors are beginning to realize that digital technology has afforded them the tools of production such as digital video recorders and multimedia software as well as the means of mass distribution such as YouTube and open content management systems. It is when language program directors begin to collaborate with their colleagues and students to produce their own pedagogical materials that new ways of conceptualizing language and language learning will finally replace outdated ideologies and practices entrenched in commercial textbooks (Train, 2003, 2007).

References

Anderson, C. (2006). *The long tail*. New York: Hyperion.

Anderson, C. (2009). *Free: The future of a radical price*. New York: Hyperion.

Baraniuk, R. (2006). *Goodbye textbooks; Hello open source learning* [Online video]. Retrieved July 30, 2012, from http://www.ted.com/index.php/talks/view/id/25.

Baraniuk, R. (2007). Challenges and opportunities for the open education movement: A Connexions case study. In T. Iiyoshi & M. S. V. Kumar (Eds.), *Opening up education*. Boston: MIT Press.

Baraniuk, R. (2012). Disruptive innovation via open education resources [Online video]. Retrieved July 27, 2012, from http://sites.la.utexas.edu/open-language/2011/disruptive-innovaation-via-open-education-resources.

Belz, J. (2003). Identity, deficiency, and L1 use in foreign language study. In C. Blyth (Ed.), *The sociolinguistics of foreign-language classrooms* (pp. 209–250). Boston: Heinle.

Blake, R. (2008). *Brave new digital classroom: Technology and foreign language learning*. Washington, DC: Georgetown University Press.

Blyth, C. (1995). Redefining the boundaries of language use: the foreign language classroom as a multilingual speech community In C. Kramsch (Ed.), *Redefining the boundaries of language study* (pp. 145–183). Boston: Heinle.

Blyth, C. (2008). Research perspectives on online discourse and foreign language learning. In S. Magnan (Ed.), *Mediating online discourse* (pp. 47–72). Amsterdam: John Benjamins.

Blyth, C. (2009a). The impact of pedagogical materials on critical language awareness: Assessing student attention to patterns of language use. In M. Turnbull & J. Dailey-O'Cain (Eds.), *First language use in second and foreign language learning* (pp. 163–181). London: Multilingual Matters.

Blyth, C. (2009b). From textbook to online materials: The changing ecology of foreign-language publishing in the era of ICT. In M. Evans (Ed.), *Foreign language learning with digital technology* (pp. 174–202). London: Continuum.

Blyth, C., & Davis, J. (2007). Using formative evaluation in the development of learner-centered materials. *CALICO Journal, 25* (1), 1–21.

Bonk, C. (2009). *The world is open*. San Francisco: Jossey-Bass.

Chun, D. (2008). Computer-mediated discourse in instructed environments. In S. Magnan (Ed.), *Mediating online discourse* (pp. 15–46). Amsterdam: John Benjamins.

Cohen, N. (2008). Don't buy that book, download it free. *The New York Times*, September 14.

Fallis, D. (2008). Toward an epistemology of Wikipedia. *Journal of the American Society for Information Science and Technology, 59*, 1662–1674.

Friedman, T. (2005). *The world is flat*. New York: Farrar, Strauss & Giroux.

Gee, J. (2003). *What video games have to teach us about learning and literacy*. New York: Palgrave.

Guttenplan, D. (2012). Big savings for U.S. students in open-source book program. *The New York Times*. February 12.

Henderson, S. (2011). The *challenges and lessons learned from Florida's open textbook initiative* [Online video]. Retrieved July 30, 2012, from http://sites.la.utexas.edu/open-language/2011/challenges-and-lessons-learned-from-florida%E2%80%99s-open-textbook-initiative.

Howe, J. (2008). *Crowdsourcing: Why the power of the crowd is driving the future of business*. New York: Three Rivers Press.

Johnson, S. (2010). *Where good ideas come from: The natural history of innovation*. New York: Penguin Press.

Kearney, C. (2012). Encyclopedia Britannica ends print, goes digital. *Reuters Online*, March 14. Retrieved July 30, 2012, from http://www.reuters.com/article/2012/03/14/net-us-encyclopediabritannica-idUSBRE82C1FS20120314.

Kelton, K., Guilloteau, N., & Blyth, C. (2004). *Français interactif: An online introductory French course*. Retrieved July 30, 2012, from http://www.laits.utexas.edu/fi.

Kramsch, C. (1997). The privilege of the non-native speaker. *PMLA, 112*(3), 359–369.

Kramsch, C. (2003). *Language acquisition and language socialization: Ecological perspectives*. London: Continuum.

Lave, J., & Wenger, E. (1991). *Situated learning: Legitimate peripheral practice*. Cambridge: Cambridge University Press.

Leland, J. (2012). Teenage master of languages finds an online fellowship. *The New York Times*, March 11.

Levine, G. 2011. *Code choice in the language classroom*. Bristol: Multilingual Matters.

Lewis, M. (1993). *The lexical approach*. Hove, England: Language Teaching Publications.

Open Access Textbook Task Force Final Report. (2010). *Report issued based on Florida state bill 7121*. Retrieved July 30, 2012, from http://www.theorangegrove.org/text_task-force.asp.

Perens, B. (1999). *Open sources: Voices from the open source revolution*. Beijing: O'Reilly Media.

Plotkin, H. (2010). *Free to learn*. San Francisco: Creative Commons. Retrieved July 30, 2012, from http://wiki.creativecommons.org/Free_to_Learn_Guide.

Raymond, E. (2001). *The cathedral and the bazaar: Musings on Linux and the open source by and accidental revolutionary*. Beijing: O'Reilly Media.

Rossomondo, A. (2011). The Acceso project and foreign language graduate student professional development. In H. W. Allen & H. H. Maxim (Eds.), *Educating the future foreign language professoriate for the 21st century* (pp. 128–148). Boston: Heinle Cengage.

Shirky, C. (2008). *Here comes everybody*. New York: Penguin Press.

Shirky, C. (2010a). *Cognitive surplus: Creativity and generosity in a connected age*. New York: Penguin Press.

Shirky, C. (2010b). *How cognitive surplus will change the world* [Online video]. Retrieved July 30, 2012, from http://www.ted.com/talks/clay_shirky_how_cognitive_surplus_will_change_the_world.html.

Tapscott, D., & Williams, A. (2006). *Wikinomics: How mass collaboration changes everything*. New York: Penguin Press.

The power of open. (2011). San Francisco: Creative Commons. Retrieved July 30, 2012, from http://thepowerofopen.org.

Thorne, S. (2008). Transcultural communication in open internet environments and massively multiplayer online games. In S. Magnan (Ed.), *Mediating discourse online* (pp. 305–330). Amsterdam: John Benjamins.

Train, R. (2003). The (non)native standard language in foreign language education: a critical perspective. In C. Blyth (Ed.), *The sociolinguistics of foreign-language classrooms* (pp. 3–39). Boston: Heinle.

Train, R. (2007). Language ideology and foreign language pedagogy. In D. Ayoun (Ed.), *French applied linguistics* (pp. 238–269). Amsterdam: John Benjamins.

Van Lier, L. (2004). *The ecology and semiotics of language learning: A sociocultural perspective*. Dordrecht: Kluwer Academic Publishers.

Wiley, D. (2009). Openness, disaggregation and the future of education [Online video]. Retrieved July 30, 2012, from http://www.youtube.com/watch?v=VcRctjvIeyQ.

Appendix 10-1. Open Educational Resources

Learning Objects

Learning objects are educational raw materials of varying degrees of complexity that can be combined with other learning objects to create more complete or comprehensive sets of learning materials.

- Connexions

A place to view and share educational material made of small knowledge chunks called modules that can be organized as courses, books, reports, and so on. All content is now available for download as the EPUB file used by most smart phones and e-readers worldwide.

http://cnx.org

- OER Commons

A network for teaching and learning materials, the website allows social bookmarking, tagging, rating, and reviewing of more than 24,000 items from 120 content providers.

http://www.oercommons.org

- National Foreign Language Resource Centers (NFLRC)

The Department of Education's NFLRC web portal for free foreign language materials.

http://nflrc.msu.edu/lrcs.php

- Multimedia Educational Resources for Learning and Online Teaching (MERLOT)

MERLOT is a project of California State University and offers peer-reviewed online teaching and learning materials.

http://www.merlot.org/merlot/index.htm

- Open Content Alliance

An archive of multilingual digitized text and multimedia material.

http://www.opencontentalliance.org

- eGranary Digital Library Project

Called the "Internet in a box," the project provides millions of digital educational resources to institutions lacking adequate Internet access.

http://www.widernet.org/egranary

- Khan Academy

A library of more than 1,600 video tutorials covering most of the K to 12 math curriculum and an increasing number of other subjects.

http://www.khanacademy.org

Open Educational Resources Encyclopedias

OER encyclopedias are edited by volunteers or invited subject area experts.

- Wikipedia

Wikipedia is the undisputed champion of user-driven collaborative encyclopedias with, according to the website, nearly 78 million visitors monthly and more than 91,000 active contributors working on more than 16,000,000 articles in more than 270 languages.

http://www.wikipedia.org

- Encyclopedia of Life

The Encyclopedia of Life aims to become an online reference and database on all 1.9 million species currently known to science with the goal of building a better understanding of life on Earth.

http://www.eol.org

- Stanford University Encyclopedia of Philosophy

This encyclopedia has both editorial and advisory boards ensuring quality of submissions, potentially qualifying it as a scholarly dynamic reference work.

http://plato.stanford.edu

Open Educational Resources Archives

Online archives are large, searchable collections of digital materials.

- Internet Archive

The Internet Archive hosts movies, texts, audio files, and a collection of websites.

http://www.archive.org

- The Alexandria Archive Institute

The Alexandria Archive institutes has created a free, open-access resource for the electronic publication of primary field research from archaeology and related disciplines.

http://www.alexandriaarchive.org

Open Text Books

Open textbooks are either authored textbooks that have been made available online (open access) or collaborative works created for sharing (open source).

- Center for Open Educational Resources and Language Learning (COERLL)

A federally funded National Foreign Language Resource Center, COERLL offers three open textbooks: *Deutsch im Blick* (German), *Français interactif* (French), and *Yòrúbá Yémi* (Yoruba).

http://www.coerll.utexas.edu/coerll/home

- Community College Open Textbook Collaborative

The CCOTC site has links to more than 545 open textbooks and the open textbook community.

http://collegeopentextbooks.org

- OpenStax College

Supported by several prominent foundations—the Gates Foundation, the Hewlett Foundation, the Maxfield Foundation, and the Twenty Million Minds Foundation—OpenStax is an initiative of Connexions.org and Rice University. OpenStax offers peer-reviewed, open textbooks for heavily enrolled college courses such as Introduction to Biology. The publication date is scheduled for late 2012.

http://openstaxcollege.org

- WikiEducator

WikiEducator has hundreds of links to free and open textbook sources.

http://wikieducator.org/Free_textbooks

Open Courses and Open Courseware

Instructional materials used to teach a specific course, including lecture notes, texts, reading lists, course assignments, syllabi, study materials, problem sets, exams, illustrations, and streaming videos of in-class lectures.

- Hippocampus

A project of the Monterey Institute of Technology, Hippocampus provides high-quality multimedia content for high school and college students on general education topics.

http://www.hippocampus.org

- MIT OpenCourseWare

MIT OpenCourseWare is the web-based publication of the content of 2,000 MIT courses.

http://ocw.mit.edu

- Open Courseware Consortium

The Open Courseware Consortium is a collaborative effort of more than 250 universities around the world.

http://www.ocwconsortium.org

- Open Learning Initiative

Headquartered at Carnegie Mellon University, the Open Learning Initiative features professionally developed "smart" courses that use feedback loops for sophisticated learner analytics. Offerings are STEM courses with a handful of humanities courses, including a beginning French course.

http://oli.web.cmu.edu/openlearning

- National Repository of Online courses (NROC)

NROC is a growing library of online course content assessed to meet standards for scholarship, instructional value, and presentational impact.

http://www.montereyinstitute.org/nroc/nroc.html

Online Tools for the Open Educational Resources Community

Tools to find, use, create, and distribute OERs.

- Center for Open Educational Resources and Language Learning (COERLL)

One of 15 federally funded National Foreign Language Resource Centers, COERLL's mission is to produce and disseminate language learning OERs for the Internet public (e.g., courses, grammars, assessment tools, corpora).

- Creative Commons

The Creative Commons website offers a menu of standard intellectual property licenses that offer creators options about how their materials can be used by others. These open licenses can be electronically appended to intellectual properties free of charge.

http://creativecommons.org

- CC Search

Creative Commons offers one-stop shopping for open content search services provided by independent organizations such as Google and Flikr. From this page, users can find all the open content they are looking for, including images, videos, music, texts, courses, and so on.

http://search.creativecommons.org

- DiscoverEd

A prototype search engine developed by Creative Commons that uses distributed curation and structured data to improve search and discovery for educational resources on the web.

http://discovered.labs.creativecommons.org

- ETUDES

Based on SAKAI, ETUDES offers turn-key, fully managed course and learning management solutions and an array or training and support options for higher education institutions

http://etudes.org

- Flat World Knowledge

A commercial publishing company that offers free learning materials while charging for printed versions and sharing revenues more generously with authors than previous industry practices.

http://www.flatworldknowledge.com

- Foreign Language Teaching Wiki

A wiki created by a foreign language teaching methods students during the fall 2006 semester.

http://flteaching.wikispaces.com

- MOODLE

Moodle is a free software package used to create online courses and teaching websites.

http://moodle.org

- Next Generation Learning

A new initiative supported by the Gates and Hewlett Foundations and involving EDUCAUSE, the league for innovation in the Community Colleges, the International Association for K–12 Online Learning, and the Council of Chief State School Officers (CCSSO). NexGen Learning "is seeking to dramatically improve college readiness and college completion in the U.S. through the applied use of technology and digital media."

http://nextgenlearning.com

- SAKAI

SAKAI is an open-source collaboration and courseware management platform that allows institutions to modify the software to meet their own needs.

http://sakaiproject.org

- Scitable

The Nature Publishing Group decided in 2009 to make a sustained effort to overcome questions about the reliability of free materials found on the Internet in life and physical science disciplines by publishing Scitable, a new type of hybrid that partners OERs with commercial publishing.

http://www.nature.com/scitable

Adapted from Plotkin, 2010.

Chapter 11

Integrating Foundational Language and Content Study Through New Approaches to Hybrid Learning and Teaching

Amy E. Rossomondo

Hybrid or blended learning, in which instruction takes place both online and in class, is typically characterized by the use of technology to facilitate those pedagogical activities that take place outside of the traditional face-to-face (F2F) foreign language (FL) classroom (Blake, 2005; Chenoweth, Ushida, & Murday, 2006; Winke, Gass, & Sydorenko, 2010). However, as digital technology use becomes ever more integrated in FL teaching and learning, this distinction becomes increasingly blurred: Is a course defined as "hybrid" because of its extensive use of technology to facilitate pedagogical activities or because many of these activities take place outside of scheduled class time? Furthermore (and although obviously extending beyond the conventional use of the term in the context of language program direction), can a course that embraces technology to promote "hybridity" and "hybridizing" with respect to both its development and implementation be understood as a *hybrid course*? Thorne, Black, and Sykes discuss how the New London Group (1996) has used these concepts to describe "the process of taking existing linguistic, semiotic, and/or cultural materials and recombining them to create new meanings" in the context of approaches to literacy teaching and learning (2009, p. 804). This chapter describes how the open-access, web-based *Acceso* project implements hybrid teaching and learning in all of these senses both inside and outside of the classroom. Through integrated use of the three categories of computer-assisted language learning (CALL) described in Garrett's (2009) comprehensive overview (tutorial, engagement with authentic materials, and communication), *Acceso* implements an approach to foundational FL study that is consonant with discussions of integrated content and language learning even at the earliest levels of instruction (Frantzen, 2010; Kern, 2000, 2002; Maxim, 2006; Meyer, 2009; Modern Language Association [MLA], 2007; Swaffar & Arens, 2005, among others). This chapter also argues for a characterization of *Acceso*'s content as "hybrid" with respect both to its collaborative development and maintenance and to how student engagement of this content is facilitated inside and outside of the classroom. Finally, the chapter discusses the benefits and challenges of developing and implementing such a project from a language program director's (LPD's) perspective, as well as directions for its future.

Overcoming Challenges of Design and Content Creation Through Collaboration

In a discussion of challenges related to incorporating content to promote lin-guistic development at lower levels of FL instruction, Allen and Paesani (2010) question the aptness of commercial textbooks, citing both a decade of scholarly criticism of "the dominance of grammatical content and lack of meaningfully in-tegrated textual content" and empirical studies that reveal "a continued reliance on form-focused, mechanical exercises and a lack of engaging content in commu-nicative textbooks" (p. 218). Moreover, the necessity for textbooks' broad appeal (as it relates to their commercial nature) privileges conservative thematic content over the exploration of more provocative topics of potential interest to college stu-dents (Allen & Paesani, 2010; Brager & Rice, 2000; Blythe & Davis, 2007). Another consideration is the medium of print itself, which is limited by its static nature: Changes and updates to any content must wait for subsequent editions, which ul-timately constrains the nature of the content itself. These pedagogical limitations, in conjunction with the fact that commercial textbook packages are increasingly expensive (students typically pay $100–$150 for a textbook and its ancillary materials), point to the need for alternative solutions.

In a 2009 report titled "Harnessing Openness to Improve Research, Teaching and Learning in Higher Education," the Committee for Economic Development Digital Connections Council explores the potential that openness and connectivity offer to higher education. The report defines open educational resources (OERs) as "digitized materials offered freely and openly for educators, students, and self learners to use and reuse for teaching, learning and research, including content, software tools to develop, use, and redistribute content, and implementation re-sources such as open licenses" (p. 15). That is, OERs are pedagogical materials, available free of cost, that can be shared, modified, and implemented as the edu-cational context warrants. When applied to the task of transforming introductory-and intermediate-level FL programs, OERs serve to reduce reduplication of efforts, thereby economizing the considerable time dedicated to materials development that would otherwise be done at the programmatic level; at the same time, the flexibility inherent in OER enables programs to modify materials or the approach to their implementation according to their own academic contexts, which renders them inherently "hybrid" if we extend our understanding of the term to include the New London Group's (1996) notion of hybridizing, or "remixing." And beyond opportunities for collaboratively created and shared content, OERs can be struc-tured to include interactive discussion forums that encourage critical reflection on teaching practices, occasioning exchanges that allow colleagues to learn and benefit from each other's experiences, both intra- and extra-institutionally.

This potential is exemplified by the *Acceso* project, which instantiates critical exploration of the culturally diverse Spanish-speaking world to promote second language (L2) development and awareness, critical cultural literacy, and opportu-nities to relate to and reflect on differing cultural meanings and perspectives in an OER that was collaboratively created for intermediate-level Spanish. All three categories of CALL—authentic materials, tutorial, and communication (Garrett, 2009)—are used to structure learner interaction with a wide variety of texts (read the term *text* here in its broadest possible sense—verbal, audiovisual, graphic, and so on). These texts include authentic materials created for a native audience that are embedded in the site or accessed on the Internet and are then framed and juxtaposed with materials that are created specifically to support and guide language learners. The result is a hybridized content environment that situates FL study "in cultural, historical, geographic, and cross-cultural frames" (MLA, 2007, p. 4) through CALL, as will be demonstrated in detail in the final section of the chapter.

Throughout the two-semester sequence, students interact with texts, their instructor, and each other to complete highly structured, reflective tasks progressing in complexity to achieve learning outcomes that target linguistic development, the capacity to critically analyze cultural content from multiple perspectives, and the ability to engage the Spanish-speaking world through applications of web-based technologies (Appendix 11-A). To direct and support learners' engagement of the curricular content and linguistic development and awareness, *Acceso*'s hybrid environment also provides (and links to) linguistic and content-focused contextual information for each of eight learning units. For example, each unit provides content-derived vocabulary lists[1] structured as searchable glossaries with contextualized examples from the site along with audio files to model the pronunciation of targeted words. Additionally, the site structures functional grammar explanations and links to other web-based learning resources for morphological and syntactic structures typically covered in third and fourth semester Spanish sequences. The open-access nature of the site does not allow for storage of student work, thus precluding the incorporation of grammar and vocabulary practice activities that can be reviewed by an instructor or assigned course credit. As a result, a complete set of tutorial CALL form-focused practice activities designed to enhance both the content and the process of working with the *Acceso* platform were developed and deployed using a commercially supported electronic learning tool. Following the more traditional structure of hybrid FL instruction, these activities are completed primarily outside of class time and feature opportunities to refine both receptive and productive language use (written and spoken) through automatically corrected closed-ended activities and instructor-graded open activities that progress from the sentence to the discourse level.

However, the *Acceso* project is envisioned not only as a vehicle for structuring and implementing the open-access curriculum for intermediate-level Spanish studies described earlier but also as an opportunity to promote graduate student instructor pedagogical and professional development through structured collaboration, as discussed in detail in Rossomondo (2011). To this end, the platform also

---

[1]These vocabulary lists are generated and updated using wordle.net, a free tool that analyzes texts to calculate word frequencies. All texts that are included in a given unit are analyzed to establish frequencies; active vocabulary words are added or modified based on their communicative functions and utility in the context of course activities.

hosts a password-protected instructor area, which transforms *Acceso* from merely a CALL resource into a complete curriculum[2] for intermediate-level Spanish that also facilitates collaboration among the instructors that shape and use it. This instructor area, which is fully available to instructors at other institutions, houses detailed lesson plans and support materials for implementing each of the 80 activities that comprise the open-access student area, a series of in-class and out-of-class writing assignments that provide opportunities for critical reflection on content and transformed practice, oral and written assessments, and rubrics for evaluating each of these. *Acceso* makes use of a common communication CALL tool—discussion fora—to promote pedagogical reflection, strategy sharing, and further collaboration (with respect to content development and revision as well as approaches to classroom implementation) among instructors.

Acceso's OER approach also allows LPDs, course coordinators, and individual instructors to select, sequence, and implement the curricular content based on their unique contexts and specific educational goals, with no pressure to use all of the materials or to contribute to their ongoing development. In other words, the extent to which this platform is used either to supplement or to replace existing undergraduate courses is completely flexible, as is the option for making use of it to foster graduate student instructor pedagogical development. This point is key in light of Frantzen's (2010, p. 33) recommendation for an incremental approach to change at institutions that are not logistically positioned to embrace the complete curricular overhaul recommended by many in the field (Byrnes, 1998, 2001, 2008; Frantzen, 2002; MLA, 2007; Scott & Tucker, 2002; Swaffar & Arens, 2005, among many others).[3] Extra-institutional sharing and collaboration provide such institutions a pathway to move in the direction of integrating language and content learning at foundational levels with considerably lower stakes and less investment (human or financial).

Collaboration and hybridity also characterize the tasks that structure undergraduate students' socially situated engagement of texts, language interpretation and use, and critical cultural inquiry through reflection on multiple meanings and perspectives both inside and outside of the classroom. This interaction and remixing is further facilitated through the use of web-based tools that are integrated into the *Acceso* curriculum (e.g., dipity.com, amplify.com, knovio.com, ask500people.com). Such applications offer a generation of students accustomed both to accessing information digitally and to using technology to creatively contribute to the participatory culture that characterizes today's social media (c.f., Facebook, Twitter, and so on) the opportunity to use and refine these skills in an academic context that promotes critical thinking. As Ganley and Sawhill argue, FL teaching should expand its focus on promoting the development of "traditional

---

[2]While recognizing that the term *curriculum* is often used to refer to the courses that comprise a four-year language major or liberal arts program of study, the term is used here to describe a specific learning program with articulated learning outcomes that include their teaching, learning, and assessment.

[3]The collaboratively realized achievement of integrating textually focused language and content learning and assessment across the entire four years of study of the Georgetown German program is one such model that has been very well documented (*Developing Multiple Literacies*, n.d.).

literacies of critical reading, thinking and communication" to include the development of "emerging literacies of collaboration, online communication and multimedia navigation" (2007, p. 5).

Yet it is critical to note that it is not merely *access* to authentic language use in texts found on the web or to tools that enable social interaction and collaboration that constitutes *Acceso*'s vision or version of CALL. Learners' interactions with these authentic texts and tools must be structured through principled pedagogical intervention to promote engaged content and language learning (Garrett, 2009, p. 723). As Kramsch and Anderson warned in reference to the incorporation of multimedia in the FL classroom:

> The computer with its unlimited capacity, rather than challenging our analytic and interpretive responsibilities, seduces us into believing that the truth is just around the corner of the next "text" that will fill the ultimate gap in our understanding. But this universe of spoken, visual, written, and printed texts is not self-explanatory. As a medium, it can only substitute itself for the living context and foster the illusion that con-text is nothing but an assembly of texts that get illuminated in unmediated fashion by juxtaposing them with other texts. Contrary to folk wisdom, understanding has not been made more immediate through the advent of multimedia technology (1999, p. 39).

It is essential to heed this prescient caution made more than a decade ago when approaching the selection, sequencing, and mediation of the texts that shape curricular content—especially in a *hybrid*, web-based environment, which allows for the sophisticated mediation (and manipulation) of meanings through the physical sequencing of texts, images, and links on a web page or the creation of multimedia mash-ups. Constant and critical reflection on the *hybridization* or remixing process is imperative, lest the mediation enabled by the digital environment inadvertently serve to fabricate context rather than reveal and problematize it. In the specific case of *Acceso*, the approach to selecting, sequencing, and mediating texts (with respect to content and genre) and contextual information is a collaborative process, not only because of the significant amount of time and energy involved but more importantly because it results in mediated content that is informed by multiple perspectives (more than 70 faculty members, instructors, and graduate student instructors to date) rather than the vision of a handful of textbook authors. Of course, all of these voices require direction and editing so that their contributions lead to cohesive and structured cultural exploration supportive of L2 development rather than a collection of random and fragmented text-based content activities.[4] To this end, the curricular content of *Acceso* is divided into eight major, geographically organized content units, each of

---

[4]The intra-institutional process by which the content is developed, structured, and edited was developed by the project leader, lead author, and editor and is discussed in Rossomondo (2011). Guidelines for extra-institutional collaborators submitting new content for inclusion in *Acceso* are available in the instructors' area. To date, extra-institutional collaboration has consisted primarily of suggestions for revisions and implementation of existing content.

which is structured by activity type (content and genre) according to an overarching theme for each semester that explicitly connects the content to the students' own cultural perspectives and experiences as Americans. The first four units explore the migration of peoples and its cultural impact in the United States, Spain, the Caribbean, and Mexico, and the final four units explore the United States' relationship with Latin America (Spanish-speaking countries in Central and South America) with respect to government intervention, trade, and cultural crosspollination.

Generating the constantly evolving content that explores these themes requires the level of departmental support discussed by Allen and Paesani (2010). In the case of *Acceso*, having the entire faculty read and discuss the 2007 MLA report at the request of the Basic Languages and Undergraduate Studies committees facilitated this buy-in. All faculty members agreed that the project would serve as a critical first step toward achieving the vision of a cohesive four-year curriculum put forth in the report. Many faculty members continue to weigh in directly through advising on text selection, and even more contribute indirectly through their mentorship of the graduate students' intellectual development and through their support of the project. For example, one faculty member specializing in contemporary Mexican cultural studies identified a newspaper article and video newscast on the Zapatista Army of National Liberation's participation in a recent March Against Violence to enhance a previously existing activity that explores the Zapatista manifesto. Other faculty members have helped graduate students develop ideas about how to approach difficult topics with undergraduate students, such as questions of cultural identities among U.S. Latinos. Nonetheless, the teamwork among the graduate student instructors, lecturers, and the LPD or project leader has resulted in curricular content driven by their own academic interests and cultural experiences. The result of such collaboration benefits all stakeholders: the tenured and tenure-track faculty enjoy teaching more broadly prepared students in major-level classes, and the graduate student instructors gain a broader, enhanced professional development as well as opportunities to explore meaningful cultural content in their own teaching. This departmental buy-in is also beginning to inspire new curricular thinking with respect to major-level courses (e.g., the need to articulate and support language learning goals in major level courses, which was discussed at a faculty retreat and is now part of the department's strategic plan for the future.) The Basic Language and Undergraduate Studies administrative committees are currently collaborating on clearer curricular articulation (with respect to content learning and linguistic development) between fourth-semester learning goals and the composition and conversation courses that serve as gateways to the major.

Intra-institutional collaboration beyond the departmental level has also been pivotal in the development of *Acceso*. The director and staff at our Academic Resource Center have supported and facilitated every stage of the project from its inception to its day-to-day technological maintenance. They also provide technology workshops and one-on-one tutoring for graduate students and lecturer-track instructors to facilitate the use of Web 2.0 technologies, including tools for facilitating student collaboration at a distance, such as amplify.com and voicethread.com; for creating mash-ups for video content, such as animoto.com and vodburner.com; for creating interactive timelines through diptity.com; and for video editing and captioning software (iMovie). Additionally, graduate students and instructors from the Department of Spanish and Portuguese have collaborated with graduate students from Film and Media Studies to learn how to effectively conduct the video interviews with native speakers that are included in each unit. Graduate students and faculty from the Title VI Center for Latin American and Caribbean Studies have also worked with the project leader and other members of the project and instructional staff on content development and outreach to regional institutions for secondary and postsecondary learning.

Overcoming Pedagogical Challenges to Implementing Language and Content Learning

Beyond structuring solutions for content creation and mediation, hybrid teaching and learning offers many creative pathways to structuring pedagogical approaches to implement this content inside and outside of class to promote language and content learning. Clearly, the challenges of integrating language and content study in foundational FL courses are numerous and vary from program to program depending on curricular goals and institutional realities. Meyer's assertion that "ideas and concepts should anchor students' intellectual and linguistic trajectories in the college-level FL curriculum at all levels of instruction," despite the inherent challenge in developing "students' thinking abilities at their intellectual levels while developing their linguistic skills in the target language, which are at a much lower level" (2009, p. 86), is all too familiar to LPDs and instructors who work extensively with these learners. In recent years, literacy-based approaches have been proposed as a route to cohesive FL instruction that embraces the complexity and ambiguity inherent in language use in cultural contexts (Allen, 2009; Allen & Paesani, 2010; Kern, 2000, 2002; Maxim, 2006; Swaffar & Arens, 2005), although to date this approach has not been emphasized in hybrid teaching and learning environments. In this framework, literacy is understood to encompass more than the ability to read and write, as Warner emphasizes: "The concept of literacy, as it is being defined in contemporary applied linguistics and L2 acquisition theory, places renewed emphasis on interpretation and critical awareness in language study, but it also maintains language use as an important objective of language study" (2011, p. 10). The textual and contextual nature of language is emphasized to promote students' ability to engage a variety of discursive communities in the target language, all of which might be deemed by some LPDs to be unrealistic in lower-division courses.

However, Kern (2000) offers a detailed roadmap of how this approach can be applied at foundational levels of instruction: Learners "design" meaning by deploying known linguistic, social, and cultural resources ("Available Designs") to engage a text (again, read the term *text* here in its broadest possible sense—verbal, audio-visual, graphic, and so on). Whether interpreting an existing text or creating a new one, learners engage in "designing" or shaping an emergent, recontextualized, and re-presented meaning ("The Redesigned"). Ultimately, learners access, apply, and recycle concepts that are either already familiar to them from their own cultural experiences or that are presented to them from the target culture in order to engage and transform the FL text, gaining in the process what Warner calls "critical language awareness" (2011, p. 11).

To realize the conceptual sequence of a literacy-based approach ("designing" meaning by accessing "Available Designs" and applying them to generate "The Redesigned"), four pedagogical strategies—situated practice, overt instruction, critical framing, and transformed practice—have been articulated by the New London Group (1996) and further elaborated for the context of FL instruction by Kern (2000, 2002). Situated practice activities promote the spontaneous use of language while accessing Available Designs, which by contrast are analyzed functionally and formally in overt instruction activities. The formal and functional analyses implicit in overt instruction activities encourage students to make use of Available Designs to construct meaning on their own and to develop critical language awareness and a metalanguage related to Available Designs. These analyses include, but are not limited to, lexical, syntactic, discursive, and genre-based features. Critical framing activities encourage reflection on the question of contexts—communicative, social, and cultural—and their role in creating meaning in texts. These activities encourage students to distance themselves from the text and their own assumptions about it in order to promote deeper learning about both (López-Sánchez, 2009, p. 34). In this way, space is created for them to operate between languages and cultures, as is called for in the MLA report (2007).

Successful iterations of this pedagogical framework have been reported when approaching language and content integration in introductory- (Allen & Paesani, 2010) and intermediate-level FL studies (Redmann, 2008; Schultz, 2004). Each of these reported successes was characterized by an emphasis on the interpretation and production of written texts, which is an inherent strength of a literacy-based approach (Byrnes, 2001; Byrnes, Maxim, & Norris, 2010; Kern, 2000). This attention to reading and writing development in introductory and intermediate courses stands in sharp contrast to the focus on oral and aural modalities and transactional language use that characterize many (but not all) current instantiations of communicative approaches, which are ubiquitous in early-level FL instruction in postsecondary institutions in the United States (Allen, 2009; Byrnes, 2006; Kramsch, 2006). As the field debates the merits and drawbacks of these and other frameworks, LPDs continue to be faced with programmatic decisions specific to their own institutional contexts.

When considering the specific context of lower-level Spanish language studies in the United States, current social and historical circumstances dictate that institutional and cultural issues unique to the study of Spanish must be taken into account. At the University of Kansas, the overwhelming majority of students (73 percent) report having no plans to continue their studies beyond the institutionally mandated FL requirements, which minimally include successful completion of fourth semester, or the last course in the basic language sequence; these students report choosing Spanish because they have studied it previously in high school or they believe that speaking it will be *useful* to them in the future either professionally or socially (Rossomondo, 2012). This utilitarian motivation presents significant challenges when determining pedagogical approaches and establishing learning outcomes that serve both this majority and the smaller but no less important group of major-track students (who either have already planned to study Spanish in greater depth or are motivated to do so based on their experiences in foundational classes). Although fully recognizing recent reconsiderations of communicative approaches to FL study (Allen, 2009; Allen & Paesani, 2010; Byrnes, 2006; Kramsch, 2006; Schultz, 2006; Swaffar, 2006; Walther, 2007), this context demands that commensurate focus on oral and aural communication (even for instrumental purposes) must be targeted, especially given the fact that by the year 2050, just under one-third of the population of the United States will be of Hispanic origin (U.S. Census Bureau, 2010). Even the majority population of students who do not continue their Spanish-language study will have ample occasion to make use of the competencies (linguistic and cultural) that they are able to develop in the required FL language sequence to communicate in both professional and social contexts. I emphasize, however, that the distinctive place of Spanish in the United States should not be understood as an argument for an "instrumentalist" rather than a "constitutive" approach to FL study, as is discussed in the MLA report (2007) and elsewhere. To the contrary, it leads us to consider how the two concepts should and can coexist. As Walther explains after relating the story of a former German student who made use of content knowledge garnered in an introductory class to land a job:

> I have no problem with such instrumental uses of foreign language study. But no matter what reasons students may have for studying a foreign language and culture, it is crucial that they receive the kind of education that will make them truly literate users of language and better interpreters of the world around them (2007, p. 13).

This sentiment is in harmony with *Acceso's* articulated learning outcomes, which seek to enhance the contribution of FL study to the general education of both groups of students—those who complete their studies after successfully completing the language requirement and those who continue their studies beyond the intermediate level. Both groups develop an understanding of why and how target cultural and intercultural awareness is critical for effective engagement with Spanish speakers, whether for the purpose of meeting their own professional and social goals with the Spanish language proficiency that can be achieved through the equivalent of four semesters of study or to be more broadly prepared for successful learning beyond the intermediate level. These learning outcomes are advanced through pedagogical strategies that comprise a literacy-based approach (situated practice, overt instruction, critical framing, and transformed practice) but are implemented in a hybrid learning environment in order to achieve contextualized language study in which learners are pushed to recognize and make sense of shifting cultural perspectives and meanings while they develop the capacities to communicate these new understandings both in virtual and F2F contexts. By enveloping "the textual within the communicative" (Allen & Paesani, 2010, p. 134), *Acceso* addresses the language learning goals of both groups of Spanish learners. Furthermore, by implementing this type of instruction in a hybrid environment, as we will see in the next section, students benefit from the added value of further developing digital literacies.

Acceso, Unit 1: Reflective Analysis of Content and Implementation

This final section of the chapter narrows its focus to exemplify how the pedagogical approaches and principles discussed earlier are actually implemented through *Acceso*'s hybrid learning environment. It should be noted that although the description below links *Acceso*'s content to a literacy-based methodology, its inherent flexibility allows for a wide variety of pedagogical applications. The analysis focuses narrowly on the implementation of the first of eight complete content units so as to offer a cohesive vision of *Acceso*'s approach. Each of the units features the same activity types, and although any of the eight units could have been featured, the first was chosen merely because it is both the students' and the instructors' first encounter with *Acceso*. To highlight the relevancy of Spanish to the students' own cultural realities as Americans, this first unit explores functions and impacts of Spanish language use in the United States, examining the multiple linguistic and cultural identities of Americans of Latino heritage and immigrants from Spanish-speaking countries. To be clear, only a very small percentage of the third semester students that use these materials at the University of Kansas are heritage Spanish learners themselves, but all students will likely be in contact with the Spanish language and fellow citizens of Hispanic origin in their future professional and social lives. The computer-mediated activities and assignments described herein are implemented during the first six weeks of intermediate-level Spanish study.[5] Although such texts and activities could be and have been used at higher levels of instruction, it is important to keep in mind that expectations for the students' engagement of the material are informed both by the developmental level of their linguistic repertoire and by their more advanced analytical capabilities. As their linguistic development progresses throughout the two-semester sequence, so do the expectations for the extent to which they are able to engage the content in Spanish.

The first activity (*Aperturas* or Openings) is a unit opener that structures learner engagement with an authentic text to foreshadow and problematize the themes explored in the unit. The text is a newspaper article from the Spanish newspaper *El País*, titled "*Más speak Spanish en Estados Unidos que en España*" or "More speak Spanish in the U.S. than in Spain." Before engaging the text, students work collaboratively (with the instructor's guidance) to generate a list of ideas about the potential content and structure of the newspaper article, thus beginning the process of accessing Available Designs. The students then engage a multimodal Flash presentation of the article, which synchs the text with images that facilitate surface-level comprehension and an audio track of a Dominican American reading the text to enhance comprehension and model pronunciation. Next they move on to situated practice in small groups, through which they collaboratively read a glossed version of the same text that defines or offers higher frequency

---

[5]It is useful for readers to understand that students at the University of Kansas enrolled in third-semester Spanish have studied an average of three to five years of Spanish before beginning postsecondary studies. Many of these students also completed an intensive introductory or review course before beginning the course that is described here. Students who place directly into the third- and fourth-semester courses score in the range of 350 to 440 on the WebCAPE foreign language placement exam.

synonyms for difficult lexical items and idiomatic expressions and signals active vocabulary words and grammatical structures targeted in the unit; one member of the group makes a list of these targeted words and grammatical structure to be used in a subsequent phase of the activity. The 800-word article is divided into four sections, each followed by comprehension or noticing questions that provide immediate feedback using a tutorial CALL tool (see Figure 11-1 for an example demonstrating how this phase of the activity functions as both overt instruction and situated practice). After an opportunity to consult with the instructor to clarify any sections of the text

Figure 11-1. Screenshot of a portion of Unit 1, *Aperturas*. When the students hover over a word or phrase in green, an explanatory gloss appears. Active vocabulary words and their derivatives appear in bold text, and links to external contextual information appear in blue. Students work in small groups to engage the text, pausing to complete noticing activities that provide automatic feedback.

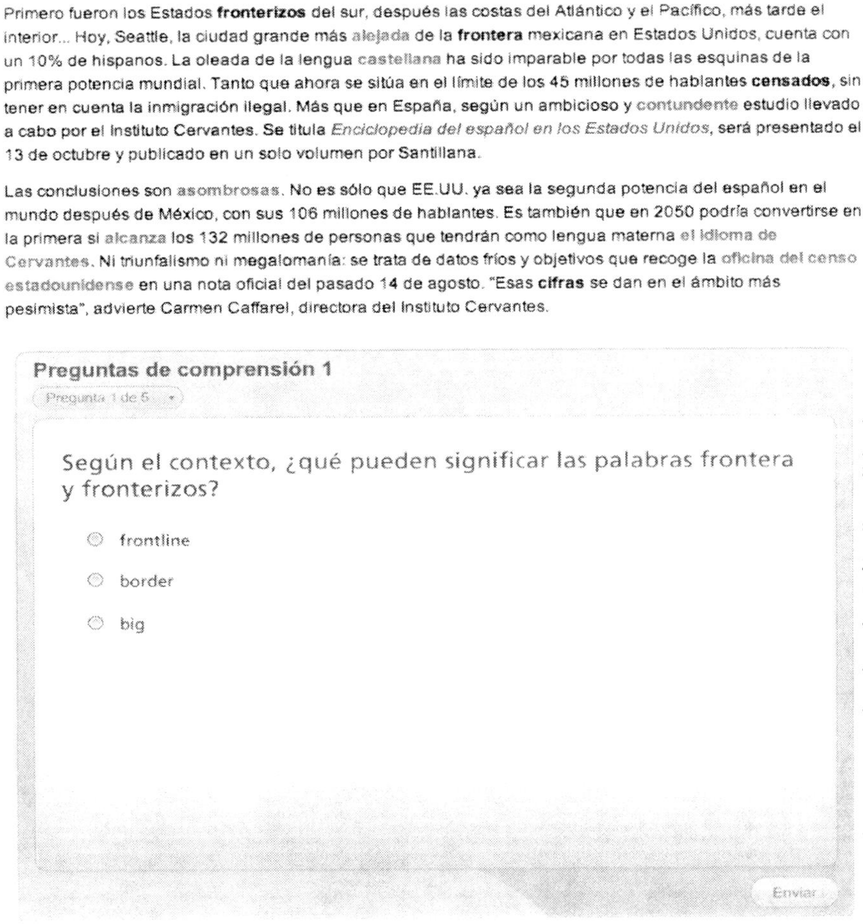

Primero fueron los Estados **fronterizos** del sur, después las costas del Atlántico y el Pacífico, más tarde el interior... Hoy, Seattle, la ciudad grande más alejada de la **frontera** mexicana en Estados Unidos, cuenta con un 10% de hispanos. La oleada de la lengua castellana ha sido imparable por todas las esquinas de la primera potencia mundial. Tanto que ahora se sitúa en el límite de los 45 millones de hablantes **censados**, sin tener en cuenta la inmigración ilegal. Más que en España, según un ambicioso y contundente estudio llevado a cabo por el Instituto Cervantes. Se titula *Enciclopedia del español en los Estados Unidos*, será presentado el 13 de octubre y publicado en un solo volumen por Santillana.

Las conclusiones son asombrosas. No es sólo que EE.UU. ya sea la segunda potencia del español en el mundo después de México, con sus 106 millones de hablantes. Es también que en 2050 podría convertirse en la primera si alcanza los 132 millones de personas que tendrán como lengua materna el idioma de Cervantes. Ni triunfalismo ni megalomanía: se trata de datos fríos y objetivos que recoge la oficina del censo estadounidense en una nota oficial del pasado 14 de agosto. "Esas **cifras** se dan en el ámbito más pesimista", advierte Carmen Caffarel, directora del Instituto Cervantes.

Preguntas de comprensión 1

Pregunta 1 de 5

Según el contexto, ¿qué pueden significar las palabras frontera y fronterizos?

○ frontline

○ border

○ big

Enviar

that remain unclear to them, small groups of students work together to answer discussion question designed to promote critical framing and (to a certain extent) transformed practice because students are encouraged to make use of language from the text section assigned to them to formulate their written answers. These answers are then projected so that the rest of the class can read and comment on them, both with respect to content and to specific vocabulary and grammar structures (e.g., answers to the situated practice questions allow for a review of the conjugation of present tense verbs). The instructor then brings the class session to a close by elaborating on the answers (refocusing when necessary) and explaining how themes touched on in the article (e.g., expansion of Spanish language use in the United States, the anxiety and pride that such expansion generates among different groups, reflection on aspects of the *Latino* experience and contributions to U.S. culture) foreshadow the content that will be explored in the unit. Before leaving class, the students answer an online poll question via text message: "Is the U.S. a Spanish-speaking country?" Their answers along with those of students in other sections (generally 400 per semester) are tabulated and revealed during the next class meeting.

The next activity type, called *Voces* or Voices, is designed to provide opportunities to work with video-based interviews, in which native speakers of a given region offer a variety of perspectives on the themes explored in each unit. All of the interviewees are Spanish speakers from the campus community. The *Voces* sections also include a limited description of the characteristics of Spanish spoken in the region in focus—in the case of the first unit, Spanglish. Before attending class, the students watch brief video clips of the interviews that are structured in a tutorial CALL question-and-answer format to both verify initial comprehension and to communicate expectations for their level of comprehension, as exemplified in Figure 11-2; students also access a contextual support article in English about Spanglish. In class, the students work together to analyze excerpts from transcripts of the interviews in order to respond to critical framing questions, which then ultimately lead to a concept-building activity. For example, a theme that emerges in several of the interviews relates to the experience of "living between cultures." Students analyze the transcripts to identify textual evidence related to this concept in order to arrive at a Spanish-language working definition of what it means to live between cultures and to assess the phenomenon's perceived positive and negative aspects. On the following class day, the focus shifts to Spanglish, a linguistic code common to Hispanic communities in the United States. Using authentic examples of Spanglish use culled from the Web, the students collaborate to interpret meanings and to discuss the necessity of understanding multiple linguistic systems and cultural contexts in order to communicate using Spanglish. They then divide into three large groups, two of which construct a brief written rationale for one of two distinct perspectives on Spanglish: (a) Spanglish is nothing more than language mixing that can lead to the degradation of Spanish language use in the United States or (b) Spanglish constitutes valid linguistic innovation that results from the expressive needs of a community that "lives between cultures." The third group (that continues to work on more Spanglish interpretation activities while the other two groups construct their arguments) then listens to the presentations of these arguments and explains orally which argument is more convincing and why.

Figure 11-2. Screenshot of Unit 1, *Voces.* Video clips are embedded within comprehension questions that direct students to listen for specific information during preparation outside of class. In class, students analyze transcripts of more extended discourse through guided activities.

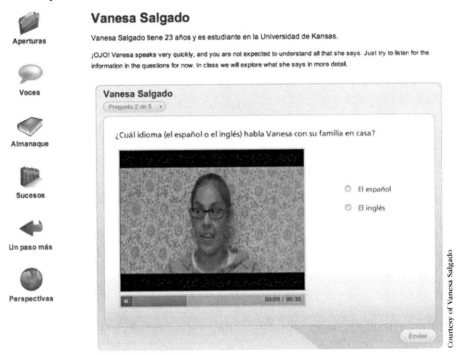

The next activities in the learning cycle, *Almanaque* or Almanac, consist of focused explorations of a wide range of present-day cultural phenomena and make use of a variety of texts to motivate guided, web-based research and collaboration inside and outside of the classroom. *Almanaque* activities are also characterized by the systematic inclusion of overt instruction activities that provide structured analysis and practice of targeted grammatical structures.[6]

In one such activity, students review and practice comprehending and producing large numbers and expressing percentages to analyze graphically represented demographic information about Spanish-speakers in the United States. To answer a series of demographic questions, the students complete a group webquest that explores the U.S. Census Bureau's Spanish language website (http://2010.census.gov/espanol/). At the end of the class period, the results of the poll from the first

---

[6]For the sake of brevity, only three such activities are discussed here in detail, but to date, there are three others: one is a structured comparison of Spanish language and English print and television commercials for the same or similar products, another focuses on the concept of *chicanidad* and features a web search for examples of Chicano cultural production and culminates in group presentations of the findings using amplify.com, and a third investigates the target audience and programming of the Spanish-language television channel *Univisión.*

day of class ("Is the U.S. a Spanish-speaking country?") are revealed and discussed in a situated practice activity, through which students reconsider or defend their initial votes.

Another activity asks students to consider the terms "*Hispano*/Hispanic" and "Latino" by analyzing graphically represented data from the Pew Hispanic Center that report the opinions and preferences of U.S. Spanish speakers with respect to using labels to self-identify. Before coming to class, they also read a brief article in English that explores the history and political implications of the two terms. In class, the students access Available Designs in small groups to complete a critical framing activity that requires them to engage several Spanish-language discussion forum posts about the terms "Hispanic" and "Latinos" to make connections with the Pew Center information and the background articles. Then in an instructor-led overt instruction activity with the whole class, they analyze specific elements of the language used in the posts (comparisons of inequality and equality). Through situated practice, the students collaborate to create conceptual maps of the two terms that explore their "linguistic baggage"; the conceptual maps are ultimately used in a transformed practice writing activity in which the students compare and contrast the terms by using the grammatical structure in focus (e.g., more older citizens express strong opinions than younger citizens).

In another *Almanaque* activity that returns to the concept of living between two languages and cultures, the students get to know a young Mexican American singer and songwriter by watching several Spanish-language music videos and interviews that are embedded in the site before coming to class. Class time is divided between situated practice, overt instruction, critical framing, and transformed practice. Students begin with the situated practice activity of sharing their oral reactions to the artist and his music. The instructor then transitions into an overt instruction activity that introduces the targeted grammar point (*ser* vs. *estar*) through which students make observations about the singer and his music. The students are then guided to consider how the concept of living between cultures is manifested implicitly in the artist's music and explicitly in the interviews through a critical framing activity. They then examine his Twitter feed and Facebook page, making note of the language use of the artist and his fans (*ser* vs. *estar*, Spanish, English, Spanglish) in another overt instruction activity. Through accessing Available Designs based on their own experiences as well as the language use modeled in the previous phase, the students then redesign texts by creating a tweet or a Facebook wall post in Spanish; those who wish to do so then have the option of posting their messages.[7] The singer himself has tweeted responses to the students each semester since the activity has been implemented, thus demonstrating how Web 2.0 tools facilitate communication CALL and serve to empower students to use their emerging Spanish language skills and cultural understanding to become participatory members of the speech communities about which they are learning.

The pedagogical decision to explore current cultural realities before introducing activities that feature historical perspectives was made so that contemporary

---

[7]Posting the message is optional in compliance with institutional regulations.

conditions might serve to stimulate interest in the historical circumstances and events that have led to them. In the *Sucesos* or Happenings activities, the students learn about history that is critical to understanding the social realities of the present Latino or Hispanic experience in the United States. Students read brief Spanish-language summaries of key events and engage interactive timelines with embedded authentic media, which were created and are updated using the hybridization tool dippity.com. The timelines include information about the history of the southwestern United States, the historical context for waves of immigration from other countries, and outstanding contributions to U.S. culture and history by Spanish-speaking Americans. The class activity blends situated practice and overt instruction as the students decide together and express which of the historical events have had more impact on the Latino experience (and why) by using the unit's grammar and vocabulary.

Each unit also includes *Un paso más,* or One Step Further, activities that provide opportunities to engage a variety of genres of literary texts that reflect themes explored in the unit. In the first unit, students read excerpts from Junot Diaz's Pulitzer Prize–winning novel, *The Brief and Wondrous Life of Oscar Wao*. Before coming to class, students watch an appearance by the author on the satirical television program *The Colbert Report* in which the host suggests that the novel is in fact an autobiography. They also watch a Spanish-language interview from a local New York City–based Spanish-language television channel. The students are directed to notice how the author interacts as a native speaker in both linguistic contexts. During class time, the students collaborate in small groups to read and analyze selected segments of the text. This analysis takes place primarily in Spanish, although English-language use is permitted to clarify specific observations that students are unable to effectively express in Spanish. Through providing written answers to guided critical framing questions (in Spanish), they consider the question of genre and genre-mixing (novel, memoir, and autobiography), language use (code switching), and the theme of marginalization. After sharing and discussing the answers, the whole class transitions into a situated practice activity that asks them to share their impressions of the text and their ideas about shifting between multiple identities in their own lives.

The final activity type of the unit, *Perspectivas*, is more experiential in approach in order to encourage students to consider a social issue from more than one perspective so that they are able to clarify and articulate their own beliefs. For Unit 1, students complete two such activities that address the topic of immigration. The first activity explores political implications of the "melting pot" or "salad bowl" metaphors as they relate to concepts of acculturation, assimilation, and multiculturalism. The students prepare by working through a series of CALL-mediated vocabulary-building activities, reading brief explanations of the metaphors in Spanish, and then watching two short videos that exemplify the two perspectives. In a structured class debate, they make use of the first unit's grammar points (present tense verbs, the contrast between *ser* and *estar*, comparisons of equality and inequality, expressing large numbers and percentages, periphrastic future) and active vocabulary to explore the two approaches to describing U.S. society.

The second *Perspectivas* activity confronts the controversial topic of undocu-mented immigration into the United States, reemphasizing that to this point the content explored in the unit focuses on Spanish-speaking U.S. *citizens*. Before coming to class, the students watch an archived episode of the television program *30 Days*, produced by documentary filmmaker Morgan Spurlock. The Spanish- and English-language episode chronicles the experiences of Frank George, a Spanish-speaking Minuteman from Arizona, who goes to live with a family of un-documented immigrants in Los Angeles for 30 days. Before watching the episode, the students are made aware that, in class, they will participate in an activity that mimics the format of a reality show reunion; each student is assigned the role of a documentary participant, moderator, or audience member and conducts directed web-based research (links for each role are provided) on their assumed perspec-tives before coming to class.

The decision to have students assume assigned roles and perspectives was made to avoid potential conflicts in class in recognition of the contentious nature of the topic. It was also thought that representing an assigned perspective would alleviate a certain amount of the frustration that the students' limited linguistic abilities would inevitably occasion if they attempted to articulate their own nu-anced points of view. Consequently, by making use of their research and observa-tions about the documentary, each student prepares a brief statement written in Spanish from the perspective of their assigned role that follows a prescribed struc-ture and includes active vocabulary and grammatical structures targeted through-out the unit. Upon arriving in class and before the simulation begins, the students collaborate in an overt instruction activity that provides structure and guidance for editing and improving the language use and content of their original prepared statements. This revision process results in condensed and refined versions of the statements, which are then read aloud during the introductions of the "reunion show" participants. The activity then transitions into an oral situated practice ac-tivity, through which the students question and clarify the differing perspectives that they have been assigned to represent.

Conclusions and Future Directions

This description of *Acceso's* creation and implementation is intended to provide a model of how meaningful content and language study can be integrated in lower-level FL study in a hybrid learning context. As we have seen, all categories of CALL are used to facilitate the teaching and learning needs of a larger Spanish-language program that serves students with distinct needs and goals. All appreciate cost savings and accessibility enabled through the OER, and the majority report that they perceive their own learning to be enhanced by the content and interaction enabled in a hybrid environment (Rossomondo, 2012). Although the benefits of integrating critical analysis of meaningful content and reflective language learn-ing among the pre-majors are self-evident, the contributions of such an approach to the general education of the students who are completing an FL requirement cannot be understated. By engaging FL study in this way, at a minimum these students can begin "to comprehend speakers of the target language as members of foreign societies and to grasp themselves as Americans—that is, as members of a society that is foreign to others . . . [and] to relate to fellow members of their own society who speak languages other than English" (MLA, 2007, pp. 3–4). This awareness better positions them for the future in any profession that they choose.

Although developing such curricula present significant challenges, the *Acceso* project demonstrates how intra-institutional collaboration can benefit all stakeholders. With respect to extra-institutional sharing and collaboration, the openness enabled by web-based technologies presents opportunities that we have only begun to explore and allows us to practice "hybridity" in new and exciting ways. To date, several institutions and numerous individual instructors at both secondary and postsecondary levels currently make use of the open-access materials either to structure or to supplement their own intermediate-level learning sequences. Most of these instructors have collaborated to suggest revisions to existing content and alternative strategies for implementing the content in a variety of educational settings (e.g., advanced high school courses, upper-division junior college courses, conversation courses at the advanced intermediate level).

However, the long-term vision for the project includes sustained extra-institutional collaboration with LPDs, instructors, and graduate students at other programs resulting in ever-evolving content inspired by their own research interests and experiences. The hybrid and web-based format provides limitless space to house expanded content for each of the seven activity types described in any of the eight learning units. To be sure, a wider selection of content would allow for far more flexible selection and sequencing of activities, so as to enable exploration of alternate themes and issues relevant to the Spanish-speaking world.[8] Other institutions of higher learning are enthusiastically welcomed to join *Acceso's* mission to enhance the experience and the impact of hybrid learning and teaching Spanish at earlier levels of instruction.

References

Allen, H. W. (2009). In search of relevance: The *Standards* and the undergraduate foreign language curriculum. In V. M. Scott (Ed.), *Principles and practices of the Standards in college foreign language education* (pp. 38–52). Boston: Heinle & Heinle.

Allen, H. W. & Paesani, K. (2010). Exploring the feasibility of a pedagogy of multiliteracies in introductory foreign language courses [Electronic version]. *L2 Journal, 2*, 119–142.

Blake, R. (2005). Bimodal CMC: The glue of learning at a distance. *CALICO Journal, 22*(3), 497–511.

Blyth, C., & Davis, J. (2007) Using formative evaluation in the development of learner-centered materials. *CALICO Journal, 25*, 1–21.

Brager, J. D., & Rice, D. B. (2000). FL materials: Yesterday, today, and tomorrow. In F.W. Medley & R. M. Terry (Eds.), *Agents of change in a changing age* (pp. 107–140). Lincolnwood, IL: National Textbook Company.

---

[8]This potential is already exemplified by the fact that course coordinators and instructors now choose which three of the six existing Unit 1 *Almanaque* activities will be implemented in class depending on the finer grained thematic focus that they wish to explore from semester to semester. This practice is used with other activity types in all eight units.

Byrnes, H. (1998). Constructing curricula in collegiate foreign language depart-ments. In H. Byrnes (Ed.), *Learning foreign and second languages: Perspectives in research and scholarship* (pp. 262–295). New York: Modern Language Asso-ciation of America.

Byrnes, H. (2001). Articulating foreign language programs: The need for new, curricular bases. In C. G. Lally (Ed.), *Foreign language program articulation: Current practice and future prospects* (pp. 157–180). Westport, CT: Bergin & Garvey.

Byrnes, H. (2005). Literacy as a framework for advanced language acquisition. *ADFL Bulletin, 37*(1), 85–110.

Byrnes, H. (Ed.). (2006). Perspectives: Interrogating communicative competence as a framework for collegiate foreign language study. *Modern Language Journal, 90,* 244–266.

Byrnes, H. (Ed.). (2008). Perspectives: Transforming college and university foreign language departments. *Modern Language Journal, 92,* 284–312.

Byrnes, H., Maxim, H., & Norris, J. M. (2010). Realizing advanced FL writing develop-ment in collegiate education: Curricular design, pedagogy, assessment. *Modern Language Journal, 94,* 1–202.

Chenoweth, N. A., Ushida, E., & Murday, K. (2006). Student learning in hybrid French and Spanish courses: An overview of Language Online. *CALICO Journal, 24*(1), 285–314.

Committee for Economic Development. (2009). Harnessing openness to improve re-search, teaching and learning in higher education. Retrieved July 30, 2012, from http://www.ced.org/issues/education/higher-education.

Developing multiple literacies. (n.d.). A curriculum renewal project of the German Department at Georgetown University, 1997–2000. Retrieved July 30, 2012, from http://www3.georgetown.edu/departments/german/programs/curriculum/index.html.

Frantzen, D. (2002). Rethinking foreign language literature: Towards an integra-tion of literature and language at all levels. In V. M. Scott & H. Tucker (Eds.), *Second language acquisition and the literature classroom: Fostering dialogues* (pp. 109–130). Boston: Heinle.

Frantzen, D. (2010). Incremental gains in foreign language programs: The role of reading in learning about other cultures. In C. Brantmeier & D. Pulido (Eds.), *The role of reading in reconfiguring foreign language programs. Reading in a foreign language* (Vol. 2 (1), pp. 31–37).

Ganley, B., & B. Sawhill. (2007). How did a couple of veteran classroom teachers end up in a space like this? Extraordinary intersections between learning, social software and teaching. *The Knowledge Tree 15,* 4–26.

Garrett, N. (2009). Computer-assisted language learning trends and issues revisited: Integrating innovation. *Modern Language Journal, 93,* 719–740.

Kern, R. (2000). *Literacy and language teaching.* Oxford: Oxford University Press.

Kern, R. (2002). Reconciling the language-literature split through literacy. *ADFL Bulletin, 33*(3), 20–24.

Kramsch, C. (2006). From communicative competence to symbolic competence. *Modern Language Journal, 90,* 249–252.

Kramsch, C., & Anderson, R. W. (1999). Teaching text and context through multimedia. *Language Learning & Technology, 2*(2), 31–42.

López-Sánchez, A. (2009). Re-writing the goals of foreign language teaching: The achievement of multiple literacies and symbolic competence. *International Journal of Learning, 16*(10), 29–37.

Maxim, H. H. (2006). Integrating textual thinking into the introductory college-level foreign language classroom. *Modern Language Journal, 90,* 19–32.

Meyer, C. (2009). The role of thinking on the college language classroom. *ADFL Bulletin, 41*(1), 86–93.

Modern Language Association Ad Hoc Committee on Foreign Languages. (2007). *Foreign languages and higher education: New structures for a changed world.* Retrieved July 30, 2012, from http://www.mla.org/flreport.

The New London Group. (1996). A pedagogy of multiliteracies: Designing social futures [Electronic version]. *Harvard Educational Review, 66*(1), 60–93.

Redmann, J. (2008). Reading Kästner's *Emil und die Detektive* in the context of a literacy-oriented curriculum. *Die Unterrichtspraxis, 41,* 72–81.

Rossomondo, A. E. (2011). The *Acceso* project: Opportunities for graduate student professional development. In H. W. Allen and H. H. Maxim (Eds.). *Educating the future foreign language professoriate for the 21st century.* Boston: Heinle Cengage.

Rossomondo, A. E. (2012). The role of formative evaluation in the development of the *Acceso* project. Manuscript submitted for publication.

Scott, V. M. & Tucker, H. (Eds.). (2002). *Second language acquisition and the literature classroom: Fostering dialogues.* Boston: Heinle.

Schultz, J. M. (2004). Towards a pedagogy of the Francophone text in intermediate language courses. *The French Review, 78,* 260–275.

Schulz, R. A. (2006). Reevaluating communicative competence as a major goal in postsecondary language requirement courses. *Modern Language Journal, 90,* 252–255.

Swaffar, J. K. (2006). Terminology and its discontents: Some caveats about communicative competence. *Modern Language Journal, 90,* 246–249.

Swaffar, J., & Arens, K. (2005). *Remapping the foreign language curriculum: An approach through multiple literacies.* New York: Modern Language Association.

Thorne, S. L., Black, R. W., & Sykes, J. M. (2009). Second language use, socialization, and learning in Internet Interest communities and online gaming. *Modern Language Journal, 93,* 802–821.

U.S. Census Bureau. (2010). Population projections. Retrieved August 9 2012, from http://2010.census.gov/2010census/.

Walther, I. (2007). Ecological perspectives on language and literacy: Implications for foreign language instruction at the collegiate level. *ADFL Bulletin, 38*(3), *39*(1), 6–14.

Warner, C. (2011). Rethinking the role of language study in internationalizing higher education [Electronic version]. *L2 Journal, 3*(1), 1–24.

Winke, P., Gass, S., & Sydorenko, T. (2010). The effects of captioning videos used for foreign language listening activities [Electronic version]. *Language Learning & Technology, 14*(1) 65–86.

Appendix 11-A. Targeted Learning Outcomes for *Acceso*

Upon successful completion of the fourth semester of foundational Spanish studies, students are able to

(1) Comprehend the main ideas of a variety of genres of authentic written texts directed at a general audience, and with guidance be able to analyze more nuanced aspects of the texts with respect to language use in its cultural context.

(2) Comprehend Spanish language use that is directed at them and be able to understand the main ideas of spoken language intended for a native audience; more importantly, students will develop the ability to identify specific areas of misunderstanding and request clarification to facilitate comprehension.

(3) Communicate their ideas both orally and in writing in such a way that native speakers unaccustomed to non-native Spanish will be able to comprehend these ideas, though this spoken and written language use will be far from error-free. Students develop and perform a formal oral presentation to share insights based on their final research projects.

(4) Develop and refine their ability to write effectively in Spanish through guided journal writing and a structured, process-oriented approach to formal composition. Students develop a 1,000-word paper informed by guided research into a topic of personal interest that relates to the content of the course. The KU Core Curriculum goals of promoting the development of critical thinking skills, written communication, and the ability to integrate knowledge into new ways of thinking are advanced through this process.

(5) Demonstrate broad cultural awareness of the Spanish-speaking world and the ability to relate this awareness to their understanding of their own cultural experiences in written work and through class activities. This outcome fosters a respect for human diversity and promotes an expanding cultural understanding and global awareness, as articulated by the KU Core Curriculum.

(6) Demonstrate the ability to analyze social issues from more than one perspective through the development of cultural sensitivity and more nuanced critical thinking skills. This intellectual development is demonstrated through the successful realization of the final research project, which serves as a comprehensive capstone assignment for the entire foundational sequence.

(7) Use technology to access the virtual Spanish-speaking world independently and effectively in order to broaden their range of information sources, which also serves to promote critical and creative thinking as well as digital fluency.

Contributors

Robert Blake (Ph.D., University of Texas) is full professor of Spanish linguistics at the University of California, Davis, and founding director of the UC Language Consortium (2000–2012). He has published widely on topics in CALL, applied linguistics, and Spanish linguistics, as well as producing materials for online instruction (*Spanish Without Walls, Tesoros, Arabic Without Walls,* and *Arabic Encounters*). In 2008, Georgetown University Press published his book *Brave New Digital Classroom.* In 2004, he was inducted into the North American Academy of the Spanish Language, an affiliate of the Royal Academy of Spanish (RAE). Email: rjblake@ucdavis.edu

Carl S. Blyth (Ph.D., Cornell University) is associate professor of French linguistics and director of the Center of Open Educational Resources and Language Learning (COERLL) at the University of Texas at Austin. His research interests include computer-mediated discourse, corpus linguistics, cross-cultural and intercultural pragmatics, pedagogical grammar, semiotics, and sociolinguistics. He has published on a wide variety of topics, including metalinguistic awareness, native and non-native role models for language learning, narrative discourse, pedagogical norms, stance taking in interaction, and open models for educational publishing. An advocate of open educational resources, he is currently developing *eComma*, an open-source software for annotating online texts to facilitate collaborative reading. His current book project is a mixed methods approach to studying French and American ways of expressing opinions. He has served as past series editor of *Issues in Language Program Direction.* Email: cblyth@mail.utexas.edu

Luis Cerezo (Ph.D., Georgetown University) is assistant professor of linguistics and director of the Spanish Language Program at American University. His research focuses on the development, implementation, and evaluation of audiovisual technology for second language learning, with a focus on type of computerized practice, corrective feedback, and learner individual differences. He is the author of *Talking to Avatars*, a computerized tutor that allows students to interact with prefilmed actors to learn Spanish in real-life situations. Email: luis.cerezo@american.edu

Lara Ducate (Ph.D., University of Texas at Austin) is associate professor of German at the University of South Carolina, where she is currently the director of Teacher Education, coordinates the lower-division German Program, and supervises the German graduate teaching assistants. Her research interests focus on teacher training, computer-mediated communication, including blogs and wikis, and more recently, mobile language learning. Email: ducate@mailbox.sc.edu

Senta Goertler (Ph.D., University of Arizona) is assistant professor of second language studies and German at Michigan State University. Her research area is technology-enhanced learning, especially computer-mediated communication and blended learning. Currently she is serving as the Interim Co-Director of the Computer-Assisted Language Instruction Consortium. Email: goertler@msu.edu

Lara Lomicka (Ph.D., Pennsylvania State University) is associate professor of French at the University of South Carolina, where she is the director of Basic Courses for French and the assistant director of Teacher Education. She currently serves as the co-chair of the American Association of French Technology Commission, is the software review editor for the *Computer-Assisted Language Instruction Consortium Journal,* and is the French section head for the American Association of University Supervisors and Coordinators. Her research interests include teacher education, intercultural and telecollaborative learning, and technology in language teaching and learning. She was recently honored as a *Chevalier dans l'ordre des palmes academiques.* Email: lomicka@sc.edu

Gillian Lord (Ph.D., Pennsylvania State University) is associate professor of Hispanic linguistics at University of Florida, where she is chair of the Department of Spanish and Portuguese Studies and directs the Lower Division Spanish Program. She currently serves on the executive committee of the Computer-Assisted Language Instruction Consortium and is the Spanish section head for the American Association of University Supervisors and Coordinators. Her primary areas of investigation involve second language acquisition, particularly of the Spanish sound system by speakers of English, and factors that can influence this process. She also has an interest in language teaching methodology and teacher training. Email: glord@ufl.edu

Jason Lee Pettigrew (Ph.D., University of Tennessee) received his Ph.D. in modern foreign languages from the University of Tennessee in 2009. He is currently assistant professor of Spanish at Middle Tennessee State University, where he teaches elementary Spanish, advanced Spanish, and grammar and composition. Email: jpettigr@mtsu.edu

Amy E. Rossomondo (Ph.D., Indiana University) is associate professor and co-director of foundational Spanish language studies at the University of Kansas, where she teaches both undergraduate and graduate courses in applied linguistics, second language acquisition, and approaches to foreign language classroom instruction. She also mentors and oversees graduate student instructors. Her research interests include the acquisition of verbal morphology, foreign language program articulation, and applications of web-based technologies to foreign language instruction. She has published articles in journals such as *Studies in Second Language Acquisition* and *Hispania* and is the creator and director of the *Acceso* project. Email: arossomo@ku.edu

Susanne Rott (Ph.D., University of Illinois at Urbana-Champaign) is associate professor of Germanic studies and linguistics and is acting associate director of the School of Literatures, Cultural Studies and Linguistics. She teaches courses in second language acquisition and language pedagogy. Her main research focus is the encoding, storage, and retrieval of individual lexical items, phraseologisms, and lexico-grammatical constructions. Her studies are based on linguistic descriptions and cognitive processes outlined in cognitive linguistics. In particular, she investigates how form-meaning mappings develop across interrelated continua that mark partial to complete, weak to robust, and non–target-like to target-like language use by second language learners in an instructed learning setting. In her studies, she assesses the effect of linguistic aspects, such as length and morphosyntactic complexity; cognitive aspects, such as attention and phonological working memory capacity; and instructional aspects, such as awareness raising, frequency, and the effect of intervention tasks. Email: srott@uic.edu

Fernando Rubio (Ph.D., State University of New York at Buffalo) is associate professor of Spanish linguistics and director of the Second Language Teaching and Research Center at the University of Utah. His research areas include second language acquisition, the integration of technology in second language teaching, and assessment. He currently serves on the Modern Language Association's Executive Committee of the Division on the Teaching of Language and on the AP Spanish Language Development Committee. Email: fernando.rubio@utah.edu

Joshua J. Thoms (Ph.D., University of Iowa) is assistant professor of applied linguistics and Spanish at Utah State University. His research interests include the effects of classroom discourse on second language learning in second language and literature classrooms, technology in second language learning and teaching, and issues related to teaching assistant professional development. He teaches courses that include topics such as foreign language teaching methodology, theories of second language acquisition, and computer-assisted language learning at the undergraduate and graduate levels. Email: joshua.thoms@usu.edu

Dolly Jesusita Young (Ph.D., University of Texas at Austin) has a B.A. in Spanish, an M.A. in Latin American studies, and a Ph.D. in foreign language education from the University of Texas at Austin. She is the language program director for Elementary Spanish courses at the University of Tennessee, Knoxville, and trains and observes graduate students in Spanish who teach first- and second-year Spanish courses in Modern Foreign Languages and Literatures. Her research areas include second language acquisition, teaching with technology, materials development, second language reading, and affective variables (e.g., anxiety) in language learning. Email: djyoung@utk.edu

AAUSC

The American Association of University Supervisors, Coordinators, and Directors of Foreign Language Programs

Purpose

Since its inception in 1980, the AAUSC has worked to:

- Promote and improve foreign and second language education in the United States
- Strengthen and improve foreign language curricula and instruction at the postsecondary level
- Strengthen development programs for teaching assistants, teaching fellows, associate instructors, or their equivalents
- Promote research in second language learning and development and on the preparation and supervision of teaching assistants
- Establish a forum for exchanging ideas, experiences, and materials among those concerned with language program direction

Who Can Join the AAUSC?

Membership in the AAUSC is open to anyone who is interested in strengthening foreign and second language instruction, especially, but not exclusively, those involved with multisection programs. The membership comprises teachers, supervisors, coordinators, program directors, faculty, and administrators in colleges and universities that employ teaching assistants. Many members are faculty and administrators at undergraduate institutions.

How Do I Join the AAUSC?

Please join online at *www.aausc.org*. Three membership levels are available.

Dues (including yearly volume)

Regular $25/year
Student $15/year
Retired $15/year

CPSIA information can be obtained
at www.ICGtesting.com
Printed in the USA
FFOW030846281112
343FF